Castles in the Air

CASTLES
IN THE AIR

MARTIN W. BOWMAN

Brassey's • Washington, DC

CASTLES IN THE AIR

First published in this edition in 2000
by Brassey's, Inc.
22841 Quicksilver Drive,
Dulles, Virginia 20166, USA.

This edition designed and produced by
Wordwright Publishing
St John's Road
Saxmundham, Suffolk
IP17 IBE
England
Designer: Simon Parry, Red Kite

Printed in Canada
ISBN: 1-57488-320-8

Front cover illustration:

Mary Ruth - Memories of Mobile,
a B-17F of the 401st BS, 91st BG.
This aircraft (42-29520) was lost to flak on 22nd June 1943.
(Thomas J. Fitton)

TABLE OF CONTENTS

Acknowledgements

When *Castles In The Air* was first published in 1984 by PSL, I wrote that most books about WWII attract a vast army of helpers and contributors that no author could do without. *Castles* is certainly no exception, and many individuals supplied me with more than I could have hoped for. Sadly, many of these same contributors, especially the Fortress aircrew veterans, have since died. Their first-hand accounts though, and memories, are proudly enshrined now in tablets of stone.

As a new millennium dawns one of the more welcome aspects of the passing of so many years is that much more information on the 8th Air Force has come to light - more than anyone could have dreamed of even fifteen years ago when *Castles* was first published. Numerous group histories have appeared, and much more detailed information on individual aircraft and crews has surfaced, notably in publications like, *Heavy Bombers of the Mighty Eighth*, by Paul M. Andrews & William H. Adams, 1995, *Pride of Seattle, The Story of the first 300 B-17Fs*, by Steve Birdsall, Squadron Signal, 1998; *Plane Names & Fancy Noses*, the 91st BG (H), by Ray Bowden, 1993; and of course, *The B-17 Flying Fortress Story* by Roger A. Freeman with David Osborne, Arms & Armour, 1998. All of these, and more, plus input from numerous other sources in recent years, have served to put more flesh on the bones, and, in many cases, cleared up mysteries and created new avenues of exploration.

Equally, I have heard from many new friends and met several more on my travels worldwide. Chief among these is Larry Goldstein, a B-17 radio operator, who flew a tour of combat missions in the 388th Bomb Group in 1943. Larry is now a vice-president on the Board of the 8th Air Force Historical Society and he still runs the New York Chapter on a daily basis, having built up the membership from scratch over the last few years. The 8th AFHS is lucky to have Larry's dynamic presence. I am indebted to him for his encouragement and for sending me many sources of information over the past ten years. He and his lovely wife Dorothy have often welcomed me into their delightful home in Queens, New York City, where visits are always special to me.

The same is true of Connie and Gordon Richards of Oakley, Bedfordshire, who have always afforded me every hospitality and assistance in the past fifteen years. I am also indebted, as always, to my near neighbour and gifted aviation artist Mike Bailey, who continues to make his vast expertise in 8th Air Force matters available to me. I am indebted to those who kindly allowed me to quote selected passages from their books; all of which are classics in the history of the USAAF at war. My thanks to General Curtis E. LeMay for extracts from *Mission With LeMay*, Colonel Budd J. Peaslee for extracts from *Heritage of Valor*, and to Paul Tibbets for passages from *The Paul Tibbets Story*. I am also grateful to Ed Hicks for kindly making his researches into the early history of the 97th Bomb Group available. Also, to Abe Dolim and "Pappy" Colby for access to their war diaries. I am especially indebted to Ben Smith Jr., for allowing me to quote from his personal story, *Chick's Crew*; undoubtedly one of the most poignant descriptions of the 8th Air Force and the 303rd Bomb Group in particular. And equally so to Lowell Watts for his compelling narrative of the 6th March Berlin mission, which will surely challenge *I Saw Regensburg Destroyed* as one of the most vivid accounts of Americans under fire.

I am no less grateful to the following B-17 crewmen, some of whom are sadly no longer in formation: Walter Austin, William D. Allen, Carl L. Anderson, Bob Browne, William Boutelle, the late Marvin Barnes, Frank L. Betz, General Harold W. Bowman, Robert Capaldi, Bill Carleton, Claude E. Campbell, Henry C. Cordery, Hugh K. Crawford, Harry H. Crosby, General Ira C. Eaker, John C. Ford, Albert J. Filiponis, Reuben Fier, Richard E. Fitzhugh, Dan Graham, John E. Greenwood, Lee C. Gordon, Hank Gladys, Frank Halm, John Hurd, Cliff Hatcher, John Holden, Robert L. Hughes, Ed Huntzinger, Howard E. Hernan, Leonard W. Herman, Henry Heckman, Herman Hager, the late Glenn B. Infield, Joe F. Jones Jr., Ivan Johnson, Loren E. Jackson, Edwin O. Jones, the late Beirne Lay Jr., Al La Chasse, Irving Lifson, Alfred R. Lea, Rusty Lewis, William B. Menzies, Emmett J. Murphy, Anthony J. McComiskey, Gus Mencow, Frank McGlinchey, Paul Montague, Ped G. Magness, James Kemp McLaughlin, Abe Millar, John A. Miller, Bob Maag, Raymond P. Miller, Gerald "Bill" McClelland, Orlo G. Natvig, Grady Newsom, General Maurice Preston, Richard Perry, Cliff Pyle, Perry Rudd, William Rose, William Sterret, Adolph J. Smetana, Lloyd B. Slimp, Edwin "Ted" Smith, Robert J. Shoens, Ben Schohan, Malvern R. Sweet, William C. Stewart, W. Griswold Smith, Bob Spangler, Ralph Trout, Leslie G. Thibodeau, Henry Tarcza, Ralph Tomek, Horace Varian, Alan R. Willis, Mike Wysoki, Joe Wroblewski, David M. Williams, Henry A. West, Richard J. Walsh, Peck Wilcox, Karl Wendel, and Sam Young.

Help came from many British sources including John Archer, a man who has probably been researching the 8th Air Force longer than anyone else, Ron Batley, Stan Brett, Stewart Evans, John Goldsmith, Cliff Hall for his help with the 94th Bomb Group, the late Mike Harvey, Ian Hawkins for his expertise and guidance on the 10th October 1943 raid on Munster, Harry Holmes, who provided many relevant photos and encouragement, and Malcolm "Ossie" Osborn for his encouragement and kindness in providing me with information and photographs on the 385th Bomb Group. Finally, my wife Paula, who, like me, could not have dreamed that *Castles* would ever take to the air again so many years later. My grateful thanks to Simon Parry for making it possible once again.

Martin W. Bowman, Norwich, England. July 1999

Chapter 1

Fame's Favored Few

On the peaceful early morning of Sunday, 7th December 1941, trainee radar operators on a rudimentary set north of Pearl Harbor in the Hawaiian Islands reported many aircraft approaching. America had broken the Japanese "Purple Code" and knew that Japan was preparing for war, but expected that the first bombs would fall on the Philippines or Malaya. The radar unit commander therefore thought the aircraft were a flight of B-17 Flying Fortresses which were expected and the radar operators were told to stand down. How wrong he was. The aircraft picked up on the radar were the first wave of a Japanese strike force, some 190 in all, heading for the island of Oahu and the American Pacific fleet at anchor in Pearl Harbor.

Shortly before 0800 hours they reached Oahu, split into elements, and made their attacks. Army personnel watched in awe, then dived for cover as Zero fighters roared over the island at low level, machine-gunning P-40s, Catalinas, and other aircraft parked in serried rows at Wheeler Field and Kanaohe. High level bombers pounded Hickham Field and torpedo planes and dive-bombers attacked Battleship Row, inflicting heavy casualties. Eight battleships were reduced to heaps of twisted, blazing metal. The *Arizona* exploded in a pall of smoke and flame and, within about twenty-five minutes, seven other battleships had either been destroyed or reduced to damaged and listing hulks.

Facing page: *B-17Es lined up at the Boeing factory. Nearest is 41-2393.* Above: *Work on the bombers was often carried out in the open in daylight hours, but work went on round-the-clock in floodlit hangars.* (Tom Cushing)

Abe Dolim had just returned from the seven o'clock mass at St Patrick's in the Kaimuki district of Honolulu when he noticed the white puffs of anti-aircraft shells bursting over Pearl Harbor. The young Hawaiian's house faced the harbor and was on high ground so he was able to witness the entire sequence of events. Thinking it odd for the Navy to be holding maneuvers on a Sunday morning, he went into the house and turned the radio set on. "I waited but nothing happened; the station seemed to be off the air. Then, in a minute or so, a highly excited announcer broke the silence with words to the effect that we were under sporadic air attack by unidentified aircraft. It was some minutes before the attackers were identified as Japanese. I watched the bombing of Pearl Harbor from our front porch. After it was over the Japanese high level bombers formed up in vics at about 8,000 feet above my house for the return to what proved to be their carriers 275 miles away.

"The next morning I was up early enough to watch the anti-aircraft batteries at nearby Fort Ruger open fire on a formation of three B-18s heading east at only 3,000 feet. No one had any idea what a Japanese aircraft looked like. A pall of black smoke hovered over Pearl Harbor for weeks. At the Hawaiian Pineapple Company, where I worked as an apprentice machinist, we began working ten hours a day, six days a week. We repaired and reconditioned dozens of huge electric motors and other types of machinery salvaged from damaged and sunken naval vessels. I spent many hours on a lathe making parts for ship's intercom systems. Work was all we had time for. Martial law had imposed a curfew at 2200 hours and anyone caught out of doors in blackout after that time risked being shot on sight

General Ira C. Eaker. Commander of VIII Bomber Command. (USAF)

- no questions asked. Fishing was banned and the beaches were barricaded with barbed wire. In a matter of weeks my island had become a huge fort, a supply dump, a trap perhaps.

"I went into military service with my eyes wide open. I remember the shame I felt that fateful December day: to realize that our military leaders, charged with the defense of our islands and the well being of their men, could have been so incompetent. Thousands of Americans died in the name of sheer stupidity. Whatever ideas I had about the supremacy of our arms and the inferiority of the enemy were destroyed in the debacle I had witnessed that awesome Sunday morning. I was destined never to fight the despoilers of my island, but yet another enemy half way around the world from my home."

That enemy was Nazi Germany, which declared war on the United States four days later, on 11th December 1941.

Although the United States could not prevent the attack on Pearl Harbor, far-reaching decisions had been made in the event that America should become involved in the conflict with the Axis powers. Between 27th January and 27th March 1941, agreements between the United States and Great Britain were made for the provision of naval, ground, and air support for the campaign against Germany. As a result, a special US Army Observer Group, headed by

Major General James E. Chaney, was activated in London on 19th May 1941. One of Chaney's first tasks was to reconnoiter areas regarded as potential sites for US Army Air Force (USAAF) installations. During late 1941 several tentative sites were explored, including Prestwick near Ayr in Scotland and Warton near Liverpool (the proposed site for a repair depot). Others, like Polebrook, Grafton Underwood, Kimbolton, Molesworth, Chelveston, Podington, and Thurleigh, all in the Huntingdon area, would soon become familiar homes to the B-17 Flying Fortress groups of the US 8th Air Force.

On 2nd January 1942, the order activating the 8th Air Force was signed by Major General Henry "Hap" Arnold, the Commanding General, Army Air Forces, and the headquarters was formed at Savannah, Georgia, twenty-six days later. Also on 2nd January, the War Department in Washington announced that United States ground forces were to be sent to Northern Ireland. On 8th January the activation of USAFBI [US Forces in the British Isles] was announced. A third announcement stated that a bomber command was to be established in England. Arnold instructed Brigadier General Ira C. Eaker to assist in the formation of a headquarters for the American air forces in Great Britain. Eaker was designated as Commanding General of VIII Bomber Command and his duties were to help prepare airfields and installations and to understudy the methods of RAF Bomber Command.

The choice of Eaker for such tasks was ideal. Late in 1941 he had spent a month in the United Kingdom as a special observer and his experience would prove useful now that he was to work hand-in-glove with his British counterparts. By February 1942, Eaker had appointed six staff officers who would fly with him to England and form the advance detachment of VIII Bomber Command. One of them was Beirne Lay, Jr. He recalls,

"I had been a 'first John', walking down the hall of the old WD Munitions building in Washington in December 1941, when Eaker stopped me. 'Want to come with me?' he asked. 'Yes Sir!' I answered, having no idea what he meant. He walked on. The next thing I knew I was packing for England.

"En route we golfed for thirteen days in Bermuda waiting for good weather for the Pan Am clipper to Lisbon. Portuguese agents ransacked our luggage at the Hotel Metropole. On 20th February we left in civilian clothes and boarded a KLM DC-3 at 0700 hours at Cintro Land airport for the one-hour flight to Porto where we were to refuel for the flight to England. I particularly remember Eaker at the gate. The gate was down, no one in sight, and our driver just sat. Eaker got out of the car, strode determinedly to the gate and raised it for us. Typical. At Porto we changed into our uniforms. At 1220 hours we were at 10,000 feet when we were nearly shot down by a

Messerschmitt 110 in the Bay of Biscay, but his engine started smoking just before he intercepted us and he headed for the French coast. We landed at 0300 hours at Whitechurch aerodrome, Bristol, and then we were flown to Hendon in a Flamingo transport aircraft piloted by a group captain. A large party, including Air Vice Marshal Baldwin, met us at Hendon. In London we over-nighted at the Strand Palace Hotel."

Initially, Eaker's headquarters was established at RAF Bomber Command Headquarters at High Wycombe on the green flanks of the rolling Buckinghamshire Chilterns. It was here, on 22nd February, that VIII Bomber Command was formally activated. Prior to military use, the headquarters had been a girls' school but there was nothing second-hand about the Americans' future air bases, proposed for the Huntingdon area. This flat, fenland stretch of countryside had originally been considered by the RAF for occupation by a new Bomber Command formation before this idea was discarded. The airfield construction program continued and these bases would soon become the launching pad for the first American four-engined bomber in Europe: the B-17 Flying Fortress.

Although Eaker's brief was, for the most part, to establish a bombing force, many of his staff officers were, in one quarter at least, thought to be unsuitable for such a task. Major General Chaney had personally checked the background of the nineteen staff officers supplied to Eaker and found that; "in general they have had only pursuit training. Moreover, a large number have come direct from civilian life without a military background of any kind. Three served with bombardment units some years ago and their bombing experience must therefore be regarded as virtually negligible."

Apart from Lieutenant Colonel Frank A. Armstrong, Jr., a regular officer who had been chosen first, the selection process for Eaker's other staff officers was unconventional to say the least. Beirne Lay, Jr., one of Eaker's original six men, explains why there were so many amateurs (as he called them) on Eaker's staff: "I recall 'Hap' Arnold had told Eaker; 'You can train a smart civilian to be a soldier faster than a dumb staff officer.' I was a writer, hence billed for VIII Bomber Command's first historian. I also filled in at first with the additional duties of Mess Officer and egg forager, PRO [Public Relations Officer], aide, and was officially also a member of A-3 [Operations and Training], and Athletics Officer. We had hotly contested bouts of volleyball, trying to ram Eaker's cigar down his throat - I got one direct hit. The four other originals were Major Peter Beasley, a successful businessman; Captain Fred A. Castle, a former Air Corps pilot, an executive of Sperry and well qualified for A-4 [Supply]; Lieutenant Harris Hull, a crack PRO, A-2 [Intelligence]; and Lieutenant William Cowart Junior, a gung-ho young fighter pilot, Eaker's first aide."

Almost six months were to elapse before the 8th Air Force mounted its first all-American bombing mission on German-held territory, so Eaker's "amateurs" had ample time in which to study RAF bombing methods and prepare to receive their own bombers. Between 31st March 1942 and 3rd April 1942, Eaker and his staff officers made a more detailed reconnaissance of the Huntingdon area and the seeds of the future American presence were thus sown.

Crew of The Red Gremlin *of the* 97th *Bomb Group on* 9th September 1942. Back row, left to right: *Tibbets, Ryan, Ferebee, Van Kirk, Hughes and Splitt.* Front row: *Peach, Quate, Fitzgerald, Gowan and Fittsworth.* (Tibbets)

Major Paul Tibbets at his desk.

Meanwhile, in America, B-17 and B-24 heavy bombardment groups were activated for deployment to Britain. The first of the B-17 groups activated was the 34th Bomb Group - at Langley Field, Virginia, on 15th January 1942 - but the group was used to train other groups and remained in America until late March 1944. On 3rd February 1942, three more B-17 groups, the 97th, 301st, and 303rd, were formally activated. It fell to these three groups, together with the 92nd (activated on 1st March 1942) and two Liberator groups, to establish the nucleus of the 8th's heavy bombardment force in England.

Lieutenant Colonel Cornelius W. Cousland had assumed command of the 97th Bomb Group upon its formal activation and, on 15th February, the fourth and final bomb squadron, the 342nd, joined the already activated 340th, 341st, and 414th Bomb Squadrons. Fortunately, many of the personnel in the 342nd Bomb Squadron were drawn from the Overseas Training Unit and were well acquainted with the B-17E, the latest model of the Flying Fortress.

At the end of March 1942, the 97th Bomb Group moved from McDill Field, Florida, to Bradenton-Sarasota AAB, Florida. The airfield was not yet completed and was located in what looked like a swamp in which palmettos abounded. Tents were pitched and all personnel were confined to base as the training program got under way. In order to meet the required 125 hours' flying, aircrews did some flying at night. Jeeps were parked near the runway so their headlights could be used to mark the end of the tarmac. By April the group consisted of only thirty-two Fortresses but, on 12th May, Colonel Cousland received his overseas orders. Aircraft and crews began flying out at once to San Antonio and Middletown, Pennsylvania, while the Headquarters Squadron returned to McDill Field. A week later the ground echelon entrained for Fort Dix, New Jersey, and on the night of 3rd June was transported to Brooklyn docks, where in the dusk the men could see the charred hulk of the *Normandie* lying on her side. Ferry barges transported them

the short distance to the Cunard liner-turned-troopship, *Queen Elizabeth*. Some 12,500 men, representing the 97th Bomb Group, the 1st Fighter Group, and the 31st Fighter Group, plus their service echelons, stumbled up the gangplanks under masses of equipment to be greeted by a member of the ship's crew who thrust into their mouths, (since their arms were full), a sheet of paper directing each man to his bunk and mess hall.

All personnel were ordered below decks where, before the war, passengers had wallowed in sumptuous luxury. There was little luxury now for the cramped soldiers and it was rumored that, officially, the *Queen Elizabeth* was returning to Britain empty. Tasks were allotted during the voyage and some 97th Bomb Group personnel were assigned to gun crews on the .50 caliber machine-guns stationed along the top deck in case of air attack. The liner made the journey safely without attacks from enemy aircraft or submarines and, on the morning of 9th June, dropped anchor in the Firth of Clyde. Lighters ferried the men ashore to Gourock where a train awaited them. As the train steamed southwards, the faces of many young Americans were pressed against the compartment windows, scanning the countryside, and showing special interest in the bomb damage to the cities and towns.

Two days later, after a stop-over at Carlisle, the men detrained at Oundle and the 97th Bomb Group divided, the 340th and 341st Squadrons traveling by bus to their new base at Polebrook, arriving at 0500 hours. The 342nd and 414th Squadrons left the train at Kettering and traveled by bus to Grafton Underwood. The Luftwaffe did its best to welcome the Americans to Northamptonshire, scattering incendiary clusters over the Polebrook base on the night of 25th June, in a raid lasting fifteen minutes. Damage was negligible and, four nights later, flares were dropped, making the night sky as bright as day, but no bombs fell. Perhaps the Luftwaffe was checking to see if the Fortresses had arrived. In fact they were en route.

The 340th and 341st air echelons had taken off for Dow Field, Maine, and those of the 342nd and 414th for Grenier Field, New Hampshire. Flying north, the 342nd Squadron encountered bad weather and was forced to put down at Mitchel Field, New York. From there they joined the 414th Squadron at Grenier Field. Meanwhile, the 340th and 341st Squadrons had arrived at Dow Field and complained that the ball turrets were malfunctioning. Repair crews were called in and, by the end of May, the B-17s and their crews were assembled at Presque Isle, awaiting orders. An attack on 1st June by the Japanese on the Aleutians changed plans dramatically and, next day, the 97th Bomb Group and P-38s of the 1st Fighter Group were scheduled for detached duty with Western Defense Command. All four squadrons in the 97th Bomb Group arrived at their destinations on 5th June and immediately began flying coastal patrol missions.

Five Fortress I's were delivered to No. 90 Squadron RAF at Polebrook in June 1941. The RAF flew twenty-four operations but by September it was decided that the Fortress was unsuitable for further bombing operations.

On 23rd June, the danger over, the 97th Bomb Group returned to Presque Isle for the flight to Prestwick via Labrador, Greenland, and Reykjavik, Iceland. Crews had a choice of routes. Either via Bluie West 1 (Narsarssuak) on the south coast of Greenland or Bluie 8 (Sondre Stromfjord) on the west coast. On 26th June, the B-17s left Presque Isle and reached Goose Bay. Three hours and ten minutes later the formation was airborne for Bluie West 1, arriving there to discover that the weather had changed for the worse, making it impossible to land. Next morning eleven of the B-17s returned to Goose Bay, having been in the air for over thirteen hours. Four crews ran into trouble in a snowstorm and had to land on a Greenland icecap and were later rescued.

After having resolved some communication problems, and having received reports of improving weather conditions moving in, the 97th Bomb Group was soon heading out over the "Great Circle" route on regular schedule. This first proving flight led to many innovations for which thousands of airmen using the Northern Ferry Route in the months to come would be most grateful. Experience was an excellent instructor and one recommendation - that all crewmen should be issued with sunglasses - became standard operating procedure. On 1st July 1942, *Jarring Jenny* became the first VIII Bomber Command Fortress to land in the United Kingdom when she put down at Prestwick. Three days later the following entry was made at High Wycombe: "Arrival of aircraft: 1 B-17 E. Total l."

The 97th Bomb Group would be based at Polebrook in Northamptonshire. There was sublime irony in its selection as the reception base for the first B-17 group in the European Theater of Operations (ETO). In May 1941 the RAF had taken possession of Polebrook airfield for the purpose of training crews for manning No. 90 Squadron, which was to be equipped with the B-17C, or Fortress I as the British referred to it. During June 1941, five Fortress I's were delivered to Polebrook and No. 90 Squadron began operations on 8th July when three aircraft took part in a daylight raid on Wilhelmshaven. The RAF flew twenty-four operations during the summer of 1941. By September it was decided that the Fortress was unsuitable for further bombing operations. Although it was an extremely well built aircraft, its defensive firepower of five manually operated .50-inch machine-guns and one .303-inch machine-gun was totally inadequate for daylight operations over such heavily defended targets on the Continent. Bombing, too, was inaccurate but the top secret Norden bombsight was deleted from all twenty models delivered to the RAF. As a result of the RAF's abortive trial period, modifications were made to the B-17 and Boeing evolved the B-17E which incorporated power-operated gun turrets and a tail gun position. It was this aircraft which now equipped the 97th Bomb Group.

Normally, the arrival of this first group would have been rapturously received by all and sundry. However, the event was somewhat overshadowed by the decision, taken on 2nd July, to dispatch six American crews from the 15th Bombardment Group (Light), together with six RAF crews, on a daylight sweep against four German airfields in Holland. It was the first time American airmen had flown in American built bombers against a German target but, although it was important historically, the 4th July raid was not an unqualified success. Two of the aircraft manned by Americans were shot down by what the RAF flight leader described as, "the worst flak barrage in my experience."

Despite the disappointing effect the raid had, the press hailed it as the start of a "new and gigantic air offensive." All the indications were that it would be, with the arrival early in August 1942 of two more heavy bombardment groups, the 92nd and the 301st. The 92nd, commanded by Colonel

Left: *B-17Es of the 97th Bomb Group prepare to take off. In the lead is 41-2578* Butcher Shop. *On 17th August 1942, Tibbets chose Lieutenant Butcher and his crew in this B-17 to lead the first Fortress raid of the war.*
Opposite: *Mr Anthony Eden (British Foreign Secretary) visits the 305th Bomb Group at Chelveston on 27th June 1942.*
(Bill Donald)

James S. Sutton, became the first heavy bombardment group to make a non-stop flight from Newfoundland to Scotland. On 28th August 1942 the last of the four squadrons landed in the United Kingdom and the 92nd set up home at Bovingdon, Hertfordshire. Meanwhile, the 301st Bomb Group, commanded by Colonel Ronald R. Walker, flew in to Chelveston and Podington in Northamptonshire.

If the press expected the gigantic new air offensive to begin at once they were disappointed. The fledgling 92nd, 97th, and 301st Bomb Groups, about to spread their wings in Europe, had been formed in the turbulent weeks following Pearl Harbor and their training had been deficient in many respects. Some air gunners had little or no training in aerial gunnery, some radio operators could not send or receive Morse, and the pilots were not versed in high altitude and formation flying. Many crews, untrained as they were, had only just got to know one another when they were pitched headlong into an air war America thought she could wage in daylight without escort.

If the crews knew little about each other, the 97th Bomb Group knew even less about a new group commander who at the end of July replaced Colonel Cornelius Cousland, who was sacked for running a "lackadaisical, loose-jointed, fun-loving, badly trained (especially in formation flying) outfit," which was "in no sense ready for combat." Colonel Frank A. Armstrong arrived from VIII Headquarters to give 97th crews a thorough training program, which would prepare them for combat over the Continent. His selection to lead the 97th Bomb Group in its pacemaker role was an excellent choice. His West Point training, his erect bearing and wind-tanned face (for the last fourteen of his thirty-nine years most of his time had been spent in the cockpits of military aircraft) commanded the respect of those who served with him. He had worked closely with his RAF counterparts during the early, formative days at High Wycombe. Once at

Grafton Underwood, Armstrong worked his new crews hard and his orders to his crewmen were direct: "There is no rank in this plane. Remember that. When we're in the air I'm just 'Doc' and you're just 'Joe' and 'Jim.' We're privates, every one of us - men on equal footing who are flying and fighting for our lives. If you want me to do something, don't just ask me to do it - tell me, and I'll do it."

Major Paul W. Tibbets, Group Flying Executive Officer of the 97th and charged with formulating tactics at Polebrook recalls: "The seven weeks of training between our arrival in England and our first raid paid off handsomely. I shudder to think of the results had it not been for the intensive practice afforded during this period." Colonel Armstrong, ably supported by men such as Major Paul Tibbets, took the group apart and put it back together again in a matter of little more than two weeks and by mid-August he was able to report that twenty-four crews were available for combat missions. The night of 9th August found the loading list (crewmen assigned to fly) on the operations bulletin board at Polebrook for the first time. Bombs were loaded into the bays, ammunition was checked out, equipment pre-flighted and procedures checked, only to have the weather "scrub" the mission. Two days later it was responsible for the loss of a 97th Bomb Group Fortress in Wales, when all aboard were killed. The often atrocious English weather was the bane of all air operations in the United Kingdom for much of the 8th's stay in eastern England.

Tension mounted again with this cancellation and the cynics spoke louder. The RAF made every conceivable effort to help the 8th get into the war as quickly as possible but had remained skeptical about its ability to bomb in broad daylight. "I remember some of the discussions held by RAF officials who tried to dissuade us from daylight bombing," said Major Tibbets. "These centered on their belief that we would be 'shot out of the air' by fighters and flak.

Consequently, most of us were apprehensive since it appeared we were up against 'super-men' and that our fate was in their hands." Critics of the American air forces were loud in their fault-finding and the continual questioning by American newsmen as to when the first heavy bomber mission would be flown was irritating the crewmen, especially when they themselves did not know the answer.

The continual wrangle as to whether day bombing would be possible over the Continent became so tense that, on 15th August, General Dwight D. Eisenhower, commanding the American forces in Europe, denied that this argument was hindering American air action. On 16th August, Peter Masefield, air correspondent, wrote in *The Sunday Times*: "American heavy bombers, the latest Fortresses and Liberators, are fine flying machines, but are not suited for bombing in Europe. Their bombs and bomb loads are too small, their armor and armament are low." He suggested that the Fortress was more suited for flying patrol missions over the Atlantic. But that night, the loading list was posted again and this time the weather held. The first Fortress strike of the war was scheduled for the following morning, Monday, 17th August 1942.

Major Tibbets and Frank Armstrong went to Grafton on 17th August to conduct the mission briefing. "We elected to take Butcher's aircraft because of its good crew and maintenance status. Frank Armstrong was not qualified in the B-17 so he elected to fly with me in the lead aircraft of the main group departing from Grafton Underwood. Twelve aircraft were designated as the main force to strike at the Rouen/Sotteville marshalling yards in northwestern France;

another six from Polebrook were to act as a diversionary force going to St Omer."

One crewman later remarked that, on the morning of 17th August, the lights of the briefing room might have been glowing from the electricity in the air. Even the briefing officer showed the tension of the moment. General Carl "Tooey" Spaatz, the American air commander in Europe, and members of his staff were present. Approximately thirty newspapermen added to the tension with their hurried scribbling as details of the historic mission were given out.

Briefing over, crews prepared to take off. At Grafton Underwood twelve B-17s were taxied out and the crews were lined up for takeoff in two flights of six. At 1526 hours Colonel Armstrong and Major Tibbets took off in *Butcher Shop*. Tibbets says: "*Butcher Shop* was not my regular airplane and I was not flying with my regular crew. My future missions would be flown in *Red Gremlin* with my regular crew, including navigator Dutch Van Kirk and bombardier Tom Ferebee, who would finish the war with me." (Tibbets was to fly an even more historic mission three years later when he piloted the B-29, *Enola Gay* over Hiroshima. Van Kirk and Ferebee flew the same positions that day.)

Tibbets continued: "It was just past mid-afternoon when we lifted off into sunny skies. All the planes were in the air at 1539 hours. We started our climb for altitude immediately and had reached 23,000 feet, in attack formation, by the time we left the coast of England and headed south across the Channel. I wondered whether or not all aircraft would make it or whether there would be aborts. However, it was a banner day with no aborts. As we departed the English coast out over the Channel, the RAF escort of Spitfire Vs joined us. Group Captain (later Air Chief Marshal) Harry Broadhurst was leading the RAF escort fighters and it was an emotional, spine-tingling event - we were off to do battle for real and fighters were there to give us protection and comfort."

General Carl Spaatz had felt confident enough to allow Brigadier General Ira C. Eaker to fly on the mission. Eaker joined the crew of *Yankee Doodle*, lead aircraft of the second flight of six, flown by John Dowswell. As the formation crossed the French coast the German radio proved as skeptical as the Allied critics by announcing that "twelve Lancasters" were heading inland.

When Lieutenant Levon L. Ray, the lead navigator, hurriedly checking his flight plan, called over the interphone: "Navigator to pilot, will you swing 220 degrees please?" Colonel Armstrong replied: "Pilot to navigator: don't just ask me to turn 220 degrees. If you want me to turn, you tell me to." The turn from the target found flak awaiting them for the second time and two Fortresses received minor damage. At Ypreville, fighters began to make their appearance and Sergeant Adam R. Jenkins, the tail-gunner aboard *Bat Outa Hell*, flying "tail-end Charlie," had his hands full. He reported later: "There were eight of them in V formation and the leader waggled his wings and came for us. When they were about 300 yards away I figured it was about time for me to do something. So I pulled the trigger and it looked like the ends of his wings came off. The other seven scattered."

One fighter was chased into the line of fire from Sergeant Kent R. West, the ball turret gunner aboard *Birmingham Blitzkrieg*, and was fired upon. West became the first American crewman to be credited with the destruction of a German aircraft. Altogether, two German fighters were shot down and five more claimed as "probables" for the loss of two Spitfires.

Ten minutes before the bomb run began, Lieutenant Frank R. Beadle, the lead bombardier, exclaimed in a singsong voice: "I can see the target, I can see the target!" Crew members twisted and turned, probing the beautiful bright blue sky for signs of possible enemy fighter attacks; a movement which would soon be known as the "Messerschmitt twist." Crews were relieved that "here was the target at last" and the tension they had been feeling began to ease. As the IP [Initial Point] was reached and the bomb run begun, Beadle again moved to the center of the spotlight for, as he

B-17E 41-9129 arrived at Prestwick in Scotland on 24th July 1942, and served with 303rd, 97th, 92nd, and 305th Bomb Groups. It was broken up after the war. (USAF)

manipulated the switch to open the bomb bay doors of *Butcher Shop*, he could be heard singing over the intercom: "I Don't Want to set the World On Fire!"

Packed into the bomb bays of the twelve Fortresses were 36,900 lbs of British bombs in the form of forty-five 600-pounders and nine 1,100-pounders. The heavy bombs (carried by three of the B-17s) were for the locomotive repair shops and the 600lb bombs for the Buddicum rolling stock repair shops. Even if the bombs missed, RAF reconnaissance photos had revealed concentrations of more than 2,000 freight cars at Sotteville. Any damage to what was the largest switching facility in northern France would make spectacular front-page news the following morning.

Bombing was made from 23,000 feet and a few bombs hit a mile short of the target. One burst hit about a mile west in some woods but the majority smashed into the assigned area. Major Tibbets says: "We caught the Germans by surprise. They hadn't expected a daytime attack, so we had clear sailing to the target. Visibility was unlimited and all twelve planes dropped their bomb loads. Our aim was reasonably good but you couldn't describe it as pinpoint bombing. We still had a lot to learn.

A salvo of 600lb bombs makes its way to the target.

"At least half the bombs fell in the general target area. One of the aiming points took a direct hit and there were a number of bomb craters within a radius of 1,500 feet. Bombs intended for the other aiming point fell about 200 feet to the south. While the results did not come up to our expectations, our accuracy was considerably better than that achieved by the RAF in its night attacks, or by German bombers in their raids on England. By the time we unloaded our bombs, the enemy came to life. Anti-aircraft fire, erratic and spasmodic at first, zeroed in on our formations as we began the return flight. Two B-17s suffered slight damage from flak. Three Bf 109s moved in for the attack but were quickly driven off by the Spitfires that accompanied us. The only German planes I saw were out of range and I got the impression that they were simply looking us over.

"A feeling of elation took hold of us as we winged back across the Channel. All the tension was gone. We were no longer novices at this terrible game of war. We had braved the enemy in his own skies and were alive to tell people about it."

Shortly before 1900 hours anxious watchers on the Polebrook control tower began counting in the formation. Down below, equally anxious base personnel, fellow airmen, high-ranking American and RAF officers, and about thirty Allied pressmen, gathered to witness the end to an historic mission. Specks were spotted in the distance and a hurried count could locate only eleven Fortresses. As the landing pattern was formed, cheers were heard, for in the distance came the straggler. Three of the B-17s, in complete disregard for air

discipline, peeled out of formation and buzzed the control tower. Under the circumstances no one seemed to mind. In came *Baby Doll, Peggy D, Big Stuff, Butcher Shop, Yankee Doodle, Berlin Sleeper, Johnny Reb, Kissey-me-Kowboy, Birmingham Blitzkrieg,* and the rest. Tibbets concludes: "Once back at base we were debriefed and then there followed a "victory celebration" at the club with some RAF fighter pilots in attendance."

Interrogation proved almost farcical as everyone seemed to want to talk at once. The crews were happy to learn that there were no losses, the most serious damage having occurred on the diversionary flight, when a pigeon smashed through the windshield of a B-17 and the fragments of Plexiglas left minor scars on the bombardier and navigator. The diversion, although not quite going according to plan, had proved successful. Three Fortresses in the 340th Bomb Squadron and three from the 341st had flown in separate elements. The latter had not been able to locate its fighter escort and, following instructions, had returned early.

General Eaker told the assembled reporters that the crew members on the bombing raid were enthusiastic and alert but nonchalant to the point of being blasé. This attitude, the General felt, was good for it meant that the men were confident, without being cocky. He added that additional drill in the use of oxygen was needed and that air discipline would have to be improved to achieve the tighter formation necessary to enable the gunners to function as a team unit. General Spaatz, elated with the success of the mission, stated: "I think the crews behaved like veterans. Everything went according to plan." The youngest man

Smoke often obscured the aiming points.

aboard, Sergeant Frank Christensen, who had not yet turned eighteen, remarked: "It's all in the day's work."

The New York Times communiqué describing the mission was placed on the front page along with the Peter Masefield story from *The Sunday Times*. Colonel Armstrong's remark upon his return, "We ruined Rouen," was without doubt an exaggeration but the raid focused world attention on VIII Bomber Command.

The first of the congratulatory messages to arrive came from Air Marshal Sir Arthur Harris, Chief of RAF Bomber Command: "Congratulations from all ranks of Bomber Command on the highly successful completion of the first all-American raid by the big fellows on German-occupied territory in Europe. Yankee Doodle certainly went to town and can stick yet another well-deserved feather in his cap."

When the news of the first bombing mission by VIII Bomber Command reached Washington, the Chief of Air Staff arranged for a memorandum (prepared for General Hap Arnold's signature) to be sent to General George C. Marshall, Chief of Staff, for the attention of Admirals Ernest J. King and William D. Leahy. This declared: "The attack on Rouen again verifies the soundness of our policy of the precision bombing of strategic objectives rather than the mass bombing of large, city-size areas." Carl Spaatz and Ira Eaker had put their careers on the line by insisting on the policy of daylight precision bombing. Eaker had been a fighter pilot before General Arnold sent him to England to study RAF Bomber Command and assess the potential for bombing the enemy around-the-clock. In spite of advice to the contrary from senior officers in the RAF, Eaker had concluded that daylight precision bombing was a gamble worth taking. It was his idea that Germany and its environs could be bombed to defeat with B-17 s and B-24s pounding them in

daylight and RAF bombers at night. In 1976, Albert Speer, Hitler's minister of armaments production, admitted that the combined efforts of VIII Bomber Command and RAF Bomber Command tied down 900,000 men who could have been used to put Russia out of the war before the Allied invasion of France.

One week after the bombing of Rouen, the Vichy Government issued a protest at the raid, claiming that fifteen soldiers had died. The typewritten communiqué blamed "American" airmen, but this had been corrected in pencil to say, "Anglo-Saxon aviators" with an additional correction that the dead soldiers were "German".

On 19th August, the 97th Bomb Group dispatched twenty-four of its B-17Es in support of the Allied landings at Dieppe. Their target was the airfield at Abbeville/Drucat in northern France, home of the infamous *Abbeville Kids*. The pilots of the yellow-nosed Bf 109s were among the Luftwaffe elite. Two of the B-17s aborted because of mechanical failures, but the rest of the group plastered the airfield, destroying a hangar and severely cratering or "potholing" the runways. Fortunately, the Luftwaffe was heavily engaged over the Dieppe area and did not show. British High Command reported that sixteen fighters were either destroyed or damaged as a result of the bombing strike and the airfield itself put out of action for a vital two hours. In addition, the controllers of the whole of the fighter area remained out of action until that evening. Air Marshal Sir Trafford Leigh-Mallory, Chief of RAF Fighter Command, added his congratulations: "The raid on Abbeville undoubtedly struck a heavy blow at the German fighter organization at a very critical moment during the operation . . .." RAF fighter pilots reported the following day that the main area of the Drucat aerodrome appeared to have been completely demolished.

The morning of 20th August brought a hurried call from photo-reconnaissance informing Eaker that 1,600 goods wagons and seventeen locomotives were parked in the Longueau marshalling yards in Amiens. Twelve Fortresses from the 340th and 342nd Bomb Squadrons were airborne and eleven bombed through slight flak. Spitfires protected the formation and a Belgian fighter pilot who witnessed the raid reported that the bombers scored at least fifteen direct hits. The bomber crews were jubilant but senior staff officers were more reserved, well aware that so far they had flown only shallow penetration missions in predominantly fine weather. The case for daylight, high-altitude, precision bombing was as yet, unproven. The indications were that the B-17s would not be able to flaunt themselves over enemy targets with impunity for very much longer.

In the early morning of 21st August, twelve Fortresses were dispatched to bomb the Wilton shipyards at Rotterdam, the most modern in Holland. Crews still felt confident, knowing that the faithful RAF Spitfires would again be on hand to protect them. But the B-17s were slow to form up after leaving Grafton Underwood. One Fortress was barely airborne when it was forced to abort and a replacement joined the formation. Three other B-17s suffered generator failures that caused the gun turrets to become inoperative and they returned to base. Sixteen minutes late for the escort, the remaining crews knew the fighters would not be able to escort them all the way to the target. The Dutch coast was in sight when the recall message came through and the Spitfires turned for home. They were immediately replaced by upwards of twenty-five German fighters in what became a prelude to a running fight, which lasted for twenty-five minutes. The bombers' massed firepower was a little more than the Luftwaffe pilots could handle and two fighters fell to the Fortresses' guns. Sergeant Adam R. Jenkins, the tail turret gunner aboard *Johnny Reb*, drew first blood. Sergeant Roy Allen, the top turret gunner, fired one burst and his guns jammed. John N. Hughes, one of the waist gunners, sucked a lump of ice into the mouth of his oxygen tube in the excitement and was forced to hold the mask with one hand and fire his gun with the other, while nearing collapse from lack of oxygen.

In the nose compartment, Harold Spire, the navigator, had just fired at a crossing fighter when a burst of cannon fire tore through the windshield. Donald A. Walter, the co-pilot, was raked from his legs to his chest and died instantly and the splinters of Plexiglas seriously wounded Richard S. Starks, the pilot. While struggling for breath, Starks managed to call for help and Edward Sconiers, the bombardier, and Sergeant Allen, came to the cockpit. Sconiers removed the dead co-pilot and took his place at the controls, hoping that what he had learned about piloting before washing out of flying school, would be useful to him now. Holding on to the stick, the pilot began giving instructions to Sconiers, while the tail and ball turret gunners continued to blaze away at their five pursuers. *Johnny Reb* lagged behind the rest of the formation with its number three and four engines hit. Despite this, Sconiers managed to nurse the ailing bomber back to England and land at Horsham St Faith, near Norwich. During the remainder of the flight, Sergeant Franky Rebellow, the top turret gunner in the lead ship, piloted by Captain Rudolph Flack, had fired away with such abandon that he had run out of ammunition. He crawled to the cockpit, slapped the co-pilot, Colonel Armstrong, on the back and screamed in his ear: "Not a bullet left!"

The press enthusiastically credited the nine Fortresses with six fighters destroyed and praised them for beating off twenty-five Focke-Wulfs. Some RAF officers, however, remained skeptical and it later transpired that only a handful of fighters had actually fired on the formation.

Yankee Doodle, *B-17E 41-9023 of the 97th Bomb Group, carried Brigadier General Ira C. Eaker to Rouen on the first B-17 mission of the war on 17th August 1942.* (USAF)

Eaker took advantage of the Luftwaffe's inexperience in dealing with American bomber formations and, on 24th August, dispatched a dozen 97th Bomb Group B-17s to the shipyard of Ateliers et Chantlers Maritime de la Seine et Le Trait. Twelve of the forty-eight bombs fell within 500 yards of the aiming point, but no material damage seemed to have been done to the yards. One wayward bomb luckily hit and sank a U-boat tied up at the docks, but overall it was the poorest bombing to date. Flak caused damage to the Fortresses and two officers and three sergeants received slight wounds. On the way home the formation was jumped from above by yellow-nosed Bf 109s.

A 20mm shell entered the cockpit of the lead ship piloted by Paul Tibbets, badly injuring Lieutenant Gene Lockhart, the co-pilot, in the hand. The top turret gunner was also seriously injured and Tibbets suffered minor wounds. All recovered and Beirne Lay, Jr. was asked to arrange an awards ceremony so that General Spaatz could present Purple Hearts to the wounded. Lay met some opposition, as he recalls.

"'Tib' was too busy to bother with me, snowed under as he was with more pressing demands. Finally, I got my dander up and accosted him in his office. 'Major Tibbets,' I said hotly, 'can you give me just five minutes?'"

"I wish I had five minutes," he growled.

"General Spaatz sent me down here to do a job. I need your okay to work out the details with your adjutant."

"Stop right there," he cut in. "I'm dealing every day with matters of life and death and I can't spare a man from the squadron for frills."

"You may call this review ordered by Spaatz and Eaker a frill, but I should think you'd have enough interest in your squadron to give them their due."

"He sprang up and advanced toward me, his face flushed, near breaking under the strain of fatigue. 'You have a lot of guts coming down here from your plush headquarters and telling me I don't really care about my squadron, because I don't have time for a PRO show!' I immediately backed up, apologizing for my choice of words. He calmed down enough for me to explain how distasteful my job was to me and that I'd much prefer to change places with him. He called in his adjutant and gave the necessary orders."

Lay and Tibbets later became great friends and collaborated on an MGM movie about Tibbets' Hiroshima experience called *Above and Beyond*.

With the good weather continuing to hold, bombing missions were becoming almost everyday events at Grafton

In England, Fortresses taxi out in preparation for another mission over enemy occupied Europe. (Tom Cushing)

Underwood and Polebrook. On 27th August, nine Fortresses returned to the Wilton shipyard at Rotterdam, which was once again working to full capacity. Although only seven of the B-17s bombed, hits were claimed on two ships and the center of the target was well covered. The following day, the 97th Bomb Group dispatched fourteen B-17s to the Avions Potez factory at Meaulte in northern France. Most of the bombs (from the eleven Fortresses that bombed) fell in open fields, although some "post-holed" the runways. The B-17s returned intact but one Canadian pilot's Spitfire was missing. It was on this mission that American fighter pilots were also represented for the first time.

On 29th August, for the third day running, the 97th Bomb Group was airborne and twelve of the thirteen B-17s dispatched bombed the German fighter base at Coutrai-Wevelghem in Belgium. The results appeared good and even the British press, which had at first been cautious of American claims, now openly praised them. However, Spaatz and Eaker refused to read too much into the Fortresses' success (claimed in some circles to have scored better than seventy percent in hits). It was early days yet and moves were afoot to transfer the 97th and 301st Bomb Groups to the 12th Air Force, which had been activated at Washington DC on 20th August. Although Eaker continued to use the two groups at

every opportunity, it meant he would have to reorganize and plan for the future.

Eaker needed a Combat Crew Replacement and Training Center. Personnel and equipment were in short supply but the 92nd Bomb Group, with its base at Bovingdon, was selected for the task. Bovingdon became known as the 11th CCR Center and, for a few important months, provided many new combat crews that the 8th was to need so badly as operations increased. This meant that the group's latest B-17Fs were no longer needed for combat and, almost immediately upon their arrival at Bovingdon, they were transferred to the 97th Bomb Group.

The B-17F was supposed to be an improvement on the B-17E. However, it was equipped with only two .30 caliber machine-gun mountings in the nose although it had additional .50 caliber sockets modified later in the field. Externally, the B-17F differed little from the B-17E, its most noticeable feature being a frameless Plexiglas nose. Inwardly, however, it incorporated over 400 major design modifications that, although making it 1,000lbs heavier than the B-17E, made it more suitable for combat. The 92nd Bomb Group personnel were disappointed to receive the 97th's battered B-17Es in return, but their time would come when they flew combat missions and became known as "Fame's Favored Few."

On the other side of the English Channel, Luftwaffe pilots await the Fortresses. The main fighter units involved in combat with the 8th Air Force were Jagdgeschwadern 2 and 26.

On 5th September, the 97th Bomb Group dispatched twenty-five of its newly acquired B-17Fs, together with twelve Fortresses of the 301st Bomb Group (flying its first combat mission of the war), to the marshalling yards at Rouen. Thirty-one B-17s bombed, six aborting owing to mechanical problems. Approximately twenty percent of the bombs fell within the target area and some hit the city. Unconfirmed reports claimed that 140 civilians were killed and about 200, mostly French, were wounded. One bomb, a dud, hit the city hospital and went through to the basement.

The following day, Eaker mounted his largest bombing mission so far, to the Avions Potez factory at Meaulte, using the 92nd Bomb Group for the first time. The 92nd scraped together fourteen ex 97th Bomb Group B-17Es and crews, filling in with ground personnel, some of them privates. They joined the twenty-two B-17Fs of the 97th in the main strike while the 301st Bomb Group flew a diversionary raid on the St Omer-Longueness airfield. Thirty Fortresses crossed Meaulte, but only six in the 92nd Bomb Group attacked the target. Enemy aircraft were encountered continuously from the French coast to the target and it was on this raid that the Americans suffered their first aircraft losses.

Near Flasselles, Second Lieutenant Clarence C. Lipsky's B-17 from the 97th Bomb Group was last seen with three fighters following it down, apparently under control. The aircraft fell near Amiens at 1855 hours. This victory, the first "kill" of an American heavy bomber by the Luftwaffe, was awarded to Hauptman Egon "Conny" Meyer, CO of II./JG26. Four parachutes were seen to open. In the 92nd formation *Baby Doll*, piloted by Second Lieutenant Leigh E. Stewart, was last seen off Beachy Head struggling towards Dover out of formation and being pursued by five enemy fighters. Victory was officially given to Oberfeldwebel Roth of 4./JG26, who carried out the *coup de grace*. Air Sea Rescue launches searched the area, but without success.

The losses had a chastening effect on both groups, as Paul Tibbets recalls: "The blow came as a personal shock to me because Lieutenant Lipsky was one of my favorites. Up to this time, the war had seemed little more than a game in the sense that we flew out in the morning and came back a few hours later after dropping our bombs and eluding enemy flak and fighter fire . . . .. Now at last the war was a bloody reality for all of us."

On 17th October 1942 the Red Cross reported that Lipsky and five of his crew were POWs.

Chapter 2
Lighting the Torch

The 92nd Bomb Group had only flown the 6th September mission because the 8th Air Force was so desperately short of aircraft, spares, and personnel. This constant drain on its resources was a direct result of the need to supply the 12th Air Force, destined for the Mediterranean theater. (Its future commander, Brigadier General James H. Doolittle, would not be appointed until 23rd September.) Unfortunately, few in the 8th were aware that the 12th Air Force was destined for *Operation Torch* and therefore had top priority when it came to spares, personnel, B-17Fs, and even training. New groups had to be trained by the 8th for eventual transfer to the 12th Air Force, a task Eaker could well have done without at such a crucial time in the 8th's history. Crews in the 92nd Bomb Group were disappointed to learn from the general that they were to continue with their training program while other B-17 groups continued flying missions to France and the Low Countries.

On 7th September, the 97th and 301st Bomb Groups were dispatched to Holland to bomb the shipyards at Rotterdam again. A storm warning was flashed to the outbound Fortresses, most of the crews receiving it and returning safely. However, seven Fortresses in the 97th Bomb Group formation continued to the target where the Luftwaffe was wait-

ing for them. The German fighter pilots hurled themselves into the fight, desperate for the kill. The lead ship of the flight, flown by Captain Aquilla Hughes, bore the brunt of the enemy attacks and the ball turret gunner was killed and three other gunners were wounded. Two engines were put out of action and the oil lines and hydraulic lines to the brakes were shot out. The radio began malfunctioning and Hughes was forced to drop out of formation. Two flights of twelve fighters each attacked the stricken B-17, but her gunners fought back tenaciously and claimed three fighters destroyed, two in flames. Although badly damaged, the lead ship and the other six B-17s managed to fight their way out of trouble and make it home safely.

Seven days later the 97th and 301st Bomb Groups were, on paper at least, assigned to the 12th Air Force, although they continued flying combat missions under the banner of VIII Bomber Command. On 26th September three squadrons of Spitfires were assigned to escort twenty-four B-17s over the harbor at Brest. The American Eagle Squadron, No.133, had moved to Bolt Head, on the south coast of England, so that the fuel supply would permit maximum time over the target. At briefing the bomber crews were told that the target would be covered by cloud and they would

Little Skunkface, *414 Squadron, 97th Bomb Group, painted in the early RAF style camouflage.* (M Bailey)

have a wind of 100mph from the south. The statement concerning the wind proved an unexplained and costly error, for the wind was out of the north, adding to their speed.

Unable to see the coastline, the navigators in the bombers flew on dead reckoning and when they were actually over their target their plotting charts had them still short of the target. Twenty-four Spitfires turned back with their assignment completed, leaving No.133 Squadron alone with the B-17s. Unable to locate the target owing to the briefing error, the bombers turned north for their bases with the Spitfires staying with them and depending on them for proper navigation. Running short of fuel, the Spitfires were soon forced to leave the formation to seek their own bases. When they broke out of the clouds expecting to be over Cornwall, they were in fact over the heart of Brest. Enemy anti-aircraft fire opened up on them immediately and, lacking fuel, they were helpless. Eleven Spitfires were forced to land in France and the twelfth, nursing his fast dwindling fuel supply, attempted to glide back to England but crashed on the cliffs of the Lizard. The Fortresses were able to buck the headwind and return to base.

Although the 97th and 301st Bomb Groups were soon to join the 12th Air Force, the complete break up of VIII Bomber Command was avoided by the formation of four new groups - the 91st, 303rd, 305th, and 306th - which were undergoing training in America. The 305th Bomb Group's training program was directed without compromise by Lieutenant Colonel Curtis E. LeMay, who had taken over the Group in May 1942 from Ernest H. Lawson (who returned to command the 305th in November 1943 and was

KIA [Killed in Action] leading the Group over Hamburg on 18th June 1944). At 36 years of age, LeMay was already a veteran of two record-breaking flights to South America in a YB-17. He had also navigated the XB-15 on a 2,839 mile flight to the Galapagos Islands in 1940, had undertaken pioneering flights to Africa, and had flown VIPs and top brass across the North Atlantic as a Ferry Command pilot of a B-24. In October 1941 he had become Group Operations Officer of the 34th Bomb Group and, later, Executive Officer of the 306th Bomb Group.

One of the officers who served under LeMay at Salt Lake City and Muroc Dry Lake, California, was Captain Clifton Pyle, who was assigned to the Group in April 1942.

"I was designated one of the flight commanders in the 422nd Bomb Squadron which was commanded by Major Thomas McGehee. The immediate mission of the Bomb Group was to train three cadres of primary flight crews, a pilot, and engineer in each, for new groups crews, that were being organized. Then we were to accept and train a new cadre of personnel, this time the whole crew, and proceed overseas.

"Lieutenant Colonel LeMay demanded the best from each man. If the man did not 'produce,' he would fire him. Several examples were made in this regard and it took little time for the entire group to start stepping in line. He was a believer in exactness in flying, abiding by the book as far as possible, but wanted the job done. He would not tolerate laziness of any type and he didn't want any 'unlucky' person on his team. He would fire a person for being 'unlucky' as quick as incompetent. All during the training period Colonel LeMay was a strict disciplinarian. He explained it was for our benefit and the best chance of survival. Most of the crews thought he was a little too rough. Colonel LeMay was soon known to all as 'Ole Iron Ass,' and referred to in public as 'Ole Iron Tail' or 'Ole Iron Pants'. Regardless of his persistent firmness, he soon gained our respect, admiration, and full support. He was one who believed in flying with his crews and did so on numerous occasions."

Other groups training for eventual movement overseas were encountering similar problems to those experienced by the 305th Bomb Group. All crews had to be declared operational by the Preparation for Overseas Movement (POM) Inspectors before they could fly the hazardous Northern Ferry Route to England. Among the first groups declared operational was the 91st Bomb Group, commanded by Colonel Stanley T. Wray. Wray had assumed command of the group on 15th May 1942, after serving with the 92nd Bomb Group as its Executive Officer. He would have to wait until early in October 1942 before the 91st had enough B-17s on strength, although one squadron began the flight to England late in September 1942. Two parent groups, the 303rd, commanded by Colonel James H. Wallace, and the 306th, commanded by Colonel Charles 'Chip' Overacker, departed for the United Kingdom during September also. The 8th Air Force desperately needed these "new" groups but it would not be until November 1942 that it could call upon all four for combat operations. Four airfields had been made available for the new groups. All were located within a twelve mile radius of Bedford, about forty miles north of London.

The 91st was allocated Kimbolton and the 303rd, 305th, and 306th - all of whose ground echelons began arriving in the United Kingdom throughout September, October, and early November 1942 - were allocated Molesworth, Grafton Underwood, and Thurleigh respectively.

Among those in the 306th Bomb Group who traveled to England was Al La Chasse, a bombardier in Lieutenant John Olsen's crew.

"On 1st September, after a good night's rest, we had taken off from Gander Bay, Newfoundland, in darkness, for a jump straight across the Atlantic to Prestwick. Previously, we had left Westover Field, Massachusetts, after weeks of preparation, shake-down, fuel consumption tests, and submarine patrols. Our trip was a "first" for a whole group to leave and arrive as one group. There were two plane losses and the loss of one crew."

After several days of waiting in Scotland, the 306th air echelon was green-lighted to go to Thurleigh. All this activity did not go unnoticed by the enemy as La Chasse explains. "The day we brought *Snoozy II* in, the English tower master said on open radio, 'I say there, American aircraft, this is your field: you are cleared to land.' Lord Haw Haw must have been listening for, that night on radio, he said: 'Welcome to England, 306th Group!'"

For administrative and accommodation reasons each bomb group would base all its four squadrons on one airfield. This resulted in the 97th Bomb Group's 342nd and 414th Bomb Squadrons having to vacate Grafton Underwood and move to nearby Polebrook to rejoin the

Eager Beaver makes the backdrop in this photo for personnel of the 368th Bomb Squadron, 306th Bomb Group.

340th and 341st Squadrons. Meanwhile, the ground echelon of the 305th Bomb Group, which arrived in the UK aboard the *Queen Mary* on 12th September, took over the vacated base and awaited the arrival of the air echelon which, early in August, had departed Muroc Dry Lake for Syracuse, New York, for six weeks' advanced flight training. At Syracuse the 305th received the balance of its thirty-five B-17Fs, but they could not be flown to England until modifications had been made. Finally, amid fears of a move to the Pacific theater minus its ground echelon, the 305th was on its way to England.

On 19th October, the air echelon departed for Gander. Cliff Pyle was among those who made the trip. "The day of departure was one day after my wife gave birth to a baby girl. It was nearly a year later before I had a chance to see her for the first time." Many men would never see their loved ones again and these thoughts were uppermost in the minds as they touched down at Gander for the flight to Scotland.

Hell's Angels in the 366th Bomb Squadron, flown by Captain C. D. Clark, was forced to ditch off Nova Scotia in bad weather after losing a propeller, but the crew literally jumped off the aircraft onto the shore. One other B-17 lost two propellers, but managed to land safely in Scotland though not at Prestwick. Cliff Pyle was another who landed elsewhere.

"Arriving over the Liverpool area, the group ran into some bad weather with low visibility and ceilings. This alone would not have deterred us from continuing to our destination, Grafton Underwood, but there were numerous balloons tied to steel cables floating around in and out of the clouds. We were not briefed on this situation. Instructions by radio advised us to land at a suitable airfield and report in by phone. My aircraft and three others landed at Pickapoo Park, just outside Liverpool. Three days later, after the weather cleared, we made it to Grafton Underwood in good shape."

Grafton Underwood offered some home comforts. The same could not be said for the bleak and under-developed bases at Kimbolton, Molesworth, and Thurleigh. Crews in the 306th Bomb Group were sent to other bases as the hard top on the runways at Thurleigh had not hardened. Air Ministry workers and US Engineers took care of expansion work and repaired the runways. The Group spent several days collecting its aircraft and flying them back to Thurleigh where they continued to use the runways during the repair work. Life remained miserable for 800 men who had to live in tents until the end of November 1942 when more suitable accommodation was finally made available.

Kimbolton airfield did not endear itself to the officers and men of the 91st Bomb Group commanded by Lieutenant Colonel Stanley T. Wray. They had arrived at the base on 1st October and soon their B-17s were breaking up the hastily built runways. The Nissen huts held damp and the men felt cut off from civilization. It was not until early October that the 91st had enough B-17s to complete its aircraft complement. Meanwhile, crews used their time wisely before beginning operations as Squadron Leader Phibbs, the RAF Liaison Officer at Kimbolton, recalls. "Their Fortresses lacked sufficient protection in the cockpit so the more enterprising among their crews stole armor plating from some British armored cars which had been left on the airfield by the RAF Regiment for airfield defense!"

On 13th October, Wray visited Bassingbourn in Cambridgeshire, a pre-war RAF station with permanent runways, solid brick buildings, and comfortable messes. Wray decided it would be ideal for the 91st and the following day 'Wray's Ragged Irregulars,' as they were nicknamed, moved in and took up residence. At headquarters, Brigadier General Longfellow was taken aback by the move and remonstrated that no decision to move the 91st had yet been taken. Wray explained there was a decision and that they had made it. Eventually, headquarters came round to their way of thinking and the group remained in Bassingbourn until the cessation of hostilities.

While the four new groups got to grips with their English bases, the 92nd, 97th, and 301st Bomb Groups carried the war to the enemy. On 2nd October, the 97th Bomb Group, now commanded by Colonel Joseph H. Atkinson (Colonel Armstrong having moved up to Bomber Command) was dispatched, together with the 301st Bomb Group, to Meaulte. Their target was again the Potez factory. The 92nd Bomb Group flew a diversionary feint along the French coast while six B-17s from the 97th attacked St Omer.

The locomotive, carriage, and wagon works at Chemin de Fer du Nord at Lille had long been earmarked as a target because of its importance to an enemy who was suffering an acute shortage of rail transport. Eaker also saw it as the ideal target to demonstrate high altitude precision bombing but it was not until 9th October that VIII Bomber Command could assemble enough bombers to destroy the target. A few weeks before, the Command could only muster twelve aircraft but, by including the Liberators of the 93rd Bomb Group and Fortresses of the 306th Bomb Group, both of whom were flying their maiden missions, Eaker was able to assemble an unprecedented 108 bombers for the raid. Furthermore, seven heavies would fly a diversionary sweep towards the Continent and the main force would be escorted by a strong contingent of RAF and USAAF fighters.

For Henry A. West, a navigator with the 352nd Bomb Squadron in the 301st Bomb Group at Chelveston, the Lille raid would be his fourth operational mission.

"The 301st was briefed to fly from Chelveston to Norwich, leaving the coast at Felixstowe and heading for Bray, France, to Mouscron, then to the target. We were to circle to the left and leave France via Gravelines and head for North Foreland and back to base. The secondary target was Coutrai aerodrome and the third target was St Omer airfield. At the general briefing later we were told that we would meet about 100 FW 190s and moderate to heavy anti-aircraft fire. I went out to the plane at about 0645 hours and worked on my maps, plotting courses, and making entries in the log and just generally getting everything in order, such as checking the guns and ammunition. We started engines on schedule but takeoff was six minutes late and we finally got off at 0753. We circled the field, getting into formation, until we departed on course. Everything went according to schedule."

The same procedure was being enacted at the other B-17 bases in the region. At Thurleigh, Lieutenant John Olsen and the crew of *Snoozy II* from the 367th Bomb Squadron, prepared for their first mission with the 306th Bomb Group. At between 0800 hours and 0830 hours, Colonel Charles "Chip" Overacker, the CO, led his crews off from Thurleigh. As they circled the airfield, Al La Chasse, the bombardier in Olsen's crew, waved goodbye to his buddy, "Butterball" Jones. "His aircraft was grounded because we were using some of its parts to fly the mission. I never saw him again. He fell out of his ship's bomb bay on a later mission to the sub-pens in France after his ship was forced into the water by enemy fighters."

The 306th joined with the 92nd, 97th, and the leading 301st with the B-24s of the 93rd Bomb Group falling in behind the formation. It was almost inevitable that an operation of this size, mounted for the first time, would be overshadowed by mistakes and mechanical problems. Seven Fortresses in the 92nd Bomb Group formation returned early

to Bovingdon and other groups also lost some of their number. Henry West in Major Dean Byerly's Fortress in the 301st formation, had no such problems.

"We picked up our fighter escort at Felixstowe, about three squadrons of Spitfires and three squadrons of P-38s. On the way to the target, as we were entering enemy territory, we had some inaccurate flak but generally we proceeded to Lille without incident. Colonel R.R. Walker, our CO, who was leading the entire mission, got fouled up somewhere and we just invited trouble by stooging around France for a while doing 180 degree turns. Finally, we found the target but, just as Arthur 'Catman Carlson,' my bombardier, was sighting through his bombsight, a formation of B-17s cut in front of us and we were forced to bomb another target. This turned out to be the railway goods terminus."

Al La Chasse, in the 306th Bomb Group formation, recalls:

"Some smoke and dust covered the target area. As we continued the run a line of B-24s out of position were coming across the target area from the east, heading towards England. Flak hit our right inboard engine and set it on fire. Norman Gates, the co-pilot, somehow extinguished it. Flak increased. I was surprised it came in so many colors. On the bomb run Olsen trimmed the ship before turning the controls over to me. After our flak hit, the Norden bombsight automatically made the corrections necessary to 'right' the ship on course. I released the bomb load, not knowing there would be several malfunctions causing bomb rack problems.

"The plane lifted, lightened by the bomb drop. The B-24s were now behind us. It was 0942 hours, time over the target as per mission plan. For *Snoozy II* the war was about to begin, and end. With only three engines pulling we began a silly 360 degree turn into enemy territory.

Hot coffee and doughnuts, brought to these 92nd Bomb Group men care of American Red Cross. The B-17 is 41-9020 Phyllis that survived many missions including courier flights to North Africa. It was eventually wrecked in a crash landing on 23rd July 1944, by which time it was serving with the 303rd Bomb Group and renamed Tugboat Annie. *(USAF)*

The difficulty of hitting a particular target is well illustrated here. Notice the number of near misses.

Where were the P-38s? - None! At about 1,000 yards at 3 o'clock there immediately appeared in line astern, a gaggle of Bf 109s with four years' war experience stalking us. 'Ass-end Charlie' was about to become a sitting duck!"

The interphone came alive with voices. Though Al La Chasse did not know their identity, they were III./JG26 led by their Kommandeur, Hauptman "Pips" Priller.

"Bandits were everywhere. 'Where are those goddam P-38s?' Sounds like typing on loose paper indicated that enemy shells were ripping into the ship's skin surfaces. *Snoozy II* began to lag behind the rest of the formation. 'Honest John' McKee's ship tried lagging back with us. Good old 'Honest John.' He tried.

"Tracers were coming and going in all directions. 'How can I toggle armed bombs in a canted ship?' I thought. They hadn't taught me that in cadet training. I thought, 'Salvo!' That's it, dump the whole damn load, bombs, shackles and all.

"Now we were headed west, towards the White Cliffs of Dover. Then, suddenly, Bert F. Kaylor, the tail-gunner, screamed: 'Jerries at 6 o'clock!' I thought: 'Boy that's right up our butts.' Out of the sun the bastards came. I could feel each gunner's position as they fired. Tail, ball, and waist gunners each took turns. Again, 'Where are those **** P-38s?' Now only Truman Wilder, the ball turret

gunner, was still firing. Oh, oh, a belly attack was coming. All at once a German fighter flew right by our nose with a dirty yellow belly and nose with a white prop' spinner and black painted corkscrew lines like a top. I tried to contact anyone on intercom but there was no sound. From behind came a hell of a thumping noise. We had taken a full burst of 20mm cannon into the flight deck."

"Pips" Priller had singled out *Snoozy II* (he identified it as a B-24!) and he pumped cannon and machine gun fire into the B-17 leaving Olsen and Gates dead in their blood-spattered cockpit.

"Shortly thereafter, the sun went by the nose as the ship went into a flat spin. We were lucky; it could have been in a tight vertical spin. Bill Gise, our navigator, got caught in the centrifugal force of the spin. Everything loose flew through the air and plastered on the side of the ship. We finally made it back to the escape hatch to bail out into the 'wild blue yonder.' I followed Gise out after some trouble with the hatch. God must have opened it. The ride down was just like the book on parachutes said it would be. Scary, but nice. I was alive!"

La Chasse, Gise, and Erwin Wissenbeck, the top turret gunner, were the only three to bail out. La Chasse was thrown into various jails including the infamous Napoleonic prison of Saint Giles near Brussels. At *Dulag Luft* he discovered he was only the eighteenth American POW. La Chasse finished the war at *Stalag Luft III*, at Sagan in Silesia.

Only sixty-nine aircraft had bombed their primary targets (four were lost) and many of the bombs failed to explode. The inexperienced 93rd and 306th Bomb Groups had placed many of their bombs outside the target area, killing a number of French civilians. Traffic control was bad and some of the bombardiers never got the target in their bomb- sights. Those who had to jettison their bomb loads in the Channel on the way home were sardonically referred to as "chandeliers" by their contemporaries at one B-17 base.

The bombardiers had been well trained by peacetime standards and the Norden bombsight was currently the best in the world. However, the "pickle barrel" accuracy obtained in the clear blue skies in Texas and Colorado was a far cry from the flak stained and cloudy conditions prevailing at 20,000 feet over Europe. Violent evasive tactics and constant flak dodging lessened the effectiveness of the precision bombsights when every degree of accuracy was imperative. On these early shallow penetration missions each bombardier had his own bombsight and bombed individually. This increased the margin for error and did not justify any complacency. Only experience and a change in application would correct the problems associated with bombing.

At the subsequent interrogations, crews revealed that they had made 242 encounters with Luftwaffe fighters and put in fighter "kills"; forty-eight destroyed, eighteen probably destroyed, and four damaged, or "48-18-4" as it was termed in AAF nomenclature. The British press in particular remained sceptical of the initial high claims. However, there was, and always would be, duplication in the number of claims and it took very careful analysis by intelligence officers to establish the correct "scores." When the heat of the Lille battle had died away the American gunners', scores were whittled down to 25-38-44 and, finally, to 21-21-15 (the Germans admitted the loss of only one fighter). At the time the figures did much to compensate for the largely inaccurate bombing.

The Lille mission placed the American bomber crews firmly in the public eye and focused attention, perhaps wrongly, on their ability to knock down fighters rather than carrying out their primary task - that of destroying important targets. The very name "Flying Fortress," conjured up visions of vast aerial fleets bent on destroying the greatest possible number of enemy aircraft, but the destruction of the enemy's ability to make war was the first consideration.

With this in mind, plans were being laid for an Allied invasion of northwest Africa. *Operation Torch*, as it was code-named, would involve both the American and British military forces which would land at Oran and Algiers. No one was certain how the French forces in Algeria would react so, in response to a request from General Charles Mast, the French Commander in Algiers, General Mark Clark, Eisenhower's deputy, and other high-ranking American officers, were flown to Gibraltar by Paul Tibbets and Wayne Connors in *The Red Gremlin* and *Boomerang*. Clark and his party then went by submarine to Algeria to confer with Mast. The mission was successful and Tibbets wrote later: "We had reason to take pride in the fact that the mission eventually saved a considerable number of lives and played an important part in lighting the 'Torch'."

Meanwhile, the U-boat pens on the French Atlantic coast had to be knocked out or crippled, so that the undersea raiders could not seriously affect the "Torch" convoys carrying men and materials to North Africa. The RAF had not even dented the U-boat lairs in 1941 and, in 1942, during a respite, the Germans had methodically reinforced the shelters with almost sixteen feet of concrete. In October that year, shipping losses rose dramatically and November was to be even worse.

On 20th October 1942, Brigadier General Asa N. Duncan, Chief of Air Staff, issued a revised set of objectives to be carried out by VIII Bomber Command. In part it stated: "Until further orders, every effort of the VIII Bomber Com-

A B-17 prepares to take on fuel prior to one of the early operations to occupied France.

mand will be directed to obtaining the maximum destruction of the submarine bases in the Bay of Biscay . . .." Duncan's crews, however, did not share the General's need for hitting the pens. They believed they should strike at the submarine yards inside Germany. However, the limited number of B-17s and B-24s available to the 8th at this time meant they would have to strike at the turn-around ports on the French Atlantic coast.

Men of the 97th Bomb Group parade for the award of the Purple Heart. Lieutenant Lockhart has the bandaged hand, and to his right is Major Paul Tibbets.

The scene, then, was set but the weather threatened to ruin any immediate relief to Allied shipping the raids on the pens might bring. Eleven missions scheduled for October 1942 were scrubbed and only one mission, on 21st October, was flown. VIII Bomber Command set fair for Keroman, a little fishing port about one-and-a-half miles from Lorient. Altogether, sixty-six B-17s from the 97th, 301st, and 306th Bomb Groups, and twenty-four B-24s, were dispatched. The two forces flew a long over-water flight across the Bay of Biscay to reduce the threat of Luftwaffe interception. However, thick cloud at their prescribed bombing altitude of 22,000 feet forced three groups to return to England.

Major Joseph A. Thomas, the 97th lead pilot, and Colonel Atkinson, who occupied the co-pilot's seat, saw no reason to turn back and descended through the cloud, breaking clear over the target at 17,500 feet. The German defenders were caught napping and, before the alarm was sounded, 2,000lb bombs were exploding in the target area, twenty-one falling within 1,000 feet of the MPI. Five hit the central block of shelters yet did not penetrate more than five feet. (Pens were poor targets, small in area and protected by reinforced concrete roofs, sixteen feet thick. A drop from 16,000 feet gave a 1,600lb armor-piercing bomb impact velocity enough, about 860 feet per second, to penetrate almost eight inches of armor.) However, three general workshops and a pair of floating docks were destroyed and two U-boats, not in pens, were damaged. Just after re-crossing the French coast, the formation of fifteen Fortresses was bounced by a swarm of yellow-nosed FW 190s, which attacked them in such a manner that the high tails of the B-17s shielded the fighters from fire positions in the radio hatch and top turrets. The attacks were ferocious and incessant and centered on the rear of the formation. First to go down was *Francis X*, Lieutenant Francis X. Schwarzenbeck's B-17 in the 342nd Squadron. The crew could have baled out but they were heading into a flock of German fighters so they kept their guns manned and managed to destroy two fighters on their way down. *Johnny Reb*, flown by Lieutenant Milton M. Stenstrom, and 41-24344 (the aircraft's official identity - not every plane was named), piloted by Captain John M. Bennett, both from the 414th Squadron, were also shot down and a further six received varying degrees of damage. The group's gunners claimed 10-4-3 but morale sagged with the knowledge that the 97th now had the highest losses of any group to date.

It was unfortunate that the 97th had flown what was to be its last mission from England under such a depressing cloud. Now they and the 301st were to come under the control of the 12th Air Force for Operation Torch. But before that happened Paul Tibbets was ordered to assemble a fleet of six B-17s for another airlift to Gibraltar. His passenger in *Red Gremlin* would be General Eisenhower, who was the

Back at the airfield after another mission with its strict no smoking law, this B-17 crew waste no time lighting up. Note the rear door which leads to the gunners' positions.

supreme commander for the operation. Mark Clark would fly in *Boomerang* with Wayne Connors.

On 2nd November, the six B-17s flew from Polebrook to Hurn airport near Bournemouth to rendezvous with the military leaders who had left London by special train. Bad weather prevented takeoff until 5th November when, although it was still not completely clear, the first landings in Africa were scheduled for early on 8th November and Eisenhower could not delay any longer.

The day long flight to Gibraltar, a distance of some 1,200 miles, was not without incident. John Knox, who had taken off forty-five minutes after Tibbets, never reached his destination. One of his passengers was Major Asa Duncan, who Tibbets remembers as a fine airman and a real gentleman, who had been chosen to play a major part in the air

war in Africa. John C. Summers' B-17, whose passengers included General Doolittle and eight British generals, had hydraulic failure on takeoff and was forced to wait until next day to fly to Gibraltar. Not long after leaving the coast of England, Summers' B-17 was attacked by four Junkers 88s. Only the B-17's top turret, ball turret, and tail guns were installed so Summers tried to outpace his attackers. A 20mm shell exploded in the B-17 cockpit, wounding Thomas F. Lohr, the co-pilot. Another shell knocked out the number three engine. Only because the Ju 88s were running low on fuel did they break off the attack and allow Summers to escape.

Tibbets' B-17 and three others arrived at Gibraltar on 6th November. Summers' disabled Fortress arrived early the following day, just in time for the invasion, which began in the early hours of 8th November. The landings at Casablanca, Oran, and Algiers were a success. Tibbets was informed that General Clark wanted to get his staff to Algiers and once again *Red Gremlin* and *Boomerang* were used, together with an escort of sixteen Spitfires. The B-17s landed at the Maison Blanche air base, right in the middle of an air attack on the city. A Ju 88 exploded and scattered the area with debris and another dropped a stick of bombs only 100 feet from *Red Gremlin*.

Tibbets had expected to return to Gibraltar and fly Eisenhower in but that task was allotted to another of the 97th's B-17s. Tibbets could only reflect: "My stint as a chauffeur for the top brass had ended. I could now go back to being a warrior."

Chapter 3
Trial by Combat

For three months the 97th Bomb Group and, to a lesser extent, the 301st Bomb Group, had pioneered American daylight bombing from England. Thanks to their sacrifices, immediate changes were made in air policy and subsequent arrivals in England would come to thank them for it. The 97th and 301st departed from England late in November 1942 for North Africa and earned undying fame with raids from the desert and later from Italy.

The future now looked bleak for the remaining groups in England. They still had to prove that high-altitude missions in daylight, often without escort (the 8th also lost four fighter groups in the transfer to the 12th Air Force), could justify further B-17 and B-24 groups being sent to the ETO. Shallow penetration missions, or "milk-runs", as they began to be called, were not the answer but, for the time being, VIII Bomber Command could not flaunt itself in force over the Continent so "tip and run" missions to the U-boat pens remained the order of the day.

On 1st November, VIII Bomber Command struck at the U-boat pens at Brest on the French Atlantic coast. Seven crews in the 91st Bomb Group formation, led by the CO, Colonel Stanley T. Wray, were pitched into the fray for the group's inaugural mission. Eaker was pulling out all the stops in an effort to reduce the number of U-boats entering the Bay of Biscay. Wray's crews came through their first mission unscathed and were equally successful the following day on a diversionary raid on the airfield at Abbeville-Drucat while the main force attacked Lille. Here, thirty FW 190s made at least two hundred attacks on the five B-17s of the 369th

Bomb Squadron, 306th Bomb Group, which chose to make a second run on the target. Captain Richard D Adams' B-17 was downed by flak.

The 91st Bomb Group's third mission, to St Nazaire, on 9th November, was to provide a much stiffer test for the "freshman" group. Bombing results had been so inconsistent on the early raids that Eaker decided to experiment with attacks at lower altitude. Instead of going in over the target at the usual 20,000 feet it was decided that the leading 91st Bomb Group formation would cross St Nazaire at 10,000 feet and the last group, the 306th, would go in at 8,000 feet. One squadron would go in as low as 7,000 feet, such was the need for pinpoint accuracy. Today these tactics seem suicidal but it must be remembered that in November 1942 the very future of the 8th Air Force was in jeopardy and even American instructors doubted their crews' ability to survive against Luftwaffe opposition in daylight. The Americans had to convince the RAF, and themselves, that daylight precision bombing was both practical and effective. In theory, these heights were between the low and high flak. However, no one seemed to have taken into consideration the agonizingly slow speed of the Fortress at such low levels, which meant they would cross the target at 155 to 160 mph, if they were lucky! With no tail wind at this height, the B-17 crews would be at the mercy of flak guns for longer than before. At Thurleigh, Colonel "Chip" Overacker, the 306th Bomb Group CO, reacted furiously to the Field Order. As soon as it appeared on the teletype machine at the base, he telephoned HQ, VIII Bomber Command, to protest.

Overacker was promptly rebuked and told that nothing would change the decision. Overacker responded that if his crews had to fly the mission, then so would he and that he would lead them! His four squadron commanders led from the front also, and they joined him on the mission.

Altogether, forty-seven B-17s and B-24s flew to St Nazaire. The force swept out over the sea towards the mouth of the Loire in Brittany at 500 feet to avoid being tracked by enemy radar. Nearing the target the groups climbed to their briefed altitudes and began their bomb runs. Unfortunately, the Germans had over fifty heavy anti-aircraft guns situated at St Nazaire and were in the process of installing more. Light flak, 20mm and 37mm, embraced the low-flying Fortress formations, but the Liberators, flying at 18,000 feet came through without any serious damage.

The heavier dual-purpose 88mm anti-aircraft guns were responsible for the most damage and the Fortresses bore the brunt. Every B-17 but one in the leading 91st Bomb Group formation was peppered with flak, but all managed to return safely to base. By the time the trailing 306th Bomb Group element crossed the target, the flak crews had correctly estimated their height and speed. Their aim was so accurate that a shell was seen to make a direct hit and explode against the nose of one B-17. In seconds the 306th Bomb Group lost three B-17s to flak in rapid succession. *Man O'War*, flown by Lieutenant James M. Stewart, went down with all of the crew killed. *Miss Swoose*, flown by Lieutenant John R. Bennett, was shot down after "Bombs Away." The intense flak succeeded in breaking up the formations and they flew back to England in disarray.

De-briefing confirmed that the 8th could never again expose itself over such a heavily defended target at such low altitudes. Bombing had been better than on previous missions but could not be justified on this kind of loss ratio. Losses would have been heavier if the Luftwaffe had intercepted and shot down the stragglers. From thenceforth St Nazaire became known as "Flak City" and bomber crews would not venture below four miles high. Missions to the U-boat lairs became an almost established routine and the Germans moved in more and more anti-aircraft guns until, by November, there were seventy-five ringed around the city alone. Gradually, the number was increased until it passed 100. Soon flak was so accurate it was even dangerous well in excess of 20,000 feet. The truth of the motto, "The higher, the fewer," was established.

On 15th November, the 305th Bomb Group was scheduled to fly a practice mission. However, there were many problems for the new group to overcome, as Cliff Pyle explains. "We had been at Grafton Underwood only a short time when the 97th Bomb Group was assigned our aircraft before they left for North Africa. We had very little time to flight-test our new aircraft before we were scheduled for combat missions. My aircraft had a peculiar problem of losing power as we gained altitude and the cause was difficult to

Waist gunners armed with .50 caliber Brownings were part of the B-17's main defense. Facing page: Bomb Boogie *of the 91st Bomb Group. This aircraft was lost on 6th September 1943.*

locate. Consequently, we named our plane *SNAFU* (Situation Normal, All Fouled Up). My crew and I were not too fond of this name and after a couple of missions we decided to change the name to, *We The People*. This name was recommended to us by the Gulf Oil Company, whose popular radio program had the same name.

"It was decided that we would fly a few diversion nights to the Channel and back. This would also provide a familiarization 'look-see' at the countryside. Our first flight on 15th November was cancelled when the commander of the 1st Bomb Wing learned that we were about to take off without ammunition on board. We had not fully realized that we were now in the war zone where the enemy could strike at any time. Next day, the group was scheduled to fly towards Brest, go halfway across the Channel, and return. I could not start my number two engine and aborted the mission. On 17th November, we flew a diversion flight to within thirty miles of Brest and returned safely."

The other Fortress groups headed for St Nazaire with sixteen B-17s of the 303rd Bomb Group from Molesworth flying their maiden mission. Unfortunately, cloud obscured the target and they returned to base without dropping their bombs. Twenty miles northwest of the target the 306th Bomb

Group, bringing up the rear of the formation, was hit by fifteen FW 190s. The Luftwaffe fighters caused mayhem and casualties. Captain Robert C. Williams in *Chennault's Pappy* was badly shot up and force-landed at Exeter. It never flew again. Next day *Floozy* in the 367th Bomb Squadron, was shot down by a combination of flak and fighters over St Nazaire and it crashed in the Bay of Biscay. Other B-17s returned to Thurleigh badly shot up and with dead and dying on board. Major Thurman Shuller, group surgeon, wrote later that, "the entire group was always emotionally jarred by the return home of the bodies of good friends." As the situation worsened, it would become a morale problem. On 25th November, the 306th Bomb Group was removed from the battle order, resuming combat operations again on 12th December. The 303rd dispatched nineteen Fortresses to their briefed target at La Pallice but, incredibly, they veered 100 miles off course and bombed St Nazaire in error. On 22nd November, seventy-six bombers attempted to hit the submarine pens at Lorient. Only eleven bombers from the 303rd Bomb Group, still smarting from their navigational error four days before, actually bombed the target.

The 303rd Bomb Group had been blooded and now it was the turn of the 305th. Cliff Pyle says, "Colonel LeMay gathered us all in one of the huts and told us that we were on our own now. He further stated that he had done his best in

training and he believed we would benefit from it. He said we would be face to face with the best of the German Air Force."

The 305th came face to face with the Luftwaffe on 23rd November, on the mission to St Nazaire. On almost every mission, bombers were hitting the target but not in large enough concentrations to damage them seriously. Experience was proving that a single bomb or even a few bombs did not have enough destructive power on their own. Colonel LeMay was determined to alter this and decided to try and achieve greater bombing accuracy by flying a straight course on the bomb run instead of zig-zagging every ten seconds, a tactic which had been designed to spoil the aim of the German flak batteries. His plan was to cross the target faster and therefore reduce the amount of time the German flak batteries had to fire on the formation. It was a big step for a group commander to take on the group's maiden bombing mission and one which caused his crews great concern.

Altogether, fifty-eight B-17s flew down to Davidstow Moor, Cornwall, to refuel before setting out for the Bay of Biscay and St Nazaire. Bad weather and mechanical problems forced thirteen B-17s to abort and one 306th Bomb Group Fortress, piloted by 1st/Lieutenant Clay Isbell, was shot down by fighters on the bomb run. Isbell and six of his crew were trapped when the bomber exploded. By the time

An anonymous B-17 of the 1st Bomb Division photographed in close formation. The notorious ball turret position can be clearly seen below the fuselage. (USAF)

the target was reached, four out of the twenty B-17s in the 305th, together with five out of the ten 91st B-17s, and four out of the eight B-17s in the 306th, had turned back. Only forty-four B-17s remained; the 91st and 306th Bomb Groups together totaling only eight aircraft. Despite this, the groups pressed on to the target.

The 305th Bomb Group carried out the longest and straightest bomb run yet seen over Europe and strike photos later revealed that they had placed twice as many bombs on the target as any other outfit. Despite their fears, no crews were lost to flak, although they came close.

On previous missions, the B-17s had been intercepted from the rear where enough guns could be brought to bear on enemy fighters. However, Luftwaffe experiments had now proved that the frontal area of a B-17 offered very little in defensive firepower and, despite the dangers of very high closing speeds, the head-on attack was considered the best method of shooting the bombers down. The B-17E was equipped with four .30 caliber flexible machine-gun mountings but they had to be operated by the bombardier who was already over-committed. Whichever mounting he used, it only offered a very poor field of fire. Navigators could also operate a flexible mounted .50 caliber Browning machine-gun from enlarged windows (often called cheek guns) either side of the nose but these suffered from the same problems

as the bombardier's position. In each case a blind spot was left in front which neither the ball turret nor the upper turret could cover.

Hauptman Egon "Conny" Mayer, commander of III./JG2, who led the attacking fighters this day, is credited with developing the head-on attack. The new tactic worked well. The 91st lost two bombers to head-on attacks. *Sad Sack,* piloted by Major Victor Zienowicz, CO of the 322nd Bomb Squadron, with Captain McCormick as co-pilot, was lost with all eleven crew. *Pandora's Box,* a 324th Bomb Squadron B-17, flown by Major Harold C. Smelser, CO of the 401st Bomb Squadron, with Captain Duane L. Jones as co-pilot, crashed into the sea about thirty miles northwest of St Nazaire with the loss of all the crew. As well as the loss of these two squadron commanders, the group navigator, bombardier, and gunnery officer were among the dead. Five men were killed aboard *The Shiftless Skonk,* which crashed near Leavesden, Hertfordshire, while trying to make it home to

Delta Rebel 2, a B-17E of the 91st Bomb Group, became one of the most famous B-17s in the 8th Air Force. (USAF)

Bassingbourn. *Quitchurbitchin* was the only 91st B-17 to return. *Lady Fairweather* of the 303rd Bomb Group was shot down in flames near the target and crashed into the Bay of Biscay with the loss of Captain Charles G. Miller and his crew.

Trial by combat had revealed weaknesses in the B-17 design, especially when confronted with head-on attacks. Enterprising armament chiefs even experimented with tail guns in the nose but the problem would only be solved when chin turrets were fitted during assembly. By the end of 1942, Fortresses arriving in England needed well in excess of 100 urgent modifications before they were considered combat-worthy.

Eaker could not wait for the new power-operated chin turrets and missions continued, weather and reorganization permitting. (Early in December the 305th Bomb Group moved from Grafton "Undermud" to the mud at Chelveston, late home of the 301st Bomb Group.) On Sunday, 6th December, the 8th struck at the locomotive factory, railroads, and repair shops at Lille, escorted by sixteen squadrons of Spitfires. Cliff Pyle remembers,

"The 305th was number three in the formation, stacked up. Major McGehee led the squadron but he had to turn back with aircraft problems and I took over the lead. Twelve

FW 190s attacked our squadron and my tail-gunner claimed two shot down and the waist gunner, one. Ten minutes from the target, the B-17 flown by Lieutenant William A. Prentice left the formation in flames and five parachutes were seen to open. (Nine men were killed and only one man survived.) We encountered very little flak in our position and there were no casualties among my crew."

Following the Lille mission, plans were formulated for an attack on the Romilly-sur-Seine air park, southeast of Paris. The Luftwaffe was using it as a large repair base and stopping-off point for pilots going to North Africa to support Rommel's Afrika Korps. Its sprawling hangars offered an excellent target and the risk in flying so deep into enemy territory was considered well worth taking. However, bad weather resulted in the cancellation of the mission on 10th December and, two days later, ninety bombers had already crossed the French coast before thick cloud resulted in a recall. Groups sought the secondary target, the marshalling yards at Rouen. Cliff Pyle says,

"My plane was out of commission so I took Lieutenant Whitson's aircraft and crew with Whitson flying as co-pilot. We led the second flight in the 422nd Squadron at the bottom of the group, which was flying lead. This forced

Christmas 1942 at the Bedford County Hospital. In this case Santa and his helpers are from the 306th Bomb Group at Thurleigh near Bedford. The lady in the center is novelist Barbara Cartland. (Richards Collection)

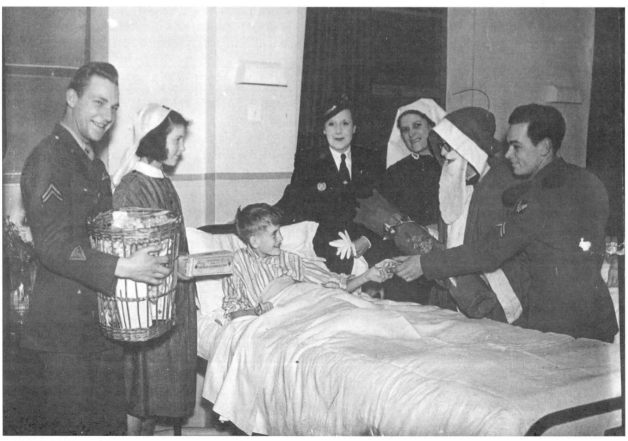

A major repair job faces this maintenance crew as they jack up a belly-landed Fortress. Note how hydraulic jacks are used to raise the aircraft a few inches at a time to allow railway sleepers to be built up under the bomber. (USAF)

the enemy planes attacking head-on to hit our squadron first. We were hit again and again from the time we crossed the French coast until we returned over the English Channel. The enemy fighters were marked with yellow noses and consisted of Bf 109s and FW 190s. Just before reaching the target, two yellow-nosed FW 190s attacked us simultaneously, shooting one of our engines out, bursting a cylinder and an oil line. They also put two holes through a prop' blade. The engine started smoking and we feathered the prop' but we couldn't stay in formation so we turned the engine back on. It was smoking furiously and consequently we drew more enemy fire than any other plane on the return trip.

"The targets, first and secondary, both had 10/10ths cloud cover, forcing us to return home with our bombs. Upon reaching the Channel, however, we salvoed the bombs, feathered the bad engine, and landed without mishap. Our crew claimed three enemy aircraft shot down. No aircraft were missing out of the 305th. Three bombers were lost by other groups and three Spitfires were missing. Nineteen enemy aircraft had been shot down - four claimed by Spitfires and fifteen by B-17s. This mission was claimed to be the hottest air battle fought so far."

Only the 303rd had bombed the marshalling yards, losing two B-17s in the attempt, so a return was ordered. However, the weather intervened again and for eight days Eaker used the time to build up his aircraft strength.

One of the airmen who flew on these early missions was Lee Gordon, a gunner with the 305th Bomb Group. He was nicknamed "Shorty" because of his five foot two inch frame but what he lacked in height he made up for in guts and determination. In October 1940, after being rejected by the RCAF because he was one inch too short, Gordon had joined the 7th Bombardment Group. When the group departed for Salt Lake City, Utah, prior to going overseas, Shorty was left behind to do three months' hard labor for being improperly dressed. On 7th December 1941, his sentence completed, he intended to join the "Flying Tigers" as a ground man. But the Japanese attack on Pearl Harbor changed all that and he threw up his job as armorer to take up aerial gunnery.

In England, Shorty's disciplinary record while on the ground did not improve and LeMay was forced repeatedly to "bust" him to private. However, the 305th needed men like Gordon. Experienced gunners were few and far between and already cooks, clerks, medical orderlies, truck drivers, etc., were being used as crew replacements. To get around the problem, when Shorty went on a mission he had his stripes returned to him but, on the ground once more, he became a private again.

On 20th December, Shorty Gordon filled in as ball turret gunner aboard *Cunningham's Coffin* (named after the pilot) for the raid on Romilly. He almost did not make the mission when one of his guns failed to work but before they reached France he had both guns in working order. A dozen squadrons of RAF and USAAF Spitfires flew cover but they were soon low on fuel and had to return to England just before the heavies reached Rouen. The B-17s were met at the coastline by yellow-nosed and black-nosed FW 190s. Gordon recalls:

"The bombardier spotted two FW 190s coming in head-on and called out the direction of the attack. I turned my turret to the front and raised my guns. Cunningham pulled up the nose so I could get at them and there was a Focke-Wulf about 100 feet away. His wings looked like they were on fire because all his guns were going at once. I thought I was a goner but I got in a quick burst and he flipped over as he went past. I tried to swing after him and get in another burst, but he was going too fast. He was only fifty feet away and I got a glimpse of the pilot in the cockpit. He was wearing goggles and had a leather mask over his face. He was looking at me and I was looking at him and that's all there was to it. But I was damn scared at the time."

For fifteen minutes the B-17 crews came under fire from head-on attacks and two aircraft in the 91st Bomb Group were shot down. One of the victims, Ralph Tomek, a waist gunner on Lieutenant Robert S. English's crew in the 401st Bomb Squadron, was on only his fourth mission.

"Sixty fighters ripped through our formation and made decisive hits on one Fortress (*Danellen*, piloted by Lieutenant Den W. Carson) flying in the rear element. The tail broke off and there was only one survivor. Salvador Dalteris, the tail-gunner, who was fortunate enough to be in the part that broke off from which he managed to bale out. Later, he told me that his pilot had told everyone that day to wear their parachutes on the mission. If he hadn't he would never have made it.

"Our ship was the next to be picked off. The fighters made head-on attacks and put two engines out of action and killed my pilot, Bob English. Our B-17 nose-dived about 1,000 feet but by some miracle, the top turret gunner, Sergeant Mandell, scrambled out of his turret and managed to get the aircraft straightened out. The two engines were on fire and we were losing altitude rapidly. Near Paris, Mandell sounded the alarm to bale out."

Ralph Tomek baled out and landed in a French garden. He was in no condition to make good his escape because he had been wounded in the hand by a 20mm shell and had broken

Facing page: *Maureen, a war orphan from London, was adopted by the 306th Bomb Group.* (Richards collection)

Farmers watch the Fortresses of the 305th Bomb Group return to Chelveston. (Bill Donald)

his ankle in the landing. Tomek was captured and admitted to hospital in Paris. Later he was sent to POW camp where he remained for the rest of the war.

Meanwhile, as the initial onslaught of FW 190s broke off to refuel, another fifty joined the running fight and continued to make attacks until shortly before "Bombs Away." Cliff Pyle, in *We The People*, saw his squadron's bombs drop short of the target. "We were using the tactics of squadron aircraft dropping on the lead squadron aircraft. However, the target was hit by the mass with good results."

The Luftwaffe fighters which had broken off to refuel, appeared again on the homeward trip and made repeated attacks on the B-17 formations until the Spitfire escort showed up to cover the bombers' exits across the Channel. Altogether six B-17s, including four from the 306th, were lost and twenty-nine damaged. Gunners once again submitted high claims and the initial score of fifty-three "kills" was reduced to twenty-one plus thirty-one "probably damaged." The accurate figure was in fact three enemy fighters shot down and one damaged.

In total, 101 bombers were dispatched to Romilly, the largest force dispatched since the Lille raid on 9th October. Of these, seventy-two had bombed the target but they had caused only minor damage to the German airfield. However, Romilly proved a turning point in the daylight aerial war in Europe. For the first time the B-17s had penetrated 100 miles into enemy territory and had successfully beaten off incessant fighter attacks without the aid of escorting fighters. It augured well for the embryonic bombing force in the months ahead.

Christmas 1942 was the Fortress groups' first in the ETO. In an attempt to integrate the English and American communities, General Eisenhower instructed all units where possible to have Christmas dinner in English homes. If the winter had been long, cold, and monotonously dark, it was temporarily forgotten as many an American airbase opened its doors to the British public.

As the year drew to a close officers and men were still working on improving methods for bombing and aerial gunnery. The two problems were linked and, at Chelveston, Colonel LeMay and his staff worked hard to find the best method of combating fighter attacks without compromising bombing accuracy and vice-versa. After trying "stacked up" formations of eighteen aircraft, LeMay finally decided upon staggered three-plane elements within a squadron and staggered squadrons within a group. This would result in a complicated bombing procedure if each aircraft tried maneuvering for accurate aiming so LeMay discarded individual bombing, which had been Standard Operating Procedure (SOP) from the outset. He replaced the technique with "lead crews," whose bombardier signaled to the rest of the formation when to bomb so that all bombs were released simultaneously, no matter what position the aircraft were flying. This simple but brilliant idea could mean all bombs missing the target but if all landed a short distance from the MPI, then a target could be successfully destroyed instead of damaged. The very best bombardiers were selected for the task and put into lead crews. LeMay's synthesis found support at Wing Headquarters where first Brigadier General Larry Kuter and later, Brigadier General Hayward "Possum" Hansell, lent encouragement. Gradually, lead crews, comprising highly trained pilots, bombardiers, and navigators, became SOP.

Unfortunately, the new techniques could not entirely allow for the vagaries of the weather and this was evident when the lead crew concept was attempted on 30th December over the U-boat pens at Lorient. The bomb run was flown into the sun and its glare gave the experienced Luftwaffe pilots a blind spot from which to attack the Fortresses. Making head-on attacks, they succeeded in shooting down three B-17s, including *Short Snorter*, a 91st Bomb Group ship flown by Lieutenant William Bloodgood. Lieutenant Floyd E. Love pulled out of the 305th Bomb Group formation to assist a loner from the 306th Bomb Group and was promptly shot down. On the return flight, the 305th formation thought it was over England when, due to a terrific headwind, it was still over France. The formation became lax and the aircraft were spread out more than usual. Fighters seized upon the lapse and badly damaged Captain Everett E. Tribbett's For-

A box of Fortresses maintain their close box formation despite the heavy flak put up by the German gunners.

tress. *Boom Town*, piloted by Captain Clyde B. Walker, was also badly shot up but managed to make it to St Eval with one dead and two wounded aboard.

For the Americans' sixth raid on St Nazaire, on 3rd January 1943, Eaker for the first time completely abandoned individual bombing in favor of group bombing. Altogether, 107 bombers were dispatched but mechanical failures accounted for many aircraft returning to base early, leaving only eight B-24s and sixty-eight Fortresses to continue to the target. Visibility was unlimited so an unusually long bomb run was ordered. B-17s and B-24s were stacked upwards of 20,000 to 22,000 feet but their airspeed was reduced by more than half due to a 115 mph gale during the run-in. The gale was so fierce that the bomb run took twice as long as that briefed and for ten minutes the bombers flew almost straight and level, taking all the flak the anti-aircraft gunners could throw at them. Shorty Gordon, in *Cunningham's Coffin*, remembers,

"There was so much flak as we approached the target that all I could see was a great black cloud that hid the formation of Forts flying ahead. It was like a big thunderstorm, thick enough to walk on. We all agreed later it was the largest and most accurate barrage ever thrown up at the Forts, over Europe. The barrage was a swell sight but it never got on my nerves.

"When I heard 'Bombs Away' from the bombardier I tried to watch them. One couldn't follow them all the way down when flying at 25,000 feet but I estimated their direction and the time they should hit. Some bombs were hitting the water near the target. One was closer, another hit the corner of the target and another two went right into the middle of it. There was a hell of an explosion and we found out later that we made a direct hit on a torpedo storage shed.

"I could hear flak hitting the ship. I knew if the flak hit me while I was looking down I'd get it in the face so I continued searching forward. About this time I heard someone on the interphone yell: 'I'm hit!' and then another say: 'I'm hit!' I thought this time we were going down in France. Everyone seemed to be shot up badly so I waited for the order to bale out. This was one mission I was wearing my, 'chute. I was still searching forward when I saw the number one engine on fire. I stepped on the interphone button but it was dead. I wondered if I shouldn't get up into the ship and tell Cunningham. It was burning on the underside and he couldn't see it. I decided to stick in the turret because there might be more fighters coming. Finally, Cunningham saw the fire through a flak hole in the wing and pulled the fire extinguisher on the engine. That stopped the fire but the prop' was windmilling out of control and I was afraid it would tear off the engine.

Delta Rebel 2 *carried on into 1943 until its pilot, George Birdsong, completed his tour and returned to Mississippi. Other crews disliked flying* Delta Rebel 2 *claiming that, "George had used up all her luck." Luck finally ran out for 2nd/Lieutenant Robert W. Thompson and his crew on 12th August 1943, when his crew and* Delta Rebel 2 *failed to return from Gelsenkirchen.*

"We were over the water on the way back when I suddenly remembered that I didn't have my Mac West and was trying to figure out how I could get ashore after hitting the water. But then I heard someone say that enemy fighters were approaching from 11 o'clock. I ran my guns to that position nearly straight ahead, and waited. I could hear bullets hit our ship but I couldn't see the fighters. That was one of the worst things that could happen, hearing the other gunners fighting but not being able to help them.

"I heard the bombardier calling out: 'Two enemy aircraft coming in low from 3 o'clock!' I turned and saw them and gave the first one a long burst at 800 yards. They were FW 190s and one was following the other. I hit the first one. Both of them saw my tracers and started to break off. Then I gave the first one another good burst at about 600 yards and saw my tracers going into his engine. He caught fire and went into a dive. I followed him for about 5,000 feet then started searching for the other fighter. One of the waist gunners saw the first FW 190 splash into the water. It was easy to see because we were only at 15,000 feet. The other fighter apparently turned back.

"My feet started to hurt pretty bad when we got down to 10,000 feet because they began thawing out. I had to take off my helmet and tear at my hair to keep from feeling the pain. My electric shoes hadn't been working. That was the fifth time I froze my feet."

The first two groups, due to strong headwinds and being somewhat off course, were forced to land at Talbenny, south Wales, with very little fuel remaining. As the last of the B-17s touched down, intelligence officers began piecing together the results of the raid. Men waited with bated breath,

none more so than at Chelveston where LeMay and his senior officers eagerly sought confirmation that the new tactics had paid off. Indeed they had, as far as the bombing went. Most of the 342,000lbs of bombs had fallen directly on the pens but seven bombers had been lost, forty-seven damaged, and two aircraft from the 305th Bomb group were so badly shot up by flak that they were left at Talbenny. These were the heaviest losses VIII Bomber Command had suffered thus far. On top of this Eaker had morale problems to consider.

At Thurleigh the 306th Bomb Group had returned to the battle-order on 12th December, followed by another week's rest from combat, until the 19th when the 367th "Clay Pigeons" Bomb Squadron lost three B-17s and twenty-nine crew. This unlucky squadron's original complement of nine crews now numbered just three. Their nick-

Back safe and sound.

name originated from an American war correspondent, who, writing in *The Saturday Evening Post*, said that the 367th Squadron reminded him of a bunch of clay pigeons. The name stuck! (Between October 1942 and August 1943, the 367th suffered the heaviest losses in VIII Bomber Command). Back at base respiratory ailments were rife and the EM grumbled about unsanitary conditions and the poor food on offer. Every military unit has its complainers, and backsliders but feeling sorry for oneself is not a condition that can be tolerated for long, especially if higher command identifies that the condition is widespread and constitutes a serious morale problem.

Of the seven losses on the 3rd January St Nazaire raid, two were 306th Bomb Group B-17s. (Navigators in the group were now in such short supply that some of the Group's B-17s flew without one). Major William Lanford, 368th Bomb Squadron CO, led the remaining B-17s back to England where bad weather forced them to seek shelter in Cornwall. Three days later, on 6th January, they set off for Thurleigh but the formation strayed south, over the Channel Isles, and the B-17s were bracketed by German flak. One B-17 was lost. It was not until 8th January that the formation finally made it back to Thurleigh. By then the 306th Bomb Group had a new CO.

On 4th January Eaker had set out for Thurleigh from "Pinetree," his headquarters at RAF Bomber Command HQ, High Wycombe, on the green flanks of the rolling Buckinghamshire Chilterns with his A-3 (Operations and Training), Colonel Frank A. Armstrong, Jr. and Lieutenant Colonel Beirne Lay, Jr. in tow. 'Things are not going well up there,' he told them. 'I think we ought to take a look a round.'

Things obviously had not improved since Eaker's last visit to the 306th Bomb Group, on 14th November, when HM King George VI and top ranking US officers toured Alconbury, Chelveston, and Thurleigh. Eaker's aide, James Parton, confirms in *Air Force Spoken Here*, his biography of Eaker, that he was unimpressed with Overacker's outfit, which unlike the other two groups, appeared slovenly and undisciplined. Parton indicated as much to Overacker and the Royal visit then went 'pretty much like the others, but there was a notable absence of spit and polish.' Eaker told "Tooey" Spaatz that he had better relieve Overacker, but the general waited six more weeks, by which time the 306th Bomb Group's bombing and loss record was the worst in VIII Bomber Command.

At the main gate General Eaker's Humber flying the red flag with two white stars of a major general was waved casually past by a sentry who neither saluted nor checked the occupants' AGO cards. At group HQ Eaker toured the base with Chip Overacker. The general was not impressed with what he saw. Eaker later recounted, "As we visited hangars, shops, and offices, I found similar attitudes as seen at the front gate. The men had a close attachment to their CO, and he to them. But there was a lack of military propriety and I could not help feel that this might be part of the problem that was being revealed in combat." The 306th had lost nine Fortresses on its last three missions.

On their return to base HQ Eaker relieved Colonel Overacker of command. "Chip" he said, "You'd better get your things and come back with me." The general then turned to Armstrong and announced, "Frank. You're in command. I'll send your clothes down." The purge did not

It is often forgotten that the majority of American personnel in England were ground support and engineering crew.

stop there. Eaker summoned Major Lanford to his HQ on 17th January and relieved him of his post. (Lanford later flew in the 483rd Bomb Group, 15th Air Force, and was shot down on his seventeenth mission to finish the war as a POW in *Stalag Luft III*). Two days later Armstrong transferred Lieutenant Colonel Delmar Wilson, 306th Bomb Group deputy commander, and brought in as operations officer Major Claude Putnam, who, like Armstrong, was a veteran of the 97th Bomb Group's early days in England. As Russell A. Strong recounts in his book *First Over Germany, a History of the 306th Bomb Group*, "The task of rebuilding the combat-decimated 306th was straight-way undertaken by Armstrong. Within a few days he had begun to restore the fading morale. He also started preparations for an event which would forever tag the 306th with the proud slogan, 'First Over Germany'."

Armstrong's stay would be short at just over a month. On 4th January other changes in command were made. The 92nd Bomb Group, less key personnel and all of the 326th Squadron, left Bovingdon and departed for Alconbury, five miles north of Huntingdon. Although Alconbury was ankle-deep in mud, morale was high because the move was generally interpreted to mean a resumption of combat missions. However, any personnel who believed this to be true, were soon disappointed. Crews were sent to the 91st and 303rd Bomb Groups as "temporary" replacements and very few ever returned to the 92nd.

Meanwhile, other groups continued flying combat missions and, on 13th January, VIII Bomber Command again visited the locomotive works at Fives-Lille. The 305th Bomb Group flew lead with Brigadier General Hansell, Commander of the 1st Bomb Wing, flying in the lead ship, *Dry Martini II*, normally flown by Captain Allen V. Martini. Martini missed the mission because of illness and the pilot's seat was taken by Major T.H. Taylor, CO of the 364th Bomb Squadron. Captain Cliff Pyle was flying his seventh mission with the 305th Bomb Group this day. "The 422nd Squadron flew the fourth position (fill-in squadron). We flew in the 'tail-end Charlie' position; the lowest airplane in the group formation. On the way over we encountered very little flak at the coast of France but over the target we received many attacks from yellow and black-nosed FW 190s which we later learned were from Abbeville. These fighter pilots were experienced and daring. They would come straight in and at the last moment would start a rolling maneuver and dive downward, firing all the time. Some of our crews believed they had armor plate on the underside of their planes.

"Everything went well until we reached the target area, then everything seemed to happen at once. Six Focke-Wulfs attacked us simultaneously, head-on, concentrating their fire on the third and fourth squadrons, while others attacked the second squadron. During this burst the number two ship in the second element in the third squadron was shot down. Our ship received four cannon holes, two in the left wing, one in the right wing and the fourth went through the floor of the bomb compartment into the pilots' compartment, bursting the hydraulic lines. Hydraulic fluid spewed throughout the pilots' compartment, blinding both myself and Lieutenant Gilbert, my co-pilot. Only moments later the windshield shattered inwardly. I believe this was caused by a hit on the side of the aircraft and was aggravated further by the top turret guns firing forward.

Many of the staff on the ground were black, and not eligible to be rostered as aircrew.

"Gunfire from two other fighters entered the lower turret, wounding Sergeant McCoy, the turret gunner. There were about 150 .30 caliber holes in the wings along with the two cannon shots. There was a hole in the leading edge about the size of a bushel basket. A tracer bullet entered the radio compartment, setting fire to the upholstery.

"Luckily, I managed to stay in formation. The number one engine was misfiring and spewing black smoke and we feathered the props immediately. The number four engine was also smoking. We feathered it for a few moments at a time until we reached the coast. Then we began to lag behind but we arrived over Chelveston in time to land with other damaged aircraft first. We had to extend the landing gear by hand. The airfoil on the leading edge of the wing was destroyed and made the action of flying the aircraft very difficult. On the final approach it required both of us to hold the plane steady. The crippled engine was unfeathered and used on the final approach. Knowing we had no brakes we lined up for a short landing. Touching down we discovered to our surprise, that both tires were flat and we landed far too short. This was lucky because we had no braking action.

"Realizing that we had to abandon the runway for other aircraft landing behind us, we blasted the engines with full power and managed to swing off and clear the runway. We ended up in the ditch and mud alongside the runway. We learned later that the aircraft landing immediately in front of us was Major Taylor's. Major Taylor had been killed by a cannon shot in the chest and his co-pilot was wounded.

"Everybody had been 100 percent sold on the B-17 before this flight but afterwards we had nothing but pure admiration for it. After all the damage, only three members of the crew were wounded by flak and flying bits of metal from the airplane. I suffered from minor frostbite after sitting in the draft of an open cockpit window with temperatures ranging from around fifty-five degrees below zero."

One Fortress from the 305th Bomb Group was lost on the raid and two B-17s from the 306th were lost in a mid-air collision over Belgium. Gunners claimed six fighters destroyed and thirteen probably destroyed. If anyone needed proof that LeMay's tactics were right, the Lille raid had proved them beyond doubt. The bombing was so effective that VIII Bomber Command never had need to return to Lille.

Despite the success, there had been talk suggesting that the small American force should be incorporated into the RAF night bombing campaign. Despite the value of daylight bombing, losses had continued to rise and many senior officers in the RAF remained unconvinced as to its ultimate success. General "Hap" Arnold, Chief of the American Air Staff, was under pressure from various quarters by those who wanted to know why Eaker had been unable to mount more missions and why it was French, rather than German, targets that were being bombed. Once again the future of VIII Bomber Command as a separate bombing force was in question and answers were desperately needed if it was to survive.

Wulf Hound, *41-24585 of the 303rd Bomb Group was seen going down over France on 12th December 1942, but it was landed safely in a field. It was later repaired and flown by the Luftwaffe for evaluation purposes.*

Chapter 4
Yanks at the Court of King Arthur

On 14th January 1943, Ira C. Eaker, who since November 1942 had been acting Commanding General of the 8th Air Force in the absence of General Carl Spaatz, received a cable from General "Hap" Arnold to meet him at the forthcoming Casablanca Conference in North Africa. Next day Captain Cliff Pyle and the crew of *We The People* were alerted to fly General Eaker to North Africa. The trip was conducted in the utmost secrecy. "We were instructed to get to a base on the west coast of Wales and await further instructions. Upon arriving at Milford Haven it was cold, wet, and windy. We were told upon our departure from Chelveston that we were to fly Mitzie Mayfair and her dancing troupe to several Allied bases. At about 0300 hours we were awakened and taken to Base Operations where we met, not Mitzie Mayfair, but General Eaker! He said we were to take off for Marrakech, North Africa, as soon as we were ready. Flight planning and checking over our aircraft took about two hours and we departed about 0500 hours. General Eaker had a cold and asked that we did not fly too high.

"Our flight en route to Marrakech was uneventful, flying in broken clouds all the way. However, one amusing incident occurred when we started test firing our guns. General Eaker's aide, Captain Parsons, jumped and his foot came down on the radio operator's table and broke the operator's watch. Landing at Marrakech we saw disabled Vichy French aircraft lying around all over the airfield. They had been shot up only a brief time before the invading Americans. General Eaker went by car to the conference site and we waited at the airfield for further orders."

The conference of President Roosevelt, Prime Minister Winston Churchill, and the combined heads of staff took place at the Anfa Hotel on a hill overlooking the Atlantic coast south of the town. Many of the villas in the vicinity had been taken over by senior officers and General Eaker found himself billeted in one called Le Paradou - The Paradise! Only two months earlier the Anfa Hotel had been the venue of the German Armistice Commission and the rooms still bore some of its furniture and fittings. Outside ran a barbed wire surround with cans containing small stones strung every few feet and armed sentries placed at short intervals.

Arnold warned Eaker that Churchill and Roosevelt had agreed that the 8th Air Force would cease daylight bombing and join the RAF in night bombing. Eaker was shattered but was determined to reverse the decision. He wrote his now famous memorandum, less than a page long, which summarized his reasons why the daylight bombing offensive should continue. Although not fully convinced, Churchill was impressed, particularly with Eaker's "round the clock" bombing strategy. The British Prime Minister agreed to extend the time Eaker needed to prove daylight bombing and the conference approved additional aircraft for VIII Bomber Command.

Upon his return to England, Eaker decided his forces were now ready to attack Germany and the target selected for 27th January was the U-boat construction yards at Vegasack on the Weser. Although the port had been heavily bombed by the RAF throughout 1942, it had long been earmarked as a possible target for the Americans. The RAF night bombers had caused severe damage to the town and had destroyed a large naval ammunition dump, but some of the U-boat slipways, dry-docks, and shipyards had escaped damage. It was an ideal opportunity for Eaker to demonstrate that daylight precision bombing could triumph over RAF night bombing.

The bombardier's position in the nose of a B-17. The single .50 caliber machine gun can also be seen.

The crews were at first astonished, then pleased, to learn that they were at last going after a German target. The mission would be led by Colonel Frank Armstrong, CO of the 306th Bomb Group, who, six months before, had led the equally momentous first American heavy bomber raid on France. Altogether, sixty-four B-17s set out over the North Sea, flying a dogleg route to confuse the enemy. As they climbed to altitude, the intense cold froze machine-guns and turret mechanisms and frosted over windscreens and bombsights. Despite their thick clothing, the men grew weak from cold and only kept their oxygen masks from freezing by rubbing them with salt. The conditions grew worse and by the time the coast came into view, only fifty-five Fortresses remained. Fifty-three B-17s dropped their bombs blindly from 25,000 feet through a German smoke screen, which drifted lazily over the shipyards, while two others bombed Emden.

The bombing was described as "fair" but the press was ready to fete the bomber crews and the B-17s in particular. The B-17 was rapidly becoming the favorite of the American public, much to the chagrin of the Liberator crews who had failed to find their target. The aircraft's popularity was given added impetus with the news that Fortress gunners had claimed twenty-two fighters shot down for the loss of only two Liberators and one Fortress, (flown by Lieutenant Vance W. Beckham of the 305th Bomb Group). Crews estimated that they had been attacked by about fifty fight-

ers, including some twin-engined fighters normally used on night interceptor missions. They did not press home their attacks and the American formation escaped lightly.

Flushed with no small measure of success, Eaker decided to crack an even bigger nut. For a year crews had referred to the industrial German heartland of the Ruhr as "Happy Valley", feared, and respected for its lethal concentrations of heavy flak. Twice bad weather postponed the strike and on 2nd February the heavies actually got into the air only for the mission to be aborted because of worsening weather conditions. Finally, on 4th February, eighty-six bombers took off and went all the way, flying a long, deceptive flight path over the freezing gray waters of the North Sea before turning for Hamm. Captain Cliff Pyle, in *We The People*, was flying his eleventh mission with the 305th (having received a credit for two combat missions and a letter of commendation from General Eaker for his flight to and from North Africa). "We took off without an aircraft heater. It was minus fifty-five degrees at 22,000 feet and it was the coldest I had ever been. Four members of my crew had to be treated later for frozen limbs."

The weather grew worse, forcing the Fortresses to seek targets of opportunity at Emden and off the coast. The Fortress formation became strung out and it became an open invitation to the Luftwaffe, as Cliff Pyle explains: "Everything went well until we were about 100 miles inland. There we were met by about fifty enemy fighters. They attacked us continuously to the target and until we were thirty miles out to sea."

On board *Sunrise Serenader*, Shorty Gordon, the tailgunner, discovered to his dismay that his guns had frozen. It is doubtful he could have fired them anyway because at 22,000 feet and a temperature of minus forty-five degrees, he had taken off his electric gloves to work on the guns. Every time the moist surfaces of his fingers touched the barrels his skin welded to the steel surfaces. When he pulled his hands away the steel tore his skin an inch. He concentrated on calling out fighter positions over the intercom for his fellow gunners. As they bore in, Shorty, who had been working on a supercharger inside the wing for most of the previous night, got so excited that he became unintelligible at times and the gunners tried to tell him to "get the hell off the air!" but Shorty's intercom switch was locked in position and he continued with his roaring, graphic description throughout the seventy-five minute air battle. "I saw a Fortress drop out of formation with four FW 190s after it. The Fort took violent evasive action. It swung up and over into a complete barrel roll. Fighters did that, not Fortresses."

The battle reached fever pitch and five Fortresses were brought down as the Luftwaffe's single and twin-engined fighters tore into the depleted ranks of the formation. A hail of machine-gun fire stabbed the air as gunners, their frozen bodies temporarily forgotten in the heat of battle, peered in all directions, seeking out their foe. The 305th Bomb Group lost two aircraft. *El Lobo*, flown by Lieutenant Cornelius A. Jenkins, was shot down, and Lieutenant William K. Davidson collided head on with a FW 190. Shorty Gordon saw it. "The Focke-Wulf was starting to roll over and go into a usual dive away from our formation when his wing hit the wing of the Fortress in the element below us. The impact cut the wing off the fighter and knocked the wing off the Fortress just past its number four engine. The Fort started into a circle, then went into a tight spin. It broke in two right at the middle and the ball turret went spinning down looking like a baby's rattle. Then the wreckage exploded."

Returning across the North Sea, *Sunrise Serenader* dropped back to protect a crippled B-17 flying on three engines. An FW 190 approached and fired a burst of 20mm cannon into *Sunrise Serenader*, almost removing its wing. The gunners shot the fighter down and the B-17 limped home with part of one wing dangling. *Sunrise Serenader* managed to put down safely at Chelveston but it was so badly damaged it could not be taxied off the runway.

Bad weather grounded the 8th until 14th February when the B-17s flew an abortive strike against Hamm. Three days later they returned to St Nazaire and, although the weather was good, most of the bombardiers missed the aiming point and the 305th formation failed totally because of a bombsight malfunction in the lead aircraft. It was not until 26th February that the weather improved sufficiently for the bombers to return to the offensive. Even so, a heavy overcast forced the B-17s to abort the primary target at Bremen and seek their secondary target at Wilhelmshaven. About thirty miles from the coast the B-17s were attacked by fighters, so determined in their mission that they kept up their attacks all the way into the target.

The lowest Fortress in the entire formation was piloted by Lieutenant George E. Stallman, one of twenty pilots in the 305th Bomb Group. About fifteen minutes from Bremen he came under attack by two Bf 109s. They made several passes and the bomber took hits in the right wing and number four engine, knocking the ship out of formation. All the gunners, including Shorty Gordon, flying as ball-gunner, returned fire but Lawrence C. Lovos, the tail-gunner, was wounded in the attack. *Arkie*, Captain Tribbett's B-17, and *Devil's Playmate*, Lieutenant Isaac D. Benson's aircraft, were both brought down. Altogether, the wing lost seven Fortresses.

Light flak also bracketed the formation and aerial mines, slightly larger than shoe boxes, were fired into the air above the Fortresses by anti-aircraft guns. After each burst they fell slowly downward, suspended from small parachutes. A burst of flak hit Stallman's B-17 as he tried in vain to catch up with the formation over the target. Glass and flying fragments cut their ball turret gunner, Shorty Gordon, and blood ran down his face. It was fortunate that he was wearing his parachute this day because Stallman gave the order to bale out. Shorty Gordon, rolled out of the turret and al-

most immediately opened his backpack 'chute at about 24,000 feet. "The silk streamed out and I felt a terrific jerk. I had not bothered to adjust the straps. If I had not had some luck I might have slipped through my harness. The opening jolt jerked my boots right off my feet and I came down in my stockinged feet."

The Germans probably came to regret capturing Shorty Gordon because he would cause them more trouble than he had Colonel LeMay! Shorty escaped from POW camp three times. Once, the five foot two inch American, disguised in Lederhosen and with hair oiled flat and chin well shaven, had little difficulty passing himself off as a Bavarian youth. He obtained a bicycle and intended riding all the way to the Swiss border. He was caught, but his third attempt was a success and, in February 1944, he reached England via France. Gordon became the first American airman to receive the Silver Star for escaping.

The mounting losses in VIII Bomber Command meant that, by the end of January 1943, casualties had exceeded replacements with only twenty-four bomber crews arriving in England to replace sixty-seven lost on missions that month. February was little better with twenty-two aircraft losses. On 4th March, four B-17s were shot down and thirty-four casualties caused during a strike on Hamm. Losses might have been higher than that but for the introduction of new armored flak vests, developed by Colonel Malcolm C. Grow, in association with the Wilkinson Sword Company of Great Britain and worn by ten crews in the 91st Bomb Group this day. The vests certainly saved the life of a radio-operator aboard one ship when a 20mm shell fragment struck his vest just above the hip. The armored vest, consisting of heavy canvas covered with overlapping plates of manganese steel protecting the chest and back from low velocity shrapnel and ricocheting missiles, was only dented. The whole suit weighed 20lbs and was cumbersome in the aircraft, but one other life at least was saved by the suit on a later raid when a 20mm shell exploded just two feet from a bombardier's chest. It peppered the vest, but the bombardier was unhurt.

In all, 300 suits, each with a quick-release mechanism, were ordered from Wilkinsons. *The New York Times* was quick to report in September 1943 that, "A London firm, specializing since 1772 in the manufacture of swords, is now beating its products into something much more useful at the moment. It is making suits of mail for American airmen . . .. Thus the cycle rolls around again, the American fighters, like the Yankee at King Arthur's Court, find themselves back in medieval armor. . . ."

On 8th March, Brigadier General Hayward Hansell flew in the 305th Bomb Group formation for the raid on the marshalling yards at Rennes to see for himself if the success gained four days earlier could be repeated. He was not disappointed. Fifty B-17s plastered the marshalling yards from end to end and effectively stopped any supplies reaching

German bases in Brittany for up to four days. Within the next five days two more marshalling yards in France were bombed, without loss to the attackers.

With morale high, plans were laid to bomb the Bremen Vulcan shipbuilding yards on the Weser, a few miles north of Bremen, on 18th March. Ranked fourth largest producer of U-boats in Germany, Eaker ordered a maximum effort and seventy-three Fortresses and twenty-four Liberators - the highest number of heavies yet, were assembled for the raid.

Near Heligoland the B-17s came under attack from the Luftwaffe and the leading 303rd Bomb Group formation of twenty-two aircraft bore the brunt of most of the enemy fighters' venom. During the bomb run the group came in for some concentrated and accurate flak. Leading the 359th and lowest squadron was *The Duchess*, piloted by Captain Harold Stouse. Up front in the nose Lieutenant Jack Mathis, the lead bombardier, crouched over his bombsight and lined up the target below. As lead bombardier, Mathis was doing the aiming for all the other aircraft in the squadron using Automatic Flight Control Equipment (AFCE) for the first time. This equipment gave him lateral control of the aircraft through the Norden bombsight's connection to the autopilot. Stouse took his hands off the control column and the aircraft was literally in Mathis' hands until the bombs were gone. Mathis called out: "Bomb bay doors are open" and then instructed Stouse to climb a little more to their bombing altitude of 24,000 feet. On the bomb run flak enveloped the 359th Squadron just seconds before the bomb-release point. One shell burst off to the right of *The Duchess* and just below her nose. It was near enough to send a large piece of flak hurtling through the side of the nose, shattering the Plexiglas and hurling Mathis and the navigator to the rear of the nose compartment. Mathis had his right arm almost sev-

ered above the elbow and he had deep wounds in his side and stomach. Without any assistance from the navigator, Mathis crawled back to his bombsight and released the bombs. The navigator heard Mathis' voice falter after he had uttered: "Bombs . . ." Thinking Mathis' throat mike had been damaged by the explosion, the navigator went forward and finished the call: "Bombs Away!" Without this confirmation Stouse would not begin evasive action, so essential after bomb release. Mathis reached over to push the bomb bay door handle to close the bomb doors but as he did so he slumped backwards into the arms of the navigator. It was only then that the navigator realized that Mathis had been mortally wounded. Two bombers were lost on the raid but *The Duchess* managed to bring Jack Mathis' dead body home to Molesworth. He was later posthumously awarded the Medal of Honor, America's highest military award, for "conspicuous gallantry and intrepidity above and beyond the call of duty."

Vegasack was officially described as "extremely heavily damaged." The bombers had dropped 268 tons of high explosive smack on the target and later photographic reconnaissance revealed that seven U-boats had been severely damaged and two-thirds of the shipyard destroyed. British Prime Minister Winston Churchill and Sir Charles Portal, Chief of Air Staff, recognized the importance of the success and seny congratulatory messages to Eaker. The next three missions did not go quite as well and eight bombers were lost.

On 22nd March, eighty-four Liberators and Fortresses attacked U-Boat yards at Wilhelmshaven. Six days later, on 28th March, seventy heavies attacked the Rouen-Sotteville marshalling yards. When on 31st March, VIII Bomber Command raided the wharves and docks area at Rotterdam, four of the six bomb groups which set out were recalled because of strong winds and thick cloud. *Ooold Soljer* and *Two*

Miss Bea Haven, *42-5257 of the 303rd Bomb Group based at Molesworth, returned Stateside adorned with the names of aircrew and ground crews.*

Captain Cliff Pyle (far right) *and the crew of* We The People, *from the 305th Bomb Group. The photo was taken on 7th March 1943.* (Pyle)

Beauts in the 303rd Bomb Group were lost in a mid-air collision. Thirty-three heavies hit the dock area. Many of the B-17s, blown off course by the strong winds, and in bad visibility, missed their objectives completely and killed 326 Dutch civilians when their bombs hurtled down into the streets of Rotterdam. JG1 intercepted the returning 305th Bomb Group formation and made one pass before their fuel was expended. *Southern Comfort* caught fire between the No. 1 and No. 2 engines. Hugh Ashcraft managed to fly the B-17 to England where the crew abandoned the Fortress safely. It crashed at Wickham Bishops.

On 4th April, Eaker switched to targets in France and, that morning, Fortresses throughout the Bedford area took off for a raid on the Renault factory in the Billancourt district of Paris. Before the war the Renault works had been the largest producer of vehicles in France and now the Germans were using it to turn out military trucks and tanks. Their output was estimated at 1,000 trucks, tanks, and armored cars a month. On the night of 3rd/4th March 1942 the RAF had destroyed the plant, but the Germans had rebuilt it in nine months by using slave labor. The Germans had even managed to increase production to 1,500 vehicles a month.

It took two hours for the four B-17 groups to complete assembly before a total of ninety-seven Fortresses departed the rendezvous point at Beachy Head. However, when landfall was made at Dieppe, only eighty-five Fortresses remained; twelve having aborted through malfunctions. For once the sky was clear and blue and many of the Spitfire escort fighters could be seen quite plainly. Others were sim-

ply vapor trails in the upper reaches of the atmosphere. From their altitude of 25,000 feet, crews could see the black mass of Paris apparently cradled by the long curved arm of the River Seine, ninety-five miles in the distance. At 1414 hours the Fortresses were over their target and 251 tons of high explosive rained down on Paris. Flak was moderate and not too accurate and crews were able to pick out the Renault works despite the industrial haze that covered much of the city. Most of the eighty-one tons that landed square on the factory were released by eighteen B-17s of the leading 305th formation, led by Major McGehee in *We The People*, flown by Captain Cliff Pyle. Before the last group had left the target, the whole area was blotted out by a thick pall of smoke reaching to 4,000 feet. Unfortunately, the groups in the rear of the formation were not as accurate as the 305th had been and many bombs fell outside the target area, causing a number of civilian casualties.

Five minutes after the target between fifty and seventy-five fighters of JG26 began attacks on the formation, which lasted all the way to Rouen. Four B-17s were shot down in repeated frontal attacks, sometimes by four and six fighters at a time. *Available Jones*, flown by Morris M. Jones, and three other B-17s in the 364th (low) squadron of the 305th Bomb Group were shot down, two of them falling to the guns of Hauptman Wilhelm-Ferdinand "Wutz" Galland of II./JG26, brother of General Major Adolf Galland. At 1433 hours the Spitfire escort reappeared to provide withdrawal support, but five of their number were shot down in a seven minute battle without loss to the Luftwaffe. The

Hell's Angels *41-24577 from the 303rd Bomb Group, was the first 8th Air Force B-17 to complete twenty-five combat missions, a number reached on 14th May 1943. The aircraft went on to survive a total of forty-eight missions before it was flown back to America to help raise War Bonds.* (USAF)

gunners aboard *Dry Martini 4th*, piloted by Captain Allen Martini, were credited with the destruction of ten enemy fighters; a record for a bomber crew on a single mission. In all, American gunners claimed forty-seven enemy fighters destroyed. The real losses were two German pilots killed and one wounded. After the raid, pictures smuggled back to England by the French Resistance showed that the Renault works had been severely damaged.

The following day, Antwerp was bombed. The 306th bore the brunt of head-on attacks by FW 190s, which shot down five of the group's B-17s - the only losses among the heavies this day. Another B-17, carrying Brigadier General Frank Armstrong, now commanding the lst Bomb Wing, who was flying as an observer, was hit by cannon fire but Major James Wilson, the 306th Air Executive, managed to bring the Fortress home safely to Thurleigh. Well aimed bombing was not possible due to the persistent fighter attacks, which forced many bombers off course. This serious situation was aggravated by problems with the Norden bomb sights in the 303rd Bomb Group, and the eighty-two B-17s that got their bombs away consequently dropped most of them on Mortsel where over 3,000 houses were destroyed killing 936 inhabitants and injuring 1,342. Only four bombs hit the Erla VII works, which killed 229 workers, with another twenty-eight missing. The Erla Werke, however, suffered little damage and within a few weeks aircraft and engine repairs were back to the normal level.

Aircrews were being lost on missions far faster than they could be replaced but fresh young crews were en route now that the 12th Air Force no longer had first call on them.

Among the new arrivals in England in March 1943 had been Howard E. Hernan, a top turret gunner in Lieutenant Claude W. Campbell's crew, which arrived at Molesworth to join the 303rd Bomb Group. "On 8th April we made our first training flight and flew three more up until the 15th. Claude Campbell was a good formation flyer and I guess they figured four training flights were all we needed. Our crew later had a theme song, *The Campbells Are Coming*. We would listen to it on the Armed Forces Network and when they signed off we would switch to 'Lord Haw Haw', who seemed to know more about us than people on our own base. He knew the theme song was being played and knew we were Campbell's crew so he would also play some music for us. He always added a little sarcasm but sometimes his music was better than that on the other ratio networks."

On 16th April, Campbell's crew flew its first mission, to Lorient. William A. Boutelle, the bombardier, wrote of the Lorient mission: "I'd heard plenty about these raids and, while a lot of the stories conflicted, knew a little of what to expect. As we approached the coast of France, though, my knees felt weak and the long time in which I had to set up my bombsight seemed to be flying by: I found myself rushing so fast that I made mistakes. I kept trying to look for the first flak and fighter and work my sight figures too. I settled down and set up my sight and looked up just in time to see the first fighters. There were two Focke-Wulfs coming up at 11 o'clock low, so I reported and grabbed my gun, even though they were a mile out of range. They soon made an attack apiece from 12 o'clock with no results on either side. I did expend fifteen rounds at one as he flashed by with his

Another veteran of the 303rd Bomb Group was Yankee Doodle Dandy, *42-5264. The* Hell's Angels *painted under the cockpit refers to the 303rd Bomb Group, which was known as the Hells Angels.* (USAF)

wings spouting 20mms like roman candles. About that time a formation of ten-fifteen fighters showed up and sat on our right wing, about 2,000 yards away. Then they came barrelassing in with a short burst for us and all they had for the group below. The tail-gunner said it was 'Some show.'"

Howard Hernan continues, "An FW 190 came in at about 2 o'clock high. The pilot could not have had much experience firing at a B-17 because he fired from a long way off. I gave him a burst at about 1,500 yards, a little further than I should have. About the same time he fired his 20mm cannon and they all went off at about 400 yards ahead of us. After he fired, he immediately flipped over on his back and down he went. It was the last I saw of him. We came through unscathed but the group lost two B-17s."

The following morning crews throughout eastern England were alerted for a raid on the Focke-Wulf plant at Bremen and a record 115 bombers were assembled. For the first time two large-scale combat wings, with the 91st and 306th in the first wing and the 303rd and 305th Bomb Groups making up the second, were dispatched. Each wing formation consisted of three group boxes of eighteen to twenty-one aircraft, flown for mutual firepower and protection. Eight bombers returned early with malfunctions, leaving the remaining 107 bombers to continue across the North Sea.

The long over-water flight was uneventful and even monotonous. Some crewmen took advantage of the lull before the storm to catch up on some sleep or letters home. William Boutelle settled down to his note pad and began writing, 12,000 feet above the North Sea. "As I write this

I'm on my way to Bremen, one of the hottest spots in Germany. Yesterday we flew in the leading and highest group. In that position we had a very calm and, for the most part, boring flight. The lower and rear groups caught some hell from flak and fighters while we only saw a few puffs of ack-ack and about twenty fighters. Today promises to be a very different story. We're in the highest but last group and have a grandstand view of all the other ships, of which I can count over 100 right now. We should really see a show today. I'll see it all I hope."

Shortly after leaving the English coast, the mass of aircraft had been spotted by a German reconnaissance aircraft and the Americans' approach was radioed to fighter controllers along the enemy coastline. The German defenses did not know where the bombers were headed but, just after the B-17s passed the Frisian Islands, Luftwaffe fighters were vectored towards them. However, the FW 190 pilots waited until after the bomb run before commencing their attacks. The reason was not long in coming, as Howard Hernan explains: "Of all the missions I would fly I never saw flak as bad as on this mission. At briefing we had been told that there would be 496 batteries around Bremen. The Germans put up a box barrage. The '88s gave off black smoke when they fired and the '105s were gray. It was just like one black cloud. The windshield was broken out and flak holes appeared in the radio compartment. I tied a pillow into a hole in the window and Campbell flew on from the co-pilot's seat. We were flying number two off the lead ship on the right-hand side and so close were we that our wing tip was in the lead ship's waist window."

The enemy fighters concentrated their attacks on the leading 91st and 306th formations. Worst hit was the 306th which lost ten bombers and one ship came home with a parachute harness tied to control cables that had been shot away by cannon fire. The 401st Squadron of the 91st Bomb Group lost all six aircraft flying as the low squadron in the 1st Combat Wing formation.

The trailing groups did not suffer loss although most aircraft had received some degree of fighter or flak damage. At interrogation, gunners put in claims for sixty-three fighters destroyed but in reality only about ten fighters were actually shot down. Howard Hernan sums up the problem. "I know that gunners made many claims and probably a lot of us got credit for planes that were not actually shot down. I think this was true on both sides. In order to claim a fighter you had to have two other witnesses. Heaven knows how many men were shooting at the same plane. Intelligence would ask what was the exact location and it would sometimes take up to forty-five minutes longer to sit in interrogation if you were claiming a fighter. By this time we were absolutely worn out, hungry, trying to get warm, and it just wasn't worth the effort. After all, we weren't there to shoot down fighters. Our primary concern was the bombing of the targets. Eventually, intelligence told us that we were claiming too many fighters. From then on I never claimed another fighter, even if I knew I'd got it."

In fact most of the parachutes that crews saw during the two-hour battle above Bremen belonged to American airmen. On the credit side, half the Focke-Wulf factory was destroyed but Albert Speer, the German armaments minister, had already issued instructions for dispersed fighter production some six months previously. Despite the continuing losses, crews received a much needed boost with the news that the 8th Air Force was to be expanded.

During mid-April 1943, four new Fortress groups - the 94th, 95th, 96th, and 351st - were dispatched to Britain. All but the 351st boasted B-17Fs with long-range "Tokyo" tanks built into their wings near the tips to hold an additional 1,080 gallons of fuel. Theater indoctrination was normally carried out at Bovingdon, but the facilities there were hopelessly inadequate for such a large influx of crews. As a result, the air echelon of the 95th Bomb Group joined the 92nd at Alconbury for combat training. They were to remain there for six weeks, during which time the ground forces of the 92nd found themselves responsible for up to ninety aircraft. The 95th flew practice missions every day, weather permitting, while the veteran crews in the 92nd found themselves in the role of instructors. Many of the experienced crews were quick to note the boyish enthusiasm displayed by the green crews. The veterans knew they would learn the hard way, through experience, that there were no milk-runs over Europe.

B-17F 41-24488 Banshee, *of the 369th Bomb Squadron, 306th Bomb Group, was lost on 17th April 1943 with Captain William J. Casey's crew. Five of the crew were killed and five were taken prisoner.* (USAF)

Chapter 5
Gaining Strength

While the new groups continued training, Eaker scheduled another attack on St Nazaire for May Day. The raid was a special one for Captain Cliff Pyle, who was flying his twenty-fifth and final mission with the 305th Bomb Group. The 305th lost two aircraft but Pyle and the crew of *We The People* came through safely. Within ten days of this mission he was attached to the 1st Bomb Wing with the title of "President, Tactical Advisory Board." The Board's primary function was to advise the commanding general about combat tactics and to monitor the preparation of the Tactical Doctrine. This eventually turned into the well known "Standard Operations Procedures."

Thick cloud over the target curtailed bombing attempts and the 306th Bomb Group flew back, unaware it was off course through a navigational error. What was assumed to be Land's End turned out to be the Brest Peninsula and as the formation began descending, it was bracketed by an accurate barrage of flak. Altogether, the 306th Bomb Group lost six aircraft.

B-17F, 42-29649 of the 423rd Bomb Squadron, flown by 1st/Lieutenant Lewis P. Johnson, Jr., was hit several times and caught fire in the radio compartment and in the tail area. Staff Sergeant Maynard H. "Snuffy" Smith, the ball turret gunner, who was on his first mission, hand cranked his turret to get it back into the aircraft. He climbed out and discovered that the waist gunners and the radio operator had baled out. He could have baled out himself but the aircraft did not show any signs of leaving formation, so Smith assumed the pilots were still aboard and he remained in the aircraft and fought the fire with a hand extinguisher.

Then he jettisoned the oxygen bottles and ammunition in the radio compartment, manned the two waist guns during an attack by enemy fighters, stopping to dampen down the fires and treat the tail-gunner. Johnson put down at Predannack near Land's End after Smith had thrown out all the equipment that was not nailed down.

For his actions this day, "Snuffy" Smith became the first enlisted man in the 8th Air Force to receive the Medal of Honor from Secretary of War, Mr Stimpson, at Thurleigh on 15th July. "Snuffy" now insisted on being saluted by officers (as is the right of an enlisted Medal of Honor recipient) and he adopted the British fashion of having his award printed after his name. He flew only four more missions before being transferred to a ground job.

Three days later, VIII Bomber Command dispatched seventy-nine B-17s on a five-hour round trip to the Ford and General Motors plant at Antwerp. The escort of twelve Allied fighter squadrons, including for the first time six squadrons of P-47 Thunderbolts, afforded the bombers good protection. This day one of Hollywood's greatest stars flew with the 303rd Bomb Group formation as Howard Hernan recalls.

"We flew on Captain Calhoun's wing (CO of the squadron) and Clark Gable flew with him and handled the radio hatch gun. Claude Campbell, my pilot, could quite easily see the Hollywood film star grinning at him over enemy territory.

Staff Sergeant Maynard "Snuffy" Smith, Medal of Honor winner. (Richards)

"The Spitfires and Thunderbolts did a wonderful job of working the Focke-Wulfs over and it was a very successful mission. One of our B-17s, piloted by Lieutenant Pence, was shot up by an FW 190 that jumped the group as we reached the English coast and the co-pilot got shot in the leg and never flew again; the radio operator got hit over the eye and in the leg. The Focke-Wulfs made a pass at us out of the sun. Every gunner had his gun out of his receiver because we thought we were safe. Never again did I take my guns out until I was on the ground. Next morning I looked over Pence's plane. It had nine holes in it and I measured them. The spread was nine feet, although they had been attacked from head-on. Captain Gable visited the co-pilot every evening at a nearby hospital to see how he was getting along."

Gable had appeared in several movies and had won an Oscar for his role in *It Happened One Night*, made in 1934. On 12th August 1942, following the death of his wife (actress Carole Lombard, who was killed in an air crash while on a bond tour) Gable, at 42 years of age, voluntarily en-

listed as a private in the USAAF. In October 1942 he graduated from the Officers' Candidate School in Miami as a second lieutenant and attended aerial gunnery school until February 1943. On the personal insistence of General Arnold, he was assigned to the 351st Bomb Group at Polebrook to make a motion picture of gunners in action. He flew a handful of combat missions and, after completing some footage for the movie, *Combat America*, returned to the States in October 1943.

May 1943 was a month of many changes for the 8th Air Force and the 92nd Bomb Group in particular. In January 1943 Major Robert B. Keck had left Bovingdon for the United States to lead back a flight of new and secret Fortresses for use with the group. Called YB-40s and fitted with sixteen machine-guns, including two top turrets, they were intended to be used as "Destroyer escorts" for conventional Fortresses. Thirteen YB-40s were assigned to the 327th Bomb Squadron and Major Keck became its CO. Their arrival also meant a resumption in combat missions for the 92nd Bomb Group.

On 12th May the overall plan for the restructuring of VIII Bomber Command began to emerge. The 94th, 95th, and 96th Bomb Groups were to form a new 4th Bomb Wing in Essex and Suffolk under the command of Brigadier General Fred L. Anderson, whose headquarters would be established at Marks Hall, near Colchester. The three groups remained in 1st Bomb Wing "country" until their new bases were completed.

The ground echelons of the 94th, 95th, and 96th Bomb Groups had only arrived in the United Kingdom on 10th May but, on the night of the 12th, orders arrived at Bassingbourn, Alconbury, and Grafton Underwood respectively, calling for a maximum effort for a mission to airfields at St Omer, starting at 1300 hours. Remarkably, the three groups managed to ready seventy-two bombers for the mission, but at such short notice problems were bound to occur. The 96th failed to complete assembly and aborted the mission. One B-17 got into difficulties and ditched in the Channel where the crew was rescued by Air Sea Rescue. Thirty-one B-17s from the 94th and 95th Bomb Groups continued to the target but they, too, were to experience difficulty. Captain Franklin "Pappy" Colby of the 94th Bomb Group, at forty-one years of age the oldest combat pilot in the 8th Air Force, was on the mission. "After many diversions and buzzing around over the North Sea to get the enemy fighters up and, hopefully, low on gas, we finally sailed across the Channel. As the weather was CAVU (Ceiling and Visibility Unlimited) we could see both shores plainly. From our height it looked like we could spit across the Straits of Dover. Major Louis Thorup led the High Squadron with me leading the second element of three ships behind him. It turned out to be a piece of cake. We saw no fighters and only three bursts of flak. However, the bombing smelled, as we completely missed the aerodrome and put the bombs out

Hollywood film star Clark Gable poses with a crew from the 351st Bomb Group. Gable enlisted as a private at the age of forty-two after his wife, Carole Lombard, died in an air crash in America.

in fields with quite a few going into the town itself. It was a downwind bomb run and apparently our lead bombardier badly underestimated the force of the wind at 20,000 feet."

The following day Eaker was able to put up in excess of 200 B-17s and B-24s for the first time, thanks to the addition of the 4th Wing Groups and the 351st Bomb Group from Polebrook. The total number of bombers available meant he could diversify his attacks with a multiplicity of options, further improved by the debut of twelve B-26 Marauders. At around 1035 hours the Marauders swooped in low over the Dutch coast and continued over the outskirts of Amsterdam at rooftop height They bombed a generating station at Ijmuiden with delayed action mines and then departed as quickly as they came. It was a curtain-raiser for a vast armada of aircraft, the like of which had never before been seen on German radar screens during daylight hours.

About an hour after the B-26s departed, the 1st Wing formation, flying without escort, was picked up, this time approaching the northwest coast of Germany. The German fighter controllers did not yet know where they were heading but the target was the Germania and Deutsch Werke shipyards at Kiel. At 1145 hours the formation turned south for the base of the Danish Peninsula. Five minutes later the German controllers scrambled their fighters when the Americans' destination became apparent.

Howard Hernan, top turret gunner in Lieutenant Campbell's crew in the 303rd Bomb Group formation, says that;

"The fighter opposition was intense and the flak heavy. We flew at 32,000 feet in the high squadron, high group; the highest I had ever flown. Most of the 88mm flak was below us. The Germans did shoot up some '105s but these were inaccurate, some going off 2-3,000 feet above us. Captain Bales, Lieutenant Campbell's roommate, flying in *FDR's Potato Peeler Kids*, was shot down twenty miles offshore.

"With Captain Bales was Mark Mathis, whose brother Jack, had been killed over Vegasack. It was for this reason that Mark transferred from a B-26 outfit to his brother's group and he even flew in *The Duchess* where he used his brother's bomb-sight. Mark Mathis hated the Germans and was determined to avenge his brother and complete his twenty-five missions for him. The Kiel raid was his fourth mission. Nine 'chutes came out of the *Potato Peeler*. Bales appeared to have all his engines turning over although one or two could have been windmilling. He came around and made a water landing in the midst of all the 'chutes. We never heard anything from them again."

Kiel was bombed at 1205 hours with "good" results. At about the same time B-17s of the 96th and 351st Bomb Groups were approaching the airfield at Courtrai in France. Just over twenty-five minutes later they returned east over Ypres to be met by Luftwaffe fighters which became embroiled with the escorting fighters. Fifty Fortresses won through and bombed the hangars, dispersal areas, runways, and workshops at the airfield and put it out of action. The B-17s then flew north and headed for the coast between Ostend and Dunkirk. By 1255 hours most of the German fighters which took part in the first attack were forced to land and refuel.

Five minutes later, German radar picked up the 94th and 95th Bomb Groups led by General Anderson, near Ostend, heading for the Ford and General Motors plant at Antwerp. "Pappy" Colby reminisces:

"With no diversion at all we headed straight in to the target. At the IP we were supposed to meet our supporting fighters but we were twenty minutes late. Finally, we saw about thirty fighters at 2 o'clock and I heaved a sigh of relief, thinking our friends had waited for us. Suddenly, they attacked and at about the same time heavy flak started exploding dead ahead. We took violent evasive action and I was so busy for a few minutes that I didn't see much of what was happening. Then I discovered that the leading three-ship element of our low squadron had drifted left, out of the group formation and I had to decide quickly whether to stay with the group or follow him. I decided to stay with the group and it's lucky I did because flak started exploding right behind him where we should have been.

"It's nasty looking stuff - like an inverted mushroom of black smoke with a horizontal smoke ring which rises from the main burst and circles the stem. I heard our guns hammering and saw little white smoke puffs just ahead of the left wingman. For a moment I thought they were from his guns and then suddenly realized they were exploding cannon shells from German fighters.

"We dumped our load of five 1,000lb bombs as carefully as possible and swung out over the coast for home. Flak followed us until we were out of range but the fighters eased up, probably because they were out of gas. Our own fighters finally joined us over the Channel, but at least one B-17 from another group was lost. My tail-gunner saw him hit the ground and explode - no parachutes. Recce photos later showed a heavy bomb concentration on the Ford factory and the nearby canal locks, and the west end of the General Motors plant also caught it."

In four hours VIII Bomber Command had attacked four targets, losing eleven aircraft and claiming sixty-seven fighters shot down. RAF Spitfires and USAAF Thunderbolts had given excellent fighter cover on the Antwerp and Courtrai raids. Not all the bombing was accurate, but for the first

time Americans had shown that they were capable of mounting multiple attacks on a given day.

Next day Eaker again diversified his forces, sending the 1st Wing to Wilhelmshaven while fifty-nine B-17s from the 4th Wing were allocated the naval base at Emden. Despite an unsuccessful attempt twenty-four hours earlier by

Stars Frances Langford, Bob Hope, and Tony Romano, pose with the crew of Lallah VIII *of the 305th Bomb Group on 5th July 1943 at Chelveston. The aircraft, 42-30242, was lost on the Schweinfurt raid on 14th October 1943. (Bill Donald)*

Liberators using incendiaries at Kiel, B-17s of the 94th Bomb Group were each loaded up with eight 500lb incendiary clusters for its raid on Emden. "Pappy" Colby was there.

"We climbed to 26,000 feet over the North Sea, turned towards the German coast in a fake attack and then turned out again. The second time we turned in, the low squadron leader in front of me missed the signal to turn and nearly ran into the lead squadron. The propellers were making heavy contrails that made visibility very bad. As we started to turn left, my left wingman, Lieutenant Eklund, apparently didn't see us and started to slide into me. All that saved us from a collision is that, by the grace of God, his right wing suddenly cast a shadow on my left window. I looked up quickly to see what made the shadow and was horrified to see his wing almost on top of ours. I dumped the aircraft down desperately and his props missed us by barely three feet. A second or two later and we'd both have had it.

"We regained formation but I stayed out to the left of the lead squadron to avoid any more fast turns. As we passed over some high clouds we saw a hole just beyond them and there, in plain sight, was our target. Everybody dumped the incendiaries but instead of the bundles dropping like bombs, they broke open and the 4lb sticks came fluttering back right through the formation, scaring the hell out of everybody. Heavy flak started bursting and for some reason the lead squadron turned right instead of left as we had been briefed and this left our low squadron out in the cold by itself. Luck-

ily, no fighters saw us and we hustled to get back into the protection of the group.

"As we crossed the German coast homeward bound, from behind us came about twenty-five enemy fighters. They passed us on our left as if we were standing still, pulled across in front of us and then dived head-on into our formation as all hell bust loose. They hit the lead squadron mostly and I saw at least ten or twelve 20mm cannon shells explode around our ships but everyone kept going. Our gunners were yelling, 'Attack 10 o'clock high; 1 o'clock high . . ..' and we were really busy. My right wingman, Lieutenant Jasper Moore, got jammed into the lead squadron again and had to fall back. Later, I found out he was hit by a 20mm in the tail which almost severed his control cables.

"Suddenly, my bombardier, Bob Gamble, let out a wild yell and I discovered later that a shell had exploded under our nose, blowing out part of the Plexiglas window. Enough to scare anyone! Two Focke-Wulf 190s started a nose attack on us and all our gunners turned loose on them while they were still out some 800 yards. The tracers flew like a garden hose in reverse and to my great surprise, they broke off the attack and turned away. We came home dog-tired and unhappy about the poor formation flying, which scared us as much as the enemy. One ship lost its tail-gunner and we all had considerable flak damage."

Left: *The air and ground crew of* Thundermug, *which lost its rudder on the mission to Rennes on 29th May 1943. Colby was the captain.* Below: *"Pappy" Colby recieves the Air Medal on 1st April 1943.*

Incredibly only one B-17, from the 95th Bomb Group, was lost on the Emden mission. Meanwhile, the 1st Wing had set a course for Wilhelmshaven. Thick cloud obscured the target and the Fortresses were forced to seek alternative targets at Heligoland, Dune, and Wangerooge Island. Heligoland was covered in only 4/10ths cloud and the flak was inaccurate. However, numerous enemy fighters put in an appearance and succeeded in shooting down five Fortresses.

On 16th May, VIII Bomber Command was stood down while maintenance was performed on the battle-scarred B-17s, blackened by two days' continuous combat. Crews were also glad of a respite, brief though it was, for on the morning of 17th May they were tumbled out of their cots for another maximum effort. Once again Eaker diversified his forces, sending the 1st Wing to Kiel and the 4th to Lorient while the Liberators, acting as an independent force for the first time, were sent to Bordeaux. In addition, eleven B-26 Marauders of the 322nd Bomb Group flew a diversionary mission to Haarlem and Ijmuiden to bomb targets they had completely missed on their debut, three days before. Fifty-five Fortresses from the 4th Wing were dispatched against the U-boat pens and the power station that served them at Lorient. "Pappy" Colby relates:

"As we came in off the sea about thirty fighters really gave us a going over. It turned out they were the famous yellow nose fighters who defended the St Nazaire-Lorient area. To my amazement I saw one come right through the middle of the group formation in front of us. What a pilot!

"We made a fair bomb run and turn out but the fighters worked us over clear out over the sea. In the middle of the fight my entire left windshield suddenly showed a million cracks and I could barely see through it. A machine-gun bullet hit it, but luckily at an acute angle, so that while it shattered the inch-thick armor glass, it only put a small hole clear through. Lieutenant Winnesheik (our Indian Chief), lost an engine but made it back. I know we got at least one of their fighters because I saw the pilot parachute out of his burning aircraft. This was the roughest raid we had yet experienced."

Midnight, piloted by Ed Spevak, became the first 94th Bomb Group Fortress to fall victim to enemy action when it was knocked down by flak over the target. An engine caught fire and the aircraft fell out of formation. Fighters attacked and set another engine on fire. *Midnight* was engulfed in flame and smoke in the tail and Spevak gave the order to bale out. "Pappy" Colby's crew counted eight parachutes. Walter Minor, *Midnight's* tail-gunner, was hit just as he was leaving the burning aircraft. He floated down and saw a wing tear free from the fuselage and continue separately to earth. He and another crew member were picked up by the French Underground and were returned to England via the Pyr-

B-17 MK.Y *of the 366 Bomb Squadron, 305th Bomb Group over the Huls synthetic rubber plant in the Ruhr on 22nd June 1943. The Huls complex was of great importance to the German war effort and produced twenty-nine percent of all Germany's synthetic rubber. 235 B-17s took off and 183 bombed the plant, causing smoke to rise to a height of 17,000 feet. Production was halted for a month and full scale output was not resumed for six months. A total of sixteen B-17 were lost on this raid and 170 more damaged. (USAF)*

enees, Spain, and Gibraltar. Ed Spevak and Don Nichols, the co-pilot, also evaded capture and were returned to England.

The B-17 groups pounded Lorient at fifteen minute intervals. Only six B-17s were lost and the bombing was described as "excellent". Unfortunately, their success was not repeated by the 322nd Bomb Group, all of whose eleven Marauders were shot down.

On 19th May, sixty-eight Fortresses of the 1st Wing went to the turbine engine building at Kiel to finish off what had been missed five days previously, while further north, fifty-five B-17s of the 4th Wing attacked U-boat pens at Flensburg on the Danish coast. Following this mission, fog and rain cloaked East Anglia and the Fens, preventing any missions being flown until 21st May when the 1st Wing was allocated Wilhelmshaven and the 4th Wing, Emden. At Wilhelmshaven weather conditions hampered the formation and it was further disrupted by constant head-on attacks by enemy fighters. The Emden force also encountered heavy fighter opposition despite diversionary ruses at the coast. Altogether, twelve B-17s were lost on the two raids with the 1st Wing coming off worst with seven B-17s shot down. Among them was *Dearly Beloved* in the 423rd Bomb Squadron, 306th Bomb Group, flown by Lieutenant Robert H. Smith. His seven gunners set a new record, downing eleven fighters before the B-17 was forced to ditch in the North Sea. All the crew was picked up by an ASR launch and returned to Thurleigh.

On 23rd May the 94th began moving from Thurleigh to Earls Colne in Essex and the 96th began leaving Grafton Underwood for Andrews Field, six miles from Earls Colne. The 95th Bomb Group was also due to move, from Alconbury to Framlingham, Suffolk, but its departure was marred by a tragic accident. At 2030 hours on 27th May a tremendous explosion shook the countryside for miles around Alconbury when a 95th Bomb Group B-17 exploded while in the process of being loaded up with ten 500lb bombs. Nineteen officers and enlisted men were killed and twenty severely injured, one of whom died later. Four B-17s parked in the vicinity of the explosion were destroyed and eleven others were damaged in the blast. Because no one in the actual proximity of the explosion survived, the cause of the disaster is unknown although an investigation board later attributed the probable cause to a defective fuse detonating from causes unknown.

The 96th Bomb Group's former base at Grafton Underwood was taken over by the 384th Bomb Group, commanded by Colonel Budd J. Peaslee, which arrived in England during late May. The 351st Bomb Group remained at Polebrook and the 1st Bomb Wing received additional "teeth" with the arrival of the 381st Bomb Group, commanded by Colonel Joe J. Nazzaro, which flew into Ridgewell on 31st May, and the 379th Bomb Group, commanded by Colonel Maurice "Mo" Preston, which took over a new base at Kimbolton.

Bad weather throughout the latter part of May restricted deep penetration missions and delayed the introduction of new groups like the 379th. Preston's group finally "got its feet wet" on 29th May when the target for 1st Bomb Wing crews was St Nazaire. Heavy cloud moving across western Europe resulted in several stop-go decisions

before the B-17s finally got the green light. Colonel Preston remembers the 379th Bomb Group's debut well (seven YB-40s also made their debut this day).

"The powers-that-be were a little concerned and skeptical about sending a new, untried unit out on its first mission to a relatively tough target like St Nazaire. So, I suppose in order to salve their consciences somewhat, they put us in what promised to be the safest position in the task force; the high group position in the last combat wing. They figured that we should sail through scot-free in that position but they underestimated the effect of their own tactics.

"A diversionary force had been sent out in an effort to induce the German fighters to take off early, thus forcing them to run out of gas as, or before, the main force arrived. Well, the tactic worked perfectly. The *Abbeville Kids* committed themselves early and soon ran out of gas. But they got back up in time to intercept us at the tail-end of the bomber column just as we passed the IP. The fighters attacked us with a vengeance then drew off to hit us again as we departed the target and before we were able to reassemble in wing formation. We lost three aircraft and thirty crew members, including John Hall, a squadron commander. Swede Carlson, another squadron commander, lost two engines near the target and suffered damage to a third, causing his aircraft to be lost later when he had to land in a brussel sprout patch in England.

"I saw flak for the first time in my life on the mission. Although it came from a little battery on Guernsey it was nonetheless real and it gave me my first big scare of the

41-24341 XB-40, the prototype for the heavily armored YB-40 gunships that first appeared with the 92nd Bomb Group in May 1943.

war. I was never quite as scared of flak again but that first view of something shot up there to kill me really got to me. The mission didn't go smoothly in all respects. There were planning errors revealed. There were personal errors. There were screw-ups and there were goofs. All of which made it clear to one young Lieutenant Colonel, out for his first exposure to the war, that we GIs didn't have our methods and procedures for fighting it down pat yet. There was room for improvement, it seemed. And maybe there was still an opportunity for some of us Johnny-Come-Latelys to make a contribution or two to the winning of the war. I was forced to wonder, at the same time, how long we'd be around to make that contribution."

The inexperience associated with any new group continued, on occasions, to manifest itself among the elder groups such as the 94th, which was briefed for Rennes this day. Problems occurred during assembly in bad weather and elements became disorientated. "Pappy" Colby, flying *Thundermug*, says that things were "SNAFU."

"We noted the high squadron had no second element of three ships. They didn't catch up until we hit the French coast. Then, just before starting the bomb run, our leader ran us in behind another group and we all got shaken up by the prop' wash. We should have been 1,000 feet higher. As the bomb run started the lead squadron made a little right turn and the high squadron, instead of turning with him, came sailing right on top of us with their bomb bays open. I took one horrified look and pulled out to the left to

get out from under them, then we scrambled to get back in place when the high squadron finally woke up. But the bombing stunk and his group leader never did release his bombs. The lack of training in formation flying displayed by some of the groups was appalling and was the cause of many of our problems.

"Right after leaving the target, the fighters came in thick but they mostly picked on the low squadron. We lost three crews and a fourth barely made it home on two engines, with a dead ball gunner and missing one man who fell out. There were two attacks by fighters dropping aerial bombs, who dove right through the formation from above. One came through between us and the second element of the lead squadron - a space of less than 100 feet - and nearly took our wing off. The second fighter was hit by Patrick, our radio-gunner, and a big piece of his wing flew off. Potts, our waist gunner, saw the pilot parachute out, so we claimed our third fighter kill. However, in knocking down the fighter, Patrick somehow put four .50 caliber bullets through the top of our rudder, breaking the top hinge and scaring hell out of Chris Thalman and myself when we felt the shock on our rudder pedals. Luckily, the middle and bottom hinges held and we got home safely.

"Since our trusty ship *Thundermug* now had a busted rudder, this meant we would fall behind the other crews in missions flown, as there were no spare ships. So I sold the Group Maintenance Officer on the idea of letting my crew swap rudders with a B-17 that was under repair waiting for parts - a "hangar queen." He wasn't happy about it but agreed finally and we made the swap with help from

one of his mechanics who adjusted the cables. Thus we were able to get *Thundermug* and its crew back in business, even though we bent a few regulations.

"General Eaker visited us and gave us a fine talk: telling us if we finished twenty-five missions we would be through with combat and assigned to staff jobs. He estimated that seventy-five percent or more would return to the States for re-assignment. (I thought it would be nearer to ninety-eight percent.) On 5th June we were visited by Brigadier General Frederick L. Anderson, CO the 4th Bombardment Wing. He awarded us the Air Medal and I was the first man in the 94th to receive it, much to my gratification. All of my crew also received the medal."

On the morning of 10th June, about thirty lead pilots, navigators and bombardiers at Earls Colne were briefed for a raid the following morning. "Pappy" Colby remembers that it was,

"very, very secret where we were going. But by 1030 hours the next morning the word was all over the Enlisted Men's Mess that we were going to Bremen. Security; ha, what a laugh! They briefed us at noon and we finally got going at 1500 hours."

Cloud and haze still filled the sky as 252 bombers headed for the target. Major Thorup led the 94th Bomb Group with the 333rd Bomb Squadron and "Pappy" Colby led the second element behind him. "We came in too close to the north coast of Germany and ran into high cirro-cumulus clouds as we turned for Bremen. The target was covered with a solid layer of low cumulus clouds down to about 5,000 feet which also partially covered Wilhelmshaven, our secondary target, so we made a 270 degree turn to the left and bombed Cuxhaven on the north coast of Germany. We hit it good and were on our way out when about twenty fighters caught up and attacked the lower groups behind us. A piece of flak flew in the open waist window on our left side and smacked against the machine-gun mount at the opposite window but luckily neither gunner was hit and no damage was caused to the mount (although it was hard on the gunners' kidneys)."

The 1st Wing, meanwhile, discovering the primary target at Bremen to be obscured, turned for the secondary at Wilhelmshaven. During the bomb run the leading 303rd Bomb Group formation was bracketed by a severe flak barrage. Colonel Chuck Marion, the CO, lost two engines and following aircraft had to maneuver violently and reduce speed dramatically to avoid a collision. Just at that moment the Luftwaffe took advantage of the now scattered formation and made repeated head-on attacks in which one B-17 was rammed by a FW 190 that failed to pull out in time. The 379th Bomb Group, flying only its second mission, bore the brunt of the attacks, as Colonel Preston remembers well.

"The enemy fighters, as expected, first appeared as the lead wing of B-17s approached the shoreline just north of the target. The fighters came in large numbers; probably several hundred. As expected, they climbed to the bombers' altitude and then a little higher as they pulled on out to the right front of the bomber column a mile or so. Then they broke off in groups of four to six and swung around in a diving turn to deliver their attack from the front. They concentrated on the low group of those at the head of the column that, as it happened, was the 379th Group.

"The fighters approached upright until they reached a point about half a mile to the front, when they rolled on their backs, fired their guns and rockets and dived toward the earth. The little puffs of 20mm shells exploding were clearly visible as the fighters approached from up front. As soon as one bunch made its pass and disappeared earthward, another bunch would roll in for its run at the B-17s. And they kept coming and coming, on and on. They attacked all during the bomb run and the subsequent reassembly and continued the attack until we crossed the coastline. Then the attacks stopped, probably because all their ammo was spent. A very typical engagement, although perhaps untypical in its severity, and an effective one.

"The 379th lost six (the 8th lost eight B-17s in all) or one-third of its strength. Our gunners claimed many dozens of fighters destroyed. A strange thing: we always claimed to inflict great losses on the enemy in the tally sheets back in the 8th Air Force headquarters. I'm sure we destroyed the Luftwaffe many times over. Yet, in my personal experience, whereas I saw many B-17s shot down by enemy fighters - perhaps a score or more - and occasionally enemy fighters destroyed by friendly escort fighters, I never once saw a fighter destroyed by a B-17 gunner - not once, and I am personally convinced that bombardment gunnery was a very ineffective weapon. It was certainly no match for the fighter."

On 13th June, the 1st Wing was assigned Bremen while the 4th went to Kiel for another raid on the U-boat yards. The 94th, 95th, and 96th Bomb Groups took off from their bases at Earls Colne, Framlingham, and Andrews Field for the last time. Heavy losses in the Marauder groups prompted their transfer further south to the three B-17 bases so that fighter cover for them could be improved. When the B-17 groups returned from the raid they would touch down at the former B-26 bases at Bury St Edmunds (Rougham), Horham, and Snetterton Heath respectively. As it turned out, the three last missions flown from the 4th Wing groups' old bases were a disaster. It had been hoped that another two-pronged attack on the coast would split the German fighter force but it turned out to be a total failure, with almost all the enemy fighters forsaking the 1st Wing to concentrate on the four combat boxes of the 4th. On the approach to the target the fight started. The leading 95th Bomb Group was particularly hard hit, losing eight of its sixteen B-17s (two having aborted early) by the time it re-crossed the coast. Among the casualties was Brigadier General Nathan B. Forrest, the first American general to be lost in combat in the ETO.

The other combat boxes also came in for repeated attacks, especially the 94th and composite boxes. To "Pappy" Colby, it seemed as if all the fighters (some 150) had ignored the two full groups in front and had singled out the 94th and composite boxes because of their small numbers.

"By this time our low squadron only had four ships, as Sabella had aborted just before the target, leaving Bill Dauth in *Wolfpack* flying left wing on Major Thorup with me in trail all by myself. Just before the target a fighter came directly at Bill from 11 o'clock and knocked out one or more of his engines. He dropped back and some think he exploded. All ten men baled out in time and survived.

"Kiel was covered with clouds again (the second straight day the weatherman missed) so we bombed an industrial town southwest of it. Then, because the briefed flight plan called for it, we made a sixty degree right turn downwind, followed by a 270 degree left turn into the wind and across the Danish Peninsula. This right turn was a tragic mistake as it kept us an extra fifteen minutes under heavy attack. Ships were going down all around us and the composite group behind us had completely broken up, with the survivors now trying to join us. Rawlinson was gone and just as we crossed the coast over Heligoland, three fighters made a rear attack on me, so I took fast evasive action. When they quit and I got back into position I couldn't find Thorup so I fell in on the left wing of somebody else. A little later we were starting to lose altitude. I suddenly discovered the ship I was flying with had left the others and we were three B-17s out in the cold all by ourselves. I immediately signaled him and the other wingman to follow me. The leader kept on for a little while and then decided he'd better follow us. About that time a Bf 109 came out of nowhere and made a pass at him but missed.

"I followed in loose formation behind the bunch I had joined (about ten ships) which turned out to be the combined remains of the 94th and the composite group. We were now down to about 3,000 feet over the sea and all relaxed, when we were suddenly attacked by four more Bf 109s. They got Hendershot, setting his wing on fire, and he spun in. All ten men aboard *Visiting Fireman* were killed. Another ship *Shackeroo* ahead of us had an engine burning so we went over to give him extra protection and discovered it was Thorup. Before we could get close they hit him again, blowing the entire left horizontal fin clear off the tail and knocking out both left engines. He managed to stagger along about ten feet off the water for a good thirty miles before his power failed and he pancaked into the sea. We flew back and forth above him to give him protection as all the rest had left. Although we saw one

The Southern Queen, *42-30248 and a formation of the 94th Bomb Group crossing the enemy coast.* (Ward)

fighter in the distance, he didn't attack us. We tried to drop our spare life raft and also our portable radio but neither inflated when they hit the water and sunk before they could be recovered. So we climbed up to where we could radio England and sent an SOS and a position fix on them. When we got home, we passed all our information on to the British ASR. One of their aircraft sighted Thorup at

2230 hours and signaled a nearby Motor Torpedo Boat who came over and rescued the boys. They picked them up after eleven hours in the water and brought them in to Lowestoft."

The other 4th Wing groups also came in for repeated attacks, but not of the same intensity which had decimated the 95th. Altogether, twenty-two bombers were lost this day including ten from the 95th (the eleventh crashed in England). The three 4th Wing groups put down at their new bases in somber mood. In the wake of the Kiel battle the new 4th Wing CO, Colonel (later Brigadier General) Curtis E. LeMay, visited the 94th Bomb Group at Bury St Edmunds. "He gave us the usual welcome talk," said "Pappy" Colby, "and left the impression of being a bit hard-nosed about things, but he had flown a lot of rough ones and had a good record. And he was trying to improve the poor formation flying which had been so troublesome."

The area around Bury St Edmunds, Horham, and Snetterton Heath offered new vistas for the men of the 94th, 95th, and 96th. There would be trips to Newmarket for a day at the horse races or to Lavenham, a famous old wool town with half-timbered houses which dovetail into winding streets, or to Thetford, birthplace of Thomas Paine, one of the sons of the American Revolution. Of particular interest to 94th Bomb Group personnel was Culford Hall, six miles from Bury St Edmunds, built by the Marquis of Cornwallis, whose surrender at Yorktown in 1781 meant victory for the Americans in the War of Independence.

The exchange of bases heralded a new era for the 4th Wing, whose headquarters was established at Elveden Hall, near Thetford, the former home of the Third Bomb Wing. The arrival of the 100th Bomb Group early that month (first to Podington, then to Thorpe Abbotts, Suffolk) and the imminent arrival of two more, the 385th and 388th, would increase the 4th Wing to six groups. Meanwhile, new commanders were posted to the 94th and 95th Bomb Groups. Colonel John "Dinty" Moore, CO of the 94th, and Colonel Alfred A. Kessler, CO of the 95th, were moved out and Colonel Fred Castle and Colonel John Gerhart, respectively, took over. Gerhart had been one of the 8th's original staff officers at its activation in January 1942. Castle had been one of the original officers Eaker had brought to England in February 1942. Both Castle and Gerhart had spent a year helping shape the 8th Air Force but both men, and Castle in particular, had yearned for combat. Their experience would be needed now as they set about lifting crews who resented the loss of their established commanders.

If anyone needed confirmation of the need to attack the Luftwaffe where it would hurt most, the Kiel debacle had proved it beyond doubt. Decisions taken at the Casablanca Conference led to the publication of Operation Pointblank, an intermediate priority objective aimed at the German fighter strength. The primary objectives listed were the German submarine yards and bases, the remainder of the German aircraft industry, ball-bearings and oil. Secondary objectives were synthetic rubber and tires and military motor transport vehicles. The objective concluded: "It is emphasized that the reduction of the German fighter force is of primary importance: any delay in its prosecution will make the task progressively more difficult." As a result Eaker decided to send his bombers on the first really deep penetration of Germany, to the synthetic rubber plant at Huls, near Recklinghausen on the edge of the Ruhr. The Huls complex was essential to the German war effort since their rubber supply in the Far East had been cut off by the Allied blockade. Huls accounted for approximately twenty-nine percent of Germany's synthetic rubber and eighteen percent of its total rubber supply. Most of the route would be flown without escort so three diversionary raids were planned to pull off most of the fighters from the main attacking force, which would still have its work cut out coping with the numerous flak guns which made Huls the most heavily defended target in the Reich at this time.

Throughout East Anglia on the morning of 22nd June, crews were awakened and ushered into briefing rooms to hear about the part they would play in the Huls mission. The Huls force assembled over England and flew a dogleg course over the North Sea to a point off the West Frisian Islands, where it turned southwest for the target. Unfortunately, the diversionary force aimed at the Ford and General Motors plant at Antwerp failed to materialize at this point. The 100th Bomb Group was delayed by ground mists and the 381st and 384th Bomb Groups, which were flying their maiden missions, were behind schedule and failed to make contact with the Spitfires and Thunderbolts which were to escort them to Antwerp. This lapse placed the small diversionary force at the mercy of the Luftwaffe, which had refuelled after an earlier raid by RAF medium bombers, and head-on attacks succeeded in shooting down four B-17s while three badly damaged survivors flew their own formation, hugging the waves all the way back to England. Two B-17s from the 384th Bomb Group were so badly damaged they were named later *Patches* and *Salvage Queen!*

The failure of the diversionary force had grave implications for the Huls force, as "Pappy" Colby, leading the high squadron of six ships in the *Thundermug*, describes.

"What we didn't know was that they had actually alerted the fighters to our force; so we got the works. They hit us at the Dutch coast and it got progressively worse. Colonel Castle rode behind me on the camp stool and took notes all through the thick of it, cool as a cucumber. When we were just short of the IP, Buck Steele, who was leading the 94th, was apparently hit and dropped away leaving the group leaderless as the deputy leader had been hit earlier. This really put me in a bind since it didn't look as though there was time for anybody else to take over the lead squadron and the group lead. We had been briefed to drop our bombs on the leader so I made a fast decision to do our own aiming and dropping and told Bob Gamble, our bombardier, to do his best. The ground was half covered with low clouds, but just about this time something big exploded on the ground, sending up a tremendous column of black smoke. Gamble hollered, "I can see it. I can see it!," and so I turned on the auto pilot so he could guide us in. We made a beautiful fifty-five second run and dropped our pattern square on the buildings alongside of the burning tank which had exploded. We were eight ships in all, as some of the others had joined us.

"Flak, which had not bothered us up to now, suddenly became very heavy, indicating that we had caught them by surprise somehow. After dropping we made the standard left turn but, when I looked for the lead squadron, there was nothing but two or three scattered airplanes in sight, so we speeded up and joined a group ahead of us for mutual protection. The remains of the lead and low squadrons strung along with us and we caught up with the 95th Bomb Group. At Rotterdam the Spitfires met us and chased off the German fighters, but it was a rough mission and we were beginning to wonder about the invincibility of the Flying Fortress. We lost two of our aircraft in the 333rd and the group lost quite a few more."

By the time the trailing groups had completed their bombing and made their 180 degree turns to the left, the smoke was as high as 17,000 feet. The bombing was highly successful and the Huls plant was put out of action for a month. Full production was not resumed for another five months after that. However, all this had not been achieved without cost. Sixteen B-17s, including a YB-40 that flew with the 303rd Bomb Group, were lost and another 170 bombers received varying degrees of damage. Fighters and flak had claimed most of the victims although the loss of the YB-40 was something of a mystery, as Howard E. Hernan, top turret gunner in *The Old Squaw* in the 303rd formation, relates.

"We were flying number five position in the low squadron. Two YB-40s flew on the lead ship's wings and another YB-40 flew in the number six slot. Just before the IP the YB-40 in front of us in the number two position suddenly went down. I couldn't understand how come he went down when there was no flak. We had not then been attacked by fighters so it wasn't a fighter. I would think he had an engine malfunction and just couldn't keep up. The last I saw of him was after he dropped below us and made a big sweeping left turn to the path that we were to take when we came off the target. He probably thought we could catch up with him after we had completed our bomb run."

The first weeks of YB-40 operations indicated that the idea of multi-gunned B-17s flying in bomber formations would not work. The additional machine-guns on each YB-40 did not add materially to the combined firepower a group formation could provide. Only stragglers were regularly attacked by the Luftwaffe and the YB-40s were unable to protect these from concentrated attacks. Howard Hernan had an opportunity to look over one of the three multi-gunned B-17s assigned to the 303rd shortly before the Huls raid and concluded later, "With all the armor plating around the tail and waist gun positions, the Martin turret over the radio room, and all the extra ammunition, the YB-40 just had to be tail heavy. Of course, it weighed the same when it got off the target as it did when it got there. When we dropped our bombs we were somewhat lighter and it made a lot of difference. I believe it was a mistake to spread the YB-40s around the groups. My opinion was that they should have been left to fly as a squadron and then if they wanted to attract any fighters, to bear out a little and let them come in. The YB-40s had a tremendous amount of fire-power but if they lost an engine they were in trouble." Losses were not made good although the YB-40s continued flying missions until the end of July 1943.

A period of cloudy weather hampered missions and then on 26th June the Fortresses were dispatched to targets in France. Again the weather intervened although some aircraft found their targets. Claude Campbell, who flew in the 303rd Bomb Group formation which went to the Focke-Wulf airfield at Beaumont, describes it as,

"An excellent mission. We were escorted by Spitfires and we met no opposition. Since we flew at 28,000 to 30,000 feet the enemy couldn't have seen us unless we were giving off vapor trails. Bombing was perfect. We hit the ammunition dumps and blew the whole works to hell. The aiming point was a cemetery just south of the ammunition dump. The best crack I heard about the raid was, 'the dead will rise tonight.'" Only four B-17s were lost and all were from the ill-fated 384th Bomb Group. The main effort this day was directed by the 4th Wing on St Nazaire, as "Pappy" Colby recalls. "There was much speculation at the briefing because only ships with the new "Tokyo" extra range tanks were going. Our target was some kind of new lock at the sub pens. I led the 333rd Squadron with the job of filling in aborts from the 96th Bomb Group. We had a hell of a time trying to pick out the 96th from all the others in the sky because they didn't answer our flare recognition signals for a long time. We finally located them, late as usual, and then had trouble following them as their formation was lousy and they were only doing 145 mph.

"We filled in several aborts and, as we approached the IP, I tacked on to the lead element of their high squadron. They made a beautiful bomb run and each ship unloaded two 2,000lb bombs on the target. Very heavy flak

The Old Squaw, *303rd Bomb Group, Molesworth. The crew are* Standing, left to right *Campbell, Miller, Ririe, and Boutelle.* Kneeling: *Hernan, Wilson, Quick, Kraft, and Backert.* (Howard Hernan)

came up and a six-inch piece of shell came up through the floor of the radio room and smacked Patrick on the fanny. Luckily, its force was pretty well spent and all he got was a big black and blue spot. It was a long way home and we were down to 300 gallons in the main gas tanks when we turned on our new "Tokyo" tanks. They brought us home with plenty to spare.

"That night after supper I was told to report to Colonel Castle at his quarters. I quickly cleaned up and wondered what had been said to put me in the doghouse again. To my great surprise, he asked me if I could take over command of the 410th Squadron and build it up to where it could become combat operational again. The squadron had lost nine out of its ten original crews and the replacements hadn't had a chance to really learn what combat operations were all about. It had lost both its COs and Ops Officer and had been withdrawn from operations as a squadron, with the new crews being used to fill in aborts. This put their people behind the rest of the group in acquiring the necessary twenty-five raids to complete their tours and made them very unhappy. I told him I would do my very best and the job certainly boosted my morale.

"Next morning I took command of the 410th and Wally Barker, the Assistant Operations Officer, was sure glad to see me. He was a big help in briefing me on their problems. That afternoon, who should show up unexpectedly but the Bob Hope Special Services Show with Frances Langford, Jerry Colonna, and Jack Pepper, their guitarist. They put on a terrific show that did us all a world of good. Unfortunately, the group had gone on a raid to Le Mans and didn't get to see the show. But when the tired crews from the raid came into the mess hall for debriefing, who was standing just inside the door shaking hands with each one, but Bob Hope and his entire cast. Some of the lads were so overwhelmed they had tears in their eyes and, personally, I'll never forget it."

On 4th July neither the weather nor the Independence Day celebrations stopped the Fortresses making a triple attack on targets in France. Altogether, 192 Fortresses of the 1st Wing were assigned the Gnôme and Rhône Aero engine factory at Le Mans and an aircraft factory at Nantes while eighty-three of the longer range B-17s of the 4th Wing went to the U-boat pens at La Pallice. Shortly after noon the two 1st Wing formations, flying parallel courses, crossed the French coast just east of the Cherbourg Peninsula, while the B-17s of the 4th Wing headed for La Pallice on the Bay of Biscay coast. At 1230 hours the 1st Wing formations crossed Laval, eighty miles inland, then split into two formations, one heading for Nantes and the other, Le Mans. The Nantes force was attacked by hordes of German fighters all the way from the IP, which did not break off until thirty-five miles after the target. The 92nd Bomb Group formation of sixteen B-17s and three YB-40s came under heavy attack and Lieutenant John J. Campbell's B-17 was believed to have hit the sea and burned. Six parachutes were seen to open and another partially opened.

This raid marked the return of the 326th Bomb Squadron to bomber operations and it came in for repeated attacks by the enemy fighters. After bombing the target, *Ruthie*, named by Lieutenant Robert L. Campbell in honor of his wife, was hit by cannon fire that punctured two fuel lines and destroyed the hydraulic system and flaps. Another 20mm shell penetrated the belly between the waist gun positions and exploded, wrecking the radio equipment. One shell also hit the ball turret and seriously wounded Richard O. Gettys in the face, chest, and groin. Despite his wounds he continued firing from the still serviceable turret until he passed out. Gettys was awarded the DSC for his action. John C. Ford, the tail-gunner, was also slightly injured in the leg. Campbell nursed *Ruthie* home to Alconbury and landed with a flat tire. He succeeded in keeping the badly damaged B-17 on the runway for as long as possible, then whirled the aircraft around in front of the control tower and came to a halt. Campbell's proud lady was only fit for scrap after that, but he promptly named his replacement B-17, *Ruthie II*.

The Le Mans force encountered intense fighter opposition fifteen minutes from the target, but the B-17s were able to pick up their fighter escort at Argentan and reach safety. For once the multiplicity of bomber attacks seemed to break up the Luftwaffe concentrations and they were able to account for only three percent of the attacking force.

The weather continued cloudy and VIII Bomber Command flew several more missions to France in the hope of spotting its targets. On 14th July, Bastille Day, groups appropriately attacked targets in the vicinity of Paris. The Focke-Wulf repair sub-depot at Villacoublay was hit and Le Bourget airport was also bombed. Le Bourget had seen the successful conclusion of Charles Lindburgh's record breaking trans-Atlantic flight in 1927 and the raid therefore had a special significance for the new breed of American aviators.

Despite the rising losses, new groups swelled Eaker's forces and on 17th July a record 332 bombers were dispatched to Hannover. This figure was made possible by the introduction of both the 385th and 388th Bomb Groups, which were flying their first missions as part of the 4th Wing. Their debuts were somewhat subdued because the mission was recalled due to bad weather after the bombers had crossed the Dutch coast and on the return leg the B-17s were hit by enemy fighters. Meanwhile, the 385th had moved to Great Ashfield, Suffolk, during the first week of July and the 388th landed at nearby Knettishall. The seventh and final group to join the 4th Wing, the 390th, flew south from Prestwick to its permanent base at Parham, near Framlingham in pastoral Suffolk. The 8th now had the means to launch an all-out air offensive. All the commanders needed was a week of fine weather for "Blitz Week" to succeed.

B-17F 42-3190 of the 94th Bomb Group, crash-landed in occupied France with a full bomb load after being shot down by Hauptman Egon Mayer on the LeBourget mission of 14th July 1943. The pilot, Captain Kee Harrison, elected to crash-land because his flight engineer's parachute had been damaged and he could not bale out. Captain Harrison, his co-pilot, and the engineer evaded capture and returned to England via Spain. (Holmes)

Chapter 6
Blitz Week and Beyond

On 23rd July 1943, General Eaker was informed that clear skies could be expected over Europe for a few days; long enough to mount the long-awaited succession of attacks which would become known as "Blitz Week." The momentous week began in the early hours of 24th July when it was revealed that the 1st Wing would bomb the nitrate plant of Nordisk Lettmetal at Heroya. Meanwhile, a smaller force of B-17s in the 4th Wing equipped with "Tokyo" tanks would bomb the harbor installations at Bergen and Trondheim. Although the latter mission would involve a 2,000-mile round trip, the longest American mission over Europe thus far, the two missions were considered to be milk runs because the targets were lightly defended.

Crews were warned of the need to conserve fuel and for this reason there was no assembly; leaders simply took off and went on course at once, flying on low power settings to enable the formations to take up position over the North Sea. Well off the coast of northern Denmark the 1st Wing flew northeast up the Skagerrak and climbed to a bombing altitude of 16,000 feet. The 4th Wing continued up the west coast of Norway to Bergen and Trondheim, not far south of the Arctic Circle. Cloud obscured the target at Heroya, but Colonel William M. Reid, CO of the 92nd Bomb Group, who flew as air commander, was awarded the Silver Star for setting up a new bomb run after Heroya had been cancelled out by the weather. The target was devastated and Colonel Budd J. Peaslee, CO of the 384th Bomb Group, wrote later: "The mission to Heroya is considered by many authorities

to be one of the outstanding missions of the war." Only one B-17, *Georgia Rebel* from the 351st Bomb Group, was lost on the raid. It was hit by flak but the crew put down safely in neutral Sweden.

Altogether, 167 bombers bombed Heroya while forty-one B-17s of the 4th Wing bombed Trondhelm from 20,000 feet. Testimony to their accuracy was provided later by an RAF photo-reconnaissance Spitfire which brought back photos of a sunken U-boat, a damaged destroyer, and gutted workshops in the harbor area. The other 4th Wing groups crossed Bergen harbor at 16,000 feet but the target was completely covered with clouds and eighty-four aircraft had to return to England and land with full bomb loads something crews were never happy about. About fifteen Junkers 88s put in an appearance on the return leg but caused no damage to the B-17 formations. Crews were upset about the failure to bomb Bergen, none more so than "Pappy" Colby, who was flying with the 94th.

The following day the Fortresses were again out in force, this time to targets in north-western Germany. One combat wing from the 1st Bomb Wing was dispatched to Kiel; the remaining groups were sent to Hamburg to bomb the Blohm and Voss shipyards. Nearing the city, crews could see a towering 15,000 foot column of smoke; a result of fires still burning after a raid by RAF Bomber Command the previous night. Crews in the first elements managed to bomb before thick cloud added to the smoke and the shipyards were well hit. However, Hamburg's notorious flak and fighter

FIESELER AIRCRAFT PLANTS
at KASSEL GERMANY
30.7.43

(SAO-94-5-2)(30-7-43)(349-6-24000) KASSEL

A photograph with original annotation, taken to record the bombing accuracy of the 30th July 1943 mission to Kassel. (USAF)

defenses brought down nineteen Fortresses, including seven from the unlucky 384th. Meanwhile, 4th Bomb Wing Fortresses headed for Warnemünde on the north German coast. Clouds obscured the target and they were forced to head for the submarine construction yards at Kiel. The 94th Bomb Group was attacked near the target by about thirty fighters and Lieutenant John P. Keelan's B-17, *Happy Daze*, was seen to ditch about sixty miles off the coast. Although badly damaged, the B-17 floated for fifteen minutes. The crew tied their life rafts together and spent the night shivering as they watched Kiel burn and the RAF making their way over Germany. About noon the following day an aircraft sighted them and dropped two more life rafts. Later a Lockheed Hudson dropped them a powered lifeboat. They sailed the boat some 120 miles, at which point they were picked up by a Danish fishing boat. The Danes agreed to take the crew to England and instead of returning to Denmark, decided to join the Free Danish Navy operating from the British Isles.

There was no let-up in the American offensive and "Blitz Week" gained in momentum. On 26th July, more than 300 heavies were dispatched to Hannover and Hamburg. Thick cloud over East Anglia hampered assembly and, despite the recent innovation of "splasher" beacons for forming up, many groups became scattered and had to be recalled. Only two combat wings won through to their targets. Other elements bombed targets of opportunity along the German coast.

Among the ninety-two Fortresses which successfully attacked Hannover were seventeen B-17s and two YB-40s from the 92nd Bomb Group. Shortly before it reached the coast the formation came under frontal attack by FW 190s. *Yo' Brother*, 1st/Lieutenant Alan E. Hermance's B-17, was seen to hit the water about ten minutes from the island of Nordenay with one engine on fire and the tail badly damaged. All ten crew perished. Captain Blair G. Belongia's B-17 came under attack from seven FW 190s and two of his engines were put out of action. Belongia nursed the ailing bomber back across the sea and ditched about two miles off Sheringham where the crew was rescued by a fishing boat after an hour in the water.

Other 92nd Bomb Group aircraft also suffered in the attack, including *Ruthie II*, piloted by 1st/Lieutenant Robert L. Campbell, who had brought the first *Ruthie* home from Nantes on 4th July, and his co-pilot, Flight Officer John C. Morgan, a six foot, red-haired Texan who had flown with the RCAF for seven months before transferring to the 8th Air Force. The navigator, Keith J. Koske, wrote later:

"We were on our way into the enemy coast when we were attacked by a group of FW 190s. On their first pass I felt sure they had got us for there was a terrific explosion overhead and the ship rocked badly. A second later the top turret gunner, Staff Sergeant Tyre C. Weaver, fell through the hatch and slumped to the floor at the rear of my nose

Captain Robert P. Bender from the 95th Bomb Group. Bender named his B-17 Spook, *and crash-landed it at Exeter on 17th May 1943.* Spook II *and* Spook III *were both so badly damaged by gunfire that they were written off. Bender ditched* Spook IV *in the sea and was rescued twenty-two hours later by Air/Sea Rescue. Subsequently, on a visit to a cinema, he went berserk when a newsreel showed FW190s attacking B-17s. On a test flight in* Spook V, *Bender froze at the controls and the co-pilot had to take control. Bender never flew again and returned to America, where he died of a heart attack at the age of just twenty-five.* (USAF)

compartment. When I got to him I saw his left arm had been blown off at the shoulder and he was a mass of blood. I first tried to inject some morphine but the needle was bent and I could not get it in.

"As things turned out it was best I didn't give him any morphine. My first thought was to try and stop his loss of blood. I tried to apply a tourniquet but it was impossible as the arm was off too close to the shoulder. I knew he had to have the right kind of medical treatment as soon as possible and we had almost four hours flying time ahead of us, so there was no alternative. I opened the escape hatch, adjusted his 'chute for him and placed the ripcord ring firmly in his right hand. He must have become excited and pulled the cord, opening the pilot 'chute in the up draft. I managed to gather it together and tuck it under his right arm, got him into a crouched position with legs through the hatch, made certain again that his good arm was holding the 'chute folds together, and toppled him out into space. I learned somewhat later from our ball turret gunner, James

L. Ford, that the 'chute opened OK. We were at 24,500 feet and twenty-five miles due west of Hannover and our only hope was that he was found and given medical attention immediately.

"The bombardier, Asa J. Irwin, had been busy with the nose guns and when I got back up in the nose he was getting ready to toggle his bombs. The target area was one mass of smoke and we added our contribution. After we dropped our bombs we were kept busy with the nose guns. However, all our attacks were from the tail and we could do very little good. I had tried to use my intercom several times, but could get no answer. The last I remember hearing over it was shortly after the first attack when someone was complaining about not getting oxygen. Except for what I thought to be some violent evasive action we seemed to be flying OK.

"It was two hours later when we were fifteen minutes out from the enemy coast that I decided to go up and check with the pilot and have a look around. I found Lieutenant Campbell slumped down in his seat, a mass of blood, the back of his head blown off. This had happened two hours before, on the first attack. A shell had entered from the right side, crossed in front of John Morgan and had hit Campbell in the head. Morgan was flying the plane with one hand, holding the half-dead pilot off with the other hand, 'and he had been doing it for over two hours!' It was no mean feat, Campbell was a six footer and weighed 185lb. Morgan told me we had to get Campbell out of his seat as the plane couldn't be landed from the co-pilot's seat since the glass on that side was shattered so badly you could barely see out. We struggled for thirty minutes getting the fatally injured pilot out of his seat and down into the rear of the navigator's compartment, where the bombardier held him from slipping out of the open hatch. Morgan was operating the controls with one hand and helping me handle the pilot with the other."

The radio operator, waist and tail-gunners were unable to lend assistance because they were unconscious through lack of oxygen, the lines having been shattered several hours earlier. Morgan's action was nothing short of miraculous. Not only had he flown the aircraft to the target and out again with no radio, no intercom, and no hydraulic fluid, he had maintained formation the whole time; an incredible feat for a pilot flying one-handed. He brought *Ruthie II* in to land at RAF Foulsham, a few miles inland of the Norfolk coast, and put down safely. Campbell died an hour and a half later. The other crew members survived, including Weaver, who was put in a POW camp after hospitalization. On 18th December 1943, listeners to the BBC's evening news heard that Flight Officer (later 1st/Lieutenant) John C. Morgan (now with the 482nd Bomb Group) had received the Medal of Honor from Lieutenant General Ira C. Eaker in a special ceremony at 8th Air Force Headquarters.

On 27th July, the 8th was stood down for a badly needed rest while the forecasters waited for the weather to improve over Europe. "Blitz Week" was resumed again on the morning of 28th July when the 8th made an ambitious attack on aircraft factories at Kassel while the 4th Wing had the dubious honor of flying the deepest penetration so far, to the fighter assembly plant at Oschersleben. The Oschersleben force was led by the 94th Bomb Group with the Group CO, Colonel Fred Castle, flying in the lead ship, *Sour Puss*. His pilot, "Pappy" Colby, recollects that,

"On my map Oschersleben was a little over ninety miles southwest of Berlin, but even with the new "Tokyo" tanks it looked a hell of a long way. The plan called for the usual diversion thrust off the Frisian Islands with a 180-degree turn back towards England and then the real attack, crossing the coast near Emden and onto the target. Things began to go wrong early in the plan. The weather was supposed to be clear but instead we were flying between layers of stratus clouds as we started the diversion. Then the navigation went wrong because, instead of turning back some sixty or seventy miles west of the Frisian Islands, we went clear down on top of them and stirred up a hornets nest of fighters based on Heligoland. They worked us over heavily, darting in and out of the clouds, and one group lost three ships from a fighter who hid in the clouds above the formation, then swooped down; and dropped an aerial bomb which exploded in their midst. The cloud layers were so thick we had a very hard time making the turn back towards England, with the result that everybody got lost and instead of leading a wing into the target, we only had twenty-eight ships.

"Colonel Castle was much upset as orders were not to go in with less than thirty aircraft. He was unhappy about my turning in towards the target, but I conned him into going, saying I could see three more of our planes in the distance (I was not about to go back after all the hell we had just been through). We just started in over the coast without asking anybody and the other twenty-seven planes followed me. The fighters followed us for about 100 miles, but as we were now in tight formation they didn't attack." The 4th Wing had started out with 120 Fortresses, but all except the 94th and some in the 96th turned back.

"So we sailed down towards the IP," 'Pappy' continued, "which was covered with about 7/10ths cloud. The navigator picked the wrong town. I don't blame him in the least, as the stupid staff people had picked the central town in a row of three all on the same railroad, and all about the same size. So we turned on the bomb run and suddenly found that the target, instead of being dead ahead, was off to our left some thirty miles away. Nobody had any suggestions so I told the bombardier to keep the target in sight while we made a 180-degree left turn to bomb it on a westerly heading. We made a good bomb run and the

Windy City Challenger, 42-3049 of the 305th Bomb Group, going down out of control on 14th July 1943. Windy City exploded seconds after this photo was taken, thowing four men clear, but seven others were killed.

Captain Claude W. Campbell, from McComb, Mississippi, the pilot of The Old Squaw. *(Hernan)*

photos showed later we did a good job hitting it in spite of the problems. Actually, the cloud cover was between 7/10ths and 5/10ths, but from 26,000 feet, it's extremely hard to pick out landmarks. Despite the press story we had no fighters over the target but heavy flak crossing the coast on the way home. We did evasive action and got home with no losses out of the 94th."

Altogether, though, fifteen Fortresses belonging to the 4th Wing were shot down on the Oschersleben raid, including one crippled B-17 which crashed into two others, bringing all three down. The 182 heavies which went to Kassel were limited in their bombing because of cloud which obscured the target. On the way home they were attacked by fighters which fired rocket projectiles, eight inches in diameter, from launchers under the fighter's wings, A long-range Thunderbolt fired a burst at an FW 190 and his bullets set off a rocket under the right wing. The rocket roared off in a cloud of white smoke as the fighter disintegrated under the onslaught of the P-47's guns. Without the P-47 escort, losses in the bomber formations would have been heavy.

On 29th July the 8th set out for the fourth time in five days; the 1st Wing visiting the shipyards at Kiel and the 4th Wing going to the Heinkel assembly plant at Warnemünde, which had escaped the attention of the B-17s four days before. The strain was beginning to tell and the 385th Bomb Group lost three B-17s in a mid-air colli-

sion during assembly at only 2,000 feet, two miles from the English coast. Only six parachutes were seen to leave the three aircraft. However, the bombing of the Heinkel plant was described as "excellent" and FW 190 production was severely curtailed. Next day, VIII Bomber Command brought down the curtain on "Blitz Week" when 186 Fortresses from the 1st and 4th Wings went to the aircraft factories at Kassel; a round trip of some 600 miles. The weather was fine and P-47 Thunderbolts equipped with long-range fuel tanks escorted the heavies almost to the target and back again. Without them losses would have been on an alarming scale because the Fortress formations were hit by a ferocious onslaught of enemy fighters as Howard E. Hernan, flying as top turret gunner aboard *The Old Squaw* in the 303rd formation, remembers.

"We were hit by more enemy fighters than ever before. The estimate was well in excess of 300. At one time I counted 157 flying off to our right. A fighter came down through our formation and then a whole *Gruppe* of them got ahead of us and started making pass after pass. Most of them we fought off and turned away at 7-800 yards. They would flip over on their backs and down they would go to get more latitude and then they would try again. Of course, the Luftwaffe painted their aircraft various colors and some were quite pretty. A snow-white Bf 109 dived on us. He had a beautiful Iron Cross painted on the wings and fuselage. He was coming so fast, with a strong tail wind behind him, that he came right through the formation and began making a turn to the right. So help me God he came between us and our wing man on the left, upside down, went between our wings and never touched either of us!"

The B-17 crews flew four of the six-hour round trip on oxygen and over enemy territory Hernan's supply ran out. Arthur W. Miller, the co-pilot, had to feed him oxygen from walk-around bottles while he tried to shoot at incoming fighters. Hernan and Quick were each credited with one fighter apiece.

On the way to the target the Fortresses had been aided by a strong wind which had given them 160 mph indicated airspeed. Now, on the homeward trip, they had to buck this wind. Howard Hernan picked out a landmark and looked down on it. Ten minutes later it was still there! Just as *The Old Squaw* finally reached the coast of England, number four engine quit, out of fuel. Campbell was forced to put the B-17 into a glide. He managed to reach an airfield just before the number two began to splutter. Other aircraft were not so fortunate, some ditching in the Channel and others having to make crash-landings all along the coast as one by one they ran low on fuel. Altogether, twelve Fortresses were lost, including some that were so badly damaged that they never flew again. *Patches*, from the 384th Bomb Group, crash-landed at the fighter airfield at Boxted and her parts were used later for other B-17s in the group.

On 31st July, groups were told to stand down after a week of exhausting raids. Crews had flown themselves almost to a standstill and were glad of the rest, however brief, as "Pappy" Colby recalls.

"Some of the boys were developing the equivalent of shell shock, in spite of all our doctor's efforts. The nervous strain of continuous raids had been more than some of them could take. It raised the very rough command problem as to how long these lads would still be fit to fly a combat mission, especially the pilots whose nine-man crews were trusting them with their lives. I finally had to go to Colonel Castle about one pilot who was rapidly coming unstuck, as the British say, and they sent him to the rest home in southern England. He didn't like it and I felt real sorry for him, but Colonel Castle agreed that it was no longer safe to send him on combat raids."

In a week of sustained combat operations, VIII Bomber Command had lost about 100 aircraft and ninety combat crews. This reduced its combat strength to under 200 heavies ready for combat. However, the losses in men and machines were soon made good and on 12th August the 390th Bomb Group from Framlingham helped swell the ranks of 330 bombers heading for targets in the Ruhr. Once again the weather was to dog the mission and cause many groups to seek targets of opportunity. Groups became strung out and the Luftwaffe seized the opportunity to strike at the widely dispersed formations. They hit groups time and again and inflicted heavy losses, particularly among the 92nd and 384th which lost four and five aircraft respectively. The anti-aircraft guns also found their mark, as Howard Hernan relates. "The flak was terrific and at no time had we encoun-

tered more attacks from fighters. I sweated out the whole trip. We lost number two supercharger before reaching enemy territory, then number one engine began throwing gas and oil badly from the oil cooler vent. Number four engine also began running roughly. Campbell had to feather the number one engine to prevent it from burning out. We lost oxygen on the right-hand side and had flak holes in several places.

"We were leading the second flight of the 303rd, which was leading the 1st Wing this day. Our hut-mates' aircraft, *Old Ironsides,* piloted by Lieutenant Arthur H. Pentz, was off our left wing. When we were this close together I could see my friend John A. Dougherty in his top turret and we would help one another. I was basically patrolling forward before we got to the target. There was quite a bit of flak around, as there always seemed to be over the Ruhr Valley. I turned my turret around and looked over at Pentz's ship. It looked as though it was on fire from wingtip to wingtip. I just could hardly believe what I was seeing. I was actually yelling at them to bale out but they were still flying along as if nothing had happened. Pentz's ship had all colors of smoke coming out of it. Although there were a few fighters on us at the time, it was flak that had got them. They flew along momentarily beside us and then dropped out of formation. I called one of the waist gunners who always had a pair of field glasses and he followed it as far as he could. The last time he saw it, it was still on fire.

"About a minute later another B-17, flying about 200 yards away and level with us at 10 o'clock, started to make snap rolls. It would snap over, level out momentarily and then make another flip. They were all to the right. I counted each one and he made twenty-one! Each time he

Picklepuss, *42-30063 of the 100th Bomb Group, one of the B-17s lost on the 17th August 1943 mission to Regensburg. Captain Robert Knox (front row, second from the left) was flying* Picklepuss *when the aircraft was shot down near Aachen. Messerchmitt 110s shot off the B-17's right wing, but four men escaped before the aircraft crashed.* (Thorpe Abbotts Memorial Museum)

The end result, a pall of smoke rises from the target at Regensburg.

flipped over every gun position fired and the tracers would come flying out. The plane looked like a porcupine. Of course, this was because of centrifugal force: as the gunners tried to hold on they would press down on their triggers. I just could not believe that this plane was still holding together. After its twenty-first flip it leveled out and started to go down in a great big sweeping turn to the left. I often try to figure out what was wrong with this 'plane as there hadn't been any fighters homing in on him and he was a little too high for flak. I can only think the pilot was trying to set up the automatic pilot for the bombardier and somehow or other it had malfunctioned.

"It was certainly an empty feeling to look over the empty bunks that night. I vowed there and then that whatever crew replaced Pentz's I was not going to make friends. I would be sociable and as pleasant as I could, but it was too hard when you lost them. Even to this day I cannot remem-

ber who moved into the hut or even what they looked like." Hernan learned later that Pentz had crash-landed his B-17, one of twenty-five lost this day, and that nine of the crew, including Dougherty, were taken prisoner.

On 15th August, VIII Bomber Command participated in the *Starkey* deception plan which was created to make the enemy believe that an invasion of the French coast was imminent. In theory it would relieve some of the pressure on Russia and halt troop movements to Italy. The Fortress formations roamed across France, Belgium, and Holland, dropping their deadly loads of bombs on long-suffering German airfields. Friendly fighter support was generally described as "excellent" and the Luftwaffe stayed largely on the ground. However, there was always the "expected unexpected" and two ships in the 390th Bomb Group collided, tearing the tail off one, and both spun in.

Strikes against enemy airfields in France and the Low Countries continued on 16th August, then early that evening, when the sound of the Wright Cyclone engines had at last died away, operations staff stood by their teleprinters, awaiting orders for the morrow; the anniversary mission of the 8th Air Force. Throughout the east of England staff waited in anticipation, none more so than at Grafton Underwood where Budd Peaslee's 384th had a special interest. Speculation had been rife on the base ever since late in July when the group had received an order from higher headquarters. Colonel Peaslee explains.

"It said: 'Select one of the best of your lead crews, stand them down. Send them to headquarters, VIII Bomber Command for special briefing, thereafter they will not leave the base nor communicate with other crews. They will fly practice flights daily and practice high altitude bombing on the Irish Sea bombing range whenever possible'"

The Field Order for 17th August caused more than a few raised eyebrows; the planners had conceived a most ambitious and daring plan to attack simultaneously the aircraft plant at Regensburg and the ball-bearing plant at Schweinfurt, vital to German aircraft production. Their selection came at a time when the enemy's operational fighter strength in the west was showing a significant increase. Regensburg was the second largest aircraft plant of its kind in Europe (the largest being at Wiener Neustadt near Vienna), and it was estimated that the total destruction of the plant would entail a nine month delay in production. Immediate results would be felt in operational strength, it was hoped, between one-and-a-half to two months. Crews were told that production at Regensburg was estimated at 200 Bf 109s a month, or approximately twenty-five to thirty percent of Germany's single-engine aircraft production. Few doubted the importance of mounting a mission against the plants, but hitherto the campaign against the German aircraft industry had been waged within reasonable striking distance from the British mainland. The original plan to bomb all three plants on one day, 7th August, had been disrupted by bad weather so the plan had been modified to bomb each target when the opportunity arose. On 13th August Wiener Neustadt was bombed by B-24s of VIII Bomber Command and on 14th August by B-24s of the 9th Air Force, both forces flying from North Africa. Not enough 1st Wing Fortresses were equipped with "Tokyo" tanks to complete the 725 mile trip, but now preparations were almost complete for the daring double strike. Such was its importance that the "top brass" would lead the heavies deep into southern Germany. Even the loss of an eye, in a bombing raid while he watched the Battle of Britain as an American observer, was insufficient to deter Brigadier General Robert Williams, commander of the 1st Wing, and he would lead his force to Schweinfurt while Colonel Curtis E. LeMay led the 4th Wing to Regensburg.

To minimize attacks from enemy fighters it was decided that LeMay's B-17s would fly a "shuttle mission" to North Africa after the target, the 1st Wing, meanwhile, would fly a parallel course to Schweinfurt to further confuse the enemy defenses and return to England after the raid. Despite this, crews remained skeptical, as Howard Hernan explains.

"We had been briefed for this one three weeks before, so naturally the Germans knew we were coming. Since the previous mission had been scrubbed we were called in every day and told not to mention the target area. Intelligence seemed to think there were a lot of spies in Great Britain." Crews realized the risks better than anyone and were made

aware how important the targets were. Claude Campbell, Hernan's pilot on the mission, wrote: "Our target was the ball-bearing factory, or rather I should say, the elimination of Schweinfurt and all its inhabitants. 'It is predicted that this is the straw that will break Hitler's back.' We were told that within three months from this date Hitler will feel the blow so seriously that he will throw in the towel."

Despite their planning, Eaker and his subordinates were under no illusions. They knew the B-17 crews would have a running fight on their hands but hoped that the fighter escorts would keep losses down. The line of bombers stretched for fifteen miles with the 96th Bomb Group in the lead and Colonel LeMay at the helm. Behind came the 388th and 390th Bomb Groups, followed by the 94th and 385th making up the Second Combat Wing. Bringing up the rear of the formation were the 95th and 100th Bomb Groups, each carrying incendiaries to stoke up the fires created by the leading groups.

At this point things began to go wrong. Four P-47 groups were scheduled to escort the Regensburg force, but only one group rendezvoused with the bombers as scheduled. The overburdened Thunderbolts could not possibly hope to protect all seven groups in such a long, straggling formation and the Fortresses in the rear of the formation were left without protection at all. The bomber crews' worst fears were about to be realized. The Luftwaffe began its attack as the formation entered enemy territory. Lieutenant Richard H. Perry, co-pilot aboard *Betty Boop the Pistol Packin' Mama*, flown by Lieutenant Jim Geary in the 390th Bomb Group, recalls,

High Life, flown by Lieutenant Donald Oakes of the 100th Bomb Group, was forced to land at Dubendorf, Switzerland, during the Regensburg raid. A 20mm shell exploded in the number three engine, necessitating a wheels up landing. This photograph was taken after the B-17 had been lifted up and put back on its wheels by the Swiss. (Hans Heiri Stapfer)

"Just after we reached the Dutch coast we were attacked by several FW 190s. A .30 caliber armor-piercing shell entered the waist gun area and went right through the steel helmet of Sergeant Leonard A. Baumgartner and struck him in the head. The bullet also shattered a rudder control cable that made our landing in North Africa very difficult later. I went to the back of the airplane to administer to him. Baumgartner took his last breath in my arms."

The 95th and 100th Bomb Groups bore the brunt of the ferocious attacks which were mostly from head-on. The unlucky Thorpe Abbotts group lost two B-17s and the 95th, one. In the hour and a half proceeding the bomb run, seventeen Fortresses were shot down. The 385th Bomb Group lost three bombers while others, so badly shot up, would barely make it over the treacherous snow-covered Alps. Aubrey "Bart" Bartholomew, a young Canadian-born ball turret gunner in *Raunchy Wolf*, was almost blown out of his turret at 19,000 feet after persistent attacks during the bomb run. Bart's turret door flew off as a result of an ill fitting hinge and only the toe of his left flying boot hooked under the range pedal of his guns saved him from being sucked out of the turret. Oxygen and intercom cables were severed and he lost contact with the rest of the crew. He somehow managed to pull himself back into his turret and attract the attention of a crewman who cranked him back into the B-17.

The 2nd Combat Wing was forced to swing around in a 360-degree turn and make another bomb run after the target had been obscured by smoke from the leading wing's bombs. The bombing was extremely accurate and might well have had something to do with the presence of Colonel LeMay, exponent of high-level bombing techniques, in the first wave. The 390th had placed fifty-eight percent of its bombs within 1,000 feet of the MPI and ninety-four percent within 2,000 feet. The last two groups over the target, the 95th and 100th, added their incendiary clusters to the conflagration, which was now marked by a rectangular pillar of smoke towering to 10,000 feet. Six main workshops were hit, five being severely damaged. A hangar was partially destroyed and storerooms and administrative buildings wrecked. Thirty-seven Bf 109s at dispersal were at least damaged, if not wrecked, and all production at the plant came to an abrupt halt. Although unknown at the time, by way of a bonus the bombing had destroyed the fuselage jigs for a secret jet fighter, the Me 262.

Betty Boop - The Pistol Packing Mama, *of the 390th Bomb Group, flown by Lieutenant Jim Geary.* (Gus Mencow)

The 96th Bomb Group crossing the Brenner Pass in the Alps after the Regensburg raid of 17th August 1943. The nearest aircraft, 42-30130, was lost on 7th January 1944. The aircraft below, 42-30372 Shack Rabbit III, *was lost in a mid-air collision over the North Sea.*

The surviving 128 B-17s, some flying on three engines and many trailing smoke, were attacked by a few fighters on the way to the Alps. LeMay circled his formation over a large lake to give the cripples a chance to rejoin the wing. Red lights were showing on all four fuel tanks in every ship and it was a ragged collection of survivors which landed at intervals up to fifty miles along the North African coast. The 100th had lost nine of the twenty-four bombers which failed to land in North Africa - the highest loss in the 4th Wing. Although they did not yet know it, the 4th Wing had encountered so many fighters en route because the 1st Wing had been delayed by thick inland mists for three-and-a-half hours after the 4th had taken off, and this had effectively prevented a two-pronged assault which might have split the opposing fighter force. The delay also gave the Luftwaffe time to refuel and re-arm after dealing with the Regensburg force and then tackle the Schweinfurt force.

The 91st Bomb Group from Bassingbourn led the 1st Wing to Schweinfurt with Lieutenant Colonel Clemens L. Wurzbach, the CO, and Colonel Cross of Wing Headquarters, flying lead in *Oklahoma Oakie*. Brigadier General Robert B. Williams, the Task Force commander, also flew in the 91st formation. The 381st Bomb Group from

Ridgewell flew low group. Following close on their heels was the 103rd Provisional Combat Wing, led by Colonel Maurice "Mo" Preston, CO of the 379th Bomb Group.

"I was positioned toward the front of the column and the 303rd from Molesworth flew the low box. The top box was a composite furnished by the 303rd and the 379th. The 379th provided the top element of six airplanes in this composite box. We began to encounter enemy fighters when we were about half way to the target and had them almost constantly with us from there until we left the target area on the way out. There was every indication that the Germans were throwing at us just about everything they had in their inventory.

"Probably as a result of introducing units that were not combat-seasoned, the tactics employed were most unusual. The fighters queued up as usual out to the right front and up high but then, instead of turn diving down for attack on the lower elements, they turned in more sharply and delivered diving attacks on the topmost elements. Woe be it to that 379th element in the composite box. That entire element of six aircraft was left in central Germany that day."

Wolf Pack, flown by Lieutenant Robert Wolf of the 100th Bomb Group, heading for North Africa after the Regensburg mission. 20mm cannon shells exploded in the tail area and also released a life raft stored above the port inner engine that caused further damage to the left tail plane. (Thorpe Abbotts Memorial Museum)

The 303rd Bomb Group flying in the low box also had its problems as Howard Hernan, in *The Old Squaw*, piloted by Claude Campbell, remembers.

"On the way over we had two abortives from our squadron, leaving it under strength. It looked bad. We had a P-47 escort part of the way in who were to pick us up on the way back. By this time they were using belly tanks and pilots would tell crews over the intercom when the fighters were due to leave. Quite a long while before we reached the target there were a lot of Me 110s. The P-47s were supposed to leave us about ten minutes previously. Out on the right of us, flying at about 2,000 yards, were six Me 110s, flying in a stacked up formation with the lead ship low. Occasionally, there would be a German fighter calling out our altitude to the ground for the flak gunners but I'm sure these were not doing that. All the time I was watching these Me 110s I suddenly saw the sun glint off four wings of planes above us. Right at that moment I couldn't identify them so I kept my eye on them. When they got above these Me 110s they dived down and I could see that they were four P-47s which were supposed to have been gone ten minutes before. Flying a finger-four to the right, they came down at a seventy or eighty degree angle, made one pass, and got all six Me 110s. They were just sitting ducks. The rear gunner in the last Me 110 evidently spotted the P-47s commencing their dive and baled out!

"Immediately afterwards three enemy fighters came in at us from about 1 o'clock. An FW 190 was in the lead and right behind him came two P-47s on his tail. The FW190 was making his turn to attack us and all six turrets were pointed at him. I'm sorry to say we got the FW 190

and the first P-47. The other Thunderbolt peeled off and headed for home. We felt bad about it and I doubt whether the P-47 pilot realized he was so close to the bomber formation. There was little flak from the target, which was battered from the bombs of other B-17s. We loosed our incendiaries into the middle of the town and as we left, huge fires were burning. The trip out was a long one and fighters were many."

The coast of England was a welcome sight for the survivors but not all the Fortresses were able to land back at their home bases. Lieutenant David Williams, lead navigator aboard the 91st lead ship, *Oklahoma Oakie*, recalls,

"Our group had lost ten aircraft and we were one of only two aircraft which were able to make it back to Bassingbourn without an intermediate landing. At that, we had part of our left wing shot off from a 20mm frontal attack which resulted in our left wing man being completely shot out of the air. We discovered after landing that we also had an unexploded 20mm in our left main wing tank. A bullet of unknown caliber (I hope it was not a .50) came through the top of the nose, passed through my British right-hand glove, through my left pant leg and British flying boot without so much as breaking the skin, then out through the floor. It paid to be skinny at the time!"

At bases throughout eastern England, anxious watchers counted in the returning Fortresses. Eighteen had taken off from Grafton Underwood but the watchers on the control tower had no need to count further than thirteen. At Molesworth things were a little different, as Claude Campbell explains. "For some unknown reason there were no losses from the 303rd. The lead bombardier was hit in the stomach forty-five seconds from the target and the waist gunner was killed and the other wounded. It was the longest, most impressive, toughest and the most important raid of the war. We got a bullet hole through our left aileron and one through the fuselage which went under Miller's (the co-pilot) seat and a fragment struck my hand.

"Following the raid the 8th got the biggest letdown of the war by the RAF. The British night bombers were to follow us and do most of the damage. Our job was merely to start fires so they could saturate the area with blockbusters. But they assumed the target was hit and enough damage done so they failed to follow. It was discovered later that Schweinfurt was not hit as terrifically as supposed. We sacrificed 600 men, sixty planes, and many injured men to start those fires."

In all, VIII Bomber Command lost thirty-six Fortresses on the raid with a further twenty-four being lost on the Regensburg strike. The total loss of sixty bombers was almost three times as high as the previous highest, on 13th June, when twenty-six bombers were lost. Hardest hit in the 1st wing were the 381st and 91st Bomb Groups which lost eleven and ten B-17s respectively. Third highest loss of the day went to the 100th Bomb Group in the 4th Wing, which lost nine Fortresses.

The Fourth Wing survivors were left to reflect on the raid as they regrouped in North Africa. Colonel Curtis E. LeMay sent the following telegram to England. "Mission flown as planned. Fighter support poor. Wing under constant attack from Antwerp to thirty minutes after leaving target. Objective believed to be totally destroyed. Detailed report impossible at this time. Airplanes have landed at a number of fields other than those scheduled due to battle damage and gas shortage." The 4th Wing's achievement earned the following accolade from General Frederick L. Anderson at 4th Wing Headquarters, Elveden Hall: "Congratulations on the completion of an epoch in aerial warfare. I am sure the 4th Bombardment Wing has continued to make history. The Hun now has no place to hide."

Arab boys salute the arrival of the 100th Bomb Group at Bone, in North Africa. (Thorpe Abbotts Memorial Museum)

Non-issue head gear for 1st Lieutenant Cruikshank's 100th Bomb Group crew. (Thorpe Abbotts Memorial Museum)

A 96th Bomb Group crew walk from their B-17 in North Africa. (Geoff Ward)

Chapter 7
Battle of the Sea Ports

Lack of facilities in North Africa ruled out any more immediate shuttle missions and VIII Bomber Command continued flying missions to France and the Low Countries. Then, on 6th September, General Eaker switched his attention to the aircraft component factories at Stuttgart. In all, 338 B-17s were dispatched. The raid was a complete "SNAFU" from the start. Cloud interfered with assembly over England and prevented accurate bombing at the target. The B-17 formations came under sporadic attack shortly after crossing the enemy coast; an indication that the bulk of the fighter force was massing further inland for a concentrated strike. Thick cloud was also building up inland and the feeling among the B-17 crews was that the mission should be aborted. However, the force carried on.

Brigadier General Robert B. Travis, who had assumed command of the 1st Wing from Brigadier General Williams, circled Stuttgart for approximately thirty minutes in a vain attempt to find the target. Claude Campbell was flying in the 303rd Bomb Group formation behind Travis.

"The plug and magneto factory we had been briefed to attack was covered in clouds so we flew around dodging flak, trying to find a hole in the overcast. Fighters were flying around as bewildered as we were. Eventually, we dropped our bombs on God knows where (they hit a wheat field) and began to fight our way home."

The 388th Bomb Group from Knettishall was flying its nineteenth mission, which would be one to remember. At the IP, flak had claimed 2nd/Lieutenant J. A. Roe's B-17 *Silver Dollar*, from the 563rd Squadron, and shortly thereafter fighters shot down the squadron's five remaining aircraft. 1st/Lieutenant W. P. Beecham's crew in *Impatient Virgin II* were interned in Switzerland, and *Sky Shy*, flown by Flight Officer M. Bowen, tried to join him but the aircraft was on fire and the tail-gunner had been killed in his turret. Nine men baled out and the radioman was murdered by German civilians. In all, the group lost eleven Fortresses, the highest loss it had sustained on a raid since joining the 8th in June 1943.

Many Fortresses came off their targets with their bomb loads intact and some 233 bombers released their bombs on targets of opportunity en route to the enemy coast. By the time the B-17s were east of Paris red lights began to show on the fuel gauges and many crews began to wonder if they would ever make England. Three B-17s in the 92nd Bomb

The Emden raid, 27th September 1943. The nearest aircraft, 42-3538, had just arrived with the 94th Bomb Group and had not yet had the "A" in a square marking painted on its tail. The aircraft was named Ten Knights in a Bar Room, *but lasted only one week before being shot down on 4th October 1943.*

Group went down over the Continent and three more were forced to ditch in the sea, out of fuel. One, which was severely damaged by flak, was successfully ditched two miles off the English coast by Captain Blair G. Belongia. It was the second time Belongia had ditched, the first being on 26th July when the target had been Hannover. All three crews were rescued and returned to Alconbury. Altogether, 118 crewmen were rescued from the "drink" this day.

The following day the 8th bombed enemy airfields in France and the Low Countries. This was the 92nd Bomb Group's last mission from Alconbury. On 15th September a motor convoy took personnel to their new base at Podington where they were to remain for the remainder of the war. The hardstands at Alconbury were filled with the B-17s and B-24s of the 482nd Bomb Group, which was to become part of the "Pathfinder Force" attached to the 8th Air Force, equipped with radar bombing aids. Eaker and his staff had professed interest in British radar bombing aids which could be used to defeat the cloudy conditions, which always seemed to obscure American targets and by October 1943 the British Gee system was being installed in B-17s and B-24s. Gee was the first of several blind bombing and navigational aids developed by the British and utilized signals received from two ground stations to give an aircraft its exact position. The second type, H2S, an airborne radar scanner, gave a crude impression of the terrain below on a cathode ray tube in the aircraft. H2S equipment was difficult to install be-

cause the radar scanner had to be extended clear beneath the aircraft. The scanner was covered with a large plastic bubble, which gave H2S equipped B-17s the appearance of having a bathtub slung under their nose.

On 13th September, VIII Bomber Command was officially divided into three bombardment divisions with the nine groups in the 1st Bomb Wing forming the First Bombardment Division. The Liberator force in Norfolk and Suffolk became the Second Bomb Division and continued to fly missions separate from the two Fortress divisions. The six B-17 groups which formed the 4th Bomb Wing now formed the Third Bombardment Division. The changes did not stop there. At Chelveston, the 305th Bomb Group lost its 422nd Bomb Squadron, which became a night leaflet squadron, dropping propaganda literature over Germany. Ten months earlier the squadron had been earmarked for such a task, but daylight operations had continued to take precedence over night operations. The 422nd was not the only outfit to begin practicing night missions. During the month the 94th Bomb Group practiced taking off in squadrons and assembling as a group at night. The reason became apparent on 16th September, when the heavies returned to the French Atlantic coast in what was then the longest trip planned by VIII Bomber Command. The first Bomb Division was assigned the port installations at Nantes while the longer range B-17s of the Third Bomb Division flew further south to bomb an aircraft plant at Bordeaux, at the mouth of the Gironde. This involved a 1,600-mile round trip lasting eleven hours and meant that their return would be made in darkness. A third, smaller, formation would bomb Cognac airfield and act as a diversionary thrust for the two larger formations.

Claude Campbell went with the 303rd Bomb Group to Nantes.

"It was our roughest raid yet. I never expected to get our ship back to England. I was leading the top squadron in our group that led the wing. FW 190s hit us hard after our P-47 escort left us but we evaded them. However, we encountered accurate flak over the target and the oil line to our number three engine was cut. We couldn't feather the propeller and the engine began to vibrate terrifically. It was so intense the bulbs in the instrument panel broke loose. Finally, the pistons seized and the propeller crankshaft broke and the prop' began to windmill at very high RPMs. We could not maintain more than 150 mph without causing excessive vibration. I expected the prop' to come off at any minute and either cut me in two or wreck the airplane."

The co-pilot told Howard Hernan, the top turret gunner, to look around for a good place to crash land.

"I took a look and if anywhere would be good it was one of the many wheat fields. But I wasn't on my twenty-fourth mission about to make a crash-landing. I was for trying to fight it back home. I told the pilots it didn't look good. With that Campbell said he was going to try and get us home. He put the nose down and dived for the deck from 28,000 feet. But the rest of the squadron stayed with us because they didn't know we had an engine out. Ordinarily, it was a, 'no-no' as they were supposed to go back with the rest of the group. It was all that saved us."

Campbell continues.

"Over the Bay of Biscay six Me 110s jumped us as we skirted Brest and made one pass at the formation, missing me but hitting my right wingman, Lieutenant Manning, and cutting his rudder cable in two. The next pass got my left wingman, Lieutenant Baker, cutting his oil lines but neither of the two ships was knocked down. By this time I had reached cloud cover which I took advantage of. One Fort, which was straggling along on our left, was knocked down by the Me 110s when they made another pass at us, which we avoided. We knocked down two of the Me 110s on their final pass and then shook the rest off in the clouds. We flew for over three-quarters of an hour with the prop' windmilling. Miraculously, the prop' stayed on and we landed at an RAF base at Exeter. Never did I welcome

terrafirma more. We had lost no planes from our group but the day's operation cost us thirteen bombers and bombing results were poor."

The third formation of B-17s, led by the 94th Bomb Group, visited Cognac airfield. However, only twenty-one bombers from the Rougham Group managed to find and hit the target because of thick cloud. The formation made its way back to England in gathering darkness but the 94th put down without difficulty thanks to its night practice mission a few days before. Groups in the force that attacked Bordeaux were not so fortunate. Just off the southwest coast of England the B-17s encountered heavy rain squalls and this and the impending darkness dispersed the formation. The storm front knocked radio altimeters about 1,000 feet out of calibration and many pilots got into difficulties. One B-17 ditched in the sea off the Northumberland coast after thirteen hours of flight, culminating in a vain search for an airfield. *Ascend Charlie*, in the 390th Bomb Group, suffered a similar fate when it crashed at Abergavenny, Wales. All of Lieutenant Herbert I. Turner's crew were killed. In the 388th Bomb Group *Sandra Kay*, flown by 1st/Lieutenant H. O. Cox, Jr., crashed just south of RAF Shobden and all ten crewmembers were killed. 2nd/Lieutenant Henry J. Nagorka's *Old Ironsides* ditched in the sea just north of The Wash. The two waist gunners drowned and the tail-gunner lost a leg. The third 388th B-17 that got into difficulty was *Gremlin Gus*, flown by Lieutenant Jarrend. It crashed into the side of a hill at North Moulton, killing Ed Baliff, the cameraman, and seriously injuring the navigator and bombardier. Three others in the crew were slightly injured.

The luckiest man on board must have been James F. Jones, the tail-gunner. Shortly before *Gremlin Gus* crashed, it touched a hilltop and Jones was thrown violently against the tail-gunner's door, which gave way, throwing him out into space as he pulled the ripcord. He spun through the air as his parachute released, the billowing silk helping to cushion his body as he hit the ground at around 200 mph. Jones was knocked unconscious and rolled almost 100 yards before stopping. About two hours later he remembered awaking and seeing a red flare in the sky. Incredibly, his only injuries consisted of a badly sprained leg and several bruises and contusions. When he arrived back at Knettishall, fellow group members listened to his story in utter amazement.

On the morning of 24th September crews were alerted for a mission to Stuttgart again. "Pappy" Colby, who on 21st September became the oldest combat pilot in the 8th Air Force at the age of forty-two, says:

"It was one of those days we should have stayed in bed, as the saying goes. The night before we had been told 'No ball game tomorrow' but at 0730 hours we were told to hurry for an 0900 hours takeoff, which was damn short notice. The 410th had been scheduled to lead the group,

B-17F Wee Bonnie II *of the 388th Bomb Group which was lost of 9th September 1943.*

but at the last minute this was changed to filling in the aborts. Everybody taxied out and two minutes before take-off the raid was cancelled, creating a small traffic jam taxiing back to the hardstands." Adverse weather had led to the cancellation and crews at bases in the east of England retired once again to their sacks. It was almost noon when they were recalled and quickly briefed for a hurried practice mission. "Pappy" Colby continues: "At 1130 they decided to have a wing formation practice mission, following a Pathfinder aircraft and bombing a simulated target in the North Sea. Takeoff was set for 1330 hours, which meant

changing the bomb loads, re-installing machine-guns, etc. Everybody rushed but only about one third of the ships got their guns in."

The same problems occurred at nearby Thorpe Abbotts, home of the 100th Bomb Group. Lieutenant J. Gossage and his crew, which had flown their first mission to Nantes the day before, headed for their B-17, *Laden Maiden*, and discovered it still laden with 500lb bombs. The unloading would not have allowed the crew time to make the mission so the crew was re-assigned another B-17, *Damdifino II*. There was no time to check out the ship completely and its ten machine-guns lay in the nose compartment. The situation was chaotic, with many 100th B-17s carrying skeleton crews, but assembly and climb went off without a hitch and the mission seemed to be settling into a routine training flight. The groups of the 3rd Division were to rendezvous with Thunderbolt escort fighters near The Wash and when ten to fifteen dots appeared heading towards six o'clock, crews naturally believed they were P-47s. "Pappy" Colby relates what happened next.

"Suddenly, we were hit by about fifteen German fighters and, of course, we had no fighter cover. They shot down one ship in the group behind me. As it glided down one 'chute came out and then it blew up. Seven Bf 109s came on through and one started an attack on us, as I was the last airplane. Luckily, our tail-gunner had gotten his twin fifties installed. He fired a long burst and the fighter turned away. There had been a sleek silver B-17 with no guns flying out to the side watching our formation and our practice bombing and evidently loaded with high ranking headquarters people. Four fighters went for him and he really put it into a fast dive into some lower clouds to get away."

In the 100th Bomb Group formation, *Damdifino II* came in for some particularly heavy attacks by fighters using the sun to excellent advantage. They raked the fuselage and a 20mm shell started a fire in the oil tank behind the number three engine. Gossage's first thought was to ditch but the wing was burning fiercely and the fuel tanks might disintegrate when the aircraft hit the water. He opened the bomb bay and ordered the crew to bale out. Theodore J. Don, the bombardier, baled out at 1,000 feet and hit the sea almost the same instant he pulled his ripcord. All except Gossage managed to evacuate the burning Fortress. Gossage tried to skim the water and extinguish the fire but the bomber hit the sea nose down and quickly began sinking. Gossage's foot was trapped by the rudder pedals, but he managed to extricate himself, crawl through the side window and surface from fifteen feet of water. *Damdifino II* floated for five minutes and sank. Don was later rescued by a flotilla of MTBs en route to the Dutch coast but the co-pilot and the navigator were dead when they were picked up. The two waist gunners and the ball turret gunner were never found.

The H2S radar trials carried out on 23rd September proved so impressive that General Eaker instructed that similarly equipped Fortresses should accompany the force of 305 bombers to Emden on 27th September. This small port was handling about 500,000 tons of shipping a month as a result of damage inflicted on Hamburg. Emden was also chosen because of its proximity to water, which would show up reasonably well on the cathode ray tubes. The debut of the H2S equipped Fortresses aroused much curiosity at Bassingbourn, home of the 91st Bomb Group. Orlo Natvig, the radio operator aboard *Local Girl*, piloted by 2nd/Lieutenant William G. Peagram, recalls:

"We got out to the planes waiting to takeoff. The weather was looking like rain and a little fog. About that time a plane came in which looked at first sight like an ordinary B-17, but when it got down on the taxi-strip and pulled up by the operations tower we had a bunch of MPs surround the Fortress. We looked from as near a vantage point as the MPs would let us and saw what seemed to be a bathtub underneath the nose. Of course, this aroused our curiosity and, as it turned out, we were told that we were going to be led by this particular B-17 on the first USAAF radar mission. We would be dropping on smoke bombs that were to be dropped by the pathfinder plane. We were quite enthused about this. It was going to be a short mission so we were quite happy about the whole affair. At briefing my tail-gunner and I had made the remark to the briefing officer, 'Well, this looks like a milk run'. As it turned out, it could not have been further from the truth.

"We went through the takeoff preparations and without any questions at all and were soon on our way over. Everything seemed like a routine mission. We made the usual approach to Germany by going out across the North

Pat Hand, flown by Lieutenant Ken Murphy of the 96th Bomb Group, took a direct hit from flak over Paris on 15th September 1943 and went down in flames into the city. (USAF)

The 390th Bomb Group at high altitude on the Emden mission of 2nd October 1943.

Sea, leaving only fourteen minutes over enemy territory. Observing the coastline we started running into fighters. There was solid overcast underneath us as we approached the target. As we were going on into the target our ball turret gunner passed out. The waist gunner and I got him into the radio room and fixed him to the oxygen system. After he seemed fully recovered we gave him a walk-around bottle and helped him back into the ball turret. We assumed he would hook up to his own system but soon afterwards he passed out again. This time we brought him up and laid him on the floor of the radio room. We decided we did not have enough time to bring him round so we just left him with the oxygen switched on. In any case, we had more serious trouble on our hands with the fighters coming in at us. We returned to our battle stations and returned fire.

"One of the fighters' first passes was made from the belly side. I suspect that the Bf 109 pilots were experienced and must have seen the twin fifties in the ball turret pointing straight down and therefore decided to hit us from this vantage point. It was not manned so they proceeded to climb at us from underneath. They hit us in the wing on one of the first passes and the second time through they came up again from below and scored hits in the gas tank,

which caught fire. We also suffered a hit in my compartment. An explosive shell entered the outer skin and all I could remember was that things started flying about and the radio-transmitter behind me was pretty well destroyed. About that time the fire in the left wing started blazing pretty well. We began to realize that we were now in very deep trouble. Our intercom was not operating; I imagine because of some of the fragments from the shell, so we were unable to converse with each other.

"The attack continued from various angles but our predominant concern was the fire in the left wing. We continued for a while but unknown to us the majority of the crew in the forward section had already left the ship. Peagram was the only one up front. He had remained true to his word that in the event of an emergency he would remain at the controls long enough to give his crew sufficient time to bale out. When the fire in the wing got so bad that I could see through the structure, I knew it was time to leave. The other waist gunner, Staff Sergeant Hutchinson, and I took the ball turret gunner and got a parachute on him. We put him through the waist door hatch, pulling the ripcord as he went. He fluttered down and landed safely. Just after we lost our left wing. Hutchinson and I found ourselves clear back down by the ball turret on our sides. The only way we could go then was to scramble up the ribs of the ship, using it like a ladder. "Hutch" went on out and I grabbed the pants of our other waist gunner, Peters, and tried to get him to come along but he would not move. I wasted no more time and went on up the ribs. When I got to the door I didn't hesitate. I just baled right on out."

Natvig drifted down and headed for a little town. As he got closer he could see that all the houses were built of brick. This was worrying because if he hit one of the houses he would be smashed against the side of the wall. (Natvig had seen some German parachutists who had baled out over London and had slammed into the sides of buildings.) Fortunately, he came down safely but was captured near Ouderdom.

"When I got down the Germans made me disrobe and then they searched us. I put my flight coveralls back on and when I ran my zipper up, it came right off by my neck. I discovered that a piece of shrapnel had come right on through my coverall and had taken my zipper out. I guess it was very fortunate for me that I wore a flak suit that day. I had never worn one before."

Larson, the engineer, and Cosgrove, the navigator, had drowned when they landed in the sea. The Germans would not allow Dutch fishermen to go out and save them. Only later were they allowed to retrieve the bodies. Pegram, the pilot, stuck to his post and it cost him his life. His body was found near the wreckage. Peters kept firing at the German fighters to the end and also went down with *Local Girl*. The other six crew members were safe and were sent to POW camps.

The Fortresses which had bombed with the aid of H2S equipped B-17s had done remarkably well. Two had flown in each of the 1st and 3rd Division formations; the inclusion of a second H2S equipped aircraft per formation was a necessary precaution because the intricate H2S sets often failed to function properly. (On arrival at Emden, only one set in each formation was still working.) Despite some confusion in maneuvering above the overcast at the approach to the target, the leading combat wing in the 1st Division successfully dropped in with the pathfinder aircraft from 22,000 feet. The 2nd Combat Wing dropped on the smoke markers while the 3rd Combat Wing found no sign of the markers and was forced to seek alternative targets. One of the three combat wings in the 3rd Division managed to bomb visually after exploiting a gap in the clouds, but subsequent photographic reconnaissance proved that only the H2S assisted formations had achieved a fair concentration of bombs on Emden, while other bomb patterns ranged as far as five miles away from the city.

The H2S sets seemed to provide the answer to the 8th's problems and Eaker was anxious to use them again as soon as possible. A period of bad weather gave the technicians time in which to iron out some of the teething troubles before the bombers were dispatched to Emden again on Monday, 2nd October, with two H2S equipped aircraft from the 482nd Bomb Group. Brigadier General Robert B. Travis led the mission, taking the co-pilot's seat aboard a 384th Bomb Group Fortress named *Little America*. This time the H2S sets worked perfectly, although inexperience resulted in one pathfinder aircraft releasing its bombs too early and many B-17s dropped their loads short of the target. Winds also carried away smoke markers and disrupted the aim of the following formations.

Despite a strong P-47 escort the Luftwaffe was again up in force. *The Eightball*, piloted by Lieutenant Bill Cabral of the 390th Bomb Group, lost its number three engine to flak and began trailing smoke. Cabral lost altitude and made a solo run on the docks at Emden. When he turned for home the bomber was still alone and therefore an easy target for preying Luftwaffe fighters. Lieutenant Richard H. Perry, the co-pilot, recalls: "It looked like the whole Luftwaffe was waiting for us at the German coast. I started calling them and our boys went to work at the guns." Soon *The Eightball* had twenty fighters on its tail and Cabral was forced to dive as fast as he dared into cloud cover at 16,000 feet below. A fighter dove in at 12 o'clock and the whole bomber shuddered with the recoil as Lloyd J. Wamble opened fire from his top turret. Wamble hit the fighter in the fuel tanks and it exploded, showering the sky with debris and smoke. For the next twenty minutes *The Eightball* came in for repeated enemy attacks and two more fighters were shot down. Finally, *The Eightball* entered cloud cover at 3,000 feet and Cabral asked the crew over the intercom if everyone was all right. Dean C. Ferris, the bombardier, replied that he was but thought he had better mention that number four engine was on fire. Orange flame covered the wing and threatened to ignite the fuel tanks. By now *The Eightball* was over Holland and Cabral asked the crew if they wanted to bale out or keep going. All wanted to keep going.

Cabral steered the ailing bomber around the flak at Rotterdam and headed out across the North Sea towards England. *The Eightball* lost altitude rapidly and soon the badly damaged bomber was so low over the sea that salt spray entered the waist windows and splashed the gunners. The engine fire threatened to engulf the number three engine and Cabral ordered the crew to take up their ditching positions. He was about to ditch, when in the distance he saw a large rolling wave and decided to fly through it, gambling that it would extinguish the raging fire. He took the B-17 in as low as he dared and the wave washed over the wing. Cabral and Perry threw the throttles forward and lifted *The Eightball* clear of the water. The fire was out! Cabral cancelled the SOS to Air Sea Rescue and flew on to the coast of

England, where he brought *The Eightball* in for a smooth landing at an emergency base. As the aircraft hit the runway, the propeller of number four engine spun off and rolled some distance down the runway. After the raid General Travis told reporters, "The raid went off like a military drill. It's not often you come back from a mission in which everything went off to perfection. I was particularly impressed by the discipline of our men. Our bombs went down together over the target. It was a good show and I was very pleased with it."

Travis had good reason to be pleased with the results. Apart from the bombing, losses had been negligible during this and previous raids on Emden. This was due mainly because the raids were carried out within the range of P-47s fitted with larger capacity drop tanks. Also, the Luftwaffe's single-engined fighter pilots, ill-trained for blind flying on instruments, had difficulty in making interceptions through overcast conditions.

Further radar bombing was delayed because the 482nd Bomb Group had insufficient aircraft and crews to participate in a major mission and there were several days on which conditions were suitable for visual attacks in western Germany. On 4th October, 361 bombers were dispatched but, without PFF, bombing was out of the question at all primary targets because of cloud. Twelve B-17s were shot down and losses would have been higher had it not been for the strong P-47 escort. Among the fifty-six fighters claimed shot down on the raid was a confirmed FW 190 kill which went to Staff Sergeant Donald W. Crossley, a tail-gunner in the 95th Bomb Group. He established a new record of twelve confirmed kills which was unsurpassed by the end of hostilities.

On 8th October, the 1st and 3rd Bomb Division were assigned the port at Bremen. The area was noted for its flak defenses and much of northwestern Germany's fighter strength was concentrated nearby. In order to split the enemy fighter force, plans called for the 1st Division to approach the target from Holland while the 3rd Division crossed the North Sea and approached the target from the northwest. The B-24s of the 2nd Bomb Division, living up to their nickname, the "Second Bomb Diversion", would fly a long, curving route over the North Sea to attack Vegasack. Unfortunately, after the P-47 escort had withdrawn, low on fuel, the B-17s were met in strength. The unfortunate 381st Bomb group, flying as low group in the 1st Division formation, lost seven of its eighteen bombers, including the lead ship. To crews in the 3rd Division, though, it seemed as if everything was going according to plan. Frank McGlinchey, the bombardier aboard Bill MacDonald's *Salvo Sal* in the 100th Bomb Group formation, recalls: "The P-47s had given us good support and things seemed rather quiet as we winged our way towards the target. Minutes passed and soon we were over the IP. With bomb bays open we turned on the target. The groups in front of us were enveloped in a large black cloud as they passed over the target and dropped their payloads. It was the most intensive flak I had ever seen."

The German flak defenses had already calculated the height and speed of the previous wing and had no need to alter those calculations as the 100th sailed over the target at much the same height and speed. Captain Everett E. Blakely and Major John B. Kidd, the command pilot, in *Just a Snappin'*, led the group through the ugly bursts of flak, so thick they formed one large oily cloud. Two minutes before the target *Just a Snappin'* was hit by the first burst of flak

Captain Murphy (kneeling, center) and the crew of Piccadilly Lily, *one of seven B-17s lost on the Bremen mission of 8th October 1943.* (100th Bomb Group Museum)

and a few moments later another burst hit the nose compartment. Further flak bursts knocked out the number four engine and caused more damage. The Fortress caught fire and fell into a flat spin. The aircraft lost 3,000 feet in the resulting dive and it took a superhuman effort for Blakely and Kidd to regain control. The deputy lead ship also started down and *Our Baby, Marie Helena, Piccadilly Lily, War Eagle,* and *Phartzac* followed in quick succession. Of the 350th Bomb Squadron, only Blakely's ship and Bill MacDonald's *Salvo Sal* remained.

Frank McGlinchey scanned the sky.

"I looked for our two wingmen but saw no one. Our whole squadron of nine ships had been knocked out. (I learned later that only the lead ship made it back to England.) Although out of formation and heading back to England by ourselves (just after the bomb bay doors had closed our ship jumped as we received a very bad hit to the rear of number two engine), we seemed to be doing all right until a flight of German fighters bounced us. Suddenly, the intercom was alive with reports of fighters bearing in from all directions. All of our guns, with the exception of the two nose guns, were knocked out in fifteen minutes. Our waist gunner, Douglas Agee, was killed by a direct hit from a fighter about two minutes after the attack started. All our left controls were shattered and we had to put out several fires. Our radio too was gone. One engine was running away and two more were just about to go. We were losing altitude rapidly and it was apparent we would not make it back to England. Suddenly, fire shot out from the rear of the undercarriage and beneath the wings. With the Zuider Zee directly in front of us, Bill MacDonald gave the order to bale out."

Incredibly, almost all the crew of *Salvo Sal* managed to bale out of the doomed aircraft. All six enlisted men were captured by German patrols shortly after landing. John James, the co-pilot, had jumped with a parachute that had been holed by a cannon shell and broke his leg in a bumpy landing. He was taken prisoner by German soldiers and hospitalized. Spicer evaded capture and made it home to England via France and Spain. MacDonald and McGlinchey also evaded capture and traveled along the evasion lines through Holland and France into Spain, only to be caught at a crossing point on the Pyrenees. They were sent to *Stalag Luft 1,* Barth.

Meanwhile, the remnants of the 100th Bomb Group formation flew on in disarray. Major Robert O. Good, the 390th Bomb Group leader, flying in *Six Nights in Telergma,* piloted by Captain Hiram C. Skogmo, had a ringside seat in the disaster. Seeing the 100th Bomb Group being decimated before his very eyes, Good radioed the other group commanders that he was taking the twenty aircraft in his group into the lead slot. The 390th made its bomb run over the

center of Bremen and then headed for the crippled 100th formation ahead. A group above covered the 390th as it made its maneuver which allowed the 100th an opportunity to slide into position behind the 390th as it passed by. The survivors in the 100th realized the plan and fell in tightly from the rear. Major Good then slowed the formation to give the stragglers a chance to form up. The maneuver prevented the loss of at least four more B-17s that might otherwise have been lost to fighters or flak. Major Good said later that it was a demonstration of the finest teamwork he had ever seen in the air.

Altogether, the 8th lost twenty-six bombers, including fourteen in the 3rd Division. The 100th Bomb Group had lost seven B-17s, including Major "Bucky" Cleven, CO of the 350th Bomb Squadron, who was later reported to be a POW. The 390th Bomb Group had lost three B-17s including *Devil's Daughter* and *Blood, Guts and Rust II.* The 96th contributed three B-17s to the division's loss. If it had not been for the installation of Carpet blinkers aboard some 96th and 388th Bomb Group B-17s, losses might well have been much higher. ("Carpet" was another British invention which used radio signals to interfere with radar-directed flak guns. Over the next two months Carpet devices were fitted to all Fortresses.)

Experienced crews could not be totally replaced, but new crews were now passing through the Combat Crew Replacement Center at Bovingdon daily. Since 1st March 1943, the 398th Bomb Group had assumed the duties of the CCRC and by December that year would have trained over 300 B-17 crews.

On 9th October, 378 aircraft were dispatched on the day's operation, which involved three targets. A total of 115 aircraft from the 1st and 41st Combat Wings were dispatched to the Arado aircraft component plant at Anklam near Peenemünde as a diversion for 263 bombers attacking the port of Gdynia and the Focke-Wulf plant at Marienburg.

The 9th October mission to the Marienburg FW 190 assembly plant in progress. Notice how the pall of smoke can be seen rising from the plant near the runway in each picture. The aircraft photographed here are from the 390th and 94th Bomb Groups.

For Howard E. Hernan and two other members of Claude Campbell's crew in the 303rd Bomb Group at Molesworth, the Anklam raid was their twenty-fifth and final mission of the war. The night before the mission Campbell had been told he would lead the Anklam raid with Major Calhoun, the 359th Squadron CO, but on the morning of 9th October Campbell discovered to his dismay that he would miss the mission altogether. Calhoun would fly *The Eightball* with General Travis, the 1st Bomb Division commander, taking the co-pilot's seat. Howard Hernan and the rest of Campbell's crew would make up the complement. The news that Campbell would not be coming with them was a bad blow, as Hernan explains.

Bombs raining down on Marienburg. Again the runway is visible to the left of the picture.

"I couldn't believe it and my morale dropped to rock bottom. It seemed so strange to fly twenty-four missions with this good man and all he had got us through to have his place taken by a general."

"When we finally got away from the crowded flight line we taxied *The Eightball* up to the end of the runway where the gas trucks met us. We topped off our tanks and took off. I was never so glad to get away. We circled the field until all the group had formed up. It was not until 0930 hours before we finally left the coast and headed out over The Wash towards Denmark. Then we were supposed to fire a green flare to let everyone know that the mission was on. I looked at the dashboard and counted seventeen green flares and two red. I said I didn't think it a good idea for all those flares to be there. If one got hit it might start a fire. I couldn't very well throw them out of the plane because they might hit one behind. General Travis said, 'Fire 'em off.' I did and it caused uproar because the rest of the group didn't know what it meant!

"We flew out over the North Sea at probably only 5,000 feet; my lowest ever raid. After we had used our gas in the bomb bay tank I disconnected the hoses and told the bombardier to open the bomb bay doors and try to salvo it. Momentarily it hung up, so I kicked it and off it went. There must have been 115 tanks washed up along the coast that day. We made landfall on the Danish coast and turned southeast to make a feint towards Berlin. By this time the enemy fighters had hit us en masse. They tried to hit us in the lead plane and I had plenty to shoot at. (Later, when I saw the general's notes, he recorded that we had been attacked 114 times, 102 of those at 12 o'clock level, no less than two planes in each attack and one time as high as fourteen.) The fourteen came at us wingtip to wingtip, firing rockets. There wasn't really much we could do about them, but I started on the one on the left and raked the entire formation.

"Just before we reached the target a Ju 88 followed us out to our left at ten o'clock, probably calling out our altitude. The General asked if I couldn't get him out of there. I informed General Travis that he was approximately 2,500 yards away and it probably wouldn't do any good to shoot at him. However, I did notice that once in a while we would make a one degree turn to the left and I asked him if he would tell me the next time he was going to turn. This Ju 88 would not immediately correct his course as it took him a moment to notice we were turning. Consequently, that would narrow the gap. I really didn't think I had a chance of hitting him, but I set up the sight for his fuselage length. The General told me he was turning and I watched the Ju 88. He didn't correct right away and I had my graticules on him and figured he was probably 1,500 yards away. As my sight was pointed towards him, I looked at my guns and they were out to my right so I knew that the sight was computing. I began firing off short bursts of four or five rounds at a time. After about the third burst the Ju 88's right engine caught fire, black smoke poured out and down he went. I don't think he crashed but the General saw what happened and I got credit for the Ju 88.

"On our approach to the target there was little flak, although there was a lot around Peenemünde. There did not appear to be many fighters either so I had an opportunity of watching the bombs drop. I very seldom did this but since we were only at 12,500 feet I figured I could follow them all the way down and see them hit. Our first bomb landed on a railroad car between two warehouses, blowing it to pieces, while others on either side of it turned flip-flops through the air. We completely saturated the target and started making our left turns to head back over Denmark and the North Sea." [The Anklam force lost fourteen B-17s, all from the 1st Combat Wing.]

The Gdynia force, led by Lieutenant Colonel Henry G. MacDonald, 40th Combat Wing Operations officer, had

Roger The Lodger II, *of the 95th Bomb Group on the Marienburg mission. Fighters have put both the inner engines out of action and the propellers have been feathered. Of Lieutenant Ralph W. Eherts' crew, two baled out but their parachutes caught fire and they fell to their deaths. Five others parachuted safely, but died in the freezing waters off the Dutch coast. The rest of the crew died in the crash.*

continued on its 1,500-mile round trip to the docks area. Flak was heavy over the target area and on the homeward trip the Luftwaffe was waiting. Bill Rose, in the 92nd Bomb Group formation, said:

"It amazed me how the German pilots could fly through the hail of shells we were firing at them. Every fifth round was a tracer. The fighters came in straight through the formation and knocked down Bill Whelan's plane. Then the fighters left the formation as if knocked down themselves. We realized that this was a game for keeps. They were out to kill us and we were going to kill them."

The third force of B-17s, which bombed Marienburg, achieved the greatest success of the day. The normally unfortunate 385th Bomb Group led the raid and lost only two aircraft, one through engine trouble. Anti-aircraft defenses, thought unnecessary at a target so far from England, meant that the force could bomb from between 11,000 and 13,000 feet. At such heights accuracy was almost guaranteed and sixty percent of the bombs dropped by the ninety-six Fortresses exploded within 1,000 feet of the MPI, while eighty-three percent fell within 2,000 feet. Before the raid, the Marienburg plant had been turning out almost fifty percent of the Luftwaffe's FW 190 production. Results were devastating and General Eaker called it, "A classic example of precision bombing."

When *The Eightball* arrived back at Molesworth, the crew was "welcomed by the same throng, possibly more, than had seen us off." According to Howard Hernan,

"I was overwhelmed and, of course, my good pilot, Claude Campbell, was there to greet us. Every man in the squadron was anxious for me to complete my twenty-five missions so they could tear my filthy coveralls off me. Everyone, including General Travis, six foot two and weighing 200 pounds, who grabbed hold of my shoulder and yanked me clear off the ground, had a lot of fun tearing those coveralls off. General Travis told Campbell. 'This is the best goddam crew I've ever flown with.'"

At Thorpe Abbotts, Major John "Bucky" Egan, CO of the 418th Squadron, had "sweated out" the mission to Marienburg. As soon as the 100th formation had landed Egan demanded, and received permission from Colonel Harding, to lead the group the next day. He was determined to avenge the loss of his close friend, "Bucky" Cleven, at the earliest opportunity. Egan wrote:

"The briefing was the same as usual, until the S-2, my good friend Miner Shaw, flashed the photo picture of the old walled city of Munster. Shaw's voice droned on that we were going to sock a residential district. At this point I found myself on my feet cheering. Others who had lost close friends in the past few raids joined in the cheering. It was a dream mission to avenge the death of a buddy. The mission had not been set up for me to kill the hated Hun but as a last resort to stop rail transportation in the Ruhr Valley. Practically all of the rail workers in the valley were being billeted in Munster. It was decided that a good big bomber raid could really mess up the very efficient German rail system by messing up its personnel."

Altogether, 264 B-17s were dispatched to Munster. Crews were told that a maximum of 245 single-engined and 290 twin-engined fighters could be expected to oppose the mission. However, they were relieved to learn that, despite a planned direct route, they would be given a strong Thunderbolt escort. Leading the 100th Bomb Group formation at the head of the 13th Wing, J.D. Brady was flying in the number one position for the first time with Egan in *Mille Zig Zag*. Egan wrote:

"The coast came up and Brady made the sign of the cross just as the first burst of flak went off . . . one of those close ones with pretty red centers. We were being covered by P-47s but the dive and zoom boys couldn't take us all the way to the target because they didn't have the range.

"From here to the target things weren't dull and occasionally a large bird would leave to land in a place he hadn't signed clearance for. Just as we approached the IP, I called out to the group that our high cover was leaving, watched them go, looked straight ahead and said, 'Jesus Christ! Pursuits at 12 o'clock. Looks like they're on to us!'"

These were the last words Egan was to broadcast for many months. Flak had knocked out the number two engine, then number one and number three. Number four proceeded to run away. Brady and Egan knew the time had come to bale out. Brady fought the controls while Egan organized the exodus. The engineer checked the rear of the ship while the bombardier made certain that those in the nose had gone. "Bucky" Egan and Brady scrambled to the bomb bay and both stood on the catwalk doing an 'after you, no, after you' act for a few precious seconds. Brady wanted to be the last out of the aircraft because it was his ship and his crew. Egan wanted to be last out because he was the senior ranking pilot. Suddenly, .30 caliber shells ripped through the fuselage six inches apart in a neat row about six inches below their feet and both men jumped without further ceremony! Egan finally landed in a wood and, after evading immediate capture, was ultimately caught and sent to POW camp where he was reunited with his old buddy, "Bucky" Cleven (who escaped to England in 1945).

The fourteen B-17s of the 100th Bomb Group had come under fire from flak batteries and upwards of 300 fighters. The German aircraft approached in *Gruppen* and broke into battle formations of between three to six aircraft that flew straight and level to their quarry. The attacks, which lasted for forty-five minutes, were made up to fifty yards range, then the fighters turned, took violent evasive action and returned for another attack. The 100th reeled under the incessant attacks, in which twelve of the group's aircraft were shot down before the target. Among them were *Stymie*, *Forever Yours*, *Sweater Girl*, *Shackrat*, *El P'sstoffo*, and *Aw-r-go*. Lieutenant John Justice's *Pasadena Nena* was shot down on the homeward leg. Only Captain Keith Harris of the 390th Bomb Group flying composite (one plane only) with the 100th Bomb Group, and Lieutenant Robert Rosenthal, flying only his third mission, had survived. These two B-17s made up the entire high squadron of the 100th. Contrary to popular folklore, Robert Rosenthal was flying *Royal Flush* this day and not *Rosie's Riveters* (which was still under repair following *Rosie's* debut on the disastrous mission to Bremen. Captain Harris's regular B-17F, *Spot Remover*, was also undergoing repairs and he was flying a borrowed B-17G). Two of *Royal Flush's* engines were shot out over Munster and a rocket shell tore through the right wing, leaving a large hole. Despite this, Rosenthal completed the bomb run and instigated a series of near fatal maneuvers to throw the flak guns off the scent.

Next to feel the full impact of the Luftwaffe attacks were the eighteen B-17s in the 390th Bomb Group formation. As the group neared the target a large formation of aircraft was spotted off to the right. At first it was thought they were B-17s but the stepped-up specks materialized into single-engined Luftwaffe fighters. While Bf 109s and FW 190s ripped through the depleted Fortress formations, the twin-engined fighters stayed out of range and fired explosive cannon shells from 1,200 to 1,500 yards. Ju 88s attacked with rockets from 800 to 1,000 yards and for the first time Dornier bombers flew parallel to the Fortresses and fired rockets from about 1,500 yards. In about twenty-five minutes the 390th lost eight of its bombers as the rockets exploded among them.

Captain Robert D. Brown, pilot of *Cabin In The Sky*, asked his tail-gunner how the rest of the squadron was doing. The tail-gunner reported back that their bomber was the only aircraft left in the squadron formation! Five of the group's eight losses had gone down in as many minutes. A few seconds later Captain Brown saw thirty-six fighters just ahead. His gunners had virtually no ammunition left and the ball turret gunner could only point his empty guns in the direction of the Luftwaffe attacks. But *Cabin In the Sky* came through the battle over Munster.

After disposing of a large part of the 390th formation, the Luftwaffe turned on the 95th Bomb Group. The fighters flew parallel to the formation, out of range, in groups of between twenty and forty aircraft, stacked up echelon-down for frontal attacks. They flew on ahead of the bombers and then peeled off, one or two at a time, attacking the lowest B-17s in the formation. Of the original 95th formation of nineteen aircraft, *Brown's Mule, Fritz Blitz, Patsy Ann III, Miss Flower*, and a fifth, unnamed, ship had been shot down. Four of them were from the low squadron. The survivors continued to the target, desperately fighting off the intense Luftwaffe attacks. In the 390th Bomb Group formation Dean C. Ferris, the bombardier, and Lieutenant Gordon H. Wharton, the navigator, in the nose of *The Eightball*, piloted by Bill Cabral, were firing their guns constantly as the battle raged. A hot shell casing from one of their machineguns landed on a fleece-lined flying jacket lying on the floor behind the two men and started a fire. Ferris pounced on the blaze and beat out the flames before returning to his gun where he continued firing despite his badly burned hands.

A live rocket entered the waist window of *Norma J*, piloted by Bruce R. Riley, but did not explode. George T. Rankin grabbed the smoldering projectile in a flak jacket and threw it back out of the window. Up front, James H. Shields, one of the few non-commissioned bombardiers in the 8th Air Force, placed his bombs on the target. During the bomb run Lieutenant Burgess W. Murdock, the co-pilot of *Miss Carry*, in the 390th formation, took over the controls. Before the IP a large piece of flak had torn a ragged hole in the thigh of the pilot, Lieutenant Paul W. Vance. Vance used the rubber extension cord from his intercom connection as a tourniquet and wrapped his white flying scarf around the wound. He managed to direct Murdock through the bombing run and helped him maintain formation during the withdrawal from the target area.

Miss Carry was fortunate. During the bomb run four ships on her wing had fallen out of formation and been lost. After the target *Tech Supply*, flown by Lieutenant John G. Winant, Jr., son of the US Ambassador to Great Britain, was hit by a rocket and exploded. It was Winant's thirteenth mission. The crew of *The Eightball* saw several parachutes leave the bomber. (Winant was among those who was made a POW). Shortly after *Tech Supply* went down, *The Eightball* was hit in the right wing by a rocket. Richard H. Perry, the co-pilot, says that, "The rocket sheared a path through the top half of the right wing (about fifteen feet from the end). The wing tip flapped up and down in the windstream and caused us to lose the lift that we should have gotten from the wing." The combined efforts of Perry and Cabral were not enough to keep the bomber from falling out of formation so Ferris was called to the controls. He stood between Perry and Cabral and managed, despite his injuries, to put a hand on each of the control wheels and help the pilots keep *The Eightball* straight and level in formation.

It was a great relief to one and all when the white vapor trails of the Thunderbolt escort could be seen directly ahead. There were few B-17s for the "little friends" to protect. The 390th now comprised a pitiful ten bombers from the eighteen that had set out and even the survivors were not sure they would make England. *Rusty Lode*, flown by Lieutenant Robert W. Sabel, had over 750 holes in her fuselage, huge gaps in both wings, rudder, and left aileron and both flaps shot away. The bomber had been hit badly before the

Me and My Gal, *returning to Chelveston with number four engine dead and the propeller feathered. This aircraft was lost on the Schweinfurt mission on 14th October 1943.*

target but Sabel forced his way home through incessant fighter attacks. However, not all his crew believed they would make it home. William L. Ellet, Sabel's ball gunner, saw three parachutes open below the aircraft. He knew they must have come from his aircraft so he climbed out of the turret and saw both waist guns hanging limp with their gunners gone. The tail-gunner had also left the aircraft. Ellet almost ran to the radio room where he found the radio operator slumped over his gun with what looked like a 20mm cannon shell burst in his face. Ellet scrambled back to the waist door and saw a blood-stained flak suit on the floor. Then the two turret guns opened up and he knew he was not alone after all! Sabel managed to land *Rusty Lode* at Thorpe Abbotts with only two minutes' fuel supply remaining. Engineering officers declared that the feat was nothing short of a miracle!

At Framlingham, *Miss Carry* landed at the third attempt in fog. Vance, his leg shattered by a cannon shell, remained in a propped-up position behind the pilot's seat, directing Murdock and the top turret gunner to the airfield. (Vance was later awarded the DSC.) Also at Framlingham, Lieutenant Riley brought *Norma J* in with two engines out and a wounded tail-gunner, whose injuries had prevented the crew from baling out. Riley put down in thick fog in a "field or nothing try" and landed safely. Bill Cabral and Richard Perry arrived over Framlingham and decided to climb to 2,000 feet to give the crew of *The Eightball* a chance to bale out if the rapidly diminishing fuel supply cut out altogether. Framlingham was completely fogged in so Cabral headed for Thorpe Abbotts where the weather was better.

He and Perry brought *The Eightball* in for a crash-landing without injury to the crew.

Despite the fog, all ten surviving aircraft in the 390th made it back to Suffolk. *Betty Boop - The Pistol Packin' Mama*, flown by Captain James R. Geary; *Rose Marie*, and *Shatzi*, flown by Harold Schuyler, all managed to put down safely. *Cabin In The Sky* also put down without incident and Captain Robert Brown put in his gunners' claims of eleven fighters shot down. Lieutenant Robert Schneider, who was flying *Little Mike* (a 100th Bomb Group Fortress) because his regular B-17, *Geronimo*, was undergoing repairs, crash-landed at RAF Wattisham in Suffolk. Some idea of the intensity of the Munster battle can best be judged by the fighter claims submitted at debriefing. Of the 180 "kills" claimed by the Third Division, 105 came from the 13th Combat Wing. In return, the 390th had lost eight of its eighteen aircraft dispatched and the 95th, five out of twenty dispatched. It had been a black day for the 13th Wing, which had lost twenty-five of the thirty B-17s shot down or written off in crashes this day. The 100th Bomb Group's loss of twelve bombers brought its total to nineteen in three days and added credence to its "Bloody Hundredth" tag.

New crews replaced those lost on the mission and were subjected to the usual "flakking process" accorded all fresh crews at bases in the region. At Thorpe Abbotts the process was probably more poignant. A new crew arrived at the base from Diss railway station in a truck to hear, as they disembarked, shouts of "fresh meat" and "meat on the table" coming from the combat barracks. Their career with the "Bloody Hundredth" had just begun.

Chapter 8
Black Thursday

The loss of twenty aircraft from the 100th Bomb Group in a week was indicative of the high losses sustained by the 8th Air Force between 8th and 10th October. In all, eighty-eight bombers had been lost on three successive days, and these at a time when Intelligence sources revealed that the German fighter strength was on the increase. On 1st October 1943 British Intelligence sources had estimated that, despite round-the-clock bombing of aircraft factories and component plants, the Luftwaffe had a first-line strength of some 1,525 single and twin-engined fighters for the defense of the western approaches to Germany. American sources put the figure at around 1,100 operational fighters. In reality, the Luftwaffe could call upon 1,646 single and twin-engined fighters for the defense of the Reich; 400 more than before the issue of the Pointblank directive. The Allies' figures confirmed their worst fears. The decision was therefore taken to attack the ball-bearing plant at Schweinfurt for the second time in three months, in the hope that VIII Bomber Command could deliver a single, decisive blow to the German aircraft industry and stem the flow of fighters to Luftwaffe units.

On the afternoon of 13th October, Brigadier General Orvil Anderson, CO of VIII Bomber Command, and his senior staff officers, gathered at High Wycombe for the daily operations conference. They were told that good weather was expected for the morrow. At once a warning order was sent out to all three bomb division headquarters with details of a mission, No. 115, to Schweinfurt. The orders were then transmitted over teletype machines to the various combat

wing headquarters. Anderson hoped to launch 420 Fortresses and Liberators in a three-pronged attack on the city of Schweinfurt. The plan called for the 1st and 3rd Bomb Divisions to cross Holland thirty miles apart while the third task force, composed of sixty Liberators, would fly to the south on a parallel course. The 923 mile trip would last just over seven hours and meant that those B-17s of the 1st Division which were not equipped with "Tokyo" tanks would have to be fitted with an additional fuel tank in the bomb bay. However, this meant a reduction in the amount of bombs they could carry. Each division would be escorted by a P-47 group while a third fighter group would provide withdrawal support from sixty miles inland to halfway across the Channel. Two squadrons of RAF Spitfire Mk IXs were to provide cover for the stragglers five minutes after the main force had left the withdrawal area and other RAF squadrons would be on standby for action if required. Despite these precautions, 370 miles of the route would be flown without fighter support. The plans then had been laid, but the success of the mission was in the lap of the gods. It needed fine weather, and above all, the fighters had to be on schedule.

During the early evening of 13th October and the early hours of the following day, all the necessary information for the raid was tele-taped to all nineteen Fortress groups in eastern England. The 96th Bomb Group, which would be flying in the van of the 45th Combat Wing, would lead the 3rd Division while the 92nd, at the head of the 40th Combat Wing, would lead the 1st Division with twenty-one Fortresses. Colonel Budd J. Peaslee, deputy 40th Wing

CO and former CO of the 384th Bomb Group, would be air commander. His pilot would be Captain James K. McLaughlin of the 92nd Bomb Group, who recalls:

"I shall never forget the many target briefings that Ed O'Grady, my bombardier, Harry Hughes, my navigator, and I, went through preparing for this famous raid. We had led our squadron (the 326th) on the first Schweinfurt raid on 17th August and, along with the others, did a pretty good job of missing the target. We had all been apprehensive of the second raid because we'd been flying missions since we'd arrived in England in August 1942 and we had first-hand experience on how the Luftwaffe would punish us, particularly when we failed to knock out a target for the first time and attempted to go back."

Among the first of the 91st Bomb Group personnel to hear the news at Bassingbourn was David Williams, who in September had been promoted captain and appointed group navigator. Like McLaughlin, Williams had also been on the first Schweinfurt raid.

"I vividly recall the operations order when it came over the tele-type in Group Operations during the wee hours of the morning of 14th October, as I had to do the navigational mission planning while the rest of the combat crews were still asleep. Thus we had already overcome the initial shock which we were to see on the faces of the crews somewhat later when the curtains were dramatically pulled back to reveal the scheduled second deep penetration to Schweinfurt."

In the early hours of 14th October the sky was still dark and windless and a heavy mist clung to buildings and the surrounding countryside as thousands of men cycled or trudged their way to the mess halls for breakfasts of powdered eggs, toast, and hot coffee. Soon they were on their way again, this time to the briefing halls to hear about the part they would play in the forthcoming mission. The news that Schweinfurt was their target brought mixed reactions from men weary from days of bitter combat and fitful sleep. There were few on the bases who doubted it was an excursion into Hell despite some officers' platitudes that it was going to be a milk-run. Lieutenant Edwin L. Smith, co-pilot in Lieutenant Douglas L. Murdock's crew, sat through the 305th Bomb Group briefing at Chelveston. "We had been briefed once before for Schweinfurt but, because of the weather, the mission was scrubbed. This particular morning, when we saw the tapes stretching that deep into Germany, we all had misgivings. The gunners knew we were in for a fight and so they lugged extra ammo boxes out to our aircraft." (The 305th was the low group in the 40th Combat Wing, flying behind the 92nd with eighteen aircraft.)

At Podington, Colonel Reid introduced Budd Peaslee to the expectant crews. Peaslee spared no punches. He told them straight out they were in for a fight. Their responsibility was to the group, not to the stragglers and there was no room for useless heroics. He tried to think of something humorous to dispel the tension that had suddenly gripped the men, but could think of nothing funny in the situation. Finally, he said, "If our bombing is good and we hit this ball-bearing city well, we are bound to scatter a lot of balls around on the streets of Schweinfurt. Tonight I expect the

The crew of The Eight Ball, *of the 390th Bomb Group pose just before the second Schweinfurt mission. Lieutenant Dick Perry is seen standing on the extreme right.* (Perry)

The crew of Sky Scrapper *of the 92nd Bomb Group. Bill Rose, the pilot, is pictured third from left in the top row.* (Rose)

Germans will all feel like they are walking around on roller skates." "It was a weak effort", wrote Peaslee, "but they all laughed loudly, too loudly, and the tension was reduced."

Crews in the 3rd Division had not flown the first Schweinfurt raid and in the words of Roy G. Davidson, a pilot in the 94th Bomb Group, they "didn't realize how bad Schweinfurt was. We knew we were in for a pretty rough time, but we had no idea just how tough it was really going to be. Despite this I really looked forward to the mission because I thought the accomplishment would be great."

At Thorpe Abbotts the 100th Bomb Group was still licking its wounds after the severe maulings of 8th October, when it lost seven crews, and 10th October, when it had lost twelve crews. Despite these extremely serious losses the "Bloody Hundredth" was still expected to make some contribution to the tonnage of bombs to be dropped on Schweinfurt, as Lieutenant Bob Hughes, pilot of *Nine Little Yanks and a Jerk*, explains.

"The call came for the 100th to mount a maximum effort but there were only eight crews available. Some of the key positions, therefore, had to be taken by personnel from other groups. The eight crews were broken down into flights. Four aircraft would be led by 'Cowboy' Roane, flying with the 390th Bomb Group, with four being led by myself flying with the 95th Bomb Group. [These two groups would fly in the 13th Wing: last wing in the Third Division task force.] The mess hall seemed virtually empty as we had our usual breakfast of dried eggs, spam, coffee, toast, and good old orange marmalade with vast amounts

of good American butter to go on that wonderful dark English bread." For many it was to be their last breakfast on English soil - or anywhere. There was little hope for any man holding low rank who wished to take the leave that was owing to them either. It was a maximum effort and everyone was needed. At Framlingham, home of the 390th Bomb Group, Lieutenant Richard H. Perry had hoped to receive a short period of leave in London after his crash four days before. "The squadron CO, Joe Gemmill, felt differently. His view was that the best way to get the 'butterflies out of our stomachs' was to participate in another mission immediately. We did fly the Schweinfurt mission, which was no milk-run, and I think in our case his approach worked fine. Later, when I became Operations Officer, I used this approach on many other crews that had rough missions."

Roy Davidson was also refused leave prior to the mission.

"I was cadging for a three day leave on 14th October but, being a second lieutenant, I was outranked by a captain who wanted leave that same day. He took his leave and I flew the mission. I flew in the low squadron of the 94th as last man - the most vulnerable spot in the entire formation. But we felt real safe because, even though we were the last 'plane in a string of over 200 bombers, there were going to be a whole lot of Liberators following right behind us. This would really put us right in the middle of the whole string, which seemed to be a pretty good spot." Unfortunately for Davidson, the unpredictable weather intervened before takeoff and hampered the Liberators' assembly. Forty-nine B-24s took off but only twenty-four arrived at the rendezvous point. The remaining twenty-five managed to link up with fifty-three P-47s from the 352nd Fighter Group, but such a small force would have been decimated by the Luftwaffe and the flak guns so both fighters and bombers aborted after circling for half an hour. The B-24s and their P-47 escort were redirected on a diversionary sweep over the North Sea as far as the Frisian Islands to aid the Fortress formations.

As H-Hour approached the tension on the B-17 bases mounted. The weather was very bad and it seemed as if the Fortresses' participation was also at an end. However, an American-crewed Mosquito, 35,000 feet over the Continent, radioed back the news that General Anderson had been waiting for. Over the secret wavelength the pilot confirmed that all of central Germany was in the clear. Immediately, the word was passed to the B-17 groups in eastern England: "Let the bombers takeoff."

Colonel Peaslee, the mission leader, and his pilot, Captain McLaughlin, sat waiting in the lead Fortress of the 92nd Bomb Group on the runway at Podington. Green flares shot skyward from the control tower and the lead bomber moved to its takeoff position. The time was 1012 hours. James McLaughlin released the brakes and throttled out toward the fading runway lights in the distance. Colonel Peaslee, sitting in the right-hand seat, listened intently as McLaughlin announced over the intercom that he was taking off on instruments. He directed Peaslee to watch the runway and if the B-17 should start to wander to one side or the other he was to overpower him on the rudder control and bring it back to safety on the runway. The lead bomber gathered speed and at 100 mph in the last hundred feet of runway it was airborne. Peaslee released the locks and pulled the "gear up" lever. They were followed by a further twenty bombers and crews peered into the overcast for recognition points on the ground. In the dimness of the approaching day there was only a brief glimpse of the dark shadows of the woodland on either side of the runway clear zone, but this was almost instantly blotted out as the bombers entered the overcast. Peaslee and McLaughlin leveled out at 8,000 feet and began craning their necks for other aircraft. McLaughlin recalls, "After we were airborne and formed up, the first warning of what the day would be like came when we discovered that some of the groups and wings had not joined up in their proper sequences and the mission thus began in confusion because some group leaders could not find their wings."

The 92nd Bomb Group had cruised to the splasher beacon over Thurleigh and formed as a group but at the second splasher, where the 40th Combat Wing was to assemble, the 305th Bomb Group failed to rendezvous. Peaslee therefore decided to continue with just the 306th Bomb Group to the third assembly area at Daventry in the Midlands and fly on at 20,000 feet to the English coast. Standing orders dictated that no air commander could send out a two-group combat wing; the risk of total annihilation of such a small defensive force was too great. However, Peaslee did not want to abort while he still had some options open to him.

Meanwhile, the 40th Combat Wing had orbited according to procedure and, at 1220 hours, led the First Division assembly line over the coast of England, 20,000 feet above Orford Ness. Further south, the 45th Combat Wing, with the 96th Bomb Group in the van, led the 3rd Division over the Naze. Behind the 45th Wing came the 4th Combat Wing consisting of the 94th and 385th Bomb Groups, followed by the 13th Combat Wing made up of the 95th, 100th, and 390th Bomb Groups. Fifteen of the 164 aircraft in the 1st Division and eighteen aircraft of the 160 aircraft in the 3rd Division either turned back with mechanical problems or became lost in the cloudy conditions. The long and complicated assembly was also responsible for diminishing the Fortresses' vital fuel reserves, especially those carrying bombs externally to make up for the lack of internal tonnage taken up by the bomb bay fuel tanks. Many of these crews were forced to dump their wing-mounted bombs in the Channel or abort the mission.

Aborts had now reduced the 40th Combat Wing from fifty-three B-17s to forty-two; one third of a complete wing formation. Standing orders in the 8th Air Force prohibited bomber commanders to penetrate the enemy defenses with less than a complete wing formation. In this situation the wing would have to abort. However, Peaslee reasoned that the loss of forty-two bombers would deprive the division of much needed firepower and, most importantly, additional bombs. He called for a report from the tail-gunner, a regular lieutenant co-pilot for the lead crew, who was acting as the eyes of the air commander by taking over the tail-gun position. The lieutenant reported that the 1st Division was in excellent position and at full strength except for the missing 305th Bomb Group. (Unbeknown to Peaslee, about thirty miles short of the enemy coast the 305th had sighted and fallen in behind the 351st and 381st Groups and were proceeding on the briefed route as the low group in the 1st Combat Wing.) Peaslee decided to continue to the target, moving the 92nd and 306th formations into the high slot just above and to the left of the 91st. In effect this would give the 1st Wing five groups. Peaslee retained air command but would relinquish the lead to Lieutenant Colonel Theodore Milton, CO of the 91st, flying at the head of the 1st Combat Wing in *The Bad Egg*, piloted by Captain Harry Lay (subsequently killed on a second tour in fighters). The air commander broke radio silence long enough to advise Milton of the plan, at the same time advising the new leader that the 40th Combat Wing would join his formation in close support, thus grouping nearly 100 bombers in a mutually protective mass. Bringing up the rear was the 41st Combat Wing, the third and final wing, led by the 379th with the 303rd in the high spot and the 384th low, in "Purple Heart Corner". In this formation the 1st Bomb Division moved across the English Channel.

At mid-Channel the lieutenant tail-gunner aboard Peaslee's ship reported, "Fighters at 7 o'clock climbing. They look like P-47s." The delay in forming up over England had put the Fortresses ten minutes behind schedule and the forty-four P-47s of the 353rd Fighter Group, which were on schedule, had met the bombers while they were some distance from the enemy coast. Over Walcheren Island more than twenty Bf 109s and FW 190s attacked the First Division, and these were soon joined by Me 110s which fired rockets into the B-17 formations. Captain McLaughlin says,

"The first big jolt came when my co-pilot riding in the tail called out, 'A large formation approaching at 5 o'clock.' We believed this to be the 40th Combat Wing but it proved to be a large gaggle of twin-engined Messerschmitts passing us on the starboard side, positioning themselves for head-on passes firing large rockets into the midst of our formations. With no fighter protection we soon became easy targets for the German rockets and, as our damaged wingmen fell behind, we could see the FW 190s finishing them off with relative ease. Under the pressure of continued heavy attacks our ranks were soon decimated. After three hours, as we closed our formation for the target run, my group looked more like a squadron. We had but twelve airplanes left out of the twenty-one we took off with."

One of the 92nd crews which survived to the target was captained by Bill Rose.
"It was indescribable. This was the first time I had any thoughts that we were in for a fight. I will always remember the tail-gunner reporting formations of B-17s flying into positions behind to protect our rear. We thought we weren't going to have the attacks on the tail like we had been getting on our last two missions. Then all of a sudden, 'Oh my God!' the Germans were letting go air-to-air rockets, straight into our group. I was fortunate in that one went right past my window. The rocket landed smack in the wing of the lead plane, right by a gas tank. I watched it burn and it wasn't long before the entire wing was on fire. The pilot dropped back and the stricken crew baled out. Eventually, the B-17 blew up. It was a terrible sight to see."

Sizzle, of the 366th Bomb Squadron, 305th Bomb Group, flown by Lieutenant Douglas L. Murdock, was lost on the 14th October Schweinfurt mission.

Henry C. Cordery, a gunner in Lieutenant Virgil Jeffries' crew, lead ship of the first element in the 423rd Squadron of the 306th Bomb Group, was also deeply shocked.

"I observed large formations of aircraft approaching from the rear. I called the navigator and asked, 'Aren't we supposed to be the last group in?' He said, 'Yes' to which I replied: 'Someone's lost or we're in for a lot of trouble:' The next voice I heard on intercom was, 'Pilot to gunner. Keep the crew advised.' The aircraft were soon identified as 'hostile.' Then it started. We were under constant attack. I don't know how long the first attacks lasted but there was a lull. I left my position to get more ammo from the radio room. Passing through the waist I found the right waist gunner, Michele, severely wounded. His leg was off. The left waist gunner was also wounded. I called Lieutenant Moon, the bombardier. He came back and we both administered first aid. I took the protective covering off the needle of the morphine only to discover it was frozen. I must have had at least five uncovered and I put them all in my mouth to thaw them. I had considerable difficulty getting them out, as my hands were numb from the cold. Then I returned to my position and just about in time, as the attacks started again."

Jeffries' B-17 survived the initial onslaught and continued to the target with the rest of the task force. The 1st Bomb Division crossed the mouth of the Scheldt at 1225 hours and continued its southeasterly course, which would take it away from the heavily defended towns of Antwerp and Aachen. Aachen was the headquarters of the German flak batteries and its units were known to be the best in Germany. At 1330 hours the 353rd Fighter Group was forced to break off near Aachen and return to England to refuel. The pilots had done their job well, beating off a succession of attacks and claiming ten fighters shot down and another five damaged or destroyed for the loss of one P-47 in combat and another which crashed in England on the return leg. Captain David Williams in the 91st continues:

The target - Schweinfurt.

"Fortunately, the undercast had disappeared at the south German border and the weather was absolutely clear for the remainder of the route to the target and withdrawal until just east of Paris. This provided us with an opportunity for precise navigation and excellent bombing but also provided a field day for the German fighters and anti-aircraft gunners. Our crew in *The Bad Egg* were extremely fortunate on this trip for I do not recall any casualties and very little, if any, battle damage to the aircraft. Nonetheless, we had a grandstand view of the entire frightening battle that once more was characterized by frontal fighter attacks. They appeared to be concentrating their efforts on the low group rather than the lead group of aircraft. In any event, we expended many thousands of rounds of .50 caliber ammo against the attacking fighters on their way to the less fortunate Fortresses of our wing."

The Third Division encountered some fighter opposition but it was not as intense as that experienced by the 1st Division. Only two Fortresses were shot down before the Thunderbolt escort withdrew. Things were much different in Peaslee's task force, however. For a little over three hours, from 1333 to 1647 hours, exceptionally large numbers of enemy fighters attacked the 1st Division. The worst of the attacks took place between Aachen and the Frankfurt area and the out-of-position 305th suffered most of all. Three B-17s from the Chelveston outfit had already turned back, one with a broken exhaust stack, one with an oxygen leak and a third that lost its way during forming up. Of the fifteen that remained, none came in for rougher treatment than Lieutenant Douglas L. Murdock's crew, flying tail-end charlie. Edwin L. Smith, the co-pilot, says,

"An explosion occurred between the number one and two engines, stunning both the pilot and myself. On coming to we recovered control of the plane but realized both engines were out and that we were way out of formation. We also realized it was impossible to get back to the formation or to the deck in time to save the crew as six or eight FW 190s and Bf 109s were chewing us up at close range. I ordered the crew out, flipped the Auto Flight Control on, and baled out myself. Murdock was to follow but I never saw him again. The bombardier and navigator had already left when I checked their positions on the way past. Bill Menzies was the only crew member I ever saw again."

Meanwhile, the 3rd Division had proceeded on a converging course with the 1st Division towards Aachen. At 1410, hours the 1st Division, now flying an almost parallel course to the 3rd Division, arrived at a point twenty-five miles north of Frankfurt where it was to change course and head south-southeast for the River Main. This was designed to deceive the German defenses into thinking that Augsburg or Munich was their destination. About ten miles south of the River Main the 1st Division turned sharply onto a northeasterly heading for Schweinfurt. By the time it entered the target area, the 1st Division had lost thirty-six bombers shot down and twenty had turned back but the 3rd had come off surprisingly lightly, losing only two bombers to fighter attacks. This left a total of 224 Fortresses to win through to the target itself. Collectively, this seems a reasonable force but most of the groups in the 1st Division had been torn to shreds by the intense fighter attacks and some were barely skeleton formations. The 306th had lost ten of its twenty-one Fortresses and by the time the 305th Bomb Group could see

Defender of Schweinfurt, the Bf 110G-2. This version of Messerschmitt's "Destroyer" had four rocket launching tubes under the wings and extra cannons in a pack under the fuselage. The drop tanks gave extra range to chase the bombers.

the city of Schweinfurt, twelve miles in the distance, it had lost its entire low squadron of five aircraft and parts of the high and lead squadrons. Only three of the original eighteen aircraft remained and they were joined by a Fortress from another group. It was not enough for effective bombing so Major Normand, the group leader, decided to join the depleted 92nd and 306th formations for the bomb run. Of the thirty-seven Fortresses in the 40th Combat Wing that had crossed the Channel, only sixteen remained and worse was to follow.

Crew members remember the dozens of great red flashes in the flak columns as they turned on the IP. Many called out that the enemy was using red flak, not realizing that they were in fact witnessing the explosions of many B-17s in the groups ahead. The enemy pilots showed complete disregard for the tremendous flak barrage over the target and made almost suicidal attacks on the bombers. For the moment the lead bombardier aboard *The Bad Egg* had to try and ignore the attacks as he set up the Automatic Flight Control Equipment (AFCE) that linked the aircraft's controls to the bomb sight. *The Bad Egg* led the 91st over the city and at 1439 hours they began unloading their deadly cargoes on the streets, houses, and factories of Schweinfurt. Budd J. Peaslee described it as "a city about to die."

The 91st was to claim the best overall bombing results for the 1st Division. However, the 351st Bomb Group, from the same wing, the 1st, was the most accurate, with Captain H.D. Wallace, squadron bombardier in part of the group formation, placing all his bombs within 1,000 feet of the MPI. Excellent visibility allowed Lieutenant J. Pellegrini, lead bombardier in the 305th formation, to pick up the actual aiming point at the IP and to instruct his pilot, Lieutenant J.W. Kane, to turn onto the bomb run. However, Pellegrini's AFCE had been badly shot up on the run-in and he was not sure if the Pilot's Directional Instrument was working so he set up his own rate and dropped on it. Only three bombers in the 305th formation remained and the bombing of the briefed aiming point would have caused them to become separated from the other groups so they bombed the center of the city instead. Immediately after "Bombs Away," the 305th Bomb Group's thirteenth victim was claimed by fighters, leaving only Major Normand and another B-17 from the eighteen that had set out from Chelveston. The two survivors turned away from the target and followed the lead group home.

Then it was the turn of the 40th Combat Wing. McLaughlin and his bombardier, Edward T. O'Grady, conferred over the intercom and, as the bomber rolled out on a heading toward Schweinfurt, they hooked up to the AFCE. Ahead of them was the daunting sight of the 1st Wing almost blotted from view by the concentrated flak barrage. Captain McLaughlin recalls,

"Looking back now I have to admire the courage of Harry Hughes as I listened to him on the aircraft intercom coolly directing Edward O'Grady to the target amidst the constant

rock and roll of the exploding flak shells and fighter attacks. We had to calm down one of our leaders whose anxiety overcame him - he began to interrupt the intercom con-
versation during the bomb run by muttering to himself
and damning the Germans!"

Flying in the number five slot in the 92nd Bomb Group
formation, directly beneath Peaslee and McLaughlin, was
Bill Rose.

"I looked straight up when the bomb bay doors opened
and could see right into the bomb bay. If his bombs had
fallen out prematurely, they would have fallen on us. Fortunately, I had told my bombardier to tell me one minute
before 'Bombs Away' so I could cut the throttles and drop
back to let the lead ship release his bombs right in front of
the nose of our plane. When all his bombs had gone and
he had closed his bomb bay doors, I pulled up again right
underneath him. In my position the German pilots had a
real hard time getting at us. The only way they could get to
us was to come underneath. I think this was how we were
able to survive; protected in every direction apart from underneath. We came home, the four of us, one right underneath another and one out on each side."

As the bombs from the 92nd Bomb Group fell away the
ships in the 40th Combat Wing turned right, away from the
target, and headed in the direction of the 1st Combat Wing,
now making for the French border. Captain McLaughlin
spoke into his oxygen mask to his tired crew and Colonel
Peaslee sitting beside him, "We've flown this far for Uncle
Sam, from here we fly for 'U.S.' - us." Lieutenant Jeffries' B-
17 was in the 306th Bomb Group formation following the
92nd Bomb Group. Henry C. Cordery was co-pilot.

"We came off the target and re-grouped. I looked around
at the group and there wasn't much of us left. In my squadron we started with six ships; two three-ship elements, and
being in the lead ship I saw all five of them go down. Out
of eighteen aircraft we had six left. I remember someone, I
believe it was Lieutenant Jeffries, saying, 'That's the government's half, now for ours.'"

The third and final wing, the 41st, added its bombs to the
conflagration and turned off the target to allow the 3rd Bomb
Division, flying six minutes behind, to take its turn. First
over the target was the 96th Bomb Group at the head of the
45th Combat Wing. Its target was obscured by smoke from
the preceding bomb runs but crews had not flown this far to
be thwarted by smoke from their own bombs and released
them anyway. The second group in the wing was the 388th
with sixteen aircraft. The lead bombardier was unable to
identify either the *Kugelfischer* ball-bearing works or the
marshalling yards located to the south so he set his sight on

Flat Foot Floogie, *42-29803,*
pictured during its time with
the 306th Bomb Group. This
B-17 joined the 381st Bomb
Group on 11th September
1943 and was the only
aircraft lost by the 381st on
the Schweinfurt mission of
14 October 1943. (USAF)

the bridge over the River Main and released his bombs slightly
to the right of the ball-bearing plant. The bombs cascaded
down into the southern half of Schweinfurt and the western
end of the marshalling yards.

Roy Davidson's crew in the 94th Bomb Group formation were in the 4th Combat Wing, the second from the
3rd Division into the target area.

"My position in the group formation as tail-end charlie
really put us in the center of the whole shooting match.
We went into the target amid very heavy flak and fighter
attacks. The fighters continued to attack us right through
to the target area. They flew through their own flak with
no let-up at all but we were able to fight them off all the

way. By the time the fight was over I think most of the gunners aboard were out of ammunition. Fred Kruger, the top turret gunner, ran out and never did get to reload."

The 13th Combat Wing was the last in the 3rd Division to cross Schweinfurt. Joey Poulin, the nineteen year-old French-Canadian ball turret gunner aboard *The Eightball* in the 390th Bomb Group flown by Bill Cabral and Dick Perry, had a lucky escape when a piece of flak ripped off his turret door. Only his slender lifebelt prevented him from falling 25,000 feet without a parachute (like almost all ball turret gunners, Poulin could not wear one in the close confines of his turret). Many gunners might have scrambled back into the belly of the aircraft but if any Luftwaffe fighters spotted

that the ball turret was out of action it would have been an open invitation to attack. Poulin chose to stick it out, praying all the time that the lifebelt would hold.

Close on the heels of the 390th were the 95th and 100th Bomb Groups, their crews eager to release their bombs and head for home as quickly as possible. Lieutenant Bob Hughes was pilot of *Nine Little Yanks and a Jerk*, in the latter group.

"We saw gas and oil fires dotting the countryside, attesting to the ferociousness of the defense and the determination of the bomber crews to place their bombs squarely on the target and not be denied. From time to time, we had seen flak from a distance but, as we neared the target area, it took on a more personal feeling. Periodically, we could see the red hearts of the bursts of 'Big Stuff.' We could now see the target area. (Lieutenant Richard E. Elliott, our bombardier, and I had attended a special briefing on the target even though we were scheduled to drop on the lead bombardier's release. This intense target study before takeoff paid off handsomely because it allowed us to distinguish the target under the most unfavorable conditions.) We had also been briefed about the smudge pots marking a dummy target area. Elliott and I recognized them for the dummies they were. They were smoking as though the whole town was on fire.

"Suddenly, our attention was diverted. The leader of the 95th was struck by flak just as we approached the IP for the final turn to the target. He descended rapidly from formation. Flak was intense and my co-pilot, Lieutenant Donald S. Davis, yelled, 'Move Bob!' I had felt the 'Whump' from the burst which had lifted our wingman's plane, and was sending it directly into us. Lieutenant Howard Keel temporarily lost control of the craft. The Good Lord kicked left rudder, down stick, left aileron, then back-stick and rolled out of a well executed diving split 'B.' It allowed Keel to pass through the space that we had occupied to execute a co-ordinated recovery. It also placed our ship on a direct course to the primary target. Dick Elliott picked up the target immediately and called, 'Skipper, target dead ahead, set up and follow PDI!'

"*Nine Little Yanks and a Jerk* was now completely alone so Hughes questioned Elliott. 'Dick, I do not have the right to commit a man to this course of action against his will. It would have to be a 100 percent volunteer.' Dick called for a vote starting with the lowest ranking man. One by one all agreed and I said, 'Gentlemen, we go!'

"We considered we had the element of surprise on our side and that we could maintain the appearance of a crippled aircraft by not opening our doors until just before 'Bombs Away.' We re-informed the crew that we were flying in a heavily defended area and the best information had it that German 'planes would not penetrate the area. We also doubted that the flak guns would fire upon the one ship but would allow us to leave the area and become fighter bait. It was our best guess that they did not want to draw attention to the steam-plant and Allied ball-bearing shops by firing on one ship. If we couldn't find it, they were not going to disclose it.

"Dick Elliott opened the doors just long enough to release the bombs. We already had our strike camera running. It was on intervolometer but our bombsight was not. Dick, knowing that he had the rate killed and course was beautiful, set the selector switch on 'Salvo.' Bombs were away at 1454. All fell in the MPI. The roar on the intercom was 'Pickle Barrel!'"

"*Nine Little Yanks and a Jerk* had just opened up the north segment of the target area and there were more bombs to follow. Our aircraft were strike photo aircraft for the 100th Bomb Group and we had picked up the 95th Bomb Group, which was still struggling, trying to get into formation. My wingmen joined me and we asked the new leader if we could be of assistance in re-forming the group, explaining that we had an experienced formation controller, Sergeant Robert L. McKimmy, riding the tail guns. The offer was graciously accepted. He lined them up for us in a hurry because we were running out of the defended area and in a very short time the 95th was formed and the 100th flight took its proper position in the high squadron. We rejoined the 390th Bomb Group and we were once again the 13th Combat Wing."

The city of Schweinfurt had soaked up over 193 short tons of high explosives and incendiaries. The 3rd Division had dropped the most bombs on target and the 390th was the

B-17 42-30727 of the 306th Bomb Group failed to return from Schweinfurt. Five of Lieutenant William C. Bissom's crew were killed.

Colonel "Mo" Preston, commanding officer of the 379th Bomb Group, listens to Major "Rip" Rohr on returning from Schweinfurt. Preston noted that Rohr, "looked harrassed, shaken, and more agitated than I had ever seen him."
(Preston)

most successful. Despite the lead ship experiencing difficulty, all fifteen aircraft placed fifty percent of their bombs within 1,000 feet of the MPI.

The Fortresses turned off the target and flew an almost complete 180 degree circle around Schweinfurt. A group of FW 190s headed for the 1st Division formation and singled out the trailing 41st Combat Wing. The leading 379th Bomb Group lost three B-17s in the first pass and another bomber also hurtled to earth after a collision with one of the fighters, which also went down. Both divisions headed for their respective rally points and began forming into combat wings again for the return over Germany and France. At 1640 hours the 1st Division crossed the Channel coast to be followed, just five minutes later, by the 3rd Division. Approaching the French coast the two surviving aircraft in the 305th Bomb Group sighted the 92nd and 306th Bomb Groups for the first time on the mission. Luckily, the two B-17s had met little fighter opposition on the way home for they had used almost all their ammunition before the target.

The Fortresses' return to England was hampered by the same soupy weather that had dogged their departure. Captain McLaughlin recalls, "This really topped it all off. Low ceilings and poor visibility loomed as an almost insurmountable problem because most of our remaining twelve aircraft were damaged and at least two had wounded on board who needed immediate attention." In all, the 1st Division lost forty-five Fortresses on the raid. At Chelveston the ground staff and crews left behind were devastated to learn that theirs had been the highest loss of the day. Of the eighteen B-17s which had taken off that morning, only two returned to base. There was not even the consolation that some crews might have put down at other bases. Second highest loss in the division went to the 306th Bomb Group with ten. The 92nd Bomb Group had lost six and a seventh was written off in a crash landing at Aldermaston. The 379th

and 384th Bomb Groups had each lost six B-17s in combat and three crews from the latter group had to abandon their aircraft over England, making nine in all. The 303rd Bomb Group lost two aircraft, including one that crash-landed after the crew had baled out near Riseley. The 91st, 351st, and 381st Bomb Groups each lost one B-17. The 3rd Division had fared a little better, losing fifteen aircraft. The 96th had lost seven, the 94th lost six Fortresses and the 95th and 390th each lost one. The 100th, 385th, and 388th Bomb Groups suffered no losses although few aircraft, if any, escaped scot-free. Of the bombers that returned to England, 142 in both divisions were blackened and charred by fighter attacks and holed by flak.

Bob Hughes, pilot of *Nine Little Yanks and a Jerk,* which put down safely at Thorpe Abbotts, concludes:

"After our strike photographs had been developed and the damage assessed by local intelligence, the results were called into division. Dick Elliott and I had been summoned to observe the strike photos. Later in the evening word was received that General LeMay wanted me to attend the critique the next day. This was to be an experience for me. I had never seen so many 'Eagles' in one room. I had never even been to a critique. In fact, I had never been out of formation over a target before.

"When the representatives from all the groups were assembled, the critique was called to order and we had just been seated when General LeMay asked, 'Will Lieutenant Hughes from the 100th Bomb Group come forward.' When I stepped upon the stage he said, 'Will you tell this group what you did yesterday.' I related how we had been forced to dive for our lives and that, when we recovered, the target lay dead ahead. How all the men volunteered so that we had a perfect bomb run and how Elliott had 'pickle-barrelled' the target. General LeMay asked how I knew we had done this. I informed him that I had studied the strike

In recognition of the 8th's heavy losses, and those of the 305th in particular, the "Rainbow Division" presented the German flag captured flying over the Kugelfischer *plant to the group at Chelveston shortly before it returned Stateside.* (W. Donald)

photos and that *Nine Little Yanks and a Jerk* was a designated strike photo aircraft for the 100th Bomb Group. He responded, 'That's right gentlemen: ten bombs MPI.'

"Stepping up to the strike map, he pulled the paper away to reveal an enlarged photo showing the strike. His next comment was, 'The lieutenant should have a commendation,' to which the reply from the back of the room in clearly enunciated words, 'The SOB should be court-martialled for breaking formation!' Those words were spoken by my now good friend, Colonel Budd J. Peaslee. Having reached the age of twenty-five I had watched enough cards to know that in poker this is called a 'Push.' If I didn't ask for a commendation, Colonel Peaslee wouldn't offer a court martial!"

Sixty Fortresses and 600 men were missing. Five B-17s had crashed in England as a result of their battle damaged condition and twelve more were destroyed in crash-landings or so badly damaged that they had to be written off. Of the returning bombers, 121 required repairs and another five fatal casualties and forty-three wounded crewmen were removed from the aircraft. The losses were softened by press proclamations that 104 enemy fighters had been shot down. The actual figure was something like thirty-five, but both the press and the planners alike were carried away on a tidal wave of optimism. Even the British Chief of the Air Staff, Air Marshal Sir Charles Portal, said: "The Schweinfurt raid may well go down in history as one of the decisive air actions of the war and it may prove to have saved countless lives by depriving the enemy of a great part of his means of resistance." Later, Brigadier General Orvil Anderson publicly stated, "The entire works are now inactive. It may be possible for the Germans eventually to restore twenty-five percent of normal capacity, but even that will require some time."

Unfortunately only eighty-eight out of the 1,222 bombs dropped actually fell on the plants. Production of the *Kugelfischer* plant, largest of the five plants, was interrupted for only six weeks and the German war machine never lacked for ball-bearings throughout the remainder of the war. As in many other German industries, dispersal of factories ensured survival and careful husbanding of resources meant that some forms of machinery needed less or no ball-bearings at all.

Four days after the raid, General "Hap" Arnold confidently told gathered pressmen: "Now we have got Schweinfurt!". However, VIII Bomber Command had to return to Schweinfurt again and again, before the end of hostilities. It was only when the city was finally overrun by US armored divisions that America could at last confirm that it had "got Schweinfurt." In recognition of the 8th's heavy losses, and those of the 305th in particular, the "Rainbow Division" presented the German flag captured flying over the *Kugelfischer* plant to the group at Chelveston shortly before it returned Stateside.

Chapter 9
The Best of Days,
the Worst of Days

The day after the second Schweinfurt mission, all heavy bomb groups were stood down to lick their wounds. At Bovingdon, Bill Rose went out to his bullet-riddled B-17 to see for himself how much damage had been caused.

"We had two of our machine-guns hit and bent back ninety degrees. I thought, 'now we could shoot around corners.' The skin of our ship had holes all through it and was so badly damaged it became a 'hangar queen.' In the afternoon a bomber came down to pick us up and we got back to Alconbury to find only three planes on the field. The officers' mess was completely empty."

The story was the same at every base. "Pappy" Colby returned to Bury St Edmunds after a forty-eight hour pass and looked over the damaged B-17s in the 94th Bomb Group.

"Most of our airplanes were spattered with flak holes and the Lockheed boys were busy patching them up. Eight replacement crews were sent in but due to heavier losses in some of the other groups five of them were re-assigned and we only kept three."

The losses and a spell of bad weather restricted the 8th to just two more missions in October and then, on 3rd November, they were assigned Wilhelmshaven. Altogether 555 bombers and H2X ships from the 482nd Bomb Group were dispatched to the port. H2X, or Mickey Mouse (later shortened to just Mickey), was a recently developed American

version of the British H2S bombing aid. Some groups carried incendiaries and, in the words of Captain Claude Campbell, flying his twenty-fourth mission in the 303rd Bomb Group in *The Eightball*, "intended to burn up the city."

Cliff Hatcher was a recent replacement co-pilot in a new crew captained by Johnny Pyles.

"We took off in *Lil' Butch* and flew in 'Purple Heart Corner.' A new crew always flew in the tail-end of the formation. 'Purple Heart Corner' was on the left wing of the second element leader of the low squadron. We were the lowest 'plane in the formation. The opposite was tail-end Charlie, which was in the top position off the right wing of the second element leader in the high squadron.

"During the mission a German fighter passed under our left wing less than fifteen feet below us. He was so close I could make out the features on the pilot's face and could see that he was wearing a light colored scarf. His guns were blazing and the black swastika stuck out sharply on the tail. Flying was in my blood. My father had been a pilot in the First World War but had joined the Air Service towards the tail-end and had not seen combat. After the war he had his own aircraft. I remember Eddie Rickenbacker, Colonel Elliot Springs, Mike O'Leary, and other aces. That cameraderie of World War One was still there when the German fighter came by. I was right in combat like Captain Elliot and the others. I sat there like a kid. This feeling persisted for two or three missions until I realized what I was into. Then I wasn't a kid any longer.

"A Bf 109 hit us and knocked out our number two engine. There were lots of contrails and we hid in them, flying behind our group. It proved successful and we got home although later our ground crew chief at Bury St Edmunds told us he found a .50 caliber bullet in the inverter beneath my seat! Obviously one of our boys in the 94th thought we were a German fighter! The group lost only one aircraft, *Margie*, Lieutenant William L. Brunson from the 332nd Squadron being set on fire by a combination of flak and fighters. One to six 'chutes were reported."

The P-38 escort all the way to the target kept losses to a minimum and crews were quick to praise their "little friends." Claude Campbell says, "I saw about twenty-five enemy fighters, but our boys kept them at bay. They came in real close and gave good protection to the stragglers. My hat's off to them and I hoped we could get more of them over to England. The target was covered by clouds and bombing results could not be determined. There were no casualties in our group and I thought, 'Bring on the next one (my twenty-fifth and final mission).'"

On 5th November, the 8th was again out in force when 374 Fortresses were dispatched to the iron foundry works and marshalling yards at Gelsenkirchen led by five Oboe-equipped pathfinders. For two weeks afterwards the weather grew worse and resulted in many abortive missions. It was not until 11th November that the 8th was in the air again, this time to Munster - scene of such devastation a month previously.

Major "Pappy" Colby led the 94th Bomb Group and Lieutenant Pyles' crew flew their third mission this day, in *Lil' Operator*. (This B-17 had the face of "Esky", the little man who appeared on the cover of *Esquire* magazine, on its nose.) Pyles' crew was assigned the tail-end-Charlie slot in the high squadron. This was reckoned to be the most dangerous position after "Purple Heart Corner." Everything went well until shortly before bomb release. *Lil' Operator* was rocked by an explosion just forward of the engines on the left side. Oil began pouring out of number two engine and streaked back across the cowling and wing area. Pyles told Hatcher to keep an eye on the oil pressure and feather the number two propeller if necessary. Quickly the pressure dropped to nothing and Hatcher punched the feathering button. *Lil' Operator* continued its bomb run and Lieutenant Adolph J. Delzoppo, the bombardier, released his bomb load over the target.

The loss of one engine had considerably reduced their speed and they were now alone. "Bandits at two o'clock" crackled over the intercom and Hatcher peered into the strong sun. Suddenly, out of nowhere appeared a Bf 109 that dived so close that for a moment the crew feared they

were going to be rammed. The German pilot opened fire and several explosions occurred in the cockpit of the B-17, filling it with smoke. *Lil' Operator* fell off to the right and dived for the ground at alarming speed. Hatcher and Pyles opened their side windows to let out the smoke and for the first time realized they were going down fast! Straining on their steering columns, they managed to right their bomber. Hatcher was sure number three engine was windmilling but three and four engine instruments had been shot out in the fighter attack.

Pyles levelled off at 15,000 feet and applied full left rudder to keep the bomber on course. Three and four engine throttles were dead, so he decided to shut down number three engine. Then Ervin Smith, the ball turret gunner, called up on the intercom to say that the undercarriage was in the "down" position. Ross Andrews, the engineer, discovered a large hole in the right forward bulkhead of the bomb bay which had been caused by two 20mm shells exploding in that area. It had cut off all the electrical supply to the right-hand side of the aircraft and only the armored pilots' seats had saved Hatcher and Pyles from flying shrapnel. Amazingly, the top turret gunner had escaped injury after fragments had whistled around his legs. Pyles lost height and headed for some clouds. One and a half engines out and a lowered undercarriage were more than an open invitation to any enemy fighter pilots. It was certain death. Soon five fighters had ganged up on the crippled bomber. Harold Norris, the tail-gunner, saw them first, approaching from the rear. *Lil' Operator* dodged in and out of cloud and was soon down to just 500 feet. Over towns and villages they flew, at rooftop height. Milburn Franklin passed up the temptation to strafe the streets and instead the gunners took it out on the enemy fighters that continued to harass them until they were clear of the coast. Two enemy fighters were claimed destroyed.

At the coast Pyles eased up to 1,000 feet and the crew began throwing out all excess equipment. As a result, the airspeed picked up a little and *Lil' Operator* flew on over the English Channel without getting her feet wet, thanks to the gentle manipulation of the number one throttle. As they approached the Bury St Edmunds control tower, Cliff Hatcher tried calling but the radios were dead. Luckily, the ADF was operating and they were able to home in on the airfield. Pyles put the *Operator* down on the concrete runway but number four engine resisted all Hatcher's attempts to kill it until the last minute. Both pilots hit their brakes hard and the aircraft stopped just short of the end of the tarmac. Smoke and dust shot into the air and the crew sat there for a few seconds until the very real threat of fire prompted them to evacuate the ship. Then came the distant scream of vehicles and the "blood wagons" with Colonel Castle at the helm. Castle made sure no wounded were on board and then demanded to know why Pyles had stopped on the runway. Other aircraft were about to land with wounded on board. Pyles explained their situation and pointed out that they could not taxi away on one engine. Colonel Castle walked across to the *Operator*, rubbed his chin and returned to the crew. He said, "You boys have had a trying day but you had better head for debriefing and then perhaps you can get some well deserved rest."

The next day Pyles' crew were given a three-day pass to London, courtesy of the Colonel. At the end of their leave and while waiting for their train at Liverpool Street Station, the crew decided to drop into a small cinema nearby. Just after the lights went out a British newsreel feature appeared on the screen. It began, "American Flying Fortress Shot Down Over Munster." At debriefing Pyles had been told that his crew had been reported missing after being seen going straight down over the target. Now they sat there in the dimly lit London cinema watching a re-run of the *Operator* going down over Munster. As it reached the frame showing the large "Square A" and the lowered undercarriage the crew jumped out of their seats as one man, startling their fellow cinema goers with cries of, "Hey, that's us!" The manager finally persuaded the "rowdy", "drunken" and "obviously combat-fatigued Yanks" to leave his premises and they never saw the movie again!

For the first two weeks of November 1943 England was blanketed by thick woolly fog and airfields were lashed with intermittent showers and high winds. However, on the morning of 16th November the bad weather front lifted as predicted by the weathermen and a mission to Norway went ahead as scheduled. H2X and Oboe sets had been proving troublesome and the break in the weather would enable crews to bomb visually. The 1st Division was assigned the molybdenum mines at Knaben while the 3rd was to attack a generating plant at Vermark in the Rjukan Valley. (Intelligence sources indicated that both targets were connected with the German heavy water experiments that would help give the Nazis the atomic bomb, although crews were not told this at the time.)

At all 1st Bomb Division bases, Fortresses were rolled from their muddy dispersal sites and lined up for the green light at the end of the runways. At Molesworth the occasion was of special significance for the 303rd Bomb Group's *Knockout Dropper*, which was flying its 50th mission. If it completed the raid it would set a new 8th Air Force record for a B-17.

Knockout Dropper was something of a "good luck" ship, but the same could not be said of *Shady Lady II*, a B-17 which had flown with the 351st Bomb Group from Polebrook on the group's first mission to Schweinfurt on 14th May 1943. Repairs to damage sustained on a recent mission had only just been completed and the original crew refused to fly it anymore. It was decided, therefore, that it be assigned to a new crew, led by Lieutenant Joseph Wroblewski, who had won his pilot's wings at Altus, Oklahoma in May 1943.

"*Shady Lady II* was the first plane assigned to the 351st with a chin turret. This cut the airspeed by 10mph and made it a very clumsy and difficult aircraft to fly in formation. Knaben was my crew's first mission of the war. I didn't expect to go with them on this one. Normally, an inexperienced pilot performed duties as a co-pilot with another crew on his first mission. The plane was heavily loaded with 2,500 gallons of gas and twelve 500 pounders, but she made takeoff easily. After forming we headed for Knaben, almost 700 miles distant. Groups of formations were scattered around in every direction leaving vapor trails. All I could see of Norway were the mountains covered with snow. This mission was flown at 15,000 feet and it was very cold. All but the co-pilot and myself wore heated suits."

Meanwhile, the 3rd Division struck at Rjukan, about seventy-five miles due west of Oslo. As the formation approached the target area there was no opposition, confirming the belief that the Germans would not be expecting a raid so far north. The 94th Bomb Group arrived ten minutes early and had to make a 360 degree turn. (Crews had been told to make certain that Norwegian workers were not on their shift when the bombs fell.) As the Fortresses crossed the target for the second time thick cloud obscured the plant from view and the formation was forced to make another 360 degree turn in the hope it would clear. Reuben Fier, the bombardier in Edward J. Sullivan's Fortress in the 94th formation, recalls,

"While doing our 360 degree turns off the coast a B-17 from the 390th began doing slow gyrations in the sky without the benefit of anyone shooting at us. It felt like we were sitting in the balcony of a theater watching an actor perform before us. The B-17 finally sliced into the water in an inverted position. We did not see any parachutes nor could we understand what caused the unfortunate incident. Small ships were seen to head out towards the crash site but we were unable to see survivors or what happened when the boats arrived on the scene.

"Our plane, momentarily attached to the 100th Bomb Group, began its run into the target behind other planes in formations before us but, due to the cloud, they were unable to drop their bombs. When the 100th approached the target the clouds drifted away and we dropped the first bombs on the target (which were what appeared to be large concrete buildings with flat roofs nestled in the mountains). As we later described to the *Stars and Stripes* reporter on our return to Bury, I could see the bombs mushroom into the flat roofs and, after a short period of time, flames of many colors escaped through the roofs. By the time we turned off the target and began flying out to sea, parallel to the course we flew in, the target area was engulfed in black smoke rising to the sky. The following groups were seen to be dropping their bombs into the smoke

The 94th Bomb Group en route to Munster on 11th November 1943. Thunderbolts can just be seen in the distance.

and licks of flame were seen coming up from the target area. Little did we realize at the time that the heavy water was essential to the Germans in their early stages of nuclear research."

The raid, comprising approximately 155 bombers, destroyed the power station in addition to other parts of the facility, resulting in a complete stoppage of the entire manufacturing process. The Germans later decided to ship their remaining heavy water stockpile to Germany. However, all 546 tons of the heavy water was sent to the bottom of Lake Timm when the ferry boat being used to transport it was blown up by SOE agents over the deepest part of the lake.

The round trip to Knaben and Rjuken was slightly shorter than the 25th July 1943 1,800 mile circuit to Trondheim and the 1,600 mile round trip to Heroya. Joe Wroblewski returned to Polebrook at 1500 hours with 750 gallons of fuel remaining. "We were lucky to draw an easy mission first time out although the going was rough coming in to the English coast with rain, snow, and low ceilings."

Lieutenant John P. Manning successfully brought *Knockout Dropper* back to Molesworth to make it the first B-17 to complete fifty missions in the ETO. Crews told waiting newsmen that the only anti-aircraft fire they had encountered had come from a single flakship in one of the fjords. Crews in the 3rd Division rejoiced over their accu-

rate bombing of Rjukan, saying that the explosion had lifted their aircraft suddenly, "as if a giant hand was pulling them upwards. As it was we hit it right on the nose."

On 18th November, 127 heavies were dispatched to Gelsenkirchen again. However, the Oboe sets aboard the leading Fortresses gave trouble and directed the formation too far north of the target. After an unsuccessful battle with the elements, the B-17s were forced to return to England. The bad weather continued over the next few days but did not prevent RAF Bomber Command bombing Berlin on the night of 22nd November. This led to rumors of an American follow-up raid being mounted on the capital the next day. Bill Rose was in the 92nd Bomb Group, which would lead the raid. "We were on stand-down and consequently we stayed in the bar and drank more than we should have done. The bar closed at 12 o'clock and we hit the sack. Two hours later there came a guy waking us to go on a bombing mission! Of course we were in no physical shape to go but we managed to get through breakfast. Imagine our surprise and sobering effect when the curtain was pulled back to reveal the target. It was Berlin! We felt that, given such a target, even if we managed to survive the fighters and the flak on the run-in we would be lucky if there was anything left afterwards. There was not too much thought about being able to return so long as the bombing part of the mission could be completed. The Luftwaffe would certainly be waiting to finish off anyone coming back.

"As it turned out, the weather was as lousy as expected on the 23rd and you could hardly see. But we went out to the planes and started the engines before the red flare was fired canceling the mission. It proved one thing though, that security on the base was very poor, because it was well known that the target would be Berlin. We were very thankful the mission was scrubbed because we would certainly not have survived."

On Friday, 26th November, 633 bombers, the largest formation ever assembled by the 8th, were directed against targets as far apart as Bremen and Paris. Two new B-17 groups, the 401st and 447th, had joined the 8th during November and the 401st made its combat debut this day. Colonel Harold W. Bowman's outfit would swell the 1st Division stream to 505 bombers briefed for the port area of Bremen while 128 B-17s of the 3rd Division would head for Paris where skies were expected to be clear. Unfortunately, the weather forecasters were proved wrong and the 3rd Division was forced to return with bomb loads intact.

A 94th Bomb Group B-17 piloted by Lieutenant Johnny Pyles, who had brought *Lil' Operator* back to Bury on one engine two weeks before, was rammed by a Bf 109 near the target, over Ivry. The German pilot was thought to be already dead as he approached the formation. The Messerschmitt flew straight at Pyles' ship and hit between the number two engine and the fuselage. Cliff Hatcher, Adolph Delzoppo, and Erwin Smith were not flying with Pyles this day. They had been replaced by three other crew members for combat indoctrination. The

only survivor was the tail-gunner, Harold E. Norris. The tail broke free during the impact explosion and Norris managed to bale out before it fluttered like a leaf to the ground. He evaded capture and was passed along the French Underground to Spain, where he recovered from frostbite and was returned to England.

The 1st Division, en route to Bremen, encountered persistent fighter attacks by up to 100 German fighters. Claude Campbell was flying his twenty-fifth and final mission of his tour with the 303rd Bomb Group this day. "Focke-Wulfs jumped us before we reached the enemy coast but I did evasive action and the boys shot 'em off. All kinds of enemy fighters were in the air, including old Stuka dive-bombers - a perfect illustration of Hitler's shortage of first-line fighters. We ran into a typically heavy barrage of flak over Bremen. The target was covered with clouds and bombing results could not be determined. P-47s picked us up and escorted us from the target so the enemy stayed away." Eighty-six enemy fighters were claimed destroyed, twenty-six of them by B-17 gunners. However, this was more than offset by the loss of twenty-nine Fortresses and five fighters.

At Bury St Edmunds, "Pappy" Colby had been waiting to fly the twenty-fifth and final mission of his tour. On 30th November, when the Fortresses were dispatched to Solingen, he finally got his chance.

"At last I was started on my twenty-fifth and final raid, to a target about twenty miles east of Dusseldorf - right in "Happy Valley" and hardly the milk-run the twenty-fifth was supposed to be. We took off in rain and pitch darkness and climbed on instruments to 19,000 feet before we got above the clouds. There were the usual problems coming

The crew of Hang The Expense, *from the 100th Bomb Group. Its pilot, Lieutenant Frank Valesh, is on the far left of the front row. The aircraft was named after Valesh had destroyed four of his previous aircraft.*

Rum Dum, a veteran of many missions with the 385th Bomb Group based at Great Ashfield. The aircraft was scrapped in May 1945. (Mike Bailey)

up through the clouds and at assembly we only had fifteen ships, while Blythe who led the A Group, had twenty. The 385th leader and his deputy both aborted and they never did form up as a group. We got clear around to the Division assembly line and there was still nobody else in sight. About this time I suddenly noticed that the whole left side oxygen on my ship had apparently developed a leak, as it showed only 115lbs of pressure but should have been over 300lbs. What to do? Should I abort or try to keep going? I was leading the 94th and this was my twenty-fifth, so I decided to keep going as long as possible.

"When we reached the Dutch coast our formation was down to nine ships as Keelan and several others had aborted. I decided to join the 95th Bomb Group for better protection and, as we sailed into Holland, we suddenly saw the entire 1st Division headed for home. Our formation now had four groups of good P-47 cover so I decided that if I could solve the oxygen problem we would keep going. I moved everybody off the leaking side but stayed on myself until it got down below 50lbs. Then I hooked into the right-side system that still had 275lbs and we stayed on it (at 28,000 feet) all the way through to the target. When we finally started to descend on the way home, we still had 110lbs, but it was kind of nerve-wracking.

"There was a glimpse of Dusseldorf through the cloud layers but it's doubtful if we were on target when we unloaded the bombs. My little formation was down to seven ships over the target; two of which belonged to other groups. It was extremely lucky that there were no enemy fighters up as they would have most certainly picked on our small formation. Apparently, bad weather at their fields kept them down.

"As long as I live I will never forget the first glimpse of the English coast which told me I was coming home for good. I remember saying to myself, 'Pappy, with God's help you made it.' When we taxied into our hardstand, who should be there but Colonel Castle (with a bottle of Scotch), Lieutenant Colonel O'Connor, (the Group Operations Officer) and Major Birdsall, (the CO of the 322nd Squadron), to congratulate me on completing my tour. A big songfest at the Officers' Club that night and I wired my anxious wife that I had finished."

The following day Colonel Budd J. Peaslee led a PFF attack on Solingen, then ground haze over eastern England hampered missions. On 11th December the weather cleared sufficiently for the 8th to set out for Emden. This was their seventh trip to the city and one of the most costly. Rocket-firing Me 110s and Me 210s made persistent attacks on the bomber formations and seventeen heavies were shot down, including *Six Nights in Telergma,* the lead ship piloted by Captain Hiram Skogmo, 390th Bomb Group. Captain Irving Lifson, one of the two navigators on board, recalls,

"We were feigning a raid on the Heligoland area, hoping to draw the enemy fighter planes up towards Denmark. Then we were to cut back on Emden. Shortly after turning back onto Emden, eight Me 110s came through the formation, firing rockets. We were hit right away and set on fire. There were eleven of us on board and only myself and Captain Donald Warren, the Group Navigator (who landed on the island of Nordenay), survived. We were picked up by German marines. Ernest Phillips, a gunner, landed in the North Sea and was picked up by a boat. Among those lost was Major Ralph V. Hansell, the 390th Operations Officer, the strike leader who was flying as co-pilot. I spent the rest of the war in *Stalag Luft I*, Barth."

Two days later the Fortresses returned to Bremen for the first of three raids that month on the German port. The 8th was stood down on 23rd December, but missions resumed on Christmas Eve when the B-17s were dispatched to mysterious targets in France which went under the code-name *Noball*. It was rumored in the world's free press and in unofficial circles in Washington that the raids were part of a "pre-invasion" blitz. Crews speculated what the concrete sites were and many dubbed them "rocket" installations or Hitler's "secret weapons." British Intelligence revealed them to be sites for launching "V-weapons" - pilotless planes packed with a high explosive warhead in the nose and aimed at London. Sources revealed that seventy such sites were being constructed and all-out raids were ordered at once.

To Joe Wroblewski it seemed as though, "every plane in Britain was up" on 24th December. The Fortress formations were further strengthened by the 447th Bomb Group from Rattlesden, which made its debut this day. As it turned out, the 447th could not have had an easier debut. Joe Wroblewski confirmed as much when he wrote, "Our third raid in five days. We had no trouble at all. There was no flak and no fighters. How we loved this type of milk-run."

On Christmas Day the festivities got into full swing throughout the region. Americans dined with their English hosts and deprived and orphaned children were invited to bases for Christmas dinner and afternoon parties. Unfortunately, the war was never very far away and preparations were already being made for the next strike. It came on 30th

December when the 8th journeyed to oil installations at Ludwigshaven, near the German-Swiss border. Cliff Hatcher, who flew with the 94th Bomb Group recalls,

"We were attacked by Me 110s, Me 210s and FW 190s, which caused a lot of damage. The German fighters lined up wingtip to wingtip off to our right, out of range of our .50 calibers. About eighteen of them were lined up like a row of battleships and when they fired simultaneously, it was like a naval broadside. They fired air-to-air rockets, one of which went right over our right wing by about five feet. I felt sure it would hit the top turret but it missed us."

Altogether twenty-two bombers and twelve American fighters were lost on the raid and twenty-three German fighters were claimed destroyed. The figures by themselves bear scant detail to the casualties on board the surviving Fortresses that made it back to England. Leslie G. Thibodeau, the flight-engineer/top turret gunner aboard *Pegasus Too* from the 388th Bomb Group, remembers,

"Lieutenant Brown, our navigator, was hit pretty badly under the armpit as he was getting in some navigational reading. The bombardier, Lieutenant Kenneth Kelly, and I had to remove our winter flying clothes to keep him warm. We gave him a shot of morphine and put a cigarette in his mouth once in a while. The flak hit an artery as the blood was about an inch thick all over his maps; of course, the blood was frozen."

On New Year's Eve, VIII Bomber Command completed its second year in England with all-out raids on airfields in France. Missions of this nature were usually considered milk-runs compared to the ones over stiffly defended targets in

Two Fortresses of the 305th Bomb Group collided during a training flight on 15th November 1943. All twenty men aboard were killed. The aircraft were 42-30666 and 42-29953.

The crew of Pegasus Too. (Leslie G. Thibodeau)

Germany. Robert "Peck" Wilcox, a bombardier in Lieutenant Marvin H. Bender's crew in *Iron Ass*, in the 510th Bomb Squadron, the 351st Bomb Group at Polebrook, recalls:

"I sat bolt upright in my bunk. The Sergeant with his GI flash-light was awakening crews. He said, 'Lieutenant Wilcox, Lieutenant Freeman, breakfast is being served. Briefing at 0230 hours.' I shook my head, trying to clear the cobwebs and get awake. My gosh! I hadn't been in the sack very long. I had got back from Peterborough about midnight and had been on a mission over Germany the day before. I hadn't hardly figured on another mission today but, Oh well! get these missions over with and back to the States. I had qualified for the Air Medal the previous day so I only had twenty to go.

"We met Bender and Grupp, our pilot and co-pilot, at the mess hall and had our bacon and eggs with plenty of coffee and not much talk. About everyone figured we would "sit down" on this, the last day of the year, and almost everyone was planning a New Year's Eve party. I know Andy, our engineer, Harold Long, the assistant engineer, and I were looking forward to going back to Peterborough for a gala New Year's Eve. In the briefing room was another surprise. A lot of high brass were there in their flying clothes and the briefing officer told us, 'We're going on a milk-run to bomb the docks at Bordeaux. We'll be flying over water most of the way at 12,000 feet. You won't have to wear oxygen masks all the time and you won't have to wear the heavy flying suits until we get ready to go in over the target area. If the target should be socked in by clouds, we'll come back and hit the secondary target, the airport at Cognac. Major Blaylock of the 510th Squadron will lead the mission. Colonel Hatcher (the CO), will be in the lead plane.'

"We were to fly number two, right off Major Blaylock's wing. After briefing we caught our truck out to our plane, stopping en route to get our .50 caliber machine-guns. At the plane everything went well except that Plunkett, our ball turret gunner, wasn't with us. He had been grounded by the medics because of a bad cold. His replacement was Collins, who had several missions under his belt and both Andy and Long said he was OK.

"The trip went well. It was good to do without flak so heavy you could get out and walk on it. We made our turn and went in over France and, sure enough, the Bordeaux area was covered with a thick cloud cover so we headed for Cognac. It wouldn't take too long to get there because Cognac is only about seventy-five to eighty miles from Bordeaux. The formation was in good shape and was pulled in close. There were some scattered clouds but no flak and no fighters. Up ahead I saw our target. Already the lead bombardier was sighting in on it and on we flew. I wondered why we weren't taking any evasive action. We were closing fast when, all of a sudden, all hell broke loose. The lead plane was the victim of a direct hit (Colonel Hatcher was later reported to be a POW). Our plane was hit; the air was turbulent. A big hole had been blasted in the nose. I dropped our bombs but no one had a chance to look down. Planes seemed to be going down all over. The formation was shot to pieces, I would say. We had an engine on fire and I remember Bender asking Collins about the damage and the fire. We made a circle all by ourselves and we were all alone. I mean all alone. What was left of the formation had headed for England but we were all of the opinion that we had lost several B-17s over the target area from some intense flak. (Altogether, the 351st lost nine B-17s.)

"Then it was Bender over the intercom, He said, 'We will be unable to make it back to England. We are too far from Switzerland to go there and the plane may explode at any time.' So he gave the order to bale out. No one questioned it. I went out through the bomb bay after Freeman and Andy." Andy Anderson walked out through Spain in one month and Harold Freeman followed him out in three months. "Peck" Wilcox remained at large in France until September 1944 when he linked up with the Seventh Army during the liberation. The rest of the crew were made POWs. After landing, the one regret "Peck" Wilcox had was, "It was a long way from home and I wasn't going to be in Peterborough for any New Year's Eve party."

Chapter 10
The Battles of Big Week

Fog and rain grounded the bombers until 4th January 1944 when the 8th visited Kiel. Bad weather interfered with the mission so the First Division returned to the port while unescorted groups in the Third Division spearheaded an assault on enemy airfields in France. The 91st Bomb Group lifted off from Bassingbourn to become the first group in the 8th to reach 100 missions, although it had paid dearly for the privilege, losing more aircraft and crews on missions than any other group.

The 94th Bomb Group was assigned Bordeaux airfield and for Cliff Hatcher, who was flying his tenth mission, in *Belle of Maryland*, it was one of the toughest missions he had flown. "For some reason the powers-that-be decided that the best route to Bordeaux was to fly straight in as if we were going to Germany, then turn due south and fly the whole length and breadth of France and out to sea, hitting the target as we went. We came under constant enemy attack from the time we hit France until we headed out to sea across the Bay of Biscay. Then we had to fly over the Normandy Peninsula and we were hit again by fighters. Three FW 190s queued up as we approached Bordeaux and the leader turned in towards our formation for a head-on attack. The two wingmen must have been trainees because they peeled off and headed for home. The leader was shot down but another three queued up, this time in front of us. They must have been veterans because they barreled in, straight at us. Trimble, the bombardier, shot at the three as they bore in and was credited with one "kill" and with dam-

aging the other. All three were burning. Our left waist gunner and our tail-gunner each claimed a Bf 109.

"When we were over the Bay of Biscay I motioned Kacsuta, the pilot, to take over but I couldn't take my hand off the throttles. I had my palm and fingers gripped over the top. My hand was literally frozen to the throttles (we had been under constant attack for maybe three hours). I finally had to take my other hand and use it to peel off each finger at a time. My hand hurt for days later. Over Normandy we ran low on ammo. Trimble had exhausted his in the chin turret and joined Ball, the navigator, in the nose. He began firing the flexible .50 caliber cheek gun while Ball fired the flexible .50 on the port side. Suddenly their guns jerked to a stop. They looked at them in disbelief only to discover that they had both been firing from the same ammo belt!" (*Belle of Maryland* made it back to Bury St Edmunds, but four other B-17s from the 94th, including *Lil' Butch*, did not.)

The 5th January missions were the last under the auspices of VIII Bomber Command. The 15th Air Force had now been established in Italy and it was decided to embrace both the 8th and 15th in a new headquarters called US Strategic Air Forces, Europe, at Bushey Park, Teddington, Middlesex, previously Headquarters, 8th Air Force. General Carl "Tooey" Spaatz returned to England to command the new organization while Doolittle assumed command of the 8th Air Force with its headquarters moving to High Wycombe. Lieutenant General Ira C. Eaker was transferred to the Mediterranean theater. Eaker had built up the 8th Air Force from nothing and Churchill told him in January 1944, "The predictions you made to me at Casablanca last February about our combined bomber missions, including 'round the clock bombing' are now being verified. I no longer have any doubt that they will prove completely valid."

Jimmy Doolittle, the famed Tokyo leader and former air racer, was well known to American airmen. His directive was simple: "Win the air war and isolate the battlefield." To help do this he was given two more heavy bombardment groups during January 1944. First to arrive in the United Kingdom was the 452nd Bomb Group, commanded by Lieutenant Colonel Herbert O. Wangeman, which was based at Deopham Green, ten miles southwest of Norwich. Close on its heels were the crews of the 457th Bomb Group, commanded by Colonel James R. Luper. By the end of the month all but two B-17s, which had crashed in Northern Ireland, had flown into their base at Glatton, Huntingdonshire.

One by one the Fortresses flew in, circling Conington village and rattling the windows with the noise of their Wright Cyclone engines. In turn each B-17 thumped down on to the concrete and rolled to a stop at its allotted dispersal point. The crews, stiff and tired and a little deaf in the sudden silence of switched-off engines, were no doubt curious and wondering what to expect as they climbed down from their aircraft. Some were anxious to get into action while others were apprehensive about what was to come, but all were united in the general disapproval of the damp Fenland murk and mud which surrounded them in that English January.

Once arrived in England, the 457th was assigned to the First Bomb Division, joining the 351st at Polebrook and the 401st at Deenthorpe as part of the 94th Combat Wing. The 452nd, meanwhile was assigned to the Third Bomb Division, joining the 96th and 388th Bomb Groups in the 45th Combat Wing. The two divisions now totaled twenty B-17 groups and Doolittle had plans to increase this number.

The first mission under the auspices of the USSAFE, was on 7th January when the B-17s were sent to Ludwigshaven. The 8th lost twelve bombers and seven fighters on the raid but considerable damage was caused to various chemical and substitute war material plants. The twin city of Mannheim was also heavily hit and damage was caused to the engineering and transport industries. Four days later a maximum effort comprising all three bomb divisions, was mounted on aircraft factories at Waggum, Halberstadt, and Oschersleben in the Brunswick area, a city notorious for its flak and fighter defenses. Since the destruction of the FW 190 plant at Marienburg in October 1943, the Oschersleben plant at Brunswick had become the principal producer of this German fighter. All bombing was to be carried out using visual sightings with the Third Division stoking up fires created by the First and Second Divisions, but, if the weather intervened, crews were briefed to bomb the city of Brunswick using PFF techniques.

Heavy rain pounded the bases in the east of England and heavy cloud began drifting across the Channel, Holland, and into Germany. Command allowed the mission to proceed in the hope that the cloud would clear. For two hours the bombers assembled into their intricate formations and then crews ploughed on across the Channel, conscious that the fighter support would be severely restricted or abandoned altogether. The fighters did manage to take off but they soon became lost in the cloud layers over England and many were forced to abort the mission. The Luftwaffe *Gruppen* in eastern Germany were not affected by the cloudy conditions and were able to takeoff and mass for a concen-

George Kacsuta's crew at Rougham, together with ground crew. Kacsuta is kneeling on the left; Cliff Hatcher is on the wing, right, Trueman Ball, navigator, is kneeling on the right and Kenton H. Trimble is standing fourth from left. (Hatcher)

Temptation of the 96th Bomb Group was badly damaged during the Frankfurt mission of 4th February 1944. It crashed at East Shropham, and was written off. The famous ball turret beneath the fuselage can be clearly seen in its lowered position. The gunner had an unobstructed field of fire below the bomber.

trated attack, the strength of which had not been seen since the Schweinfurt battles of October 1943. With the American escort seriously depleted the order went out to the Second and Third Divisions to abandon the mission, but the First Division, which was about 100 miles from Brunswick, was allowed to continue. The First Division was being led by the 303rd Bomb Group and Brigadier General Robert Travis flew as Task Force Commander aboard *The Eightball*, piloted by Lieutenant Colonel Bill Calhoun, CO of the 359th Squadron. Just past Dummer Lake the formation was bounced by over 200 enemy fighters. General Travis was to tell newsmen later,

"The fighters . . . in spite of our escort, came at us in bunches. Our first attack was from four FW 190s, the next from thirty FW 190s, then twelve and they just kept coming. They attacked straight through the formation and from all angles without even rolling over. They seemed to let up just a little when we started our bombing run. There was a period of three minutes only, from the time the fighters first started to make their attack until they left us, when they were not around."

Joe Wroblewski flew in the lead position of the low squadron in the 351st Bomb Group at about 19,000 feet.

"One wing was ahead of us and we were second with most of our fighter escort. Just ahead of us planes kept falling, spinning and exploding from somewhere up above. Our fighters and the enemy were dog fighting just prior to the recall message. Then our fighters left us. I saw one crippled B-17 going back below us escorted by two Bf 109s. The

Fortress had its landing gear down as a signal that the crew was going to bale out. The German fighters were flying alongside to allow the crew to leave the aircraft before shooting it down.

"Any bomber that fell out of formation was a dead duck. I watched a B-17 off to our right by itself. An Me 110 got on its tail and really poured tracers into the bomber. It caught fire and, as the flames licked around the tail, I could see the tail-gunner still firing back at the Jerry. Finally, the bomber climbed straight up and fell off into a spin, burning and breaking up. One yellow-nosed Bf 109 came in between us and our wingman with his guns blazing. He must have put a few holes in our tail but no one was hurt. Our waist gunner fell back away from his gun for a second when he saw this plane so close and when he did start shooting again he shot through our tail and through the B-17 flying next to us. The enemy fighters kept falling and exploding all around us but still they kept coming in without giving us a breathing spell. They tried real hard to break up our formation but we hung together for dear life. All I could hear over the intercom was, 'Fighter coming in at 5 o'clock, one at 7 o'clock, another at 9 o'clock low. Fighter coming in at 10 o'clock level!' It was almost useless to call them out. There were so many coming in from every direction.

"At about this time many thoughts began to go through my mind. My parachute was just behind my seat and the temptation to snap it on and get the hell out of it was very strong. But then I thought about the other crew members. I don't doubt that they were just as scared as I was but at least they could shoot back. I thought about the training that had led to our present situation and about how we had looked forward to being in combat. But that was before all this. Right then I would have settled for being just a potato peeler, mess cook, or whatever, washing kettles for the duration. Then Saxon said, 'Lead him Henkel, lead him a little more!' The tail-gunner came in with, 'I got him! I got an Me 210! The pilot's baling out!'

"Somehow one of our P-51s got separated from his group so he tagged along with us. We were very grateful because he fought as long as his fuel permitted, chasing the enemy until his ammunition was gone. Then he just dived after the fighters to divert them from the B-17s. Watching this one fighter escort bolstered our confidence in survival and we all admired his guts. Later we learned his name was Major Howard. He got back to base safely.

"Our group got separated from the wing for just a short time while ready to bomb and in the mix-up we dropped our bombs on a small town. There were two holes in the railroad and three in the main highway. It was a great relief just to get rid of the bombs under the conditions."

Meanwhile, the 94th Bomb Group, flying at the head of the 4th Combat Wing leading the Third Division, was only twenty-five miles from its objective at Waggum when the order to abort was given, so Lieutenant Colonel Louis G. Thorup, flying in the lead ship, decided to press on to the target. The remaining groups in the Third Division and the entire Liberator force withdrew leaving the 4th Wing to continue alone. Only forty-nine Mustangs remained to provide support over the target area for the two groups that were left. A squadron of Lightnings managed to rendezvous with the bomber stream but had to turn back before the bombers reached the outskirts of Brunswick. Cliff Hatcher flying *Belle of Maryland* in the number seven position of the 94th Bomb Group formation says, "It was a typical SNAFU mission and finished with some 94th aircraft flying in other group formations. Two of our crews flew with the 447th and we started off with another group. The target was clouded over and Thorup decided to do a 360 degree turn over the target. When he turned, the 385th and the 447th did not follow."

The 385th and 447th bombed the target with devastating results, the former group placing seventy-three percent of its bombs within 1,000 feet of the MPI. Then it was the turn of the 94th. Nineteen B-17s placed seventy-three percent of their 100lb incendiaries within 1,000 feet of the MPI to cause widespread damage to the Waggum plant. The bombing of the Junkers plant at Halberstadt was described as "good" and the results at Oschersleben were even better.

On the route home the B-17s were subjected to continual aerial assaults by the Luftwaffe and few bombers escaped punishment. Cliff Hatcher continues,

"Before the battle was over the three aircraft in front of me were gone. We were attacked by almost every type of German fighter and lost seven of our bombers, including the one that was flying with the 447th. Our aircraft was involved in one hell of a fight on the way out. 20mm shells punched heck out of the nose section and how our navigator and bombardier survived, I'll never know. The shells started electrical fires and punched two gaping holes in the left side of the plane. Trimble observed that the right side was in an even worse condition! We got back to Bury with an engine on fire and the ship was in such a badly damaged condition it never flew again. We counted over 1,000 holes in the *Belle of Maryland*, not including the two big ones. The ship was cannibalized and made the group's losses eight in all."

For its action over Brunswick, the 94th received its second Presidential Unit Citation, as Hatcher recalls.

"We paid a hell of a price to get it. I knew I was lucky to be alive and the air war had changed for me. Shortly afterwards I was sent for a 'flak furlough' at Coomb House in southern England. We were in such bad shape our flight surgeon, 'Doc' Miller, went along with us. He too was getting 'flak happy' riding along with his boys!"

Other groups also paid a hell of a price. The 303rd lost ten bombers and the 351st, seven. In all, thirty-four of the 174 Fortresses dispatched to Oschersleben were shot down while two wings assigned the plant at nearby Halberstadt came through practically unscathed. In August 1944 all the First Division groups that took part in the raid were awarded Presidential Unit Citations.

Vast banks of strato-cumulus clouds covering most of Germany prevented visual bombing of targets so attacks on targets in France throughout the remainder of January and early February became the order of the day. One exception was on 30th January when the 8th returned to the aircraft factories at Brunswick. A record 778 heavies were dispatched and bombing was carried out using PFF techniques. Of the twenty-nine missions flown during January and February 1944, thirteen were to V-1 flying bomb sites. These strikes were no longer regarded as milk-runs because the Germans, having realized their vulnerability to air attack, moved in additional flak batteries and the bombing altitude was raised to 20,000 feet.

On 5th February the ranks of the bomber formations were swelled by the addition of the 452nd Bomb Group. The reinforcements were needed badly for Doolittle had been biding his time, waiting for a period of relatively fine weather in which to mount a series of raids on the German aircraft industry. The meteorologists informed Doolittle that the week 20-25th February, which was to go down in history as "Big-Week," would be ideal for such an offensive.

All American, *42-30173 of the 95th Bomb Group, failed to return on 10th February 1944.* (Glenn Infield)

Like so many mornings in England, the sky in the early hours of 20th February was clear but a few stray clouds drifting in from the North Sea gave warning of an instrument assembly above 10/10ths cloud by takeoff time. A force of over 800 heavies was assembled as the anticipated cloud scudded across eastern England, bringing with it snow squalls which threatened to disrupt the mission. The First and Second Divisions were briefed to hit the Messerschmitt 109 plants at Leipzig, bombed only a few hours earlier by RAF Bomber Command. The Third Division, meanwhile, would fly an equally long and arduous route to Posen in Poland.

Lieutenant Lowell Watts, pilot of *Blitzin' Betsy* in the 388th Bomb Group, who would be flying his nineteenth mission this day, viewed the map in the briefing room at Knettishall with a sense of foreboding.

"The map was covered as always but there was an extension on the right-hand side of it. Our regular map, which reached from England to east of Berlin, was too small for this raid! The cover was pulled away and there it was! The red tape ran out from England, over the North Sea to Denmark, across it, out over the Baltic Sea, then back in over eastern Germany and into Poland. Posen was our target. It lay almost 1,000 miles away.

"'Men,' Colonel William B. David (the CO) was saying. 'Your bomb load is 5,000lb; gas load, naturally, maximum. Don't start your engines before you have to. You'll need all the gas you have. Altitude is 11,000 feet. Over the Baltic you'll climb to 17,000, which is your bombing altitude. If you lose an engine over or near to the target check your gas and, if you don't think you can make it, head for Sweden. Our wing is bombing Posen. The 13th

The crew of Blitzin' Betsy *of the 388th Bomb Group. Standing, left to right; Watts, Kennedy, Murphy, and Kelly. Kneeling; Ramsey, Hess, Finkle, Sweeney, Brassfield, and Taylor. Hess, Sweeney, Brassfield, and Taylor were killed in action during the 6th March raid on Berlin. The rest of the crew were taken POW.* (Watts)

Wing will go part of the way but are bombing about where you will hit the German coast, so you'll be alone all the way back. The rest of the 8th will be bombing targets all over central and southern Germany. You'll have no fighter escort so shoot at anything you see in the way of a fighter. Keep on the ball and good luck to all of you.'"

"I was very careful that morning to leave my personal belongings in the safe keeping of the PW room. Our chances of needing them that night seemed rather slim. Out at the plane we double-checked everything with unusual care and threw in a couple of extra boxes of ammo. For the first time on a combat mission we noticed a box of 'K' rations in the ship. We'd need some food before we got home on a haul like this one. Just before taxi time we started the engines. We'd run them up while lining up for the takeoff. There was no point using any gas we could save. We took off, climbed through the clouds and assembled. The rendezvous time was cut in half and we started out over the North Sea, tightening up the formation more as we went along and climbing to 11,000 feet before leveling off. We used the lowest possible power setting and the lowest rpm possible and flew as smoothly as we could in an effort to make our gas last.

"Near Denmark the clouds began breaking up and, by the time we crossed the Danish coast, it was clear as a bell beneath us. Something else met us besides good weather - Jerry fighters. Off on our left a group was under heavy fighter attack. Two bombers went down. Later, we saw ten 'chutes drop from another crippled plane but, pilotless as it was, this ship, slowly losing altitude, continued on eastwards and not until we were across the Danish peninsula did we lose sight of it.

"The FW 190s attacking us kept sweeping in until we were well out over the Baltic and the quaint red-roofed villages of Denmark had blended into the horizon behind us. We changed course to the southeast and climbed to 17,000 feet. Clouds were piling up beneath us again and the German coast was covered by them. On and on we flew. We were almost to Poland now and Ju 88s, Me 110s and Me 210s had replaced the Focke-Wulfs, making steady, unrelenting diving attacks on our formation. Nowhere could we see a break in the overcast. There was a ruling that no target in an occupied country would be bombed except by contact bombing. Targets in Poland came under this category so, after flying those hundreds of miles, many of them under fighter attack, we had to turn back, still carrying our bombs, tired, hungry, with the fighters still on us and a feeling of frustration in the knowledge that Posen's factories would still be turning out Focke-Wulfs on the morrow.

"We checked our gas tanks. They were less than half full and we were still lugging our bombs. The loss of only one engine would be enough to make us run out of gas. As it was, it would be nip and tuck. We should just make it but maybe we wouldn't. We were still at 17,000 feet, using a lot more gas than we would had we dropped our bombs and gone back down to 11,000. Sixteen of our twenty-one planes were still in formation. Our other two groups were a little better off. We had lost the left wing and the 'diamond' ships in our element, the second element of the low squadron. The VHF crackled to life. 'Wolfgang Yellow, Wolfgang Yellow, this is Wolfgang White calling. Open bomb bay doors. We're approaching our target.' Now over Germany, we were going to bomb a secondary target by PFF through clouds.

"Our bomb doors swung open as we fell in behind the 96th Bomb Group which contained the PFF ship. Suddenly, flak appeared - big, ugly, mushrooming billows of black, blossoming out around the angry red flash of the shells' explosions. The flak became thicker and more accurate as we neared the point of bomb release. Our ship bounced as the sound of ripping metal brought a lump to our throats. A big jagged hole had made its appearance between our number one and two engines. The number two gas gauge still showed no indication of a leak. There were two rips in the number two cowling but the oil pressure was up and the engine was running smoothly. Ahead, two long streams of white arched down beneath the lead ship in the 96th formation. Those were the marker bombs of the PFF ship. In a few seconds we were nearing those markers. As we passed them we dumped our bombs, happy to feel the plane leap upwards, free of its load. The flak pounded us for about a minute longer, then it began to disappear. At last we were heading home, free of our bombs and able to cut down on our power settings. Only a few Ju 88s were around. Now and then they would lob a rocket at us, careful to stay out of range of our .50s. One formation of the 88s lined up behind us and started pumping rockets at us. The projectiles sailed into the high squadron, bursting like flak. Fire broke out on the right wing of one plane. It flew for a minute longer, then rolled up on one wing and started down. Suddenly, there was a flash, a huge billowy puff of smoke, and jagged pieces of broken, twisted metal fluttered aimlessly earthwards.

"The hours dragged on. We'd been up almost eight hours now and we were crossing Denmark with the North Sea still separating us from England. Leaving the coast we let down to 10,000 feet and loosened the formation as the fighters fell away. A glance at the gas gauges was anything but heartening. It would be a close one getting back today. We checked everything we might need if we should have to ditch. The sun was riding low in the west as we neared England. Every few minutes one of our planes would drop out of formation to save gas. A few we heard calling pitifully to Air Sea Rescue and soon, below us, one of the lone planes would glide with a splash into the sea, its gas exhausted. 'Pilot from navigator, we're over England. You can see a spot of coastline off to our right through that little hole in the clouds.'

"We watched the radio compass swing around, telling us we were passing over our field. Our squadron leader zoomed gently up and down. His left wing ship peeled off and was followed by the squadron lead ship, his right wing ship and then our plane. The ships were letting down on a heading of ninety degrees, disappearing one by one into the fluffy folds of white below us. Soon we were skimming the clouds, then we were in the soup, dark, lonely and uninviting. I was watching only the instruments now, heading ninety degrees, flaps one third down, wheels down, air speed 150, vertical speed 500 feet per minute. Down, down, down we went, the gloom darkening each second. At 1,000 feet we were still on instruments. We were all dead tired but during the let-down we forgot it for the moment while eager eyes tried to pierce the murk for signs of the ground or other planes which might hit us. At 750 feet we broke out. It was raining but visibility was fair. We turned almost 180 degrees until the radio compass read '0' and flew on until landmarks became familiar. Finally, we saw flares up ahead and soon the runway became visible. A plane was

42-37796, Fletcher's Castoria II of the 100th Bomb Group, after its crash in Holland during the mission to Brunswick on 21st February 1944. Following the crash the aircraft was badly damaged by fire which destroyed the rear fuselage. Fletcher and his crew were made POWs. (USAF)

The 452nd Bomb Group during a raid on the airplane assembly plant at Romilly. (Sam Young)

on its approach. Another, too close to it, pulled up and went around again. We started our approach and let down with the fuel warning lights on and the gas gauges reading almost empty. We couldn't stay up much longer. Kennedy turned the turbos full on in case we should need the power if we had to go around again. Old *Blitzin' Betsy* settled down, floated a second, then touched the runway. We rolled to the end of the runway, another mission completed. Then we realized how tired we were."

The same tiredness prevailed on the First Division's effort at Leipzig. As the formation crossed into Germany it encountered single and twin-engined fighters of almost every type, including Stukas, He 111s, Dornier 17s and Focke-Wulf 190s. The German pilots adopted American single-engined fighter tactics in an effort to gain favorable attacking positions. Joe Wroblewski was in the 351st Bomb Group formation.

"About twenty Bf 109s hit us just before the target and came in four at a time head-on. They flew right through our formation and slow-rolled beautifully while shooting. In the excitement some gunner from our own formation shot through one of our engines, cutting a gas balance line and mixture control cable. Besides having a few screwed up indicators on the panel and a worried mind, everything was okay."

In a last resort to deter the First Division, the Germans employed cable bombing methods. They did not work. The leading 401st Bomb Group, led by Colonel Harold W. Bowman, the CO, at the head of the 94th Wing, flew on to the briefed point west of Brunswick and diverged to bomb the target. Despite a heavy flak barrage during the bomb run, which heavily damaged Colonel Bowman's aircraft, the formation bombed with excellent results. Colonel Bowman recalls,

"Because the weather was uncertain we were provided with a PFF crew especially trained for instrument bombing. The weather en route was indeed bad and preparations were made for aiming by instrument means but, as we approached the target area, the clouds opened up to 'scattered' and a visual sighting was made. The result was, for our group, 100 percent of our bombs within 1,000 feet of the aiming point."

(Direct hits were achieved on the principal assembly shop at the Erla Maschinenwerk Messerschmitt production factory and its other large assembly building was observed to be on fire as the bombers left the target area.)

Over the target 42-38109 of the 364th Bomb Squadron, 305th Bomb Group, piloted by 1st/Lieutenant William R. Lawley, Jr., was hit by an 88mm flak shell which did not explode when it went right through the left horizontal stabilizer and cut the control cable. Suddenly, the B-17 became very nose heavy. At "Bombs Away" the bombs refused to go and Lawley tried to salvo them but this failed. (The racks had moisture on them and they were frozen). In the meantime, the rest of the formation had moved out because when they released their bombs their B-17s "jumped" a hundred feet or so. Lawley managed to get back into formation once, but he knew he could not get home like this as he was pulling too much power.

Enemy fighters singled him out, and on the first head-on pass they were hit all over. A shell came through the right windshield and hit Lieutenant Paul Murphy, the co-pilot, in the face and exploded. He put his hands over his face and fell forward, hitting the control stick and knocking it out of

Lawley's hands, forcing the B-17 into a steep spiral. Almost immediately, the B-17 dived from 28,000 feet to 12,000 feet. The left windshield was covered with blood, but Lawley's view was clear and by looking out he realized that they were descending and that the aircraft was in a turn. Lawley was able to correct it. He got the dead co-pilot off the controls with his right hand while bringing the aircraft out of its dive with his left. The group reported that they had spun in. Murphy's death slump had sent the B-17 spinning down, which the enemy fighter pilots must have thought was a fatal dive, because they passed up the stricken B-17 and did not attack again. By the time the B-17 had leveled out Lawley had already rung the alarm bell to signal the crew to get out and then he received word that two gunners in the back were too critically wounded to bail out. Harry G. Mason, the bombardier, came up and said, "Can we make this thing fly." Lawley replied, "I don't know. We'll try." All the crew agreed to ride out their luck. Two engines that had been set on fire were extinguished and Harry Mason managed to salvo the bombs. There seemed a good chance they could make it safely to England. The bombardier later took over the controls when Lawley was on the verge of unconsciousness, but he recovered sufficiently to pilot the stricken bomber to the east coast of England, where one engine died of fuel starvation. As Lawley made his approach to a Canadian airfield near Grimsby, Lincolnshire, the first available airfield, another engine burst into flames. Despite this he belly-landed the B-17 safely on the one remaining engine and all the crew were rescued. Lawley was awarded the Medal of Honor.

Two other Medals of Honor were awarded for actions this day. During an attack by enemy fighters a cannon shell entered the cockpit of 42-31763 *Ten Horsepower*, a B-17 of the 510th Bomb Squadron, belonging to the 351st Bomb Group. Flight Officer Ronald E. Bartley, the co-pilot, was killed instantly. The right side of the pilot's face, 2nd/Lieutenant Clarence R. Nelson, was torn off by spinters rendering him unconscious. Sergeant Joseph F. Rex, the radio-operator, was also wounded in the attack and the bomber suffered severe damage. 2nd/Lieutenant Joseph R. Martin, the bombardier, decided that *Ten Horsepower* was finished and told the crew to bale out. Martin salvoed the bombs and then left the aircraft through the forward escape hatch. Staff Sergeant Archie Mathies, aged twenty-five, the Stonehouse, Scotland born ball-turret gunner, and Sergeant Carl W. Moore, the top turret gunner/engineer, decided to see what could be done for the pilot. They clambered into the cockpit. 2nd/Lieutenant Walter E. Truemper, the navigator, had also remained in the aircraft and went up front to help Mathies. After much effort the body of Bartley was dragged out of his seat and placed in the nose.

The windshield was smashed but Mathies, who had a couple of hours flying experience, took over the wheel. He believed he could fly the bomber back to England. Mathies and Truemper took it in turns to fly *Ten Horsepower* while the rest of the crew struggled to remove the dead co-pilot. His limp body forced both men to crouch on the floor between the seats, using only the elevators and ailerons to keep the B-17 airborne. Mathies had the greater knowledge of how to fly a B-17 and completed most of the route home. At times the cold became so intense, because of the smashed windshield, that Truemper and the others had to take it in turns at the controls. Mathies and Truemper did not know how to land a B-17 so, when they reached Polebrook, Mathies called up the control tower and told them of their

Begin the Beguine - She Dood It, of the 306th Bomb Group. This aircraft later served in the 381st Bomb Group at Ridgewell.

predicament. The crew was told to bale out over the airfield but, because of the injured crew, Mathies and Truemper volunteered to remain aboard and try to bring the crippled bomber in for a crash-landing.

Colonel Eugene Romig, CO of the 351st Bomb Group, Colonel Elzia Ledoux, tower officer and a flight engineer, took off in B-17G 42-30499 *My Princess* with the intention of flying alongside *Ten Horsepower* and assisting in the landing by radioing instructions to Mathies. Unfortunately radio contact could not be made between the two bombers and visual directions were impossible because *Ten Horsepower* was flying too erratically to allow Romig to get in close. Romig decided the only course of action was for Mathies to fly the bomber towards the sea and bale out. Mathies and Truemper still refused to leave their pilot and elected to try and land. The tower radioed a set of instructions and the now crowded flight line waited as Mathies came in for the first approach. *Ten Horsepower* was too high and he had to abort. At this point five of the crew baled out, three of them sustaining broken legs. *Ten Horsepower* was by now far to the south of Polebrook, and heading for Molesworth airfield. This second approach was also too high so Romig and Ledoux, via the tower at Polebrook, instructed Mathies and Treumper to head north and try to land at their home base. However, *Ten Horsepower* drifted northeast, passing Sawtry, the A1 road and Glatton airfield. Here the B-17 veered off to the left in a sweeping, diving, turn past the control tower. Believing the crew were attempting to land, ground staff fired off red flares. *Ten Horsepower* recrossed the A1 and headed towards the village of Denton, seven miles from RAF Upwood.

From the actions of the errant B-17, which suddenly throttled back, it was obvious to Romig and Ledoux that Mathies and Treumper were going to attempt to put the B-17 down in a field (near Denton Hill). At 1700 hours, in a very large open field just south of Stilton, *Ten Horsepower* touched down. Romig and Ledoux estimated that the aircraft was traveling at 200mph when it hit. The B-17 rolled for fifty yards or more before hitting a mound of earth and then it cart-wheeled before breaking into pieces. Mathies and Truemper died in the wreckage. Nelson was reportedly still alive when rescuers reached the wreckage, but he died later. Mathies and Truemper were posthumously awarded the Medal of Honor.

That night the crews in the 351st went to their barracks and caught up on some much needed sleep. Joe Wroblewski planned on taking a short catnap before dinner but he was so exhausted after the mission it was not until the following evening that he awoke again. Such exhaustion could quickly lead to total breakdown and flight surgeons were ever-watchful for the first signs of combat fatigue. Bill Rose, in the 92nd Bomb Group, recalls,

"The squadron flight surgeon drank with us and palled around with us but kept a very watchful eye on us. He knew what shape we were in, how many combat missions we had flown and what the crew situation was. He was the one who dispensed the pills. In February-March 1944 I was on pills to put me to sleep and on the morning of a mission I was on pills to wake me up and get me going. Sleeping on pills at night became so bad that we started taking pills from our escape kits."

Usually, crews known to be "flak happy" were sent to rest homes. Sometimes the exhaustion and tension of flying so many missions during a short period such as "Big Week" had a disastrous effect on crews. Bill Rose continues,

"We had four officer crews in one Nissen hut. The night before a mission I would go over to the barracks and write letters and get some early sleep because you never knew when you would be alerted to fly a mission the next day. One night one of the officer crews packed all their belongings. It made me wonder what insight they must have had to know they would not survive the next mission. Sure enough, the next day they went down.

"We had another crew who went on a bombing mission to southern Germany. After bombing the target we turned around and came home but this crew took off for Switzerland. When we got back I checked their clothes in the hut. Everything was there except for their Class A uniforms which they had worn on the raid to prove their identity. They had just given up fighting."

There was no let-up in the campaign against the German aircraft industry and on 21st February the heavies were out again. The bomber stream was swelled by thirty-six B-17s of the 457th Bomb Group, which was making its debut, and principal targets were the aircraft factories at Brunswick. However, thick cloud obscured the objectives and bombing had to be completed using PFF techniques. Many groups attacked targets of opportunity and airfields and aircraft depots were heavily bombed.

The following day the elements were responsible for collisions during assembly and the Third Division was forced to abandon the mission completely. However, the First Division, led by Colonel "Mo" Preston, CO of the 379th Bomb Group, continued to the Junkers works at Oschersleben. Colonel Preston says,

"There was pretty solid low undercast so as Strike Force Commander I directed strikes on targets of opportunity. Thereafter, the problem became one of finding our way home, The overcast extended indefinitely in all directions and we simply had no way of navigating except by dead reckoning and guesswork. Somewhere in our wanderings the wing in which I was flying suddenly came under fire -

big black heavy intense flak. Inside the lead airplane it seemed that we could feel every burst as it went off beneath us and bounced our plane around. Ahead and very close to us we could see not only the black cloud of each flak burst but also the flash of the explosion. This was unusual, for normally one doesn't see that much. We took evasive action and it may have helped but it didn't seem to get us out of the flak pattern.

"Meanwhile, my tail-gunner was reporting planes going down, one of them at least, as a result of a direct hit which exploded the plane. On this one there were no parachutes. Finally, we came out of it but not until we had lost four planes. This was the worst flak I ever saw and the heaviest loss to flak I ever experienced. I had already taken a piece of flak in my right foot from an isolated burst or two we had encountered on the way in to the target. Now I got another piece as a souvenir. It was about three inches long and an inch wide and hit me in the side, knocking the breath out of me but not penetrating the skin. Fortunately, it was spent when it got there. A Purple Heart for the piece in my foot but nothing for the piece in my hand. It was subsequently calculated that we got the flak from the guns at Cologne. I never wanted to go back to Cologne. I still flinch when I get near that place. A few terrible moments can leave an imprint on a fella.

"The First Bomb Division had scored a notable success at the Junkers works at Oschersleben and Bernberg but lost thirty-nine Fortresses in the day's raids, including seven from the 306th Bomb Group. Enemy fighter interceptions were high despite the hope that a simultaneous attack on Regensburg by the 15th Air Force would split the German fighter force. The 8th had also taken the precaution of flying a diversionary raid, sending some Fortresses to Aalborg in northern Denmark. Bill Rose, who flew with the 92nd Bomb Group, was with them. "The lead pilot took the whole group into 10/10ths cloud, which went all the way up to about 20,000 feet, instead of staying out in the clear and making a 180 degree turn to avoid them. All I could see was the wing of the man we were flying on. In cloud you lose complete orientation and I did not know whether we were up, down, sideways, or anything else. In all the years of flying this was the one and only time I suffered vertigo.

"The sound indicated we were in a screaming dive but I believed in my instruments and rode it out. Eventually, we lost the man we were flying on. All we could do was make a 180 and come out. We broke out of the cloud and I found myself stretched way over in the seat but the plane was flying straight and level just as the instruments indicated. One plane coming out of the cloud flew straight into another plane going in and collided. It looked like a huge oil tank fire at 20,000 feet with nothing but black smoke."

On 23rd February, crews received a much needed respite when weather conditions were the prime reason for keeping the heavies on the ground. Maintenance crews worked around the clock, attempting to get every bomber possible ready for combat. They were needed the next day, 24th February, when Doolittle again dispatched in excess of 800 bombers to targets throughout the Reich. The Second Bomb Division was allocated Gotha, and the Third Division, targets near the Baltic coast. Hearts sank at First Bomb Division group briefings when the curtains were pulled back to reveal their target - the factories at Schweinfurt! However, losses were light and events overshadowed by the Liberator's success, and high losses, at Gotha.

The following day, 25th February, marked the culmination of "Big Week" when the 8th flew its deepest raid into Germany thus far. The First Bomb Division was assigned the Messerschmitt experimental and assembly plants at Augsburg and the fighter plants at Stuttgart, while the Third Division returned to Regensburg for the first time since 17th August 1943 when the B-17s had suffered such devastating losses. The shadow of Schweinfurt and Regensburg was still uppermost in the minds of all the B-17 crews and this time the Third Division would share the bombing role with the Italian-based 15th Air Force, which would bomb Regensburg an hour before the English-based force arrived over the city. The Germans had given top priority to the reconstruction of the Regensburg plant and within six months had restored production to something like its previous output. Although most of the old buildings had been destroyed, several main buildings had been rebuilt including a long assembly shop on a site where three had once stood.

News of the Regensburg strike came only hours after crews had logged twelve hours' flying time during a mission to the Baltic coast. It had not only been the longest raid they had flown so far but also one of the roughest. Lowell Watts and the crew of *Blitzin' Betsy* at Knettishall were still very tired, as all crews were, when they were roused from their fitful sleep at 0300 hours, but the prospect of flying to Regensburg did not seem to sink in.

"Crews had arrived at that mental state", recalls, Watts, "where one more extra long, extra tough raid, meant nothing to us. It was just another raid. As for myself, at least, I'd grown calloused. The tougher the raid now, the better I liked it.

"Beautiful weather greeted us as we assembled over England and headed off across the Channel. We crossed the coast at 21,000 feet, our formation assembled and everything was working OK. It was one of those rare days in the European theater when visibility was unlimited by either fog, clouds, or haze. Just as the enemy coast began passing beneath us, a murderous barrage of flak started coming up. We were supposed to cross the coast between Dieppe and Le Havre but we were evidently too close to Le

Havre. We'd been through heavier flak before but the accuracy of this stuff was hard to beat. They had our altitude perfect. Then they began tracking us and in a matter of seconds those black puffs were riding right along with us. The ship jerked a little to the sound of ripping metal. We'd been hit and hit hard. Our left wing showed a big, ragged hole. A few more bursts got in close enough to leave other hits showing in the nose and fuselage. Givens, flying our left wing, peeled off and headed for England. He'd probably make it back from our present position but he hadn't lasted long. Sweeney turned his ball turret to the front and looked over the bottom of our wing. 'Pilot from ball turret; there are a lot of holes in the wings, especially the left one, but I can't see any gas running out.'

"All four of our engines kept purring away and we were seemingly in pretty fair shape as we flew out of range of the flak. It was time now for our fighter cover to be showing up but they were nowhere in sight. For another thirty minutes we kept flying to the east and still found ourselves out there alone. Something had gone wrong with the timing. Then we began to see fighters but they weren't our own, they were Jerries. Focke-Wulf 190s, Ju 88s, and Messerschmitt 109s were beginning to circle in ever increasing numbers, then they pulled up ahead of us and started their attacks. One B-17 dropped out of formation and lost altitude. 'Chutes appeared beneath it. As we watched him he started burning, leaving a long trail of black smoke behind. The crippled plane dropped fast then seemed to level out a little, sailed over the hills beneath and finally disappeared into a mass of flame and debris which scattered itself over almost half a mile as it hit and exploded. Another B-17 was hit and exploded, almost in the formation. A B-24 seemed to fall apart as the Jerries took on one of the B-24 formations.

"As time wore on we could see the FW 190s peel off from their attacks, dive almost straight down, leveling off just above the ground, make a brief half circle and land on the nearest field. They would taxi in, sit there for five to ten minutes and then we could see the dust behind them as they started up again. In another five minutes they would be back to the attack. It was sort of fascinating to watch that circle complete itself but at the same time very discomforting to realize that these fighters that were hitting us might follow us all the way in and out unless they were shot down. Of course, some of them were, but not enough. There was still no sign of our fighter cover.

"It was almost 1200 when we sighted a column of smoke rising almost to our altitude. It was dead ahead. If that was smoke from Regensburg, then the 15th Air Force had hit it and no question about it. The Alps were clearly discernible to the north of us now. They reminded me quite a little of our own Rockies. About then I was wishing they were the Rockies too. Upon reaching our IP we could easily see the 15th's target. All we had to do was follow that column of smoke down to the earth and there it was, what was left of it at least. We turned in for our bombing run and there above us was the most welcome sight I'd ever seen on a mission; a group of P-38s. At last, our fighters had found us!

"Up ahead the flak was getting thicker and thicker. One of our squadron leads was hit and peeled out of the formation so quickly that his whole squadron was scattered. Only half his planes got back into formation during the bombing run. Back behind us his second element of three ships was trying to catch up with us but they were too far behind. Then the flak got too heavy for us to worry about anyone but ourselves. We settled down on the last of the bomb run. The target was spread out beautifully below us in perfect visibility. A chance like this was a contact bombardier's dream come true. The bombs went out, we closed our bomb bay doors and turned away from the target. Behind us were those three planes, making a bomb run of their own. They looked so vulnerable and all alone back there but they made the run and pulled in with another formation without losing anyone.

"Below us our target was rapidly looking like the other one which had been hit by the 15th Air Force before we had arrived. Smoke was pouring upward, rising to about 20,000 feet. The Jerries were still making things quite interesting, but with our own fighters in the skies, a lot of their attacks were diverted. Now the strain began to tell. We'd done a lot of combat flying during the week and we were beginning to feel its effects. Kennedy and I began trading off on the flying. Both of us were so tired that after about fifteen minutes we just couldn't hold formation, Never in all my missions had I reached the stage where I was absolutely too tired to fly, but I reached it on this raid. During a lull I looked around the formation. Several ships were missing and in three of the missing spots was a queer-looking sight. Three P-38s were flying formation with us. Each of them had lost an engine and had pulled into our formation for protection.

"Hours later we circled Knettishall and set *Blitzin' Bettsy* down on good old terra-firma once again. Every man on the crew was completely fagged, sleepy, stiff, sore, and just generally all-in. We taxied up to our hardstand and tumbled out. Those holes were even bigger and uglier-looking than we had realized. Quite obviously our wing was badly shot up. The gas tank had been hit in several places. Tired as I was, at that particular moment I could have taken my hat off to the engineers who had never seen combat but who had developed the bullet-proof gas tank. Our story of this particular day would have been quite different had those tanks never been designed."

All three divisions of the 8th Air force exacted a heavy toll on the German aircraft plants for the loss of thirty-one bombers. Thereafter, cloud banks over the Continent brought a

42-31134, 569th Bomb Squadron, 390th Bomb Group, en route to Rjukan on 16th November 1943. The aircraft was lost over Nuremburg on 10th September 1944. (Ian McLachlan)

premature end to "Big Week" and enabled higher command time to weigh up the results and implications of their actions over the past five days. Although the 8th had flown some 3,300 bomber sorties and had dropped 6,000 tons of bombs during "Big Week" the destruction was not as great as at first thought. Luftwaffe *Gruppen* were certainly deprived of many replacement aircraft and fighter production was halved the following month, but it had cost 400 bombers and 4,000 casualties to achieve. Unfortunately, the small size high explosive bombs destroyed only the factories, leaving machine tools, lathes, and jigs virtually untouched be-

neath the wreckage. It was only a matter of time before this equipment was recovered from the wrecked plants and put into full production again. However, Doolittle and his staff officers believed the 8th had dealt the German aircraft industry a really severe blow and they now felt confident to strike at Berlin, the biggest prize in the Third Reich.

Chapter 11
Bomb Bays over Big-B

A raid by the 8th Air Force on Berlin had been scheduled for 23rd November the previous year but had been postponed because of bad weather. RAF Bomber Command had been bombing the capital nightly for some time but Berliners had never before been subjected to the round-the-clock bombing which had devastated so many other German cities. "The very thought of making a raid on Berlin was almost terrifying," recalls Robert J. Shoens, a pilot in the 100th Bomb Group. "Rumors began flying thick and fast several weeks before the day arrived, adding to the apprehension and anxiety. Each day we would walk into the briefing sessions wondering if the tape on the wall map would stretch to 'Big-B' that morning. A great sigh of relief could be heard from the crews when the briefing officer pulled back the curtain and the tape went somewhere else. But sooner or later it was sure to come, and it did." The momentous day arrived on the morning of 3rd March 1944. At bases throughout eastern England briefing officers pulled back the curtains to reveal red tapes reaching like groping fingers all the way to Berlin in the heart of Nazi Germany. Whistles and groans greeted the news. "What a birthday treat," thought Cliff Hatcher, as he sat through the briefing at Bury St Edmunds. Only the day before he had celebrated his 21st birthday.

Hatcher was one of thirty-one crews readied at Bury St Edmunds for the raid and the B-17s began taking off in marginal weather conditions. As crews flew on over the North Sea, conditions grew worse. Eventually, the mission was 'scrubbed' but not before a tragic accident occurred. Hatcher says,

"We were midway in the stream in the vicinity of Kiel and kept trying to climb above the fog and cloud. It was hard trying to stay in formation. Unfortunately, we did not get the recall signal until after the groups in front of us and they turned before we did. Suddenly, I looked up and saw what looked like hundreds of B-17s heading straight for us. Lieutenant Donald L. Ahlwardt's ship collided with an approaching B-17 and I flew right through the middle of a black cloud. I could feel the heat from the explosion. We bounced all over the sky and I thought we had had it but, incredibly, we survived and began heading back. We were maddened by the wasteful and needless collision."

The 94th Bomb Group disrupted into chaos after the recall and aircraft flew home in twos and threes, dropping their bombs en route. Hatcher dropped his bombs over Heligoland.

"Coming back we ran into horrendous weather again. Half way across the North Sea we saw a front ahead of us. We were at 30,000 feet. The temperature was about sixty or seventy degrees below outside the aircraft so we decided to go over the front. We thought maybe we could find a hole between the thunderheads.

"We climbed and climbed and we still couldn't see the tops. We thought we'd have to go under it. We got down to about fifteen feet off the water but ice built up and we got slower and slower. All our de-icer boots had been taken off the B-17 when we had entered combat because they slowed the aircraft down. It was thought that the chances of icing up were negligible but this was one time they were wrong. We even used some flap to keep her airborne because we were so close to stalling. The only de-icing equipment we had was for the propellers. If we hadn't got that we wouldn't have made it. Eventually, we broke clear and just made it back. It was hell after the mission to have to fly like that. When we got back to Bury we looked the aircraft over and it was covered in burn marks. It was a miracle. How lucky could we get?"

There was another shock in store for the returning crews.

"Next day, 4th March, I walked into the Briefing Room at Rougham as scared as hell," says Hatcher. " 'Big-B' was splashed all over the target map and I thought, 'I won't make it.'" However, the weather intervened again and crews were recalled. One wing, composed of two squadrons from the 95th Bomb Group and one from the 100th Bomb Group, either did not receive the call signal or chose to ignore it, and continued to the capital alone. The 100th Bomb Group's code-name at this time was "Fireball."

Robert J. Shoens was in the 100th Bomb Group. "I was part of 'Fireball Yellow' and we received the recall and brought our bombs home. It wasn't until we landed that we learned that 'Fireball Orange' (the second group of aircraft in the wing) had not received the call and had somehow made their way to Berlin."

Fortunately, some of the Mustang escorts were still with the wayward bombers and provided support in the target area. There is no doubt that their appearance prevented a debacle. Fourteen minutes from the capital, "Fireball Orange" was attacked by German fighters. The 95th bore the brunt of the attacks and lost four aircraft. However, the 100th lost only one: Seaton's *Sad Sack*, piloted by Stanley M. Seaton, who had been Shoens' best man at his wedding in May 1943. A short time later Shoens received news that Seaton was a POW. Those aircraft that did get through to the capital claimed to have dropped the first American bombs on Berlin. They were right. The 95th Bomb Group was awarded its third Presidential Unit Citation and the 100th was similarly awarded later.

Returning crews were well aware that the German defenses in and around the city had now been fully alerted and a rough reception could be expected next time the heavies ventured to "Big-B." The Germans knew only too well that any target which was not bombed because of a recall could be expected to be hit again at the earliest opportunity. That opportunity came only two days later, on 6th March, when the 8th dispatched 730 heavies escorted by almost 800 fighters. The First Division was assigned the ball-bearing plant at Erkner, a suburb of Berlin, and the Third Division was assigned the Robert Bosch Electrical Equipment factory.

Life in a POW camp. The man at the field kitchen is 1st Lieutenant John C. Morgan, Medal of Honor. Morgan had won the award on 26th July 1943, when he brought Ruthie II *back from Hannover after the pilot had been killed. He was shot down again on 6th March, 1944 by flak. This time his aircraft exploded in the air, killing eight of the crew. Morgan was thrown out of the plane while carrying a parachute under his arm and succeeded in putting it on while in free fall.*

Throughout the east of England Fortresses and Liberators began taxiing from their hardstands to take up position on the runways. The First Division groups would be in the van of the formation with the Third filling in behind them and the Liberators of the Second Division bringing up the rear. The bombers crossed the English coastline and the gunners tested their .50 calibers. The Channel passed beneath then the Dutch coast dropped under the wings and fell away. They sailed over the Zuider Zee and were almost over the German border when the storm broke.

Over the Dummer Lake, the First Division was attacked by fighters which concentrated on the leading groups and the 91st, 92nd, and 381st were given a thorough going-over. The 457th Bomb Group was met by head-on attacks, one 109 which did not pull out in time crashing into 2nd/ Lieutenant Roy E. Graves' B-17. The combined wreckage fell on 2nd/Lieutenant Eugene H. Whalen's Fortress and all three fell to earth. Next it was the turn of the Third Division groups to feel the weight of the enemy attacks. The leading 385th Bomb Group at the head of the 4th Combat Wing came in for persistent fighter attacks. Brigadier General Russell Wilson was flying in a 482nd Bomb Group H2X-equipped Fortress and his crew included Medal of Honor recipient John C. Morgan, now a 1st/Lieutenant. Just as the formation approached the Berlin area the flak guns opened up and bracketed the group. Wilson's aircraft was badly hit but continued on the bomb run with one engine on fire. Major Fred A. Rabbo, the pilot, gave the order to bale out after the bomber began losing altitude, but before they could take to their parachutes the aircraft exploded killing six of the ten-man crew. Incredibly, John C. Morgan survived, being somersaulted out of the aircraft with his parachute pack under his arm. He managed to put it on after several attempts and was saved from injury when a tree broke his fall. Morgan was captured and sent to *Stalag Luft III*.

The unprotected 13th Combat Wing, comprising the 95th, 100th, and 390th Bomb Groups, now caught the full venom of the enemy fighter attacks It was another black day for the 100th in particular as Robert J. Shoens, in the 351st Bomb Squadron, which flew lead, well remembers.

"I was part of 'Fireball Yellow' again and the group was going in with twenty planes - one short. It was a spectacular day, so clear it seemed we could almost see Berlin from over England. Somewhere over eastern France we suddenly realized that we hadn't seen our fighter escort for several minutes. We had been without escort for about twenty minutes, which meant that a relay had not caught up with us. (The German fighters had engaged them somewhere behind us, knowing it would leave us without fighter escort.)

"The reason wasn't long in coming. Ahead of us, probably ten miles away, there appeared to be a swarm of bees - actually German fighters. Guesses ran to as much as 200. They were coming right at us and in a few seconds were going through us. On that pass they shot down the entire high squadron (350th) of ten planes. When an airplane went down you had to shut out the fact that it took men with it. On this raid it became most difficult because so many were lost. One loss in particular was an example of this. The crew from our own barracks were flying off the right wing of our airplane. Suddenly, during one of the fighter passes, their entire wing was on fire. In the next instant there was nothing there. The fighters made two more passes and when it was over *Our Gal' Sal'* was all alone. The last airplane from the group that I had seen flying was Captain Swartout in the 351st Squadron lead. He was struggling along with about six feet missing from his vertical stabilizer and was the only other airplane from the squadron who came back with us.

"We saw another group ahead of us, so we caught up with it. The airplanes had an 'A' in a square on the tail so they were from the 94th. We flew on to Berlin with them and dropped our bombs. The flak was heavy but over Berlin the sky was black. The target was on the southeast side of the city. For reasons we couldn't figure out, the group we were with chose to turn to the left and go over Berlin. Since we were not part of the group we decided to turn to the right and get out of the flak. When we did that a German battery of four guns started tracking. They fired about forty rounds before we got out of range. None of them came close because of the evasive action we had taken. Higher up and ahead of us we saw another group so we climbed and caught up with it. It was also from our wing, having a 'J' in a square on its aircraft's tails (390th). We flew the rest of the way home with them without further incident. It was still a beautiful day and with a chance to relax we began to wonder what had happened to our group. It couldn't be that we were the only survivors of 'Fireball Yellow.'"

In thirty minutes the enemy pilots had shot down twenty-three Fortresses from the 13th Wing, or had damaged them so badly that they were forced to ditch or crash-land on the continent. Worst hit had been the 100th Bomb Group, which lost fifteen B-17s in all.

The 452nd Bomb Group formation of six B-17s flying as the high squadron also suffered loss, as Hank Gladys, the bombardier aboard *Flakstop*, flown by Lieutenant Charles F. Wagner, recalls.

"Flying back from the target we were about half-way through Germany when our fighter escort had to leave us as we were behind schedule because of our second pass over the target. Immediately the Germans came up after us. Later I learned that there were thirty-three of them after us. *Flakstop* was hit during a ferocious fighter attack. The first attack came from the rear, killing our tail-gunner,

Sergeant G.L. James. Then the attack shifted to the front where they knocked out our left engine and damaged our wing on the right side."

Allan R. Willis, the co-pilot, says, "The German fighters came like the proverbial swarm of bees. Six 109s and FW 190s took the 452nd as their quarry and the fun really began. Virtually all passes were made from 10 to 12 o'clock high. Our intercom was *kaput* and I could make no attempt at fire control. A second pass raked the fuselage from nose to tail. The third did the crucial damage. It must have hit the starboard side oil, electrical, and fuel lines because both starboard engines, numbers three and four, began to splutter. The tachs immediately indicated nearly total loss of rpms. I hit the feathering switches but nothing happened. The props simply windmilled. The wide variation in rpms started *Flakstop* vibrating and we fell out of formation. Both Charlie Wagner and myself fought the vibrating control columns to try and maintain straight and level flight. There was no panic yet. We could see the Zuider Zee on the horizon. We didn't want to bale out over Germany because of the stories we had heard about the German treatment of downed fliers.

"I saw one of our gas caps fly off. The only explanation I could think of was that the intense vibration had loosened them. The airstream over the starboard wing must have set up a siphoning action and the gasoline and the hot oil might have come together. What I did know was that the entire starboard wing was, in a flash, a sheet of orange flame! In that single moment *Flakstop* gave up her role as a mighty

Flying Fortress and became a flying coffin. It didn't take an aeronautical engineer to inform us that it was much safer outside than in. As I hit the bale-out bell (thank God that was working!) I glanced at the altimeter; 1,400 feet over Holland!"

Clyde J. Martin, the navigator, was first out of the front escape hatch.

"After I opened my 'chute a German fighter was still flying around us. I watched to see if his guns would fire on me but they did not. I landed in a pasture at about 0330 hours near the little Dutch town of Staphorst. I hid my 'chute and started walking." Allan R. Willis continues. "By the time I got down to the forward escape hatch, the engineer and the navigator had already jumped. Hank Gladys was about to go. He took one look at me, said, 'I've forgotten my cigarettes.' and went back into the nose. I swung out of the hatch (the wrong way!), got into the slipstream, and nearly got cut in half by the bomb bay doors. After some frantic fiddling with a pilot 'chute that did not pop out, I finally felt the violent snap that tells you the 'chute has opened. When I hit the ground, Hank Gladys was there waiting for me!" Gladys says, "During all this, Lieutenant Wagner was trying to set the automatic pilot as he didn't know what the situation was in the other part of the plane. Right after I'd baled out, *Flakstop* went into a spin and crashed within my sight. Of the four remaining crew members in the back, three were killed and Sergeant Lloyd Freeman, our ball-turret gunner, was seriously wounded. He landed near Sergeant Donald Porter, the flight engineer,

Lady Be Good, 43-37563 of the 452nd Bomb Group, photographed through the waist gun window of another B-17 riding through thick flak over Berlin on 8th March 1944.

who was advised by Dutch Underground workers to leave him, as the Germans were very near and searching for us. Porter and Martin were taken into the Dutch Underground and in September 1944 were liberated by the British Army. I never learned the fate of Sergeant Freeman. The Dutch Underground said that one of our 'chutists was strafed and killed by one of the attacking FW 190s while floating down. Two other crew members' 'chutes failed to open after they baled out."

Six months later, Willis and Gladys were liberated by the American Army.

The first American air raid on Berlin had certainly flushed out the Luftwaffe, just as Doolittle had hoped it would. The Fortress gunners and the fighter pilots claimed over 170 German fighters destroyed but the Americans had suffered record losses. The First Division had lost eighteen B-17s while the Third had lost thirty-five. The "Bloody Hundredth" had again suffered unmercifully at the hands of the Luftwaffe, losing fifteen B-17s. Air Chief Marshal of the RAF, Arthur Harris, sent a message to his opposite number, Carl Spaatz, at High Wycombe: "Heartiest congratulations on first US bombing of Berlin. It is more than a year since they were attacked in daylight, but now they have no safety there by day or night. All Germany learns the same lesson."

The record loss of sixty-nine bombers, and a further 102 seriously damaged, meant that the survivors had lost many close buddies. It quickly developed into a morale problem and for those who remained the nightmare would soon begin again. John A. Miller, a seventeen-year-old gunner who had flown the first Berlin mission with the 100th Bomb Group, explains.

"Lovin, a gunner from Captain Sumner Reeder's crew, I believe, and I were the only two left in the 349th Squadron spare gunners' hut. Lovin rotated to the States a day or two after that. I was alone in that hut and was going nuts. I told Captain Reeder that I couldn't take any more. 'Take what?', he asked. I told him my problem. He got teed off right there (he was then our CO) and told me to take a forty-eight hour pass to London. I went to London and I was really down. All alone in a crowd. I met a good, decent, Irish girl working at Rainbow Corner and out of thousands of GIs, she liked me. (I would always see her when I made it to London. The first part of July 1944, she was killed by a 'buzz bomb'. All the damn luck!)

"I took the last train, returning from my pass on 8th March. When I checked in with 'Irish,' the night CO, he said, 'My God, what are you doing out?' I said, 'forty-eight hour pass to London why?' 'You're flying, that's why.' Whew! I ran over and took a cold shower, got dressed, grabbed a bike, and headed for briefing. Too late for chow, too late for briefing also. I changed and made it out to the hardstand, just in time to take off. After we had formed up and left the English coast I introduced myself on the intercom (this was a new crew, Townsend's, on their first mission) and told them I'd just got back from London. I asked them what was the target for the day. Back came the answer, 'Berlin!' I felt sick."

Though he did not know it, Miller was aboard one of 600 bombers which had been prepared for the third raid on "Big-B" that week. The Third Division would lead the 8th to the VKF ball-bearing plant at Erkner in the suburbs east of Berlin with the First Division flying in the middle and the Second again bringing up the rear. Lieutenant Franklin L. Betz,

Vapor Trail, 42-31363 of the 306th Bomb Group. This damage was repaired, but Vapor Trail *was lost on 27th March 1944 when it crashed in the Bay of Biscay. Lieutenant Rene C. Fix's crew were all taken prisoner.*

4th March 1944. Vapor trails stream out behind these B-17s on their way to Berlin on the first daylight mission. They are flying at an altitude of 25,000 feet. The air temperature at these great heights fell to sixty degrees below zero.

a navigator in the 379th Bomb Group at Kimbolton and part of the First Division force, was flying his first mission this day.

"Promptly at 0915 hours the lead plane took off. Taxiing behind a line of Fortresses that one after the other soared into the gray sky, the pilot, Captain Douglas H. Buskey, swung our plane onto the runway as the B-17 before us started on its way into the 'wild blue yonder.' The four 1,200 hp Wright Cyclone engines roared and our heavy bomb-laden plane shuddered as Buskey pushed the throttles forward. Bobbing gently, it rolled down the runway with increasing speed, the ride becoming smooth as the massive bulk lifted gracefully above the Huntingdonshire farmland.

"Climbing steadily, one by one each of the eighteen planes slipped into its designated place of the group formation; six in the lead squadron and six each in the high and low squadrons. Wide-eyed, my heart racing from excitement (or was it apprehension from the realization that I'd soon be departing the friendly shores of Britain), I was awed at the magnificent sight of the vast air armada stretching for miles in precise formations against the frosty blue sky. The palms of my hands were moist when we headed over the English Channel and I noted in my log, 'altitude, 20,000 feet, time, 1106 am, ground speed, 170 knots.'

"Scattered flak greeted us at the Dutch coast a few miles north of Ijmuiden. Happily though, the fighter planes we saw were identified as our 'little friends', P-51 Mustangs. On we droned, due east, and the Dummer Lake in western Germany loomed ahead. Suddenly, black splotches darkened the sky around us a few miles north of the lake. Flak! The concussion from exploding shells rocked the plane. Fragments of flying steel tore through its aluminum skin. The oil line of number one engine was cut and, gushing like a geyser, the oil covered the cowling and adjoining wing surface, quickly congealing on the metal in the minus 30 degree temperature. Promptly, Buskey feathered number one engine as he called over the intercom, 'Number two engine's only pulling half power.' We were flying on two and a half engines! Fortunately, none of the crew was hit. We learned upon our return to Kimbolton that flak had damaged the vital induction pipe of the turbo-supercharger, reducing the engine's thrust. 'Pilot to navigator, what's the estimated flying time to the target?' Consulting my map and log I applied pertinent data to my E-6B computer and made a calculation. 'Navigator to pilot', I replied, 'It's approximately two hours flying time at our present ground speed'.

"The plane rocked gently. 'Bandits at 2 o'clock high', the engineer called. Warily, I watched the two 109s, as yet out of gunfire range, while I manned the right nose gun. Flying high and ahead of us, suddenly they peeled off into a screaming dive, the front edge of their wings from which the tips of machine-gun barrels protruded, lighting up like firecrackers when they fired. In a flash they were way below us and out of range. Lucky! All the Fortresses in the formation continued droning determinedly toward Berlin. If any of them had been hit by the 109 gunfire, none had gotten it fatally this time.

"'Pilot to crew. Despite the flak damage to two engines, the plane's flying well. We'll continue to the target in formation instead of dropping out and trying to get back to England alone. It could be tough going.'

"Breathing heavily from the excitement of my first major encounter with flak and fighters, I slid onto the seat by the navigator's worktable to make entries in the log. Peering through the window over the worktable I saw twin-engined P-38 fighters engaging enemy fighters, keeping them away from the bomber formations. A reassuring sight. High above the peaceful-looking German countryside we flew, in tight formation. Our course to the IP took us far enough south of Berlin to avoid the formidable anti-aircraft defenses. A lump rose in my throat when we turned onto the IP for the thirteen mile run to the target. Five miles above the ball-bearing factory, the Germans had the sky enveloped in a murderous box barrage of flak and the air was filled with black puffs of exploding shells and unseen fragments of deadly steel.

"The formation flew in a straight and unwavering line to the target. There was no turning back, no evasive action. The lead bombardiers were busily aiming their Norden bombsights on the target and the lethal loads of bombs would drop automatically from the bomb bays when the cross hairs in the exquisite bombsight centered on the buildings far below. At that moment, bombardiers in other planes of the group would release their bombs by flipping a toggle switch and the destructive explosives would hurtle toward the doomed factory. Ahead of us, planes in precise group formation entered the pall of smoke from bursting flak. Suddenly, a brilliant ball of orange lit up the sky. Hit by flak, a bomber exploded! No 'chutes were seen. Off to the right, one of the splendid aircraft, out of control, spun lazily to its destruction. It reminded me of a seedpod drifting from a tree. One, two, three 'chutes emerged from the plane, as it disappeared into a cottony cloud. Sweat from my brow trickled into my eyes.

"The plane rocked from the concussion of bursting shells as we entered the envelope of fire. 'Bomb bay doors open,' the engineer called. 'Bombs Away!' cried the bombardier. The plane lifted perceptibly when the tons of bombs dropped from her belly. Ahead of us, bombers emerging from the flak barrage in ragged formation were attempting to close up for maximum protection against the Luftwaffe fighters circling above us. As we pulled away from the target area, the plane perforated by flak but the fliers unscathed, Buskey said, 'We've got to get the bomb bay doors closed quickly. There's too much drag and with only two and a half engines, I may not be able to keep up with the formation.'

"Closing the massive bomb bay doors was no easy job. The engineer had to crank them shut since the electrical system which powered the motor that normally closed them was out. In a cramped space 25,000 feet above Germany, temperature way below freezing, wearing a weighty fleece-lined flight suit, gloves, flak vest and helmet, an oxygen mask with the hose dangling like an elephant's trunk and hooked into the life support system, wires from his throat mike and earphones to contend with, plus a parachute strapped on his back, it was an interminable task. 'Pilot to crew. Someone help the engineer close the doors.'

"'Yes Sir', the right waist gunner volunteered. This meant he had to disconnect from the plane's oxygen system and hook on to a walk-around bottle that provided about eight minutes of the life-giving element, a routine any time a crewman left his position to go elsewhere in the plane. The walk-around bottle was an aluminum cylinder six or eight inches in diameter and about thirty inches long. Really cumbersome. To get to the engineer and help him, in his bulky flight gear, the waist gunner had to shuffle through the radio operator's compartment, then into the bomb bay, balancing precariously on a narrow catwalk, squeeze between V-shaped bomb racks, the bomb bay doors below him only partly closed, until he reached the engineer's station behind the cockpit.

"Buskey continued to do a magnificent job of flying the disabled aircraft and managed somehow to stay in formation. The engineer, Sergeant George Thomas, was slowly and laboriously cranking the bomb bay doors closed. Those of us on the guns were warily watching the enemy fighters in the distance, who fortunately, didn't attack. Sergeant George Thomas said, 'Engineer to pilot. I see the waist gunner on the catwalk. He's stuck between the bomb racks. He can't move.' Sergeant Louis J. Kyler, the radio operator, closest to the helpless waist gunner, attempted to extricate him but his oxygen bottle fell through the partly opened doors and he had to go back to his position and hook into the plane's oxygen system. Private Willis Volkeming, the left waist gunner, on his twelfth mission, the only experienced combat crewman aboard, came forward and tried unsuccessfully to rescue his buddy who had fainted from lack of oxygen. Somehow he had freed himself but unfortunately he had toppled off the catwalk and dropped part of the way through the bomb bay doors that were nearly closed.

"The radio operator came back again and tried once more to save his pal but to no avail. He had to go back to his position for much needed oxygen. 'Radio operator to pilot. We can't get the waist gunner out of the bomb bay. He's unconscious. You'll have to hit the deck if he's to live.'

"'Pilot to crew,' Buskey called, his voice faltering. 'If I leave the formation and try to go it alone at 10,000 feet or lower, where we don't need oxygen, we may not make it back to England. German fighters will jump us. It means losing one of us with the hope that the rest of us will get back.'

"The waning winter sun of late afternoon shone warmly through the transparent nose of the battle-scarred B-17 as we approached our airbase. The red flare fired from the plane by the engineer alerted the ground personnel that we had a casualty aboard and the tower gave the pilot priority to land. The plane dropped smoothly to the concrete runway and the tires screeching on touchdown sounded like a whining protest against the terrible ordeal the plane and its crew had endured. Buskey taxied the splendid Fortress to its dispersal area. The medics removed the dead body of the right waist gunner and took him away. I dropped to the ground from the plane's nose hatch, somber and weary after more than eight hours in the plane. I realized the hardening of a naive airman to combat in the crucible of war had begun."

The leading Third Bomb Division had encountered the fiercest fighter opposition on the raid, losing thirty-seven Fortresses, including sixteen from the 45th Combat Wing. Curtis E. LeMay, the Third Division Commander, singled out the 45th Combat Wing for special praise in the Daily Bulletin, No 69, dated 9th March 1944.

"The crews of the 45th Combat Wing delivered a punishing blow today to the morale of all Germany. In successfully putting bombs on the enemy's capital and his vital plants they furthered the war effort more than any of us can adequately evaluate. At the present writing, the major part of the hurt to the Third Division forces fell on the gallant crews of the 96th, 388th, and 452nd Bomb Groups. The spirit and fight these units displayed made it easier on the other wings who wanted to share the brunt of the battle with them. Convey to all officers and men who participated, my deep admiration for the courage and determination with which they pushed the air attack into the heart of the enemy's territory and blasted Berlin."

Worst hit group in the Third Division during the series of Berlin missions had been the 100th Bomb Group. In the first American operation to Berlin on 4th March the "Bloody Hundredth" had won through to the target with the 95th while all the others had turned back. It had lost one B-17 that day but successive raids on the capital that week cost the group another sixteen aircraft. It was for its "outstanding performance of duty in action against the enemy in connection with the initial series of successful attacks against Berlin, 4th, 6th, and 8th March 1944 . . ." that the 100th was awarded its second Presidential Unit Citation, on 3rd March 1945.

On 9th March 1944 the 8th was again dispatched to Berlin but 10/10ths cloud prevented visual bombing. The Luftwaffe was notable for its absence, licking its wounds after the sustained American offensive of the past few days and all nine heavies lost were victims of flak. Cliff Hatcher's crew in the 94th Bomb Group was relieved at the lack of opposition because it was their twenty-fifth and final mission. The crew of the *Grand Old Lady* had not been to "Big-B" before, having been forced to return early on 6th March. The 94th lost no aircraft and Hatcher declared that he was "Happy as hell" to have completed his tour. He had made it, with the help of a little luck. He had missed the battles of "Big Week" and had survived the Berlin gauntlets but, he concluded, "I felt a nervous wreck after my last four missions."

Life expectancy was put on average at eleven missions at this stage of the war. Hatcher was one of the lucky ones. As if to confirm his good fortune, on 18th April, during yet another raid on Berlin, the *Grand Old Lady* was one of eight B-17s taken from the 94th. Of the eleven aircraft Cliff Hatcher flew during his tour, nine had gone down with other crews. Hatcher wrote later, "Lady Luck has certainly been with me. Of the fifty-four crews in the original Snow Provisional Group, only four survived their missions."

"Lady Luck" had also helped bring Bill Rose of the 92nd through twenty-four combat missions. On 8th March he had been flying *Black Magic* when he was forced to abort after all four superchargers failed. He jettisoned his bombs and returned to Podington, hugging the sea all the way. Luckily, P-38s were in the vicinity and chased off any fighters in the area, then some P-51s escorted them back across the Channel. When the rest of the group returned, Rose was in the officers' bar and they told him he had been reported going down over Germany. But now the end was in sight.

"Everybody wanted to see our crew make it. We waited for a milk-run to complete our tour. On 19th March we went to Frankfurt and we made it. As we entered the flight pattern over Podington, we broke away to buzz the field. There was a definite pattern for this. We went ninety degrees to

the landing runway and right at the tower where we pulled up, went around, and landed. Of course, we had to be last in the formation to do this and have no wounded on board.

"On an earlier mission we carried a bombardier who was on his twenty-fifth. Now, on our twenty-fifth, there were six of us who were flying their last mission together. It was a great day and we duly buzzed the tower. Then we parted until our papers came through. What we didn't realize was that we were war weary. My weight going into combat was about 160lb but I was now down to 140lb."

Bill Rose and his five fellow crew members had completed their tours just in time because four days later the 92nd lost five crews to heavy flak and fighter attacks during a raid on Herben-Hamm. Four of the crews were from Rose's squadron, the 326th. (In 1945 Rose returned to the 92nd Bomb Group and flew part of a second tour.)

On 22nd March 1944 the heavies again sought the rich industrial targets of "Big-B." Almost 800 B-17s and B-24s were dispatched, led by H2X-equipped bombers flying their last mission under the control of the 482nd Bomb Group. Thereafter, each of the three bomb divisions operated one pathfinder squadron apiece. The First Division assigned the task to the pioneer 305th Bomb Group at Chelveston while PFF responsibilities in the Third Division were allocated to the 96th Bomb Group at Snetterton Heath. Altogether, the 8th Air Force dropped 4,800 tons of high explosive on Berlin in five raids during March 1944. The raids cost the 8th scores of experienced crews and valuable aircraft to say nothing of the mental scars on those who survived. Berlin would be indelibly printed on their minds for days, months, even years, to come. By 19th May 1944, John A. Miller of the 100th Bomb Group would have completed six missions to the German capital; the greatest number of Berlin missions in one tour by any 8th Air Force member. "Altogether, we started out for Berlin seven times. Twice our co-pilot went nuts and tried to crash us into the sea. These times the crew fought him off the wheel and we aborted. After the second time he didn't return to our crew. He wasn't a coward; he just couldn't go back to Berlin."

The disintegrating wreckage of B-17G, 43-37883 Blue Streak *of the 486th Bomb Group tumbles to the ground near Merseburg on 2nd November 1944. 2nd Lieutenant David Paris and his eight crew were all killed..*

Chapter 12
Eighth over England

After the Berlin raids of early March 1944, the weather closed in over the Continent and shallow penetration missions to V-1 sites in the Pas de Calais became the order of the day. It was a time when the 8th could take stock and, during April, overall command of the Combined Bomber Offensive and the 8th Air Force officially passed to General Dwight D. Eisenhower, newly appointed Supreme Allied Commander. During the month, despite the obvious drawbacks in mixing two different types of heavy bomber - the B-17 and the B-24 - six new B-24 groups joined the Third Bomb Division. Doolittle wanted to bring the 8th up to full strength using just B-17s but there were simply not enough to go around. In contrast, by the late spring of 1944, five B-24 plants in America were producing more than enough Liberators. This uneasy marriage was to last only four months, by which time Doolittle had gone some way to achieving his all-B-17 force.

Also in April 1944, Generalmajor Adolf Galland, the Luftwaffe fighter commander, revealed to his superiors that since January that year the day fighter arm had lost more than 1,000 pilots. He estimated that each enemy raid was costing Germany about fifty aircrew and at that rate the time was fast approaching when the Luftwaffe would lose air control over Germany.

Unfortunately, any new 8th Air Force offensive was curtailed by the weather and it was not until 8th April that the heavies were able to assemble in force when 644 bombers were dispatched to the aircraft depots throughout western Germany. Then on Easter Sunday, 9th April, the First

Division was assigned Marienburg and the Third Division, Poznan. The FW 190 plant at Marienburg had been the scene of a successful bombing attempt by the First Division earlier in the war but the component part of the plant had escaped the attentions of the Third Division because a thick layer of cloud had obscured it from view. This time the Third Division was not to be beaten by the weather. Despite the loss of one combat wing and some combat boxes from another, it managed to place seventy-one percent of its bombs within 1,000 feet of the PI. Leaving the target, the Third Division received radio orders to join the Marienburg force for the homeward journey for mutual protection but, before it could do so, the Third Division came under heavy fighter attack. The leading 45th Wing bore the brunt of the attacks but stout defending by the Fortress gunners kept losses down to just two aircraft. The following day crews were "rewarded" with a milk-run when 730 aircraft went to airfield targets in France and the Low Countries. The 457th Bomb Group flew to Evre airfield at Brussels and the mission was so low-key that Perry Rudd even had time to take snaps of the city while he waited for "Bombs Away." Then things changed.

"We made three runs over the target despite the heavy flak. I was sitting in the camera well. Just after 'Bombs Away' sounded a piece of shrapnel, which had come through the bomb bay doors and through the radio room wall, hit me in the back about two inches above the bottom of my flak suit. The whole ship was shot up and we later counted more than 100 holes. Number three and four gas tanks

Sergeant John L. Hurd, the ball turret gunner aboard Battlin' Betty *of the 401st Bomb Group.* Battlin' Betty *was shot down on 11th April 1944.*

leaked and number four supercharger ran away coming home. The left horizontal stabilizer had a hole in it and another through the elevator. When we got back to Glatton the ship was sent to a sub-depot."

On 11th April well in excess of 900 bombers were dispatched to six Junkers and Focke-Wulf assembly plants in eastern Germany. Eighty-eight Fortresses from the First Division were assigned Cottbus and Sorau. Joe Wroblewski in the 351st Bomb Group viewed the mission philosophically.

"The 11th of each month always seemed to be my day for missions. I was picked to fly with a new crew that had just arrived at Polebrook. It was usually standard procedure to take a new pilot and his crew on their first mission. We went to Arniswalde, Germany, which was our secondary target near the Polish border. We flew at 15,000 feet, descending to 12,000 feet at the target. That gave the German anti-aircraft gunners a field day. They got their share of B-17s over Hannover. Bombers were blowing up, burning, and falling out of control all around us. We all got scared as hell when a four-inch piece of flak came right through the nose and cut the oxygen line on the right side. The whooshing sound of the escaping oxygen under pressure made plenty of noise. The new pilot grabbed the controls from me and about pulled us out of formation in panic. I almost had to beat his hands off the yoke. I told him that if we did get out of formation by ourselves the enemy fighters would be on us like a pack of wolves. Some of our crew members had to use portable oxygen bottles after losing half our supply. Enemy fighters did not bother us although we could see other groups under heavy attack."

One of these groups was the 401st from Deenthorpe. Flying his eleventh mission this day was John L. Hurd, the ball turret gunner aboard Lieutenant Francis L. Shaw's *Battlin' Betty*.

"My squadron was hit hard by flak and we lost four B-17s in this action. There were many flak bursts around our ship. From my position in the ball turret I was able to watch under the wings for fires. Immediately the number three and four engines started smoking and shortly afterwards my ball turret was hit and I was injured in the right butt! Our bombs were salvoed to guard against explosion just as one of our B-17s blew up. *Battlin' Betty* finally came clear of the flak and we slowed down and lost altitude. I was asked to leave the ball turret and have the radio operator look at my injury. He was unable to do anything as I had too many clothes on. About this time the pilot gave the order to bale out. I hooked on my chest type parachute and placed my GI shoes inside my 'chute harness. We were over flat country and somewhere east of Hannover. I looked out of the bomb bay and then decided to jump out of the waist door. We were somewhere between 15,000 and 18,000 feet. The two waist gunners and I were waiting to jump when I heard a loud crash. The ship started to rock to the left and knocked us against the left side of the ship. I thought to myself, 'It's now or never,' so I gave a big push and all three of us went out the door. It was very noisy as I left the ship and shortly after I pulled the rip-cord. The 'chute opened and then the world was quiet."

Hurd landed, injuring his ankle and was captured immediately. He finished the war at *Stalag Luft 17*, Krems, Austria.

Meanwhile, other groups were suffering loss in the ferocious flak barrage, as Perry Rudd in the 457th formation, recalls.

"We were knocked out of formation and fell a thousand feet before we recovered. We leveled out just in time to witness a burning B-17 fall off its right wing directly over us. Lieutenant Matterell, the co-pilot, pulled our ship up on the left wing and we fell another 3,000 feet. The burning B-17 missed us by only a few feet. A piece of flak had entered the cockpit before exploding and had set the nose on fire. The flames spread through the open radio hatch of the doomed ship, leaving a trail of smoke as it spiraled down. Two men got out. The tail-gunner went through a wing and a pilot banked his plane to let him by. Neither 'chute opened, if indeed either of them had them on."

Colonel Preston talking with Major Meyer on 11th April 1944.

At the target, the Fortresses were bracketed by more flak. The lead bombardier in the 351st Bomb Group was hit in the arm, which had to be amputated later. Perry Rudd's B-17, meanwhile, had to salvo its bombs.

"The bomb doors would not close and we headed back to Belgium alone. We received about twenty flak hits on the homeward run. The right aileron was knocked out of position, the rudder was holed and the right flap was put out of commission. Lieutenant Hovey did a remarkable job of getting us back. We took our crash landing positions but it was a great landing at Glatton despite the damage, although the plane was later declared a sub-depot job."

The most remarkable feat of all was performed by 1st/Lieutenant Edward S. Michael and Lieutenant Franklin Westberg of the 305th Bomb Group, who brought *Bertie Lee* home to England after it had been devastated by cannon fire and had plummeted into a 3,000 foot dive. Michael crash-landed at an RAF airfield near Grimsby despite his undercarriage and flaps having been put out of operation and the ball turret stuck in the lowered position with its guns pointing downwards. The airspeed indicator was not working and the bomb doors were jammed fully open. Fighting off unconsciousness, Michael skillfully brought *Bertie Lee* down safely on

42-97083 of the 452nd Bomb Group crash-landed on the shore of the Baltic Sea during the Rostock mission of 11th April 1944. (Hans Heiri Stapfer)

Lieutenant L. Brown celebrates the completion of his tour with the 379th Bomb Group, Kimbolton. His last mission was flown on 11th April 1944.

"I kept seeing the English coast all the way back across the North Sea. It must have been a mirage. It seemed like we would never get back. I was dead tired when we eventually did get back and I passed out in the sack and slept like a log."

But crews barely had time to catch up on some much-needed sleep when, a few hours later, they were told to prepare for another long mission. Once again the targets were aircraft plants in central Germany. Men dragged themselves out of their beds and took off but the weather intervened and the bombers turned back early. Although some crews came under fire none were sorry the mission had been "scrubbed." It meant another day to live.

The respite was short however, for on 13th April the First Division was sent to the ball-bearing plants at Schweinfurt for the third time. Its leader, Colonel (later General) Maurice "Mo" Preston, CO of the 379th Bomb Group, flying at the head of the leading 41st Wing, encountered strong fighter opposition.

"In all probability they made a direct head-on approach from a distance of some fifteen to twenty miles. The first we saw of them they were among us and already firing their guns. They made only a single pass and then went on through the lead wing, maintaining an upright position, thus abandoning, for at least this one time, their practice of attacking inverted and then pulling out in an earthward dive.

"The great majority of attacks were concentrated on the high box (384th Bomb Group) presumably because it was separated some distance from the remaining boxes. I made a determined effort via the radio to induce the element leader to get back into formation, but to no avail. (Whether or not he received my orders is something else.) He and his entire formation paid dearly. Every single aircraft [eight] in that formation was shot down on that single pass made by the German fighters. I never saw such a thing happen before or since. One pass; scratch one entire formation!"

The Third Division was also badly hit in the bombing of the Messerschmitt plant at Augsburg in southern Germany, being subjected to heavy and accurate flak barrages. Ten Fortresses were forced to head for Switzerland and many others were either shot down or badly damaged. Despite the losses, however, the raid on Schweinfurt had been a great success, as Colonel Preston recalls.

"It was on this mission that we finally achieved a direct hit on the number one prime building, the elimination of which would do the greatest good. At least one 379th bomb went

its belly. His miraculous feat earned the second Medal of Honor awarded to a member of the 364th Bomb Squadron, 305th Bomb Group.

The 92nd Bomb Group, which had been assigned the industrial area of Stettin, also suffered loss. Six aircraft in the 325th Bomb Squadron, flying as the low squadron of the high group, were shot down during vicious and persistent attacks by fighters and a concentrated flak barrage. The 13th and 45th Combat Wings in the Third Bomb Division force were confronted with bad weather in the Poznan area and were forced to bomb the secondary target at Rostock. Rocket-firing Me 410s and Ju 88s took advantage of a lapse in fighter cover and wreaked havoc among the leading groups. The 96th Bomb Group was worst hit, losing ten of the twenty-five bombers shot down this day. Most of the crews who got back to England had been in the air for more than eleven hours and tiredness had already begun to take effect during the last stages of the homeward leg. Joe Wroblewski says,

The Smith family over-wintered at Yelden, their lives seemingly little disturbed by the arrival of the 8th Air Force. The aircraft is Dinah Mite, *which was written off after being damaged by fighter attacks on 15th May 1944.*

into that prime building. It probably didn't make a great difference to the war effort, but it's little successes like these that spice things up for the participants."

Thereafter, the weather intervened and provided a much-needed respite for weary crews, ever conscious that soon they would be flying yet another mission, days, maybe even hours later. The waiting was as bad for raw crews as it was for the experienced. Among the new arrivals at Bovingdon in March 1944 had been Lieutenant Anthony "Chick" Cecchini's crew. It was here that they began to get disquieting news, as Ben Smith, the radio operator, recalls.

"We heard about a hard-luck group called the Hundredth, which was continually being wiped out. Daily we saw formations coming over, headed north, some with props feathered, others trailing smoke. Once I saw one with half the horizontal stabilizer shot off, keeping its place in the formation. We fervently prayed not to be sent to the Hundredth. Each day two or three crews would be sent out to take their places.

"Finally, it was our turn. We did not fly to our base, we took the train from Bovingdon to a station near Molesworth (to join the 360th Bomb Squadron, 303rd Bomb Group) and were ignominiously carried there in trucks. When we came to our squadron area, we were not greeted by the familiar, 'You'll be sorry,' which was the customary greeting Stateside. The men we saw gave us only a few incurious glances and said nothing to us. Our hearts sank. We were assigned a barracks shared by two or three other crews. Six empty cots gaped at us. These had been occupied by a crew that had not returned from the mission the day before. We were not prepared for this sobering reality. In progress was a non-stop poker game. The players did not look up or acknowledge our presence in any way. We were accorded a few glum nods from some others who were lying in their sacks reading. About that time the door flew open and a bevy of uproarious drunks fell inside. It was the lead crew - Lieutenant Brinkley's crew. I had seen many drunks but this was a different kind of drunkenness. These men were veterans of the great missions of Schweinfurt and Oschersleben. They had seen too much

Abe Dolim, on a mission over Germany in 1944. (Abe Dolim)

and it showed. I had the sudden feeling that things were far different from what I had been led to believe. I was right.

"We were not referred to as Lieutenant Cecchini's crew. Instead, we were called the 'new crew,' which continued to be our status until we had flown about eight combat missions. New crews were given the most vulnerable places in the formation and had a way of disappearing after a few missions. We heartily resented this callous treatment, but after winning our spurs, we were as bad as the rest."

On the night of 17th April, Cecchini's crew was placed on the operations bulletin board at Molesworth and the target on the morrow was hardly a milk-run; it was Berlin! That night Ben Smith looked up and down the row of bunks.

"There were many cigarettes glowing in the dark. There was not much sleeping going on. In the early hours of 18th April the door flew open and this cheery CO named 'Fluke' came in, switched on the lights and started calling off the crews who were to fly on the day's mission. He yelled, 'Cecchini's crew!' and my heart sank within me. I felt like a condemned man. We donned our flying coveralls, heated suits, and boots and headed to the mess-hall down the road where the cooks were putting on a mission breakfast. The chefs were very solicitous seemingly jovial. We could have pancakes, eggs sunny-side up, or any way we wanted them.

Sort of like, 'It's your last meal-you can have what you want.' To me it seemed a somewhat macabre occasion, and I found their jollity very disquieting and out of place. I could eat none of the breakfast anyway. Even to this day I have butterflies before breakfast.

"All of the crews, officers, and non-commissioned officers, were briefed together. The radio operators were also given a separate briefing at which time they received a canvas packet with coded data in it called a 'flimsy.' In the main briefing hall the target remained covered until the Intelligence Officer came in. He was a dapper individual, sporting a moustache, and quite hearty in manner - for a good reason; he didn't have to go. These Intelligence Officers were non-flying personnel with some useful information and a lot more that was useless. His first move was to peel back the cover from the map, which act was always met with a loud groan from the assembled crews. They were a lively bunch, and time had to be allowed for them to get over the initial shock, sound off, and cuss a little while. After a time they subsided and he began. We could see that the red lines pinned on the map went deep into Germany. The target was the Heinkel plant at Oranienburg in the suburbs of Berlin. We were told we could expect heavy fighter opposition, with flak at the target described as 'intense.' In other words, the target was heavily defended. We could see from the diagram that we were flying 'Tail-end Charlie' in the high squadron. There would be a lead squadron and a high squadron.

"Briefing over, we got up and started out. We climbed into trucks and headed out for the hard-stands where the Forts were parked. The ground crews swarmed over our B-17 getting it ready. The armorers were arming the bombs in the bomb bay. It was still pitch dark. We put our machine-guns into their casings and attached the gun belts. When this was done, we went to the dispersal tent and lay down on the canvas cots that were there for that purpose. We tried to log a little sack time before 'Start Engines.' The signal for this was a red flare from the control tower. These quiet moments in the dispersal tent were always the worst part of the mission for me. I was always inflicted with an unbearable sadness at this time. I can still hear the clanking coughs of the aircraft engines as they struggled manfully in the damp mist and then caught up. We were on board and soon taxiing out in trail until we reached the end of the runway. Every thirty seconds a Fort would gun its engines and hurtle down the runway into the black darkness. Finally, it was our time. We always sweated takeoff as we were heavily laden with gas and bombs.

"We climbed through the mist on a certain heading until we reached a predetermined altitude. At 10,000 feet Chick told us to go on oxygen. Thereafter, we had periodic oxygen checks with each position checking in. We learned the value of this on a later mission when the ball turret gunner did not check in. We pulled him out of the turret unconscious and almost dead. His hose had become disconnected.

"During all this time there was complete radio silence, as the German interceptor stations were monitoring constantly. Looking back, I doubt if we ever fooled them. The planners would go to extreme lengths to conceal the mounting of a mission but I doubt if they could conceal something of that magnitude. I imagine the Germans had ample notice from their own agents in England of every mission we flew. I don't remember their ever being asleep when I visited Germany.

"So far I was fine. It was a bright, clear day marred only by the contrails of the bombers ahead of us in formation. I can recall a certain amount of exhilaration and pride. The great battle formations were something to see! As far as the eye could see there were B-17s, some of them olive drab Fs, others the new silver Gs. The scene was innocuous enough. Nothing about it even hinted of danger. A formation of P-38s slanted overhead, adding to my feeling of security. It seemed that we had been flying for hours without incident. We chatted a little on the intercom until Chick told us to shut up.

"I heard it before I saw it. Whomp-whoosh! Simultaneously, the bombardier shouted, 'Flak, 12 o'clock. Christ look at it!' By then we were at the IP and turning on the bomb run. A rush of cold air blasted the radio room as the bomb bay doors came open. The plane began to lurch and reel with the continuous explosions. Now I could see it. Oily, black bursts of crimson blossoms in the center. Everywhere there were literally thousands of bursts as far as the eye could see. I was throwing chaff out of the chute. I couldn't see that it did any good at all. They had our range perfectly. It did keep me occupied, however. Just before 'Bombs Away' a moving shadow caused me to look up and through the open radio hatch. A bomber had moved directly above us. Horrified, I was looking directly into his bomb bay. I called Chick and we slid over in the nick of time. The bomber lurched as the bombs went away. I stood up in the door of the bomb bay to see if the bombs had all gotten clear. As soon as I did, a jagged piece of shrapnel sliced the command radio set in two and struck me directly in the chest. I was wearing a metal flak vest that was all that saved my life. It spun me around and stunned me momentarily. I saw that I was bleeding. A piece of spent metal had lodged in my neck, and this was where the blood was coming from. I was not badly hurt and I felt no pain at all, but I had had a close shave.

"On the way home we had some more excitement. We strayed over Brunswick, which was not on our itinerary and got flakked again. We eventually crossed the enemy coast and started letting down from altitude. It was a relief to take off the oxygen mask and relax for a bit. I ate a Clark bar and felt better at once. We had been on oxygen for about eight hours. The hydraulic system was damaged, so we knew we were going to have some problems getting down. Fortunately, we were using the long runway. We touched down; after slowing a bit, Chick headed her off the runway onto the grass. We circled to the right, kept circling, slowing gradually; and finally she gave up the ghost and stopped. We got out and looked her over. It was unbelievable. She was one more lacerated lady. That morning she had been a lovely girl without a blemish. The ground crews could do wonders with a shot-up B-17 but they had their work cut out with that one. Sometimes when one was shot up too badly, they made her a 'hangar queen' and cannibalized parts off her. I remember the ground crew laid some rueful looks on us."

The wreckage of aircraft littered the routes to the main targets in Germany. This B-17G, 42-38005 Stormy Weather *of the 351st Bomb Group, crashed at Sose Odde during a mission to Berlin on 24th May 1944. Capatin Robert B. Clay and his crew were taken POW.* (USAF)

The Luftwaffe had generally forsaken the First Bomb Division and had concentrated on the luckless Third Division instead. The enemy fighter pilots were aided by the weather which forced the Division to split and, in the resulting confusion, the escort became disoriented. The 4th Wing flew on in thick cloud which topped 30,000 feet but other groups were forced to turn back and bomb targets en route. When the Fortresses finally pierced the cloud front, only the 94th and 385th combat boxes remained. Both were alone and without fighter cover. The Luftwaffe assailed the unprotected Fortresses for over half an hour and shot down nineteen of the bombers, including ten from the 94th Bomb Group. Captain Lundak brought his battered B-17 back to Bury St Edmunds as one eye-witness put it, "shot to hell," and minus his tail-gunner who had baled out when the aircraft had nose-dived from 25,000 feet.

Since 11th April the 94th Bomb Group had lost about fourteen crews in combat or rotated home. Among the replacements at Rougham during April was Abe Dolim, a navigator, who three years before, had witnessed at first hand the Japanese bombing of Pearl Harbor. Such was the urgency for replacement crews that Abe Dolim had only to wait until 22nd April, fifteen days after disembarking from the *Queen Elizabeth* in Scotland, to fly his first combat mission, to the marshalling yards at Hamm. Unfortunately, the weather was to play a large part in shaping the mission and was responsible for its ultimate fate. Crews were apprehensive from the start. They were awakened in the middle of the night because the mission was scheduled for the usual early morning start. It was later postponed for several hours while Command waited for the bad weather front over the Continent to clear. After several stop-go decisions, it was in the afternoon that final clearance was given. Crews, who had been awake since 0200 hours, had their briefing updated with more recent weather information and began assembling for takeoff.

The Liberators of the Second Bomb Division led the 8th this day and began taking off from their Norfolk and Suffolk bases between 1615 and 1630 hours. They were followed by the Fortresses from nearby Third Division bases and First Division groups further west. At Bury St Edmunds, Lieutenant Scannel's Fortress lifted off from the rubber-stained runway and climbed to altitude. Abe Dolim was the navigator.

"We took off in beautiful CAVU weather topped with high cirrus clouds. On VHF I heard a weird chatter unfamiliar to me. Phrases like 'Fireball,' 'Vampire Violet,' 'Clambake Yellow,' 'Hotshot Red,' (our group code) and, 'Rotate' (our squadron code) badgered the radio waves. As we assembled over the 'splashers' and 'bunchers' the sky became dotted with colored flares, singles and doubles, while hundreds of aircraft tacked onto flights, squadrons, and groups. Finally, after more than an hour of forming, we took our

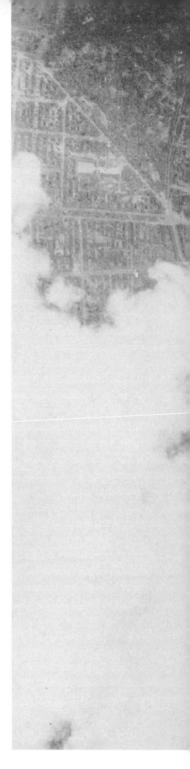

During the Berlin mission of 19th May 1944, bombs falling from Trudy, *flown by Lieutenant John Winslett of the 332nd Squadron, severed the tailplane of Lieutenant Marion Ulysses Reid's* Miss Donna Mae. *The aircraft fell into an uncontrolable spin. At 13,000 feet a wing broke off, sending the aircraft and the ten men inside crashing into the city below.* (Abe Dolim)

place at the lead of the 4th Combat Wing and proceeded at 150 mph indicated airspeed. Our fighter escort of P-47s and P-38s picked us up just north of Ijmuiden on the Dutch coast. There were no reports of enemy fighters as we turned at the IP and opened our bomb bay doors for the bomb run. From the IP onward there was absolutely no evasive action,

"We saw the flak before we spotted the target. The 88mm explosions looked like double black mushrooms as though the shell exploded in the middle and worked itself

out at both ends vertically. The railroad marshalling yards at Hamm, the chokepoint to 'Happy Valley' was three-and-a-half miles long, the largest in Germany, so large that we bombed in combat wing formation-three groups abreast. Flak was not too accurate and we were lucky to be the first over the target. Our bombs blanketed the yard; only a few appeared to go astray. As we turned off to the rally point, I looked toward 5 o'clock and saw a sky full of flak with two B-17s in trouble, one in a shallow dive afire and the other exploding after a short vertical dive. I watched several para-

chutes descend to German soil, then looked for my chest pack - it was not within reach. I made a note to stack it between my position and the emergency hatch against the bulkhead next to my navigation table. The trip back was uneventful, the 94th suffering no losses."

A few fighters were scrambled to harass the bombers as they left the target but the escorting fighters were more than a match for them. Perry Rudd, flying in the 457th formation, says,

42-97167 of the 339th Bomb Group was lost on 12th May 1944. Only one of Captain Jack E. Link's ten man crew survived when the aircraft crashed at Hahnsatten, in Germany.

"Thirteen wings hit the target and really blew it off the map. There was little flak over the target but I saw two planes going down. We hit the target from 22,000 feet and dropped twelve 500 pounders. Some planes in the distance got hit by heavy flak while we received only an occasional burst. The homeward trip was really rough, coming back in almost total darkness. At the coast some P-47s went down and silenced some flak guns - nice piece of work. We finally got back to base at 2235 hours but such was the confusion we had to put down at an RAF base."

The confusion was caused not only by the almost total darkness, something the majority of crews had never flown in before, but also by German intruder aircraft which mingled with formations after the target. Me 410s of KG51 waited until they were nearing the English coast before firing into the helpless American bomber formations. Many B-17 and B-24 crews were in the process of removing their guns when the first intruder struck. The B-17s generally avoided the intruder strikes, which were concentrated on B-24 bases in Norfolk and Suffolk. However, some Third Bomb Division bases in the vicinity also came under attack, as Bill Carleton, Engineering Officer at Thorpe Abbotts, remembers.

"At about 9 o'clock the planes of the B-24 base near us were late in returning from Hamm. As a result, it was necessary to turn on the runway lights. When those poor fellows started on their final approach they were shot down by the Jerries like sitting ducks. While all our planes were in, we were a little careless with our blackout and at least one German saw the lights near our Operations Building.

He strafed the building as well as part of the field, but no-one was hurt. Our perimeter defense threw themselves into action along with ninety percent of the base personnel, all of whom carried either a carbine rifle, a Browning automatic machine-gun or a Colt .45. A few minutes later a B-24 flew over and our perimeter defense opened up along with hundreds of other guns. Fortunately, they were all poor shots and the plane was not hit, but I quickly surmised it was getting pretty dangerous on the ground. Strafing was one thing, but to have 4,000 'dingalings' shooting into the air was too much. I ran for cover in my newly dug foxhole, tripped over the mound of dirt and fell into the hole on top of Sergeant Spangler, the line chief, who had evidently taken refuge some time earlier!"

The wreckage, considerable at some bases, was cleared away and conditions returned to normal. Also on 22nd April, the air echelon of the 398th Bomb Group, led by its CO, Colonel Frank P. Hunter, landed at Nuthampstead to join the 1st Combat Wing in the First Bomb Division. April is not one of England's better months and the squally showers and cold damp days soon turned Nuthampstead into "Mudhampstead." Fortresses began arriving ten a day until the group was up to full complement. After the system of deploying aircraft in long straight lines at their Rapid City base in the heart of the Black Hills of Dakota, the system of dispersal in England made life very difficult.

While new crews began their indoctrination lectures, the established groups were assembled on Monday, 24th April, for yet another raid on the aircraft plants in the Munich area. Altogether, 750 bombers were dispatched while from Italy another strong force hit targets in the Balkans. Perry Rudd was in the 457th formation that struck at Erding, northwest of Munich.

"There was no flak over the target but the fighters really gave us the works. I saw two B-17s go down. One had a direct hit on the vertical stabilizer and we could see right through it. There were lots of 109s that succeeded in breaking up a couple of our formations. Over Augsburg, Lechfeld and other towns nearby you couldn't pick out the formations for flak. One group struggled over Munster and had the heaviest concentration of flak I had ever seen. It blotted out the sky."

The 41st Bomb Wing, which bombed the Dornier repair and assembly plants fifteen miles south of Munich, bore the brunt of the attacks carried out by an estimated 200 enemy fighters. The 384th Bomb Group suffered the worst casualties, losing seven of the wing's fifteen losses before the Luftwaffe concentrated on the 40th Combat Wing. The 92nd Bomb Group lost five bombers in the resulting aerial battle including *Lil' Brat*, flown by Lieutenant James E. King who tried in vain to reach neutral territory but exploded over Baltenswil, Switzerland. Three days later a funeral service was held for the crew in Berne and their bodies were interred at the US cemetery at Munsingen. Altogether, thirteen Fortresses landed in Switzerland this day.

On 27th April, when the 8th flew two bombing missions in one day, and the following day, the heavies bombed targets chiefly in France. On the 28th April raids the 100th Bomb Group was assigned a "Noball" (V-1 flying bomb) site at Sottevast, near Cherbourg. John A. Miller, right waist gunner in Lieutenant Larry Townsend's crew, was one of many at Thorpe Abbotts who could not believe his luck, as he explains.

"A milk-run! The briefing officer described our mission and our route and it really sounded sweet. We would start our run over the water and only be over land a few minutes. 'There are only about eight guns there that will be able to reach you,' he said. Wow! This was really great! We wondered how the 'Bloody Hundredth' happened to get such a soft mission.

"Colonel Robert H. Kelly, fresh from the States, had just joined our group as CO on 19th April. At the morning's briefing he stood up and told us, 'There'll be no evasive action when we're on the bomb run.' Jack Swartout, a squadron CO, was to be the mission's air commander flying with Bill Lakin's crew, but at the last moment Colonel Kelly bumped Swartout from Lakin's crew and said he would fly as command pilot. Colonel Kelly had only been in command for nine days but in that short time we had learned to dislike him. Of course, none of the regular aircrews even knew the man but Kelly had come to the group with the idea of straightening it out. The worst part of this

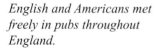
English and Americans met freely in pubs throughout England.

for us was that we would fly a combat mission and when we returned he would have us take off again on a practice mission! (We also noted that Kelly had not yet flown a mission with us.) This was for our own good, of course, and we did start flying the tightest formations you ever saw (anything to stop those practice missions), but at the time we were really angry. As we left the briefing room you could hear comments that 'Kelly sure picked a sweet milk-run for his first mission.'

"It was a beautiful day. We took off and soon we were starting on the bomb run. The flak was way below us as we made our run and there wasn't much of it. Then on the intercom I heard Townsend say that Kelly had called off the bomb drop and that we would have to go around again. We must have made the longest 360 in recorded history. Kelly took us far out over the water and it took forever. We came back in on the bomb run at the same speed, same altitude, and the same course, flying in rigid formation as Kelly ordered. The Kraut flak guns got us good! The Kelly-Lakin lead B-17 received two direct hits, one between the number two engine and the cockpit and the second back toward the tail position. The plane disintegrated and fell to earth. Colonel Kelly was killed. A second Fortress, flown by Lieutenant James W. McGuire, had its number one engine knocked from its mounting. The engine landed back on the left wing, setting it on fire. As he dove out of formation the left wing snapped off and the plane tumbled, a ball of fire, into the clouds below. The way that B-17 went down, the gyrations, how could a bombardier, of all people, get out and live to tell about it? But he did. John Jones, wherever you are, you're a walking miracle! I did not see any other 'chutes. (Six of the crew shared our hut with us in the 349th Squadron and all were KIA.)

"The flak over Sottevast was unbelievably accurate! Every plane received hits and damage. Bernard Palmquist, the ball gunner on Ralph W. Wright's crew, was hit, the flak going through his shoulder. He told me later that he had never seen such flak. This was the only time he could actually smell it. (Palmquist was still in hospital on 7th May when we started out for Berlin. just as we were leaving England I watched the old '17 his crew were flying dive out of formation. Somehow the flares, carried in the passageway to the nose, had exploded. All of Palmquist's officers were burned to death. The gunners baled out after much trouble.) When we returned to Thorpe Abbotts we were one shook-up bunch of fliers. At interrogation we told our story about the milk-run Colonel Kelly had chosen for his first mission with us. The intelligence interrogators were awed and amazed. One was heard to say, 'Colonel Kelly hasn't even unpacked yet.'"

On 29th April, Doolittle again unleashed his bombers on Berlin. Perry Rudd, in the 457th Bomb Group formation, says,

"Germany announced the raid as soon as we hit the IP, eighteen minutes at least from the target. There was little flak going in but plenty over the target. Their aiming point seemed to be in the lower boxes and we were in the higher box so we didn't get touched. The mission was planned for PFF but we could see the target quite clearly. Plans seemed to change at the last minute and we made a 360 degree turn near Berlin and went in thirty minutes late. We dropped three 1,000lb demolition bombs and six 500lb incendiaries which hit near a river bridge in the center of the capital. Each plane dropped three tons right on the target. The place must really have taken a beating: three divisions of ten wings bombed different sections and I saw only one plane go down, right over the target. It was in flames and broke up after a direct flak hit. There must have been 600 planes and even more fighters. I couldn't see how the city could be standing that night."

Once again the 8th had paid dearly for its accuracy. Part of the 4th Combat Wing had strayed off course and near Magdeburg FW 190s had wreaked havoc among the unprotected formation, shooting down or fatally damaging seventeen Fortresses in twenty minutes. The 385th Bomb Group, which was flying its 100th mission this day, lost seven bombers and the 447th Bomb Group, eleven. The latter group's losses brought its monthly total to twenty-one aircraft lost. The 94th and 96th Bomb Groups' losses for April 1944, the 8th's heaviest of the war, were also twenty-one bombers apiece.

Despite the heavy losses in April, May Day 1944 marked the beginning of a series of all-out raids on the enemy's railway network in support of the Pointblank Directive. On 1st May, 328 heavies were dispatched to marshalling yards and railway centers in France and Belgium but the offensive failed to gain momentum when bad weather fronts over the Continent halted deep penetration missions. The offensive was resumed with a vengeance on 6th May. The 398th Bomb Group at Nuthampstead made its aerial debut just thirty-one days after leaving Rapid City, Dakota, and only fourteen days after the group had arrived in England; a truly remarkable achievement. Then, for two consecutive days, on Sunday 7th May (when 1,000 American bombers were dispatched for the first time) and on 8th May, the 8th blasted Berlin. The following day 772 heavies were dispatched to enemy airfields and transportation targets and, on the 11th, 973 bombers were dispatched to marshalling yards in Germany and the Low Countries.

Next day the First Division sought synthetic oil plants in the Leipzig area while the 13th and 45th Wings of the Third Division went to oil targets at Brux in Czechoslovakia and two composite 4th Wing formations went to an FW 190 repair depot at Zwickau. This simultaneous attack on oil and aircraft was in keeping with Eisenhower's policy of pounding two of Germany's most valuable assets. Both had to be knocked out or crippled if the invasion of the Continent was to succeed.

Abe Dolim in the 94th Bomb Group was among those who went to Zwickau.

"We took up the low position in a composite group with a 385th Group squadron leading and a 447th Group squadron in the high position. After crossing the enemy coast at Ostend we received reports that the Luftwaffe was up in force. Near Koblenz our escort of P-51s departed to chase bogies. Some minutes later, Lieutenant Maybank spotted a small formation of unidentified fighters at 3 o'clock level. I stood up to be close to my .50s and, as I squinted out toward 2 o'clock, I was shocked to see about six jet-black FW 190s flying right through the high squadron, attacking from 12 o'clock level. The group closed up – no one seemed to be hurt. About ten minutes later, ten more black FWs attacked the lead squadron from 12 o'clock level, some of them fish-tailing to rake their targets. Kelch, Long, and I fired as they went by at 3 o'clock. One of the Focke-Wulfs rammed the number six aircraft in the lead squadron and both exploded. Two more B-17s dropped out of formation. One began a shallow trailing dive with all ten men baling out. The other maintained speed with the group about 500 feet below the lead squadron and dropped its landing gear to communicate air surrender. After some minutes, it retracted its landing gear and rejoined the group which was then about twenty miles southeast of Frankfurt.

"At our altitude of 19,000 feet there were some stratus layers, ideal for the enemy and, as I scanned at 11 o'clock level, I spotted a large formation of fighters approaching from 2,000 yards heading for our low squadron. I got on the intercom and notified the crew - Messerschmitt 109s, about thirty of them in three flights. We opened fire at about 1,200 yards and I picked the far left 109 in the lead flight. Two of them were shot out of formation before they approached within 500 yards. A string of cannon shells, so close I heard their sharp cracks, exploded just in front of our nose. I fired about sixty rounds at the 109 until he passed by our number one engine forcing me to quit. He was closing fast from out 100 yards when I yelled at Wehrfritz to get him. He poured .50s into the Messerschmitt at point-blank range. Apparently, the enemy pilot was not firing at this point or he would have raked us. His aircraft stalled after passing us and our tail-gunner saw it go down and crash - the pilot did not bale out.

"The 332nd was lucky to be intact, having suffered no losses. The bomb run to the target was a question mark as preceding bombers created fires in the repair plant, forcing our lead bombardier to aim through the billowing smoke. Near Weimar, the low group to our right took a pass from 6 o'clock level by ten 109s with no apparent effect. The floor of our navigator-bombardier compartment was covered with empty .50 caliber casings and in moving about I felt I had roller skates on my fur-lined boots."

Over 200 enemy fighters attacked the two composite formations for half an hour and the 4th Wing lost eleven bombers, including seven from the 447th Bomb Group. The Fortresses that won through to the target achieved a highly effective bomb drop. Pride of place went to the 385th, led by Colonel Vandevanter, the CO. He slowed down his own formation so that other, disoriented, groups could re-form on them before commencing the bomb run. The 385th stole the bombing honors, placing ninety-seven percent of its bombs within 2,000 feet of the MPI. This feat earned the group a Distinguished Unit Citation.

The 13th and 45th Wings, meanwhile, carried out the long and grueling mission to the oil refinery complex at Brux. Mike Wysocki in the 94th Bomb Group was flying his twenty-sixth mission this day and was angered by the ten-and-a-half hour round trip.

"General Doolittle had said missions were now getting shorter and easier! We were under constant fighter attack for four-and-a-half hours but we weren't so badly off as the Luftwaffe attacked us from the tail position. They would sit out of range of our gunners and lob rockets at our formation. I had a ringside seat of the 45th Wing who were right in front of us. B-17s, P-51s, 110s, and 109s were going down all over the place. I heard that the 452nd really took a beating. When we finally got back, after debriefing and cleaning up I went to the officers' club and proceeded to get gloriously drunk."

Long penetration missions were apparently the order of the day for, on 13th May, American crews were dispatched to Politz on the Baltic coast to bomb more oil refineries, while the Third Division was assigned the marshalling yards at Osnabruck. Perry Rudd in the 457th Bomb Group recalls the trip to Politz.

"The clouds were 7 to 9/10ths so we headed for the secondary target at Stettin instead. The town center and the docks were hit and our 1,000lb demolition bombs seemed to wreck the whole works. Flak over the target was light but they really knew how to use it. Every burst was just off our wing tips at exactly the right altitude. We came off the target with open bomb bay doors that we had to crank down. There were no escorts after the target but we could see Sweden off to our right and it looked really peaceful. Coming back across Denmark there must have been some Danes on the guns because they fired at us plenty but a mile low and off to the left of us. Two or three guns opened

Colonel James R. Luper brought the badly damaged Rene III *home from Ludwigshaven on 27th May 1944, and landed her at Glatton on only one wheel.* (USAF)

up on a P-51 and gave him a really tough time. It was as if they were showing us they could do it if they wanted to but didn't."

On 14th May the weather grounded all three divisions and for five days missions were scrubbed. For Joe Wroblewski, waiting to fly his thirtieth and final mission in the 351st Bomb Group, the wait was almost unbearable.

"After getting up at 0100 hours for three straight days each mission was scrubbed. All would have been milk-runs or easy raids. Then, at briefing on 19th May, when the weather finally cleared, I sat through briefing and the target was Berlin! What a way to end my tour! I cursed the weatherman all the way. He said we would have an overcast at the target with clouds coming up to 25,000 feet. We went in at 27,000 feet with a temperature of about minus forty degrees centigrade. The clouds were nowhere to be seen, except for a puff here and there. Just before we got to Berlin about thirty enemy fighters came up and made a pass at the group just ahead of us, knocking down two bombers. I broke out in a sweat and was glad to get into the flak before they could make another pass. Flak was the lesser of the two evils. It was heavy but inaccurate and we only picked up a few holes, though one piece tore away the tail-gunner's shoe. He received no injury.

"Bombing was made visually. After 'Bombs Away,' the trip back was uneventful. We got a good look at Berlin and saw bombs from the groups ahead exploding in the city. This being our last mission, we shot a green flare upon returning to Polebrook. It sort of upset Colonel Romig,

because this was against orders. He threatened us but all we had to do for penance was go on a practice mission two days later."

On 20th May, the 8th roamed far and wide, bombing targets in France. Bomb groups were stood down on the 21st but the following morning the heavies were assigned Kiel after bad weather had ruled out targets in France. On the 24th, the bombers returned to "Big-B" yet again. The Luftwaffe was up in force and inflicted savage losses. Cloud and thick contrails caused the 381st Bomb Group to lose contact with other groups in the 1st Wing and eight Fortresses were shot down by fighters. The "Bloody Hundredth" also suffered badly, losing nine Fortresses from the day's total loss of thirty-three Fortresses. The next day crews correctly anticipated a milk-run to the Low Countries. Despite perfect weather, some Fortresses in the 390th and 401st Bomb Groups bombed using radar. Command needed to know how successful PFF methods could be on D-Day if targets were obscured by cloud. It all served to increase speculation, at Framlingham and Deenthorpe at least, that the invasion of *Festung Europa* was imminent.

On 27th May the German rail network once again came in for a pounding by the Fortresses. Colonel James Luper, CO of the 457th, led the "Fireball Outfit" and the First Division to Ludwigshaven in *Rene III*, the 1,000th B-17 built by Douglas and named after Luper's wife. The flak was heavy and fighters made head-on attacks that verged on the suicidal. *Rene III* was badly shot up but Luper managed to nurse her back to Glatton. During final approach, however, only one undercarriage leg would extend despite repeated attempts to lower it. Finally, Luper had to land *Rene*

III on only the one wheel, skillfully keeping her straight and level for as long as possible before the left wing began to sag. The Colonel killed his ignition switches just before the Fortress dipped and ploughed an arc across the airfield. The entire crew was unhurt and was able to walk away unscathed. *Rene III* was repaired and flew again, but three other B-17s in the 457th failed to return and nineteen were severely mauled. The 457th's tale of woe continued on 28th May when three more crews were lost. This day the 8th dispatched a record 1,282 bombers to seven oil targets in Germany. The Luftwaffe again concentrated their attacks, in this instance on the leading wings of the First and Third Bomb Divisions. The escorting fighters were overwhelmed and the 94th Wing at the head of the First Division was assailed by over 300 fighters. Altogether, twelve bombers were lost, including seven from the 401st Bomb Group.

Next day the bombers were dispatched to oil plants at Politz and three Focke-Wulf 190 factories in the Reich. The long, arduous missions took their toll and those crews due some leave were glad of a respite. When the opportunity arose, combat crews headed for London. The English capital was very popular with combat crews who normally received a three-day pass about every forty-five days. Ben Smith remembers that American airmen slept most of the day and spent most of the night in the pubs and clubs that stayed open until seven a.m.

"We dressed in our ODs and ventured out into the night. Even in the blackout, throngs of people were surging up and down the street. Wartime London was a melting pot for the armed services of every nationality and their uniforms were colorful, often picturesque. In the United Kingdom women were drafted into the services, so most decent girls were in uniform. Only prostitutes and elderly ladies were in street dress.

"The conviviality of wartime is unimaginable if one hasn't actually experienced it. People who had not seen each other five minutes ago became comrades. Romantic attachments were formed on the spot, sometimes with no more than a searching look. Complete strangers drank out of the same bottle with no thought of disease. Virtuous girls (in another context) quickly availed themselves of the chance of dinner and dancing and a one-night stand with boys who would be dead within the week. Australians, Canadians, and Yanks prowled the city together, denigrating their English cousins and declaring their undying friendship. Language was no barrier; the bottle was the universal language bestowing upon Pole, Norwegian, Free French, and Yank alike; perfect understanding and instant communication.

"I remember vividly a slender English girl who let me take her home. She told me that I was nothing but a baby, which news took me aback. No matter - she was very tender and sweet to the 'baby' and I never forgot her. We

Piccadilly Circus, London, center of activity for GIs on leave. (Royal Frey)

went from one pub to the other drinking gin and Guinness, a standard affectation of the English but a pretty neat drink withal. One thing sure, it would get the job done. I loved the uproarious good humor of the Cockneys. These people are a breed set apart, quite unlike the other English I had met. Hitler had not been able to break these people's spirit. They thrived on adversity. We had a grand time together but inevitably time would run out on us. Of all sad words of tongue or pen, saddest were these: 'Time please, Lideys and Gentuhlmen!' Oh, how we dreaded to hear the familiar closing words.

"Each night, at least once or twice, the air-raid siren would begin its mournful dirge and the ack-ack would start up. As searchlights plied the sky, we watched from the roof of an hotel, in our drunkenness scornful of shelter or succor. My companions were Australians or Canadians. The English always went dutifully to an air-raid shelter. It was not

The streets of Kimbolton did not hold the same appeal as the sights of London, but these three airmen from the 379th Bomb Group are out to make the best of the local life.

that they were afraid; they were cool customers under fire. It was just that they always did what they were supposed to do, exactly as they were supposed to.

"Something moralistic about my make-up made me eschew the favors of the army of prostitutes who thronged Piccadilly. I never liked the idea of buying sex; however, they didn't lack for customers simply because I was squeamish. They were ignored by the 'Bobbies' who wisely knew that this had to go on in a war. These 'ladies of the night' were in every doorway with a cigarette lighted so you would know they were there. They never left the doorway; when they got a customer, the trick was turned on the spot - in a standing position. They could turn five tricks that way while turning one in an hotel room. Our lads called them 'Piccadilly Commandos,' a name that stuck."

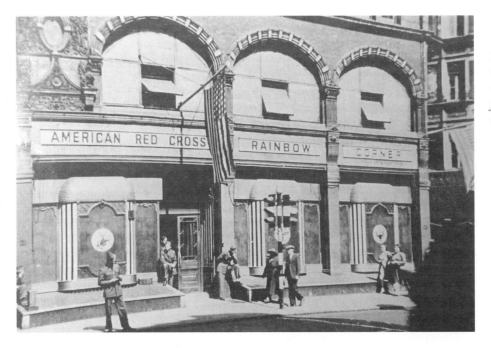

The famous American Red Cross Club at Rainbow Corner, a favorite stopover for GIs on leave in London. (Richards)

Chapter 13
The Great Crusade

When crews returned from leave they usually had riotous tales of revelry to tell. Men stationed at Fortress and Liberator bases who had taken forty-eight hour passes to London returned with vivid accounts of vehicles of all descriptions jamming the English roads and country lanes. Passenger trains were being withdrawn and trains out of the capital were crammed. For some weeks now the headlines in the London press and the *Stars and Stripes* had proclaimed that invasion of the Continent was imminent. Certainly, recent events seemed to point to a grand offensive and crews sensed that the day when the Allies would assault Hitler's *Festung Europa* was not far off. They knew it would come some time in 1944 but they did not know where the thrust would pierce the enemy stronghold. They could only take side bets, little knowing that higher command had already decided upon a stretch of the Normandy coastline from Quineville to just south of Caen. "Invasion fever" spread throughout East Anglia as preparations were put in hand at the American air bases. The number of air crews and available aircraft were kept at peak strength while training, especially of new crews and PFF crews, was stepped up. All this supported the belief that the invasion was "Go!"

Beginning on 30th May, American bomber crews as well as RAF Bomber Command, made all-out attacks on the invasion coast. Both were careful to place twice as many bombs on targets further afield as they did on the Normandy coast, for fear that the German defenders would learn where the assault would come. The enemy knew that invasion was

imminent but suspected that the first wave of troops would land in the Pas de Calais, further north. So, while the German defenders on the Atlantic Wall played their guessing game, the heavies continued their strikes on "Noball" sites in the Pas de Calais.

Late on 29th May Mike Wysocki, a lead bombardier in the 94th Bomb Group who had flown his twenty-ninth and penultimate mission to Leipzig earlier in the day, was called to a special briefing. It revealed that the target for the morrow would be a rocket storage site at Watten in the Pas de Calais. B-17s were to carry a special load of six 1,600lb SAP (armor-piercing) bombs to penetrate the roof. Only Wysocki and the other lead bombardiers in the 410th Squadron were privy to the information. On the morning of 30th May crews were called a little later than usual, had their breakfasts and then went out to their Fortresses after briefing. While Wysocki's fellow crewmembers were getting ready to fly, the ground crew smuggled a couple of extra flare guns aboard in anticipation of the crew completing their tour. Mike Wysocki dropped his bombs on the rocket site.

"I am very nosy - I like to see what happened so I put on my steel helmet and looked. All I could see was dust in the target area. I was disappointed to think on my last mission that all I dropped was a bunch of duds! (A couple of months later Major Stevenson, the 410th Bomb Squadron CO, called me over and told me those damn Navy bombs went through the roof right down to the cellar and blew the joint out of operation!) When we came back our B-17 was like a Roman Candle with all the flares going. It looked like a good old fashioned 4th of July, only it happened to be Memorial Day!" Mike Wysocki's tour was over but for thousands like him, the missions to France continued. On Monday 5th June, the 8th went to the Pas de Calais. The raid was one of many similar ones flown over the past few days and that night Abe Dolim, a navigator in the 332nd Bomb Squadron, recorded in his diary: "There have been all sorts of rumors about an imminent invasion of the enemy coast."

The rumors gained credence that night, as Ben Smith in the 303rd Bomb Group at Molesworth, explains. "We saw RAF aircraft and gliders coming over, wave after wave. We knew we would be going in the morning and thought there would be hell to pay. We didn't sleep much that night."

At Kimbolton, Franklin L. Betz, a navigator in the 379th Bomb Group, was one of thousands awakened in the early dawn.

"To be awakened about 0400 hours for a mission was pretty much routine but to be hauled out of the sack at only 0130 hours to report to briefing - well, 'something unusual must be up,' I thought as I groped sleepily for my clothes. The atmosphere at briefing was invariably somber. Sitting quietly on benches, dozing or languidly puffing on cigarettes that glowed eerily in the soft light of the starkly furnished rooms, there was very little talk while the fliers, officers, and enlisted men, waited for the CO, Colonel Preston, to arrive.

"'Tenshun!' someone up front bawled when the CO strode in. Everyone arose, standing erect, eyes straight ahead. 'At ease' the Colonel said. The men sat down quietly, tensely awaiting roll call and the removal of the cover from the huge map of Europe on which the course to and from the target had been traced. If it showed a deep penetration of Germany, which meant dangerous fighter attacks and flak encounters throughout the flight, a groan arose from the dry throats of the airmen, a groan that trailed off into excited whispers as briefing continued. But at 0230 hours, when the briefing officer announced 'This is it! This is D-Day!' it was different; a lusty cheer shattered the quiet of the moment before. Whoops, whispers, and yells echoed from the gray walls. It was an unprecedented and ecstatic vocal demonstration by the fliers who had doggedly been carrying the war to Germany for many months with considerable losses of men and planes. It was the day they had waited to share with the ground forces and together they would assault the Nazi war machine, hopefully gaining a foothold on the mainland with the ultimate goal of driving the Wehrmacht back to the Fatherland and crushing it."

The same scene was being repeated throughout the rest of the First and Third Bomb Division bases, nestling in the low-lying Suffolk, Norfolk, and Essex countryside (the Liberators of the Second Bomb Division were to lead the 8th on this momentous day). At Horham, Suffolk, Henry Tarcza in the 95th Bomb Group was awakened some hours before daylight.

"I thought this was just another routine bombing mission over enemy-occupied Europe. Shortly after 0300 hours I enjoyed a breakfast of bacon and country fresh eggs, a wartime delicacy reserved only for the combat flying personnel. We entered the maximum security briefing room around 0400 hours where the huge map on the wall was covered with yards of thick drapery. After all the noise of shifting chairs had ceased the briefing officer calmly pulled the covering material towards him and a long moan from all the flying men echoed throughout the room, followed by a hoarse whisper of 'invasion.'

"The red streamers on the map ran from every air base in England and crossed the Channel, converging on one tiny spot near Cherbourg. The briefing colonel pointed toward that area with what happened to be an old billiard cue and said, 'Yes, gentlemen. This is the day you've been waiting for and this is the spot that has been selected.' It was a relatively short briefing because the navigators had already been given separate instructions. Before unlocking the exit doors the briefing officer smiled and said, 'Good luck, gentlemen, and give 'em Hell!'"

At all bases in the three divisions the following telegram from General Doolittle was read out. "The 8th Air Force is currently charged with a most solemn obligation in support of the most vital operation ever undertaken by our armed forces. It will be necessary during certain stages to attack with tremendous intensity the area immediately in front of our advancing troops. Because of the intensity required, no other agency except the 8th Air Force can undertake this task. The required materials and skills are ours, yet it must be recognized that bombardment accuracy has never faced a more severe test. Every individual keenness, every refinement of technique, and every aid to accuracy must be exploited so that the pattern of our attack is exactly as ordered, and that there are no gross or avoidable errors to bring disaster to our troops on the ground. The necessary hazards have been accepted. They can be minimized only through exalted performance on the part of our air leaders and bombardiers. I have every confidence in you."

The 8th was required to fly three missions. The first was primarily concerned with neutralizing enemy coastal defenses and front-line troops. Subsequent missions would be directed against lines of communication leading to the bridgehead. The bombers would be in good company with no less than thirty-six squadrons of Mustangs and Thunderbolts patrolling the area. Initially, they would protect the "big friends" but would later break off and strafe ground targets. It was evident that there could be no delay and that any stragglers would be left to their fate. Any aborts were to drop out of formation before leaving the English coast and then fly back to base at below 14,000 feet. It was a one-way aerial corridor and the traffic flow intense. Aircraft would fly to and fro over the length of England dropping various colored flares to denote the aerial corridors. If a Fortress had to be ditched, only those ships returning to England from the bridgehead would stop to pick up crews. Crews were told that if they were shot down they were to wait in uniform until they could join their own troops in France.

Finally, a message from General Eisenhower, the Supreme Allied Commander, was read out. Perhaps it was the tension brought on by the big occasion but not all crewmen were impressed. Ben Smith recalls, "At briefing we heard Eisenhower's inspirational message to the departing troops. At least, it was supposed to inspire. I remember thinking that Churchill could have done it with a lot more class."

Briefing over, a line of trucks was assembled to take crews to their waiting Fortresses. "Little was said by our crew of ten as we proceeded to our bomber in a canvas-covered truck," Henry Tarcza remembers. "I'm sure they all felt as I did. If the Germans shared my secret at that moment it could have altered the destiny of mankind. As we boarded our bomber we all did a good job of maintaining our composure so that the ground crews might not suspect that D-Day had, in fact, arrived."

The pre-dawn calm of the countryside around the farmlands and in the towns and villages near the bomber bases was shattered by the roar of thousands of Wright Cyclones and Twin Wasps being pre-flighted at all points of the compass. Overhead the moon shone through a thick black undercast. Henry Tarcza walked out to the waiting Fortress at Horham.

"Our B-17 bore none of the usual fancy paintings. On her nose were the simple words, *El's Bells*. Our aircraft commander was Mathew McEntee, who had named our plane in honor of his girlfriend back home in New York City and whom he later married. We waited in line on the runway for our turn to takeoff. As we left the ground I had that very comforting feeling that I was coming back safely to England that day. As we circled to gain altitude it was early daylight and the sight in the vast sky staggered my wildest imagination. The air was thick with eastbound aircraft for as many miles as I could see in all directions. We joined in and headed toward France."

Meanwhile, Frank L. Betz in the 379th Bomb Group formation had lifted off at 0445 hours.

"The lead plane roared down the runway, lifting gracefully into the gray light of the early morning. The remaining Fortresses, lined up like dancers in a conga line, swung on to the runway in turn and followed. Aboard No. 003 my heart raced from the excitement of knowing that I was involved in an undertaking that, if successful, would be a

Forbidden Fruit, of the 452nd Bomb Group drops its bombs on Schwerte, Germany, on 31st May 1944. (Sam Young)

D-Day. *News of the invasion is given in the packed briefing room at Thurleigh on 6th June 1944.* (Richards)

major turning point of the war. It took until 0604 hours for the formation to assemble over the awakening English countryside. Departing Molesworth at 11,000 feet and climbing, the planes headed south. Flying in tight formation I noted in my log that we crossed over the coast between Portsmouth and Brighton at 0637 hours, altitude 15,000 feet.

"The fluffy layer of clouds below hampered visibility but there were some breaks in them and I could see the choppy dark waters of the English Channel. Droning steadily toward the Continent, I gasped when a huge opening in the clouds revealed ships and boats of all sizes dotting the water as far as I could see. 'Hundreds - no, there must be thousands,' I thought. Although no one type of ship could be identified from nearly three miles high, I was to learn later practically the whole spectrum of powered vessels from battleships to motor launches made up the Invasion fleet. Landing ships carrying thousands of troops, tanks, guns, vehicles, and ammunition, were positioning for the daring dash to the Normandy beaches. Barrage balloons swayed lazily above the ships, to which they were attached by stout cables.

"More holes appeared in the clouds and the awesome spectacle continued to unfold. I arose from my seat in the navigator's cramped work area in the left rear of the B-17G's nose to get a better view from the right waist window. Fascinated, I saw puffs of white smoke snort from the huge guns of battleships and cruisers aimed toward the mainland. A moment later massive explosions could be seen a short distance inland where the shells landed, kicking up a fountain of debris that, I reflected, must be a mixture of steel and stones, flesh and bones when the targets were hit.

"The Fortress, swaying gently, throbbed on. No sign of Me 109s or FW 190s but our 'little friends' were out in force. The Lightnings, Thunderbolts and Mustangs, their invasion markings - blue and white stripes on wings and fuselages-very prominent, were providing an aerial umbrella for the landing forces. Strafing the enemy positions up and down the coast and for some miles inland, they were determined to help the GIs embarking on the great crusade.

"The white capped wake of hundreds of circling landing craft awaiting the order to head to the shore contributed to the drama of the scene."

Henry Tarcza was another gazing in awe at the hundreds of ships and boats off Omaha Beach below.

"All were headed toward the beach landing site and it appeared from our altitude that one could almost step from one vessel to another and walk between England and France. Our group of about forty B-17s in close formation began to ease its way into the narrow corridor for the bomb run. At this time the bombardier instructed me to activate the bombs. I climbed out onto the catwalk and, after cautiously removing the safety pins from each bomb, notified the bombardier that they were now 'live.' For the first time since takeoff I experienced a sense of fear. This was mostly for the unknown because I now began to wonder what the Nazis had in store for us in that critical area. As we reached Omaha Beach the lead plane released a smoke bomb which was a signal for all forty aircraft to drop their bombs simultaneously. Thus, more than 100 tons of bombs exploded in a matter of a few seconds. This was the only mission over Europe when I actually felt the concussion of our own bombs. The explosions caused our aircraft to bounce and vibrate."

Meanwhile, groups in the First Task Force of the First Bomb Division prepared to bomb their allotted targets in the Cherbourg peninsula. Perry Rudd's B-17 was one of a record forty-eight dispatched by the 457th Bomb Group this day.

"We were plenty tired after getting no sleep the night before, having been forced to land at a B-26 base following a raid on Paliscau on 5th June. We had flown back to Glatton that night and were unable to get to bed at all before being awakened for the raid on the Cherbourg peninsula. We flew over our target at 16,400 feet and dropped thirty-eight 100lb demolition bombs through overcast. The landing troops hit the beach fourteen minutes after we dropped our bombs. There were reports that some of our bombs were still exploding as the boys went in."

Excited crews began touching down at their bases and pouring out their stories to receptive ground crews and newsmen. Henry Tarcza and his fellow crewmembers became a little apprehensive on the return trip because of their diminishing fuel supply. They left the formation and landed at an RAF base in southern England where they refueled before flying on to Horham. At the Suffolk base, Tarcza and the rest of the crew gave an Associated Press reporter their views on the historic mission.

"Emotions varied among our crew members. Many of our thoughts, feelings and opinions we kept to ourselves. I like to recall the words of our worthy pilot, Mathew McEntee. As we all parted for our respective quarters he said, 'Thank you, men, for your fine co-operation as a combat crew. It is doubtful if any of us will ever in our lifetime, participate in an historic undertaking of this magnitude.'

"So far, nobody has."

There was no sleep for those left behind. A second mission was being planned and this was to be followed by a third. There was no respite at all for the ground crews who, after a hasty breakfast, were out again working on the returning aircraft. Ironically, amid all this activity, the German radio station at Calais was on the air playing a song called *Invasion Day*.

The Liberators of the Second Bomb Division managed to get off for the second mission but the weather deteriorated and not all the Fortress groups made it. Ben Smith in the 303rd Bomb Group was one who did get a second look.

"We flew two missions on D-Day and did not see a single German fighter or even a burst of flak. Amazing! I could see a battleship out in the Channel (I believe it was the

Bombs tumble towards their targets below.

Texas), firing at shore targets. There was a solid mass of ships offshore and we could see the beach-head landing craft and others streaking in with their precious burdens."

The destruction of German railways was of great importance if reinforcements were to be stopped from reaching the Normandy front. This German marshalling yard has been all but destroyed from the air.

Altogether, 2,362 bomber sorties were flown on D-Day, for the loss of only three Liberators. The Luftwaffe was noticeable by its absence and the Fortresses suffered no loss. An indication of the success of the operation was contained in a message sent to all bomber bases that day from Lieutenant General Doolittle.

"Today the greatest effective strength in the history of the 8th Air Force was reached; an overall effectiveness of approximately seventy-five percent of all crews and airplanes assigned. Please extend my congratulations to all members . . . for their untiring effort in achieving this impressive strength."

On 7th June the Luftwaffe again failed to appear as the heavies helped consolidate the bridgehead with strikes on communication targets such as a railway bridge over the Loire at Nantes. Tactical targets in France continued to be attacked until 15th June, when the 40th Combat Wing was dispatched to Nantes to finish off the railway bridge, and the Third Division attacked an oil refinery at Misburg. The First Division, meanwhile, struck at targets in northern France, mostly airfields that could be used to launch Luftwaffe attacks on the Normandy bridgehead. At Le Bourget and Melum airfields near Paris, five B-17s of the 457th Bomb Group, including the lead ship flown by Lieutenant Malcolm Johnson, which also carried Colonel Cobb of the 94th Wing, were brought down by flak. One of them ditched in the Channel but five of the crew drowned before ASR could reach them.

After the D-Day missions and continued raids on oil and tactical targets throughout the first three weeks of June, it seemed nothing was beyond the reach of the 8th Air Force. Such was the strength of this powerful striking force that, even while a record 1,402 bombers were being dispatched to oil targets on 20th June, plans were being finalized for a second shuttle mission which would surpass even the Regensburg-Africa-France shuttle of August 1943.

Chapter 14
Frantic

For the 8th's second shuttle mission, the 13th and 45th Wings of the Third Division would bomb a synthetic oil refinery just south of Berlin and then fly on to landing fields in Russia. The Italian-based 15th Air Force had already flown a shuttle mission to Russia on 2nd June but the 8th was forced to wait until now, 21st June, because of the demands made upon it by the Normandy invasion. Five of the groups (the 452nd formed the sixth) had flown the first shuttle mission, to Africa, in August 1943. The Regensburg shuttle leader, General Curtis E. LeMay (as he now was), had been transferred to the Pacific early in June 1944 and his place at Third Bomb Division Headquarters was taken by Major General Earl E. Partridge, under whose direction the second shuttle was to be flown.

The plan, code-named Frantic, was impressive. The 13th and 45th Combat Wings were to provide 163 Fortresses, each equipped with a long-range bomb bay tank, for their journey to Russian airfields at Poltava, Piryatin, and Mirgorod, all east of Kiev. Their return would be made via Italy and France. The 4th Combat Wing and a composite from the Third Bomb Division would lead the 8th Air Force to Berlin with the First Bomb Division next in line, then the Second Bomb Division, with the rest of the Third Division bringing up the rear. After Berlin they would return to England, leaving the 13th and 45th Wings to fly on to Russia, escorted all the way by seventy Mustangs of the 4th and 352nd Fighter Groups. It was hoped that the RAF would join in the massive daylight strike on Berlin in retaliation for the V-1 attacks on London, but lack of fighter support for the slower Lancasters with their limited firepower would prevent their participation. Even so, the 8th was able to assemble 1,311 bombers for the momentous mission.

News of the second shuttle soon spread and some ground crew members learned that they would be flying with the shuttle force to service the bombers when they touched down in Russia. Mustang ground crews would fly as waist gunners and would service the fighters. At least one ground crewman would fly in each bomber. The number of ground crews alarmed the sensitive and highly secretive Russians and the shuttle only got the green light after several problems had been ironed out by diplomatic means! The shuttle meant that at least one airman who was holding down a desk job, would be allowed to fly on the mission. Harry H. Crosby, group navigator and veteran of many of the 100th Bomb Group's more harrowing missions, explains.

"At one point in the air war, the high command decided that rotating leadership was a waste of training. A command was issued prohibiting anyone with the rank of major or above from going home after flying his missions; instead he would be re-assigned somewhere in the ETO, which usually meant an almost enforced volunteering for a second tour. I was only a captain but, since it was believed (rightly or wrongly) that I knew something about lead navigation, the 'Powers Up There' neatly solved the question of how to keep me on duty by grounding me after my twenty-second mission. I convinced Tom Jeffrey, the CO, that I was necessary on the mission. Most importantly, I pointed out that missions there and back would still not bring my total up to twenty-five and they'd still have me around. So it was settled, I could go.

"The 0130 briefing was orderly, swift, a strange note of festivity perceptible. Besides the usual views of the target, briefings about the group, wing, and division rendezvous, and reports of enemy resistance, there were also a few words to be said about which Russian ranks to salute. On the blackboard was a space for the estimated time of our return. Colonel Bennett, the air executive, jokingly inserted 4th July in that space, little realizing how prophetic he was.

"Each ship had some particular item to take care of for the group. Some carried the engineering kits, some the field rations, others the luggage of the P-51 Mustang pilots who were going to escort us all the way. The plane whose safe arrival was most desired was the one that carried our entire supply of toilet paper. At takeoff time there was a taxi incident, which dashed the hopes of two crews for this jaunt. Naturally, the only officer who spoke Russian was on one of these crews."

The bombers flew the northern route to Germany, climbing northeast to a point above the Frisian Islands, then heading due east as though to southern Denmark. All went according to the flight plan until the bombers reached the German coast near Cuxhaven where four aircraft in the 452nd Bomb Group were involved in a mid-air collision. Harry Crosby says,

"We penetrated the German coast between Flensburg and Bremen. Of course, although we were miles from it, Bremen threw flak and smoke screens all over the place. From the German coast on, the wisecracks subsided. Gunners scoured the skies for fighters. If they were friendly we relaxed. By now we were on oxygen and in our heated clothing. With all those wires, if you turn around twice in the same direction you feel as though an octopus has you. There is a maze of intercom cords, oxygen tubes, electric heating lines, and parachute harness all tangled about you. Every fifteen minutes or so I gave a position report: 'There's Kiel off to the left. We're in the middle of the enemy twin-engine belt. Keep your eyes peeled.' Or: 'There's Brandenburg. We're 15 minutes from the IP. Some P-51s are due. Watch for them.' Occasionally, the bombardier requested an oxygen check and each crew member called in to let us know he was okay.

"During the trip to the target, the most impressive sight was our glimpse of Berlin. As we passed by, we all vocally pitied the poor devils who drew it as their target for the day. There was the usual cloud of flak to wade through,

and there's no rougher job. We saw a few B-24s go down as their turn came."

In the 94th Bomb Group formation, Abe Dolim waited for the bomb bay doors of his Fortress to open.

"Our bomb run was a straight forty miles long at ninety knots ground speed due to a stiff headwind, instead of a tailwind as briefed. We unloaded our delayed action GPs and incendiaries over the Charlottenburg district while heavy flak from the 900-odd 88mm cannons around Berlin gave us the most accurate and sustained fire we had encountered to date. We watched one of our bombers drop out of formation and head for the deck. As we turned away from the target we saw many brightly blazing pin-points of fire in the heavily built up residential area below.

"The demolition bombs used were fused to explode from one to seventy-two hours after impact. These, coupled with the incendiaries, created the maximum hazardous situation for the enemy fire-fighting and UXB demolition crews. The 500lb incendiary canisters were designed to disintegrate after dropping about 1,000 feet and spew out approximately 200 two-and-a-half pound thermite bombs which literally rained death on the enemy. Some thermite bombs had anti-personnel fragmentation devices to discourage countermeasures. They exploded in contact with water and could only be put out by smothering with non-combustible material. Under no circumstances were we allowed to return and land with a load of delayed action bombs as they were sensitive to shock. These are murderous weapons to use against civilians and there are many among us who are not proud of the day's accomplishment."

Despite the intense fighter cover, the Luftwaffe managed to make a few attacks on the Berlin force. Near the capital, Me 410s swooped on the rear of the First Division formation and made several attacks on the B-17s. Altogether, forty-four Fortresses and Liberators were shot down on the raid. Meanwhile, the shuttle force, consisting of the 13th, 45th, and Composite Wings, headed for their target, the Ruhrland-Elsterwerda synthetic oil plant some fifty miles south of the capital. The 388th Bomb Group from Knettishall, with the task force commander, Colonel Archie Old, at the helm, provided an "A" Group, which led the 45th Combat Wing, plus the low and high squadrons of a composite group which was low group in the 13th "B" Wing led by the 452nd Bomb Group.

Bombs fell from the bellies of the 388th and 452nd Bomb Group Fortresses and were joined by those of the 100th Bomb Group. Harry Crosby recalls,

"The groups of our wing were in trail, the lead bombardiers synchronizing on the target. The corrections to course were rocky and the pilots found it difficult to keep our squadron in place. There was a tense order every once in a while like, 'More manifold pressure', or 'Watch number three engine. It's running high,' or a burst of exasperation as one of our wingmen overran us. Then, 'Bombs Away!' . . .. The bombardier hit the switch. Lights on the instrument panel flashed. The plane jerked upward as the wings were suddenly released from their 6,000lb burden. A sudden turn to the left. Eardrums cracked as we lost altitude to confuse the flak. Bomb bay doors closed. The flak, black, ugly, and angry, grew worse. We'd been over these gunners for twenty minutes and many of the planes were racked by bursts."

Lieutenant Alfred R. Lea, navigator aboard *BTO in the ETO* in the 452nd Bomb Group continues,

"Our seventy-five B-17s had bombed what turned out to be the wrong target. We rejoined the other groups afterwards and headed for Poltava. While over Poland, those in command decided it would be good for the morale of the people in Warsaw if we went off course and flew far enough north to fly over the city. It caused riots in the streets; the first Allied planes to fly over since their own did it in 1939! Unfortunately, it gave the Luftwaffe time to rise up against us. Near Swory and Biala Podlaska we were attacked by fifteen 109s and, despite Lieutenant Sibbett, a valiant P-51 pilot who went down defending *BTO in the ETO*, we were shot down. The Poles gave Sibbett a hero's burial and made a wooden cross marker with an emblem depicting wings and a propeller. Three of our crew were so badly wounded they could not escape the German forces and were taken prisoner. I and the other six (including Sergeant Robert Gilbert, a P-51 crew chief who was flying with us) evaded capture. We were picked up by Polish partisans of the 34th Regiment and served as infantrymen for forty days, attacking German forces and pillaging Russians preying on Polish civilians. Our adventures were all under extremely adverse circumstances as the 34th was limited to rifles, machine-guns, pistols, grenades, and plastic explosives. The Germans had unlimited resources and personnel but were unable to restrain our 200 - 300 man unit. Our opponents included the Gestapo, Wehrmacht and the Luftwaffe. At one time plans were being laid to take over a Luftwaffe base long enough for the seven of us to commandeer a Ju 88 and fly it to England! We had captive pilots' manuals to study but we called it off because it would have been too costly in partisans' lives for just seven of us to get away. The planes looked very tempting as we surveyed them from our hiding places in the adjacent forest!

"We finally made our way, with the 34th Regiment Commandant 'Zenon's' help, into Russian-held territory, thence with the Red Air Force from base to base to Poltava. We were awarded the 'Kryz Walzyuch' (Cross of Valor) by the Poles for our infantry service. Later we were also awarded the 'Memorial Medal of Armia Krajowa' by the Poles for our services in the AK (Resistance Forces). When we got back to England we lectured on evasion tactics for a month before being sent home to the States."

Harry Crosby, meanwhile, in the 13th Wing was grateful for the Mustang escort after the target.

"We lost a few thousand feet of altitude, which improved living conditions. Then eastward across Germany we went and into Poland. Our P-51 escort was with us, and what a feeling of security their presence brought. The Mustangs were eager for a fight. We could hear the pilots chattering over the radio as they looked for opposition. In eastern Poland they found it. Just as we passed a few miles south of Warsaw, the skies changed. Huge fair-weather cumulus piled up high and awesome. From behind them suddenly careened a flight of enemy fighters. Messerschmitt 109s!

"After seven-and-a-half hours of flying, the bomber pilots had relaxed to loose formation, but at the first sight of the enemy they snapped back into position like the snap of a plumb line. The Mustang pilots yelled with delight and dove after the bogies, ratio about eight to one, P-51s to 109s. Seven bogies went down and the others went home.

"Visibility cleared as we crossed the Dnieper River and we saw plenty of evidence that war had been to Russia. From the Polish border to central Russia every hill had a slit trench and every plain a battlefield. The trip's duration was just about the limit of our fuel capacity. When we reached Kiev, four planes had to peel off and land. Our maps were unsatisfactory and the radio facilities just as bad, so that finding our field was difficult. The relief was tremendous, when, after about eleven hours of flying, we landed at Mirgorod, our destination. Each plane was met by an American master sergeant and a Russian enlisted man. For all we knew he was a general, so everybody saluted everybody else and shook hands all round. We were gathered up in army trucks, taken to a tent headquarters for interrogation and indoctrination by Colonel Witten, the 13th Wing CO. Then we were caravaned to the town where we were to be quartered and deposited before a battered schoolhouse. Half an hour later we were asleep."

A few hours after the 45th Wing had touched down at nearby Poltava, while crews were attending debriefing sessions, Soviet anti-aircraft batteries were heard close by. Crews dismissed the barrage as a practice but they were, in fact, firing at an He 177 high-altitude reconnaissance aircraft which had shadowed the formation about 400 miles into Russian territory. The Heinkel was too high even to be seen and flew off into the clouds to report its findings. The Fortress crews thought no more about it and went to bed. A few hours later sixty Luftwaffe bombers droned over Poltava and proceeded to drop flares. The Russian defenses offered little in the way of resistance and the Germans were able to drop over 100 tons of bombs on the airfield at will. For two hours the German pilots made run after run, picking off aircraft one after the other, the heavy caliber shells of their machine-guns exploding and adding to the general chaos and noise. Ammunition dumps were blown up and the fuel dump, containing 450,000 gallons of fuel, exploded in an angry orange mushroom of flame and debris. More bombs, more flares and, as each wave completed its run, there was a series of three blinding flashes as they took photos of their bombing.

The heaviest loss in personnel occurred among the Red Army men and women stationed on the base. They completely disregarded the bombing and attempted to extinguish fires and move aircraft. Twenty-five Russian soldiers were killed, including several Red Army women, some of whom were manning an anti-aircraft battery which received a direct hit. American casualties were incredibly light, considering that combat and ground crews were billeted in tents and their only protection was slit trenches. One American was killed instantly by a stick of bombs that fell squarely in the hospital area and another died later as a result of his injuries. About twenty others received minor injuries.

The early morning light revealed hundreds of butterfly bombs littering the airfield. American and Russian personnel were told not even to approach them and Russian sappers exploded them with long poles. Major General Alexander Perminov, commander of the airfield, was among those who inspected the damage. Skeletal remains of the Fortresses were clustered around the airfield like carcasses. Some were only a collection of engines and twisted propellers that marked the spot where once bombers had stood. Altogether, forty-four of the seventy-two bombers that landed at Poltava were completely destroyed and another twenty-six riddled with machine-gun bullets and bomb fragments.

Fifteen other American and Russian aircraft were also destroyed during the raid. Further losses to the 13th Wing Fortresses at Mirgorod and to the Mustangs at Piryatin were, however, avoided, as Harry Crosby explains.

"German reconnaissance planes droned over the fields. There was little or no anti-aircraft for our newly constructed fields. Our few Airacobras with Russian pilots were not sufficient defense, so Colonel Witten and Colonel Jeffrey had a brilliant idea. Shortly before dark we took off and flew, low enough to escape the German radar screen, 150 miles further south to Zaporpozhe, distant enough to be safe. It was this idea that saved us. That night raiders dropped a flare over the deserted field and bombed under that chandelier for an hour and fifty minutes."

The German raids led to serious disagreements at high level between the Americans and Russians. The Americans complained about the lack of fighter support, radar, and searchlight facilities at the bases. The Soviets pointed out that they were all badly needed at the Front. General Carl Spaatz was to concede later that the Poltava raid was the "best attack the Luftwaffe ever made on the AAF."

Harry Crosby continues.

"It was bad enough to have lost so many planes but there were other problems. The only fields in Russia long enough for us to lift bombs off were masses of craters. Since the Germans knew where we were, we couldn't stay there for long. Some time or other our small remaining force would have to make a break for it. Colonel Witten and Colonel Moller kept us pretty well informed of our situation. At one of the frequent meetings the two Colonels told us that our main base would soon be repaired. At another we were

The Stork, *44-6142 of the 96th Bomb Group based at Snetterton. This aircraft survived the war and returned to America where it was broken up.*

B-17s of the 96th Bomb Group en route to the Haute Savoie to drop supplies to the FFI on 25th June 1944.

informed that communications had been established and it was again possible for us to get bombs and fuel. And then at the final meeting we were alerted for a mission the following day. We were to leave Kharkov that evening and go to the nearby field where our planes were parked, sleep there until dawn, then return to our main base and be briefed while our planes were being refueled and loaded with bombs.

"Kharkov gave us a grand farewell. All the women who had them wore gaily colored dresses. Some of them dug up rouge and lipstick. And they all hurled roses at our trucks. Little girls gave us bouquets. And the entire populace called not merely 'goodbye', 'Do spedanye', but also, 'Farewell, till we meet again', 'Poka du solve stra.' At Mirgorod it was evident what an attack we had missed. The runways had been repaired but the field itself was pitted like the side of a colander. And all the time we were there the demolition squads were exploding delayed action and dud bombs. That day we rested. In the evening we flew again at low altitude to another town that had an airfield. For our supper we had C-rations. Yet that supper clings to my memory. It was cold, so we ate in the waist of the plane. It was dark, so we turned on one little flashlight. Nobody said very much. We would see a hand reach out

into the arc of light, pick up something and withdraw. There was only breathing, or a quiet word or two. Outside was Russia. Tomorrow was Italy. We were very young. The United States was very far away. We had seen so much, fought so long."

At around 1215 hours on 26th June, the surviving Fortresses took off on the next stage of the shuttle to Foggia, Italy, with a raid on a Romanian oil refinery en route. For a time it looked as if Harry Crosby's Fortress would have to remain in Russia, as he explains.

"At taxi time our number three engine cut out completely. For a while it looked as though our hopes for a mission that day were dashed. We should have been very disappointed. Actually, we all felt a guilty surge of elation. We saw visions of our one single plane being held back a day, then having to go back by the ATC route, maybe to Tehran, Cairo, and Casablanca. There would be hotels, expense money, and good food: a regular tourist's trip! However, Sergeant Picard climbed out and changed a whole bank of spark plugs in ten minutes; a superhuman feat which gave us plenty of time to catch the formation. I don't think he understood at all the coolness which greeted him when he crawled back into the plane."

Larry Townsend's B-17 *Lady Luck*, in the 100th Bomb Group, carried an unexpected guest, as John A. Miller recalls.

"A Russian officer came with us in the nose to study the way we navigated and flew a mission. The top turret gunner and the bombardier could talk to him in a language he understood so that's why he flew with us, I guess. The Russians didn't have electrically heated high altitude flying suits. When the time came to board our plane he took an Eskimo suit out of a bag and put it on. We wondered how in hell we would get him into the airplane, let alone in the nose. We were leading the second element of the lead squadron. Townsend and Ed Fehrenkamp, the pilots, flew the tightest formation anyone ever saw. On the bomb run they had our nose crammed right up under the leader. With 'Bombs Away' we were in big trouble! The first bomb from the leader's bomb bay was a smoke bomb, the acid from which clouded all of the Plexiglas in the nose, flight deck, and top turret! Townsend said, 'What the . . .. Can you see anything?' to the co-pilot. 'Not a damn thing,' came the reply. 'Hell! We've got to get out of this formation somehow! Ed, slide open your side window. I guess we'll have to fly with our heads hanging out of the side!' We managed to pull out of our formation without incident and dropped down to about 12,000 feet so we could remove our oxygen masks. It would also be warmer for the pilots with their heads out of the side windows."

Harry Crosby was in the same formation and continues.

"The mission was as uneventful as a mission can be. We hit our target. The flak was bad. We lost no bombers but one plane lost an engine. Captain Bucky Mason was in the plane and having a high time. We all heard him call by radio to Colonel Jeffrey's plane and ask to talk to Major Rovegno, our doughty old ex-Marine pilot, now our engineering officer. When Major Rovegno answered, Bucky said, 'Hey you old coot, you better have your hammer and nails ready. This duck I'm riding is about to fall apart.'"

Crews reported seeing a large column of smoke and flames shooting skywards after the attack. They had to make it alone from the target but another B-17 with markings never seen in the 8th Air Force, appeared, as John A. Miller recalls.

"It would try to move over and we would slide away. We had been playing the game of "chicken" for a long time and I told myself that this '17 was full of Krauts and should be shot down. I was tired of this game. The next time it made a move I was going to open up and the top turret would too, the best he could. But the strange B-17 peeled off to the right and headed back whence it came. Then we were mad we hadn't blasted it. It was full of Krauts.

"We flew the course as briefed. It took us near Ploesti an at 5,000 feet we flew just east of Bucharest where we got a wonderful view of that ancient city and its bridges over the river flowing through its center. South of Bucharest we set a course to the west for Italy. To this day I will never understand why we were not attacked by any enemy fighters! The credit has to go to God and our guardian angels.

"When we reached Italy we landed at the first bomber base we saw. After we crawled out of *Lady Luck*, an officer came up at great speed in a jeep. He was very surprised and asked, 'Where in hell did you come from?' Of course, he knew nothing of the shuttle raid. Then he saw our man in the Eskimo suit. He was dumbfounded and decided he must have a picture of this. He sped away in his jeep to get a photographer from the PR section. We all posed for the

Two photographs of 43-37523, of the 388th Bomb Group, which crash-landed at Knettishall on 26th June 1944. The aircraft was repaired and returned to America in 1945 when it was broken up.

picture but then the officer decided that we gunners looked too raunchy. So he told us to get out of the picture. 'Officers only!' That day I flew my thirtieth mission. In Russia we had been bombed, we had slept on the ground of a large barn-type building near Kharkov, we had eaten K-rations, we had suffered dysentery, in Kharkov we never saw a bathroom, and we had just flown alone to Italy from Poland. And this officer says we looked too raunchy! I'm still angry."

The crew was driven to Foggia Main, where the majority of the force had landed, but *Lady Luck* had to stay where she was until her Plexiglas was replaced and her engines inspected. "The next time we saw our ship," Miller continues, "the painting of *Lady Luck* had run down and streaked the side of the nose. After we had got settled in Italy, Larry Townsend told us there wasn't supposed to be a smoke bomb in the load of the leader's B-17. Someone had goofed! Well, we could believe that . . . ."

At Foggia Main, repairs were carried out to aircraft damaged in Russia and during the raid on the oil refinery. Some aircraft were too badly damaged for further combat and had to be sent back to England by the much coveted ATC route via Cairo and Casablanca. The appropriately named, *Belle of the Brawl*, in the 388th Bomb Group, touched down at Payne Field, Cairo, with over one hundred linen patches glued over holes in her fuselage. In the meantime, crews took advantage of the lull in combat missions and caught up on some much needed leave. Two days later, on 5th July, the 13th and 45th Wings took off from Foggia on the final leg of their shuttle. Crews flew quite low over Rome and then headed for the marshalling yards at Beziers, in France. Some 109s approached the bombers but were taken good care of by the P-51 escort. Harry Crosby whistled all the way across France.

"All the way I kept rejoicing that my promotion had never come through. Since I was a captain and my tour was over, I could go home. When we got to England the White Cliffs never looked so good. When we passed London I told it goodbye. I was on my way home. When we got back over Thorpe Abbotts, Jack Kidd was at the flying control tower. When we came onto radio I heard his voice. I called out to him. 'Jack,' I said excitedly, 'I got in an extra mission. I am sorry but now I have twenty-five. I will have to go home.' His voice came back clearly, 'No you won't Major!'"

Some of the crew of 43-37523 examining flak holes in a shoe and a flak jacket. Left to right: *Bessett, Kelley, Isaacs, Dean, and Woodsum.*

Chapter 15
Oil!

Harry Crosby was not the only crew member in the 8th Air Force on 5th July to receive such a shock. During the shuttle force's absence, tours had been raised from thirty to thirty-five missions. This "Catch 22" situation was a shattering blow as John A. Miller explains.

"When we took off on the Russian shuttle raid the limit was thirty missions. When we returned I had thirty-two missions. Thank God I had made it! Then they gave me this stuff that it had been raised while we were gone and that I had to do thirty-five. I said, 'No way,' as they would pro-rate it like when it was raised from twenty-five to thirty. I was called into Group Operations and the officer I talked to said I would have to fly three more missions. I objected. He said, 'It's Bennett's order and you know how he is.' It looked like either the Krauts or Bennett was going to get me for sure. I flew three more missions and Townsend had a couple more to go. They went down on their last mission. During my time in the Air Force I missed going down with five different crews and sure death with three of them! I was the only one from Townsend's crew to complete his missions and return to the States."

The news of the increase in missions affected crewmen like Ben Smith in the 303rd Bomb Group.

"I was now an old combat veteran; and though only twenty-one years old, I had seen enough for a lifetime. I had literally grown up in the war. More of my friends were dead than alive. A seemingly endless procession of crews had come and gone out of our squadron. Only a handful of them had completed a tour of operations. I had seen them come and go, but always on my mind was the specter of Lieutenant Long's crew, who went down on their final sortie. The same thing happened to Lieutenant Holdcroft's crew. I was getting closer and closer to the day when my tour would be complete. Now that it looked like I had a chance to finish, I began to sweat it out. I had finished twenty-five missions and had collected my DFC. Before I had completed the required thirty missions the brass said we were going to fly unlimited missions (as did our friends, the RAF). This was so disastrous to morale that they finally relented. I actually had to fly thirty-one and was given credit for four I didn't fly. I don't know how they figured it; it made no sense to me."

Headquarters also announced that deep penetration missions would rank equally with the short-haul raids in the table of missions per tour. Eventually, a fairer method was evolved when headquarters took into account the greater risks involved in flying deep into Germany. One of the more

Lieutenant Colonel James Dubose (standing in for Colonel Preston) with Her Majesty Queen Elizabeth and the young Princess Elizabeth during a visit to Kimbolton on 6th July 1944. (USAF)

immediate ways of shortening a tour and earning a thirty-day rest and recuperation leave was to "volunteer" for a second tour. On Tuesday, 11th July, Abe Dolim and the rest of his crew at Bury St Edmunds were among many who were approached. Dolim had recently spent a week's "flak leave" at Aylesfield House and elected to take the thirty days' R&R and return to fly combat. "To refuse meant flying eight more missions and I'd had my fill. My home was in Honolulu, Hawaii, and I calculated what with slow convoys and Patton on his way to Paris, the war in Europe might be over before I had to return."

In the meantime, the 8th continued its bombardment of V-1 sites in the Pas de Calais and also made supply drops to gallant groups in the French Resistance movement. On 14th July, Bastille Day, the B-17s took off for "Area 9" near Limoges where the 8th had made its first drop only three weeks before. The Maquis had since gained control of an area 100 miles square; the equivalent of an entire French Department. They had succeeded in keeping the Limoges-Orleans railway closed since D-Day and had been extremely successful in cutting communications. Now they needed replacement arms and ammunition to continue the fight.

Flying his first supply drop this day was Bob Maag, pilot of *Skinny* in the 94th Bomb Group.

"Our eighteen-plane formation split into three-plane elements to make the drop. The drop site was located in a valley at Valance and we took the big birds down to 3,000 feet. The guns, ammo, medical supplies, and other essentials for guerrilla strikes, were packed into parachute canisters. As the 'chutes floated down we could see figures, pulling two-wheeled carts, dart out of the woods, retrieve the canisters, and scurry back to cover. As we came out of the valley we were so low that I had to lift my left wingtip to clear the trees. My navigator pointed out Lake Geneva to us. The large body of water looked beautiful from the air.

"The mission was an enjoyable experience, made even better by the fact that we encountered no enemy action. However, not all missions that summer were as enjoyable. That familiar phrase, 'sweating it out' was no idle collection of words. When I was flying combat in the summer of '44 I literally had grainy salt deposits on the outside of my thick leather GI shoes! I'm not ashamed to admit that I was sweating every minute we were over enemy territory!

When the flak bursts were thickest and closest I'd sing 'Home on the range' over the intercom (probably off key!) to relieve the tension."

The tension Bob Maag felt on missions was possibly none greater than on another mission to France which still angers him to this day.

"I've concluded that Command decided to make 'guinea pigs' of myself and my crew without our permission. Fuel supplies were tight but I was surprised when my Form 1 this particular morning listed 1,700 gallons for the mission instead of the usual 2,100 gallons. I called for the gas truck to bring my tanks up to 2,100 but was refused. Instead I was told that there was a new field order allowing each plane only 1,700 gallons. So, we took off and, after forming and reaching the coast, two-thirds of my gas had been consumed. I called for permission to return to base and permission was denied. After we'd cleared the Channel I again called for permission to return and was told to turn on my 'Tokyo tanks' at which time I informed the leader that there was no fuel in my 'Tokyo tanks!' It was only then that I discovered that we were the only plane in the formation with empty 'Tokyo tanks!'

"The target was cloud covered so no bombs were dropped. But I knew that we had to lighten our load if we were going to have a prayer of making it back to Bury, so I repeatedly requested, and was finally granted, permission to dump our bomb load through the clouds. I've always hoped that bomb dump didn't cause casualties among innocent civilians! In a further effort to conserve fuel I had the crew leveling off the four fuel tanks, switching fuel between tanks for as little as ten to twelve second intervals. The stress level was high as we all wondered whether we'd land in the drink, be forced to make an emergency landing, or make it back to Bury. As the fuel supply inexorably diminished and we were switching between tanks, our bombardier, Lyle Haines, asked, 'What do you want me to do skipper; make the next transfer with an eye dropper?'

"We left the formation at the Channel and made it back to Bury with fifteen minutes fuel to spare. But I was furious at the fact that we'd been jeopardized in this fashion. I demanded an explanation from the crew chief, the line chief and the engineering officer, but never got a satisfactory explanation, so I can only assume that some character with rank had decided to see whether a mission to France could be made with 1,700 instead of 2,100 gallons of gas."

Also during July, the 8th flew missions to Germany in search of oil and other strategic targets in an ever-diminishing Reich. For three successive days, beginning 11th July, the heavies blasted industrial sections of Munich. The Bavarian city was important to the Germans at this stage of the war because the aircraft engineers and designers were building new weapons for the final aerial battles between the Luftwaffe and the Allied air forces. Jet aircraft and experimental works dotted the vicinity of Munich. The hub of the complex was the massive *Allach* aero engine works which, with assembly plants and Luftwaffe airfields close by, made Munich a top priority target. On the 16th July mission to Munich, the 1st Scouting Force of Mustangs and Mosquitoes, developed and led by 42-year-old Colonel Budd J. Peaslee, was used for the first time. Peaslee's scouting force flew just ahead of the main bombing force, transmitting up-to-the-minute weather reports back to the task force commander to prevent him leading his bombers into heavy weather fronts which could disrupt the mission and, in some instances, lead to its cancellation.

Peaslee's weather scouts also proved effective on the 18th July mission to the principal German research and development center at Peenemünde on the Baltic coast, where German scientists were trying to create the atomic bomb. The MPI was well-covered with bomb hits and smoke was reported rising to 12,000 feet. The bomb pattern brought acclaim from General Spaatz, among others, who described it as, "one of the finest examples of precision bombing I have seen." General Williams added, "On this vital operation the First Division again demonstrated its ability to

B-17G, 42-107073, 452nd Bomb Group, Honington, crashed on 30th July 1944.

B-17G, 42-598357, Super Rabbit, *100th Bomb Group, Thorpe Abbotts, crashed on 28th July 1944.*

destroy the assigned objective regardless of its location or enemy opposition." Peenemünde was the furthest penetration into northeast Germany and it was not until after the war that its importance was fully realized.

On 19th July, some 1,200 bombers attacked targets in south-central Germany again, and two days later the 8th went to Schweinfurt. Peaslee's weather scouts were instrumental in preventing the First Bomb Division entering a cloud belt that towered to 28,000 feet. Unfortunately, the Second Bomb Division did not receive the radio signal put out on the fighter-bomber frequency and twenty-six Liberators failed to return as a result of collisions and enemy action. In sharp contrast, the First Division lost only three bombers and the Second and Third Divisions wasted no further time in forming their own scouting units.

During July, the 8th flew seven tactical missions in support of the Allied armies in northern France. On 24th and 25th July the largest formation of bombers since D-Day dropped thousands of fragmentation and 100lb GP bombs on German positions in the St Lô area, just ahead of advancing troops of the US 1st Army. On the first raid weather severely hampered bombing and the 379th Bomb Group was forced to make three runs over the target before it found a gap in the clouds to bomb through. Accuracy was essential and many bombers returned with their bomb loads intact rather than risk dropping them on their own troops. The aerial armada paved the way for the breakout and several days later Allied and German troops clashed in the Battle of Brittany.

During the last week of July, General Doolittle carried out the first stage of his plan to convert all Liberator groups in the ETO to Fortresses. The 486th Bomb Group at Sudbury and the 487th Bomb Group at Lavenham, which together formed the 92nd Wing, were taken off operations and, by the end of the month, were ready to begin combat missions in Fortresses. Between the end of August and mid-September the three B-24 groups of the 93rd Wing, the 34th, 490th, and 493rd groups, also changed over to the B-17. At first crews resented the change-over but they quickly grew

to like the improved flying characteristics inherent in the B-17 and they praised the more spacious nose compartment and improved heating,

August followed the same operational pattern as July with bombing raids on airfields in France and strategic targets in Germany. On 1st August, while heavy bomb groups struck at airfields in France, some B-17 groups again parachuted supplies to the French Resistance movement. On 5th August, the 8th returned to strategic targets with all-out raids on eleven separate centers in central Germany. Next day the B-17s struck at Berlin and oil and manufacturing centers in the Reich. On this occasion, seventy-six Fortresses from the 95th and 390th Bomb Groups hit the Focke-Wulf plant at Rahmel in Poland. After the bombing the two groups flew on to their shuttle base at Mirgorod in Russia, scene of such devastation two months before. During their stay they flew a raid to the Trzebinia synthetic oil refinery and returned to Russia before flying to Italy on 8th August, bombing two Romanian airfields en route. Four days later they flew back to Britain on the last stage of their shuttle. Toulouse-Francaal airfield was bombed on the flight back over France. This third shuttle by the 8th Air Force proved more successful than the disastrous shuttle of June 1944 with not a single Fortress being lost.

Meanwhile, on 9th August, the English-based B-17 crews were summoned to the usual daily briefing. Bob Maag in the 94th Bomb Group was flying his twentieth mission this day.

"We learned that our target was Stuttgart again, though it seemed highly unlikely to me that the mission would come off as planned. The weather officer informed us that the cloud cover over the target would extend to 40,000 feet, at which altitude bombing would be impossible. Furthermore, they told us that, when we returned to base, all of England would be socked in from zero to 20,000 feet, making landing impossible!

B-17G 42-102619, Report to the Nation*, 306th Bomb Group, damaged on 9th August 1944.*

B-17G 43-37615, Elizabeth's Own*, 306th Bomb Group, wrecked on 27th July 1944.*

Royal Flush, crashed at Clamart in France on 11th August 1944. This photograph was taken by a local photographer.

"We'd be taking our own *Skinny*. We didn't know at that time that she was something of a legend (the first B-17 in the 94th to complete 100 missions), but realized that she was a venerable veteran. We assumed she got her name from the fact that she was an anomaly - a B-17G with no chin turret. We sometimes speculated whether *Skinny* had lost her chin turret in an earlier battle, or had been built that way. We all felt at home on *Skinny* and liked having her for our missions because her missing chin turret gave us the advantage of lower fuel consumption.

"When we arrived at the hard-stand we weren't surprised to learn that takeoff had been delayed, first for one hour, then another. We were still dubious when we received orders for takeoff and fully expected to be recalled. The forming and flight to the target area were routine and uneventful. When we approached Stuttgart we found that the cloud cover did indeed extend to 40,000 feet. Since we could not bomb the target and no secondary target had been communicated to us, the formation turned for home. In Luxembourg we were led over some flak guns mounted on railroad cars and all hell broke loose. I don't know how many hits *Skinny* took but one that came through the Plexiglas caught me on the left side of the face and wounded George Byczkowski, the top turret gunner, in the leg. I lost my left eye and the co-pilot, Ivan Walker, had to take over the controls. Lyle Haines and Smitty, the bombardier and navigator, somehow managed to get me into the nose of the plane where they did what they could to keep me alive.

"During the trip back under these emergency conditions the crew performed magnificently. Since this was the sixth consecutive day we'd flown a combat mission with only two or three hours' sleep a night (between 6th July and 9th August we'd logged 167.55 hours), it was all the more remarkable that everyone handled the emergency so well. I know Ivan and I were so wiped out at that point that we had been alternating at the controls at the same time! I was conscious during that hairy trip home and remember lying in the nose and worrying about the weather over England and the fact that this would be Ivan's first attempt to land a B-17! I needn't have worried. Not only did Ivan get us down safely, he made sure that *Skinny* was the first to land, thus ensuring that George and I would get medical attention at the earliest possible moment. For their actions, Walker, Smith, and Haines were awarded the DFC.

"After our mission of 9th August, *Skinny* was sent to the hangar to be used for parts - but a changed decision saw her repaired for combat. She flew her 109th mission in December 1944 to January 1945. It was then decided to send her out one more time to make it an even 110 and on that mission three of her engines failed and the pilot put her down somewhere in Belgium. I don't know whether those miracle men of the ground crew were ever able to get *Skinny* airborne again. I do know I'll always have a warm spot in my heart for her and my wonderful crew."

From 19th to 24th August, a low pressure system gathered over the British Isles and Western Europe and prevented any missions being flown. During the five days of stand-down it was announced that Paris had been liberated and it was reported that the Romanians wished to seek peace. It seemed the war would be over by Christmas, this year. To maintain the Allied push through France during late August and early September, the 8th began "trucking" supplies to the troops. The bulk of the operation was completed using Liberators, whose cavernous fuselages were ideal for the task, but some Fortresses were also used. Third Bomb Division groups also dropped supplies to the Maquis and in mid-September Fortress pilots had to call upon all their experience to fly a mercy drop to beleaguered Poles in the ruins of Warsaw. The Polish capital was cut off from the outside world with the Germans on one side and the Russians on the other. Russia had requested General Bor to rise against the German occupiers but had then stood by while the gallant Polish Home Army was gradually being annihilated. Allied airmen in RAF squadrons operating from Italy supplied the Poles in August but then operations ceased because of the danger to crews. Operations were re-started after Polish protests but it was not until early September that the Russians finally agreed to co-operate and allow the B-17s to fly on to Russia after the drops.

An attempt to reach Warsaw on 15th September was aborted because of bad weather and it was not until three days later that the 13th Wing was able to fly all the way. Colonel Karl Truesdell of the 95th Bomb Group led the B-17s over Warsaw and the supply drop was made from between 13,000 and 18,000 feet amid limited but accurate flak. The strong American fighter escort was unable to prevent the Luftwaffe attacking the 390th Bomb Group, which was flying as the low group on the dropping run. One Fortress was shot down and another landed at Brest-Litovsk. However, the remaining aircraft succeeded in reaching their shuttle bases at Mirgorod and Poltava. On 19th September they took off again for the now familiar return flight via Italy and France, but this time without bombing because all French territory had fallen to the Allies.

Bad weather throughout the rest of September severely limited missions and only fourteen were flown during that month. It was one of the worst months of the war for the 92nd Bomb Group. On the mission to oil refineries at Merseburg on 11th September, savage fighter attacks cost the group eight B-17s while another four crash-landed or were abandoned in France and Belgium. Next day the Third Division journeyed to Magdeburg to attack the oil refinery and marshalling yards at Fulda while the First Division was assigned oil targets at Brux in Czechoslovakia. Colonel Maurice "Mo" Preston, CO of the 379th Bomb Group, led the 41st Wing to Brux. He recalls,

Betty Jane, 42-32027 of the 303rd Bomb Group, failed to return on 19th September 1944 with 2nd Lieutenant C. W. Heleen's crew. One man was killed and the rest made POWs.

"Somewhere in central Germany, at a time when we were without friendly fighter escort-cover, a gaggle of German fighters came up to meet us. As luck would have it, they zeroed in on my wing. As they ganged up to the right front, well forward and above us, I was figuring what to do. I could turn toward them, hoping to make them steepen their turn into the attack and leaving them with only a minimum of time in which to shoot, or I could turn away from them by pulling off to the left, thus making them deliver a quartering attack rather than a head-on one. But if I did that I'd run right into the prop wash coming from the other wings ahead. We were already riding right on the fringes of the wash.

"Then the idea struck me! Why not make those fighters fly through that wash in order to attack us. No telling what it might do to them. So I did it. Just as the fighters started their left turn I eased off to the left with my formation. And just as those fighters were rolling on to their backs preparatory to firing, they hit the wash! One after another they wobbled and flipped and squirmed and jiggled - then pulled off downward, breaking off the attack without firing a shot. We jiggled and wobbled too but everyone in our formation could see what happened and under the circumstances I doubt that many pilots were upset by the rocky road I was leading them on. We didn't lose a plane!

"Another problem occurred right at the target. About the time bomb release was expected, my aircraft, which was flying through medium intensity flak, suddenly filled with smoke. This was coming from the bomb bay, which suggested that there was a fire. And the bombs were still there! This was one of those situations that were occasionally encountered and for which, therefore, an approved procedure for handling had been developed. It involved simply; first, try to salvo the bombs and second, if this was ineffective, get out of the airplane! So I tried to get rid of the bombs using the salvo switch on the pilot's side panel. It didn't work! I tried calling the bombardier to have him hit the salvo lever. The intercom was dead! So I hit the alarm bell, calling at the same time over the intercom for the crew to bale out. The call was fruitless, of course, just as the call to the bombardier had been.

"About this time I remembered the formation, so I called them on the radio asking that they assemble on the deputy leader. This too was fruitless, for I had no radio. But I looked out of the window and saw that I no longer had a formation. Very wisely, the pilots in that formation, on seeing what looked like fire in the lead craft's fully loaded bomb bay, had decided to leave the vicinity. My plane, my crew, and I were very much alone in the skies over Czechoslovakia. I too had to get out of the plane so I reached for my parachute. But then I noticed that my co-pilot was still with me. And then, looking over my shoulder, I saw move-

ment and concluded that others were still with me. Then I noticed that I had not heard the ringing of that bale-out alarm bell. That didn't work either. So I hit the co-pilot on the arm to get his attention and then, pulling my oxygen mask to one side, I hollered at him to take a portable oxygen bottle and run around and tell the crew to get out.

"Just then we felt an upward lurch of the airplane, after which the smoke quickly cleared away. It seemed that the top turret gunner (the flight crew chief) had gone back and released the bombs using a screwdriver. It further seemed that there was no fire in the bomb bay. The smoke had come from a flak hit on one of the smoke bombs carried by lead aircraft to mark the release of the bombs. We had taken a hit or near miss just before the bomb release line. The flak, in addition to releasing the smoke from the bomb, had knocked out the electrical system, thus rendering the bomb release system inoperative, as well as preventing any type of electrical release of the bombs. It also KO'd the interphone and the radio. Thank God for inoperative alarm bells!

"Then it came home to us that we were all alone in the skies over Czechoslovakia with no formation to shelter us and several hundred miles to traverse through very hostile territory. (The remainder of the formation had assembled on the deputy leader who had then taken them back to the IP for a second run at the target - all in the best tradition of the 379th.) However, the trip home was long, fearsome and lonely but otherwise uneventful. We saw many German fighters, including a two engine jet fighter (my first view of one), but they didn't seem interested in us, strangely enough. Also, we passed along by the Alps off to our left. They stood out clearly visible to us as did the friendly refuge of Switzerland, which seemed to beckon us. But in the best tradition of the 379th we passed it by. 'As long as the airplane will fly, fly it toward the target and then toward home base.' A sacred rule."

On 27th September, the 92nd Bomb Group completed its 200th mission with a raid on the marshalling yards at Cologne and Lieutenant Colonel James W. Wilson assumed command from Colonel Reid, who was still suffering from a flak wound sustained on a mission to Gelsenkirchen on 26th August. On 30th September the 100th Bomb Group celebrated with a 200th mission party at Thorpe Abbotts. There was an alert before celebrations had got into full swing and at 0930 hours the 100th took off for a raid on an ordnance dump at Bielefeld. It seemed ironic to many of the combat crews that they should be going to war from a field filled with the carnival spirit but no one missed the party. At 1523 the formation, led by Major J. Wallace, droned over the field and cheers went up when a quick count revealed that no aircraft were missing.

Crews were still making merry after their long haul to Germany. Bill Carleton, the 351st Bomb Squadron engineering officer, recalls that the party was a gala affair to which all the brass and all the civilians in the surrounding community were invited.

"An English carnival was set up on the field and we had an American barbecue, including a beef on a spit right on the airfield. Three bands were brought in and there were dances in the hangar, the non-coms' club, and the officers' club. Official contact was made with the other Allied groups and special invitations were issued to the ATS, the WRENs and WAAFs. General Doolittle and General Spaatz were on hand as were many other dignitaries."

Elsewhere there was little to celebrate. On 28th September, the Luftwaffe had succeeded in penetrating a strong force of American fighter escorts and had shot down eleven Fortresses belonging to the 303rd Bomb Group en route to Magdeburg. The tragedy was repeated eight days later when the 8th ventured to Berlin. At the IP near Nauen, the Third Division formation was forced to lose altitude to prevent flying through thick cloud. Unknown to the B-17 crews, in this layer of cloud lurked a strong force of enemy fighters. Using the cloud cover to excellent advantage, the German fighters were vectored by ground controllers right into the 385th Bomb Group formation, flying as the high group of the last combat wing. The surprise was total. To make matters worse, the 549th Bomb Squadron was in the process of turning on to the target and had become separated from the rest of the group. Most of the eleven B-17s shot down belonged to this squadron. Only the arrival of the P-51 escort prevented further carnage.

Despite mounting losses there was increasing evidence that the 8th's bombing offensive, against oil targets in particular, was reaping rewards. During August 1944 German oil production had fallen to a paltry 16,000 tons compared with 195,000 tons in May that year. The Luftwaffe was therefore forced to live off stocks accumulated during the winter and spring and began to feel the bite as the fuel crisis grew. During September 1944 German oil production plummeted to only 7,000 tons and draconian measures were called for. Reichminister Albert Speer was given 7,000 engineers from the army and an unlimited number of slave laborers to reconstruct the synthetic oil-producing plants. Hundreds of additional flak guns were erected around the *Hydriesfestungen*, as the plants became known, and workers, who now came under the direct supervision of the *SS*, built deep shelters in which to take cover during air raids. Plants quickly demonstrated a remarkable ability to regain full production quotas and between bombing raids were able to produce 19,000 tons during October (39,000 tons in November).

Doolittle continued to apply pressure on the German oil-manufacturing industry and on 7th October the First and Third Bomb Divisions were assigned refineries at Politz and Merseburg respectively. The Merseburg mission was 20-year-old Karl W. Wendel's second of his tour with the 447th Bomb Group. The young navigator had made his debut the day before when the 8th attacked Berlin. Merseburg was in the same class as "Big-B" when it came to flak, and American crews gave it a healthy respect. Wendel's ship, *T.N.T. Kate*, was going well when someone sang over the intercom that the flak was thick enough to land on. The group leader was shot down and Karl Wendel found himself in the position of lead navigator; the youngest in the 8th Air Force and on only his second mission! However, his new role was taken from his grasp as quickly as it had been thrust upon him. A direct hit knocked out *T.N.T. Kate's* oxygen system and there was an almighty scramble to connect the masks to an alternative supply.

The intercom came alive with frantic calls for help. The ball turret gunner could not breathe. The radio gunner helped him. "Engineer to pilot, gas leaking like hell from the wing tanks!" Likewise, "There's a hole big enough to drive a jeep through back here," reported the waist gunner. The heavy flak kept tracking them. Number three engine was out and number two's propeller was out of control and windmilling frantically. Oil flowed like venomous bleeding. From his position in the nose Karl Wendel could see it congealing. *T.N.T. Kate* dropped out of formation and the crew started throwing out all loose equipment to lighten the ship. On two engines they could not keep their altitude of 28,000 feet. Then the bombardier salvoed the bomb load over the suburbs of Merseburg as the formation pulled away and proceeded to the alternative target because clouds obscured the primary. Wendel frantically began working out a new course. "Navigator to pilot, course two-nine-zero, heading to nearest safety is 290 degrees." He added, "If we can make it." "Roger," sounded above the noise of the engines and flak as *T.N.T. Kate* turned on the new course. Before the new course could be followed, number four engine was hit and caught fire. The stricken B-17 fell like a stone. Among all of this Wendel could hear the prosaic sound of a ringing bell which added to the confusion and excitement. The navigator was first on the intercom. "Are we baling?" he asked. His question went unanswered in the cockpit. The lonesome kid in the tail-gun position was scared and yelled repeatedly, "Are we baling?" Karl Wendel waited no longer and shouted over the intercom, "Bale out! Bale out!" He had seen the bombardier beckon to him then slip out of the navigator's hatch. Within seconds Wendel had followed him. Dropping through the hatch as he usually did when the crew landed, it felt odd to find that his feet did not touch the ground as he left the aircraft.

Millie "K", 42-37878, of the 388th Bomb Group, was lost on 28th September 1944. All nine men were POWs.

Wendel struck the roof of a house on landing and bounced off it into a back yard. He was soon captured after being surrounded by an angry mob that wanted to beat him. Being able to speak German was probably the only thing that saved him from being beaten to death. He learned later that two of the crew had been murdered in this way. All except the bombardier, ball turret gunner, and the engineer, were put on a train for Frankfurt and finally POW camp.

The simultaneous mission by the First Division on Politz also met with disaster as Staff Sergeant Adolph J. Smetana, a tail gunner in the 351st Bomb Group at Polebrook, testifies.

"Nearing the target I saw this 'boiling mass' of flak. We started to make a 360-degree turn and I thought, 'Thank God we don't have to fly through it.' However, I was soon to discover that another group had cut us off and we were only waiting our turn. God it was awful! I could see planes falling from all over the sky. When the first flak burst was at our altitude I knew we had just 'bought the farm.' It was a hell of a ride through that stuff. Our group just simply dissolved. We finally got through after what seemed an eternity. We found ourselves flying in formation with only one other plane and that was all in flames. If it had exploded we would have gone up with it. I was so scared that I couldn't even tell the pilot to get the hell out of here. (We were breaking in a new officer crew that day, flying their first mission.) Finally, 'Pops,' the top turret gunner, screamed over the intercom to 'get his bloody ass out of it or we would never see Polebrook again.' He shouted many other choice words but our pilot did what 'Pops' said and broke off.

"Out of the corner of my eye I saw cripples heading for Sweden but mostly my eyes were focused on the flying coffin in front of us. It finally went out of control and started down. Tears welled up in my eyes and I prayed that nine spots would come out of that plane. One who didn't was our usual waist gunner who had been with us since we had been grouped together at Ardmore AFB, Oklahoma. It was his very first mission in action."

Colonel James R. Luper, CO of the 457th Bomb Group, led the "Fireball Outfit" in *Rene III* with the Group Surgeon, Major Gordon Haggard, the Group Navigator, Captain Norman Kriehn, and the Group Bombardier, Captain Henry Loades among others, as crew. The 457th crossed Politz and became enveloped in the heavy flak barrage. *Rene III* was hit in two engines, which caught fire. The bomb bay doors were closed and Luper managed to keep the crippled bomber level for a moment but the fires spread and engulfed the starboard wing, causing the outboard engine to fall away. Four men, including Luper, jumped from the nose of the doomed B-17 and another three went out through the waist windows. One man who baled out of the waist had his parachute on fire as it fluttered open and was soon engulfed in flames. The remaining sections of *Rene III* hit the water in Stettin Bay and the fuselage, which still contained the bomb load, exploded on impact with the water.

Altogether four bombers in the 457th Bomb Group were lost over the target, including Luper's wingman and the deputy lead ship piloted by Lieutenant Moland. Luper and Captain Kriehn survived and were taken to *Dulag Luft* for interrogation and eventual shipment to *Stalag Luft IIIA*. Politz was a disastrous raid for the 457th. The thirty-eight aircraft that returned to base were badly damaged and sixteen required sub-depot repairs. Only four ships came through unscathed. A short time later Colonel Harris E. Rogner assumed command of the "Fireball Outfit."

While raids on oil centers did not noticeably diminish the Luftwaffe's fighter capacity, it seriously hampered He 177 bombing operations in the east, so although Doolittle's oil raids were not directly aiding the 8th, they were helping to shorten the war. Ironically, the only units not greatly affected by the oil campaign were the Me 262 *Jagdverbande* which used the low-grade petrol still in abundance. During September Hitler had reconsidered the Me 262's role as a fighter rather than the fighter-bomber he had once envisaged. Forty were immediately formed into a fighter unit, commanded by the Austrian fighter ace, Major Walter Nowotny. "Kommando Nowotny," as it was known, became operational in October 1944 and, during the first month of operations, shot down an estimated twenty-two American bombers.

During October 1944 many familiar personnel in the established groups returned to the States after completing their tours. Among the fresh, green, replacements were a few veterans with a first tour in the ETO behind them. Abe Dolim who, on 17th October re-joined the 94th Bomb Group at Bury St Edmunds, fell into this category. The young Hawaiian had left for his native island in July 1944 for thirty days R&R, hoping that the war would be over by the time his leave had expired. However, a second tour brought compensations.

"It was good to be back among my comrades. People back home did not comprehend air warfare." Dolim was informed that a second tour in the ETO would involve flying twenty-four missions; a stiff target for a man who had already flown twenty-seven missions over some of the most heavily defended targets in the Reich. Dolim was still only 22-years old but felt much, much older."

Bad weather throughout November slowed down the Allies' advance all along the western front and severely hampered missions. When they were flown they were usually against oil targets. On 2nd November, the heavies were dispatched to the vast *I.G. Farbenindustrie's* synthetic oil refinery at Leuna, three miles south of Merseburg. It was rated the number one priority target and was estimated to be producing ten percent of all Germany's synthetic oil and a third of all the enemy's ammonia and other chemicals. At briefing crews were warned that German fuel and replacement pilots were in such short supply that Hermann Goering, the Luftwaffe chief, was massing his forces to strike a telling blow on a single mission. All they needed was an opportunity.

The thirty-five aircraft in the 457th Bomb Group formation were blown thirty-five miles off course and away from the target by a 50-knot wind. They flew on alone and sought the secondary target at Bernberg. The "Fireballs" were out on a limb and at the mercy of more than 400 fighters that were in the vicinity. At 1248 hours the "Fireballs" had still not joined the rest of the divisional bomber stream and came under attack from about forty German fighters. Attacks were made on the low squadron from 6 to 8 o'clock low. The American gunners opened up on the 109s and 190s and some fighters did go down. But then, one by one, the "Fireballs" fell out of formation and hurtled down. *Lady Margaret*

Colonel James R. Luper, Commanding Officer of the 457th Bomb Group until he was taken prisoner on 7th October 1944.

had its fin severed by the wing of a passing FW 190 and several other hits sent it down in flames. It exploded shortly afterwards with only two men baling out in time. *Prop Wash* followed her down and another seven B-17s exploded or crashed with a further nine being badly damaged. Only the timely intervention by Mustangs saved the group from total annihilation.

It was for his actions this day that Lieutenant Robert Feymoyer, a navigator in the 447th Bomb Group, was posthumously awarded the Medal of Honor. Feymoyer's B-17 was rocked by three flak bursts, which showered the aircraft with shrapnel. Feymoyer was hit in the back and the side of his body but refused all aid despite his terrible wounds so that he might navigate the Fortress back to Rattlesden. He was propped up in his seat to enable him to read his charts and the crew did what they could for him. It was not until they reached the North Sea that Feymoyer agreed to an injection of morphia. He died shortly after the aircraft landed. Losses were so bad on this mission (the 91st lost twelve Fortresses), that groups were stood down for two days following the raid.

On 9th November the heavies returned to tactical missions in support of General George Patton's 3rd Army halted at the fortress city of Metz. The 8th was called in to bomb German lines of communication at Saarbrucken and also enemy gun emplacements to the east and south of Metz to enable the advance through Belgium to continue. The mission was deemed top priority and at bases throughout East Anglia Fortresses taxied out in the mist and bad visibility. The conditions were instrumental in the loss of eight

bombers during takeoffs and landings and further disasters befell some groups as the mission progressed. While on the bomb run over Saarbrucken, the 452nd Bomb Group encountered an extremely accurate and intense flak barrage.

Lady Janet, flown by 1st/Lieutenant Donald J. Gott and 2nd/Lieutenant William E. Metzger, had three engines badly damaged and the number one engine set on fire. It began windmilling and the number two engine was failing rapidly. Number four showered flames back towards the tail assembly. Flares were ignited in the cockpit and the flames were fuelled by hydraulic fluid leaking from severed cables. The engineer was wounded in the leg and a shell fragment had severed the radio operator's arm below his elbow. Metzger left his seat and stumbled back to the radio room and applied a tourniquet to stop the bleeding. However, the radio operator was so weak from pain that he fell unconscious. The bombs were still aboard and Gott was faced with the prospect of the aircraft exploding at any moment. He therefore decided to fly the stricken Fortress to Allied territory a few miles distant and attempt a crash landing. The bombs were salvoed over enemy territory and all excess equipment was thrown overboard. Lieutenant Metzger unselfishly gave his parachute to one of the gunners after his had been damaged in the fire. As *Lady Janet* neared friendly territory, Metzger went to the rear of the Fortress and told everyone to bale out. Staff Sergeant Herman B. Krimminger, tail-gunner, had died when his parachute had opened accidentally and snagged the blazing B-17's tailplane when he was pulled outside the bomber. Metzger then went back to his seat and the two pilots prepared for a crash landing with only one engine still functioning and the other three on fire.

An open field was spotted and Gott brought *Lady Janet* in. At about 100 feet the fire took hold of the fuel tanks and the bomber exploded, killing Gott, Metzer, and Technical Sergeant Robert A. Dunlap, the radio operator, instantly. Both pilots were awarded posthumous Medals of Honor.

Other crews came through unscathed, or so they thought. Flying his first mission this day was 19-year-old Lieutenant Bob Browne from the 487th Bomb Group at Lavenham.

"The excitement of my first mission over enemy territory crowded out almost all thoughts except an expectation of seeing fiery Messerschmitt fighters flashing past with cannons blazing. But all my expectations were in vain. Nothing exciting happened. No fiery fighters, no flashing cannon, no exploding anti-aircraft shells nearby. Frankly, I was disappointed. At approximately 1500 hours I was swinging my B-17 about the circular concrete hard-stand and the big ship halted in its sharp arc. As the engines were being cut, I could already see my crew chief, Sergeant Jim Haley, racing down the taxi strip in a jeep, heading towards our Fort. I believe he got his jeep training at Le Mans! He stopped just short of the number one engine propeller arc, just as the props were coming to rest, and was coming to meet me as I swung down through the bomber's forward escape door, seven feet to the concrete below.

"'Boy,' I yelled at him, 'if all my missions are like this milk-run, I've got it made.'

"Jim was a veteran. He had already wet-nursed six Fortress crews, efficiently keeping their ships running smoother than any in the group. I detected a rather incredulous look on his face as he said, 'Lieutenant, let me show you something.' Then he methodically guided me on a tour around the Fort. Before we were finished, he had shown me no less than twenty-seven jagged shrapnel holes in my ship, all from enemy anti-aircraft fire!"

On 16th November the 8th returned to western Europe to provide support for the advancing US and British armies. The mission was very carefully planned to avoid bombing friendly troops near the targets just east of Aachen. After the "softening-up" bombardment by the heavies, the ground troops would advance on the enemy strongholds. The Allied artillery would fire red smoke shells every 500 yards along the front and barrage balloons were also placed along the edge of the area. Other devices, such as radio signals on the SCS-51 sets normally used for instrument landings over England, were implemented. The use of the radio was especially worthwhile when 8/10ths cloud covered the front lines, and helped ensure accurate bombing. General Doolittle congratulated all groups, saying, ". . . the 8th Air Force performed one of its most outstanding operations. The force took off under extremely adverse base weather conditions and successfully attacked targets on the immediate front of our ground troops almost exclusively by instrument technique with very good results. Ground commanders were highly pleased and report all bombs on or near the targets. Only one bomb fell wide but did no damage, with no injuries to friendly troops. It was a difficult task well done and I commend you for the capable and efficient manner in which it was conducted."

On 21st November, the 8th returned to Merseburg for the first of three more raids on the refineries in a week. Merseburg had become synonymous with flak and crews hated all missions to the city. Herman L. Hager, radio operator in Lieutenant Wismer's crew in the *Nutty Hussy* in the 603rd Bomb Squadron of the 398th Bomb Group, had already been there on two previous occasions and knew what to expect. "To say the least, shivers always ran up and down our spines when we saw this mission on the map. Like Schweinfurt and others, this was one mission on which you could count your blessings if you returned unharmed."

The 398th Bomb Group dispatched thirty-seven Fortresses this day, led by Major Templeman flying lead with the 602nd Bomb Squadron. Assembly and flight to the target were as briefed but, as the three squadrons started to take interval prior to the IP, dense and persistent contrails and a

43-38172, of the 398th Bomb Group made it back to Nuthampstead after a flak shell exploded in the bombardier's position. 1st Lieutenant Lawrence de Lancey regained control of the bomber over Cologne on 15th October 1944.

heavy layer of cirrus cloud were encountered. The group climbed through the cloud layers to 30,000 feet but the squadrons became separated in the process. The 602nd and 603rd Bomb Squadrons dropped their bombs on secondary targets using PFF while the 601st bombed targets of opportunity. Shortly after the target, the 603rd Bomb Squadron began moving back into a defensive formation for the return home. About ten minutes after leaving the target, at an altitude of 29,000 feet, the 603rd was still flying alone. Suddenly, ten Focke-Wulf 190s shot out from the clouds and made a frontal attack on the squadron, shooting down seven Fortresses. Among them was *Nutty Hussy*. Herman Hager recalls, "We received a direct hit in our left wing. The great amount of smoke seemed to fill up the entire aircraft. We didn't seem to be able to maintain the speed nor the altitude needed to stay with the formation so Fred Wismer left his position and tried to hang on at 'Purple Heart Corner.'

"Moments passed which seemed like hours. We hung on for dear life, at least hoping to make France. However, our luck ran out and six fighters took us on for a sure kill. We requested fighter support but not soon enough, I suppose. It was 1157 hours and *Nutty Hussy* seemed to be burning everywhere. The magnesium alloy skin was actually on fire. I looked back towards the tail to see that Dave Labey, the tail gunner, had baled out. I left my position only to find the ball turret gunner, John Butler, without electric power to position the turret so he could get out. I immediately started hand-cranking so he could exit and, after a brief signal of thanks, he lost no time in baling out. Marvin Clarke, the waist gunner, had released the emergency handle on the waist door and insisted I go first. By this time the ship was flat spinning. I sat at the threshold of the door and rolled into space. After pulling my ripcord the only other figure to come out of the waist must have been Marvin

Stingy, 42-31053, of the 96th Bomb Group, over its home base at Snetterton Heath, Norfolk. The aircraft was lost on 9th October 1944.

Clarke. His 'chute blossomed at approximately a quarter of a mile away at about 23,000 feet. There was 10/10ths cloud cover so the earth was not visible. I found out later that the tops of the clouds were at about 10,000 feet and the base at about 600 feet."

Hager enjoyed only the briefest of freedom before being captured in the Leipzig area by an SS trooper on a motorcycle. Later, he was marched through a throng of about 300 irate villagers and had a tooth knocked out by a rifle butt after turning to look at an Me 109. He was taken to a jail in Erfurt run by Gestapo before being sent to *Dulag Luft* for interrogation. He subsequently became a guest of the German Government at *Stalag Luft IVA*, Keifheyde, in Pomerania.

On 25th November, the 8th set out for Merseburg yet again but the bombing was so poor that on 30th November the heavies were once again dispatched to the oil plants. The plan called for the leading First Division force to attack the synthetic plant at Zeitz while the Third Division was to strike at Merseburg itself, twenty miles to the north. By now Bob Browne, in the 487th Bomb Group at Lavenham, had completed five missions and thought, "only thirty to go" as he prepared for his sixth during the early hours of 30th November.

"It was still dark at 0400 hours when the corporal shook me, saying, 'It's time to go sir, briefing is at 0500 hours.' I looked at my Air Corps issue watch, just one hour to dress, bike over to the mess hall a mile away, get breakfast (probably the usual powdered eggs and spam), then race to the operations building for the mission briefing. Ice on the roads made the bike trips almost as hazardous as the combat missions. And there was always that cold, penetrating English fog that permitted about ten yards' visibility, at best.

"The large briefing room was quiet in anticipation, as Colonel Robert Taylor III, the CO, walked up on to the platform. Without saying a word, he yanked repeatedly at cords at one side of the 30-foot-wide curtains, parting them until the large map of western Europe was completely unveiled. There was a sudden outburst of mixed moaning and profanity. There was a sinking feeling within as I traced the bright red wool yarn fixed with pins, showing the proposed route for the day's mission on the map. The red yarn started about forty miles northeast of London, at our base, and after several turns, aimed straight at the heart of Germany, to the city of Merseburg. The veteran pilot seated at my right turned to me and said, 'Serves us right, I guess, for goofing that last raid five days ago.' He was referring to the 25th November mission to the same target, when one of the poorest displays of 8th Air Force 'precision bombing' resulted in such minor damage that Germany's hottest target - the synthetic oil refinery at Merseburg - was in full production again only twelve hours later.

"The Colonel spoke. 'OK, your attention please. Now, you all realize the fiasco of the last attempt to destroy this target. I'm personally leading this one and we're going to give the Krauts their hardest blow today. It's been said before but, I repeat, destroy Merseburg and the German war machine will stop in its tracks. This plant is so important to the Germans that they rush in their repair crews and have always had the damage repaired before sun-up the next day.' He paused briefly, then added, 'Intelligence tells us the place is seething with activity, indicating a massive anti-aircraft effort. And we already know from experience that if you even look like you're headed for Merseburg, they put up a maximum effort with ack-ack and fighters too.'

"An hour later, my crew and I were at our positions inside *Fearless Fosdick*, as our Fort was named. A four-foot-high vivid picture of 'Lil' Abner' with a four-leaf clover, wishbone, horseshoe, and a rabbit's foot, was painted on each side of the fuselage, just aft of the Plexiglas nose. I, along with the other crew members, had completed all the required oxygen mask and electrically heated flight suit connections and we were waiting for the green flare from the control tower to start engines. Sergeant Haley and his ground crew had completed turning each propeller through several revolutions and were standing by with fire extinguishers. The armament specialists had long since loaded

The .50 caliber gun hangs limply from Harry Thoms' waist gun position on Hank's Bottle, *43-38316, of the 493rd Bomb Group. Gunfire from Luftwaffe fighters hit the B-17 and killed Thoms at his post on 2nd November 1944.*

twelve 500lb demolition bombs in the bomb bay and thousands of .50 caliber machine-gun rounds for the thirteen guns on board.

"Suddenly, there was the signal! It left a green trace gracefully arcing from the walk high up on the control tower and drifted towards the center of the runways. Almost as one, the forty-eight four-engined bombers of the 487th Bomb Group began starting engines. The same thing was happening at many airfields peppering the southeast English countryside. Soon, our bombers were working their way single file towards the takeoff position. One by one, at about thirty second intervals, a bomber would take position at the end of the runway, hold hard brakes until all throttles were wide open and engines straining, then release brakes and take off, disappearing into the dark fog. After what seemed like hours, my turn came and, with engines wide open, the big craft accelerated to attain takeoff speed. The 5,000 feet runway was really too short for a Fortress with a crew of nine, three tons of bombs, and tanks topped off at 2,850 gallons of gasoline. Through the fog the emergency steel matting could be seen just a few feet ahead. The end of the asphalt zipped past and the big tires vibrated as they rolled across the perforated steel matting. Just 300 feet of runway left and a tug on the control column indicated that the big bird wasn't about to part with the runway. I reached down instinctively for the flap switch, holding it in the 'down' position until the indicator showed one-third flaps. I pulled back steadily on the control column and the Fort shuddered sickeningly off the runway.

"I quickly switched on the prop de-icers. This was always disconcerting. It sounded as though the fuselage was being peppered with a massive volley of shotgun pellets as the props threw ice particles at high velocity. Flipping the

landing gear switch upward, I watched the indicator until it showed full retraction. There was a disturbing resonance in the drone of the four 1,200 horsepower Wright Cyclone engines. Adjusting the throttles returned the engines to a pleasing synchronous drone. Climbing eastward, red and yellow flares could be seen arcing southward. These came from the colonel's ship which would maintain a spiraling climb, firing flares at five minute intervals, until his bomb group had formed in four squadrons of twelve airplanes each echeloned behind him.

"An hour later we were crossing the Channel, headed southeast for the French coastal town of Calais. Our altitude now was 26,000 feet. We would continue a southeast course to Verdun, where Patton's artillery and tanks at this very moment were probably pounding. At Verdun, we climbed to our mission altitude of 28,000 feet and leveled off, adjusting engines to cruising. Suddenly, the colonel's Fort began a long left turn. Several bursts of 88mm anti-aircraft rounds could be seen about half a mile ahead. That was the usual line flak from the dual-purpose guns below. Normally, it wasn't too accurate at altitude. However, the next bursts came uncomfortably close as the city of Metz passed under my right wing. We were now in enemy territory! All crew members were tense now and adrenaline was running fast. Messerschmitt 109s and Focke-Wulf 190s could be expected any moment. It was very comforting to see our fighters instead of German ones."

Both divisions had flown the route as briefed as far as Osnabruck but the leading First Bomb Division formation flew on instead of turning for Zeitz. The Third Division wings were some five to fifteen miles south of the briefed route. The error placed the Third Division within range of

Winter at Deenthorpe, home of the 401st Bomb Group. The winter of 1944 to 1945 was the worst in England for over fifty years. Snow and bad visibility hampered operations against the German counter attack in the Ardennes.

some ninety flak batteries at Zeitz and the Fortresses were subjected to an intense and accurate barrage. A strong head wind reduced their speed and aided the German defenses.

Bob Browne in the 487th continues. "Our escorts followed us to a point approximately twenty miles northwest of Merseburg. As we turned onto a southeast course at this point, it had become apparent where our target was. It was eighteen miles straight ahead. The sky was so full of ugly black explosions that none of the blue sky could be seen through it!" Watching the terrible sight ahead and knowing that he would be in the middle of it in less than three minutes, Bob Browne says,

"An almost hopeless feeling welled up inside of me. It occurred to me that only God could see me through it safely. In desperation I silently bargained with God. 'Lord, if you'll bring me through this alive, I'll serve you for the rest of my life.' This hasty communication brought much relief from the almost unbearable anxiety. Now, our bomb group was at the IP, the point where the ten-mile-run began in meticulous sighting and correcting for target alignment. Flak now was bursting all around us. Several bursts exploded right in front of the nose. More bursts right on top of the right wing. Another group burst straight ahead. Black puffs were everywhere. Forts were going down all around us. The colonel had already lost his right wing man. Didn't even see him go. There were two giant white balls of smoke about a mile ahead, showing where two Forts' gasoline tanks had exploded, probably taking other Forts with them. They were still falling. Even through the oxygen masks you could smell cordite. Enemy fighters were waiting outside the flak corridor, not daring to follow us through the seemingly impenetrable barrier of flying steel.

"'Bombs Away!' There was the usual upsurge of the craft, bringing instinctive reflexes for forward control wheel, as the 6,000lbs of bombs dropped free. What an awesome sight, as thousands of 500lb bombs fell in train simultaneously! Now the formation was in a steep bank to the right. The Colonel's voice could be heard over the airwaves, 'Let's get out of here!' The flight back was relatively uneventful. What a relief to park old *Fearless Fosdick*. But I dreaded having to inspect the old bird for battle damage. Sergeant Haley was always so obviously distressed when the Fort's skin was even scratched. How much more if she looked like the sieve I expected? As I left the forward escape door I could hear ambulances as they raced to pick up wounded and dead from other aircraft. Sergeant Haley was already at the nose of *Fearless Fosdick*, looking her all over. As I approached him, I could hear him muttering something. As he turned to me, I finally heard what he was saying. 'I can't believe it,' he muttered over and over. It was the sergeant's way of expressing the fact that he could not find a single scratch on *Fearless*. The old Fort sat there all shiny and spotless, as though she had never left the pad that day!

"It took about two weeks before the 487th could repair enough aircraft for another mission. The 8th and 9th Air Forces had just lost twenty-nine Forts and Libs and over forty fighter planes on this bleak day. But Merseburg had suffered its greatest damage too. And no doubt this helped considerably to bring the terrible conflict to an end."

Chapter 16
The Silver Bullet

December 1944 brought the worst winter weather in England for fifty-four years. Water froze in the pipes and a thin film of ice coated runways at bases throughout eastern England. The temperature dropped to as low as minus eighteen degrees centigrade, but the worst feature of the weather was lack of visibility during missions. The weather was also held responsible for the loss of Major Glenn Miller, the famous American, band leader, on 15th December. Miller's AAF band gave what was to be their final performance together, on the night of 14th December, at the Bedford Corn Exchange. It was a cold, dark, night and the hall overflowed with American airmen from the nearby Fortress bases, plus a sprinkling of US sailors and WRACs. Famous movie stars David Niven and Humphrey Bogart were also present. The Miller band went through the whole gamut of melodies and the encore was greeted with pandemonium and spontaneous applause. The band left after the concert for their next engagement in Paris. Miller, having several business arrangements to conclude, left in a light aircraft the following day. He was never seen again.

The following day, 16th December, Field Marshal Gerdvon Rundstedt and his Panzer columns punched a hole in the American lines in the forests of the Ardennes. The operation was similar to his advance into France in 1940 and opened up a salient or "Bulge" in the Allied front lines. The bombing force in England was grounded by fog, just as Hitler had hoped, and was unable to intervene. It was not until 23rd December, when traces of fog still shrouded the

bases, that many groups managed to take off and offer some hope to the hard-pressed infantry divisions in "The Bulge." The heavies were dispatched to communication targets in an effort to stem the tide of troops and materials entering the salient. The First Bomb Division's attack on the marshalling yards at Ehrang, Germany, earned a commendation from Brigadier General Howard M. Turner.

"I wish to extend to you and all officers and men of the bombardment groups which participated in the mission of 23rd December 1944 my congratulations for the excellent manner in which the mission was executed. Operating in extremely adverse weather conditions, these units exhibited a high degree of determination and skill in clearing the Division area, attacking the marshalling yards at Ehrang and landing in weather conditions equally as adverse, without the loss of a single aircraft. Excellent bombing results were obtained. Convey to participating officers and men my appreciation of a job well done . . .."

On Christmas Eve 1944, the Field Order at all bases called for a maximum effort, to meet which most groups put up all available aircraft, including war-wearies and even assembly ships. Doolittle wanted to throw as much weight as he could against the German airfields to prevent any missions being flown by the Luftwaffe in support of the German land forces in the Ardennes. However, controllers had to work overtime at some Third Bomb Division bases that were still

A B-17 of the 95th Bomb Group returning to England.

congested with First Division Fortresses. Many had landed there after the mission of 23rd December when their home bases had been "socked in." Visibility was still poor and led to many accidents during takeoff. At Podington, for instance, Lieutenant Robert K. Seeber's Fortress crashed into a wood about 200 yards to the left of the runway. The wood had not been visible during takeoff because of the thick fog. About two minutes later Seeber's B-17 exploded, killing six of the crew. At Glatton the 457th managed to get six aircraft off in reduced visibility but the seventh crashed at the end of the runway and operations were brought to a halt for a time.

Despite these setbacks the 8th was able to mount its largest single attack in history with 2,034 heavies participating. In addition, 500 RAF and 9th Air Force bombers participated in this, the greatest single aerial armada the world has ever seen. The First Division would be involved in a direct tactical assault on airfields in the Frankfurt area and on lines of communication immediately behind the German "Bulge." Crews were told that their route was planned on purpose to go over the ground troops' positions for morale purposes.

Brigadier General Fred Castle, former CO of the 94th Bomb Group and now commander of the Fourth Wing, drove to Lavenham airfield and elected to fly in the 487th formation, even though he carried a thirty day leave order in his pocket, and lead the Third Division on what was his thirtieth mission. Soon, Castle was in the air, flying with Lieutenant Robert W. Harriman and crew in *Treble Four* (44-8444). All went well until over Belgium, about thirty-five miles from Liege, when the right outboard engine burst into flames and the propeller had to be feathered. The deputy lead ship took over and Castle dropped down to 20,000 feet. At this height *Treble Four* began vibrating badly and he was forced to take it down another 3,000 feet before leveling out. The Fortress was now down to 180 mph indicated air speed and being pursued by seven Me 109s. They attacked and wounded the tail-gunner and left the radar navigator nursing bad wounds in his neck and shoulders. Castle could not carry out any evasive maneuvers with the full bomb load still aboard and he could not salvo them for fear of hitting Allied troops on the ground. Successive attacks by the fighters put another two engines out of action and the B-17 lost altitude. As Castle fought the controls in a vain effort to keep the stricken bomber level, he ordered the crew to bale out. Part of the crew baled out and then the bomber was hit in the fuel tanks and oxygen systems, which set the aircraft on fire. Castle attempted to land the flaming bomber in an open field close to the Allied lines but, nearing the ground, *Treble Four* went into a spin and exploded on impact.

Brigadier General Castle was posthumously awarded the Medal of Honor; the highest ranking officer in the 8th Air Force to receive the award. General Henry H. Arnold, Chief of the US Air Forces, later dedicated Castle AFB in his honor. His loss was felt greatly by many in the 94th Bomb Group at Bury St Edmunds where he had taken over a

Three of the losses on New Year's Eve 1944. Right: Fools Rush In, *from the 100th Bomb Group, was one of four bombers lost in collisions over Hamburg. It was flown by Lieutenant Floyd E. Henderson and collided with Lieutenant Williams' Fortress.* Facing page, left: *43-38459, 100th Bomb Group. Shortly after this photo was taken the aircraft was shot down.* Facing page, right: Morgan's Raiders, *yet another loss on the New Year's Eve mission to Hamburg.*

demoralized outfit after relinquishing a staff job, and had knocked it back into shape. At the end of the war one of the prisoners held in a POW camp near his former base at Bury St Edmunds was, ironically, Field Marshal von Rundstedt.

Overall, the Christmas Eve raids were effective and severely hampered von Rundstedt's lines of communication. The cost in aircraft, though, was high. Many crashed during their return over England as drizzle and overcast played havoc with landing patterns. Tired crews put down where they could. Any who felt like joining in the festive spirit on the bases were disappointed because another strike was ordered for Boxing Day, 26th December. Ground crews worked right around the clock but it was all in vain. The weather and the widely dispersed groups resulted in only 150 aircraft being dispatched. The following day the wintry conditions were responsible for a succession of crashes during early morning takeoffs. At 0840 hours a 390th Bomb Group Fortress crashed on takeoff from Framlingham and plummeted into the center of nearby Parham village. The crew perished in the explosion that shattered the windows of every home in the vicinity of the crash but, miraculously, none of the inhabitants were harmed.

On 30th December, the 8th again attacked lines of communication and on the final day of the year the First Bomb Division kept up the attacks while Third Division crews returned to oil production centers. This time they were assigned Hamburg, the scene of another disaster for the 100th Bomb Group, as William B. Sterret, flying as navigator in Lieutenant Billy R. Blackman's crew, recalls.

"31st December 1944 is one day in my life I will never forget. When the map was uncovered in the briefing room we all gave a sigh because we knew that Hamburg was a rough target. For some unknown reason I believe that all of the crew had a feeling that this was going to be our last one. We could not fly our own ship because an engine had been burnt up the day before so we flew a ship belonging to another squadron. When we had finished all of our last-minute checks, we gathered in the tent and waited by the fire until time came to start our engines. It was our usual procedure to kid one another and 'shoot the bull' but everyone was very quiet on this particular morning. We never told the ground crew where we were going, because this was against security regulations, but they could guess just about what the target was by the way the crew acted. I am sure that they knew we were 'sweating this one out.' They were a swell bunch of fellows and would do anything they could to help you get back home.

"We took off at 0715 and went through the usual procedure of assembling over England. We left the English coast at 0900 and went up to the North Sea. The weatherman had told us that conditions were not so good, which was evident when we got in the air. The wind was supposed to be about 150 knots at altitude but it was actually much stronger than that. Consequently, we drifted about thirty miles south of our course that put us almost over Holland. The lead navigator began to correct our heading which made us fly directly into the wind. This reduced our ground speed to about 100 mph. We were supposed to come in above Heligoland Island but instead we came in below it and had to turn directly into the wind to reach our IP. We were all talking over the intercom and wondering what was going to happen next. Heligoland was our secondary target and even though we knew that the two islands were well defended we were wishing we could drop our bombs there.

"We finally got to our IP, turned on our rack switch, opened the bomb bay doors and started down the bomb run. At this point we all usually cut off our heated suits because the nervous energy was enough to keep you warm even though it was fifty degrees below zero. Our turn to get on the bomb run was to the right and we were on the outside. This caused us to lag behind a little but finally we were able to get back into position. The target could be seen from our IP even though it took us about ten minutes to actually get over it. A group hit an airfield off to our right. We could also see the groups in front of us getting shot at and we knew that we would soon be in the middle of it. No one was saying a word. We were all just hoping and praying that we would come through without any trouble.

"Finally, we got into the flak, which was really accurate. We could hear the shells as they burst, which is too close for comfort. On our mission to Frankfurt I had told

the boys that I could hear the pieces of shrapnel beating on the side of the ship and they had all said I was getting 'flak happy.' I knew they would agree with me this time. At 1133 the lead ship dropped his smoke bombs, which was a signal for all of the wing ships to drop their bombs. Andy hit the toggle switch and out went our bombs. You always felt better as soon as the bombs were gone because you felt like your job was done."

One by one all the Fortresses in the 100th Bomb Group formation began dropping their bombs. *Fools Rush In*, piloted by Lieutenant Floyd E. Henderson was struck while on the bomb run and dropped sharply, crashing into the B-17 flown by Lieutenant C. Williams, which was cleaved in two. Both aircraft fell to earth in flames. The sky over Hamburg was filled with accurate bursts of flak and Lieutenant Bill Blackman's Fortress was struck on the number three engine. Bill Sterret continues.

"We started for our rally point but had only flown about two minutes when Carson, the ball turret gunner, called Bill and said oil was pouring out of number three engine. The oil pressure gauge verified this fact so Bill feathered the engine. As soon as number three had stopped running Carson called again and said number four engine was also losing oil. Bill feathered this engine too. We were unable to keep up with the formation with only two engines but we could hold our altitude. Bill Blackman called us all and said, 'Stick with it boys. We'll get this thing home yet.' I told him to keep the same heading because it would bring us back out over the North Sea. Bill called for fighter escort but he couldn't contact any because they had been unable to get off the ground in England due to bad weather. He turned back on the intercom and said, 'Bandits in the area!' At this instant, Joe Pearl, the engineer, yelled, 'They're coming in at 6 o'clock!' I looked up through the astrodome and saw two FW 190s coming in on our tail. I turned around and grabbed my gun hoping I would get a shot in. No such luck. We could see tracers as they passed us. 20mm shells were also flying around. We all realized that our chances of getting through were really slim.

"A 20mm shell exploded in the cockpit and knocked all the insulation between the pilots' compartment and the nose into the section where I was. The ship was also on fire and started spinning. I realized that it was time to leave. When I got to the escape hatch Bob Fortney, the radio operator, was lying on his back on the catwalk. I thought he was hurt so I started to help him but he got up and told me to get out so I put one foot on the door and pushed it out. Then I jumped. As soon as I cleared the ship I took off my helmet, pulled my ripcord and looked back to see the ship blow up.

"Bill said that he reached behind his head to fire the Verey pistol to call for help and a 20mm shell exploded and knocked him out. When he came to he rang the bell and then managed to get his 'chute on. When he got down to the nose the ship blew up. He came to falling through the air and pulled his ripcord. The next thing he remembered he was on the ground and Krauts were standing around him. They told him that another boy (Bob Freshour) had been found with his 'chute open but he was dead."

Basil Numack, one of the waist gunners, and Joe Pearl were killed by fighters. Carson was unable to get out of the ball turret and Fortney did not have his 'chute on. Andy Herbert, the tail-gunner, and Tom Pace, survived and were made POW. Tom Pace was blown out of the ship. The last thing he remembered he was lying on the floor in the waist and could not move. When he recovered consciousness he reached for his ripcord but the concussion had broken his shroud and his parachute was dangling above his head. He finally gathered his senses and pulled the ripcord.

"I landed in the middle of a field which was surrounded by woods. I took off my 'chute and started into the woods but the Krauts were coming from all directions with rifles. This was enough to make me stop. There was also about six inches of snow on the ground. They searched me and said, 'For you the war is over.' I did not realize the significance of this statement until later."

In the sky above, the rest of the 100th Bomb Group Fortresses were in the midst of a furious air battle. Lieutenant W. Wilson's B-17 was hit and started down. Lieutenant W. Mayo had two engines knocked out and was last seen over Speikeroog Island. FW 190s and Me 109s attacked in elements of two, three, and four, meeting the bombers 300 yards out before breaking off to reform and come in again. Gunners blazed away at the enemy fighters and scored a few kills but, without close fighter support, it was only a matter of time before they too were knocked out of formation. Lieutenant P. Carroll's Fortress was hit and dived straight down. It temporarily recovered and was last seen heading in a westerly direction. It did not return to Thorpe Abbotts.

Lieutenant J. Morin's B-17 headed for Holland with two wounded men aboard. *Faithful Forever*, piloted by Lieutenant Leo D. Ross, went into a tight spin and all nine crew baled out safely. Lieutenant Charles C. Webster's B-17 plummeted to earth in flames and exploded on impact. Lieutenant Whitcomb's right wing began to burn and the bomber circled for two minutes under control before spinning down enveloped in flames. Lieutenant McNab and his co-pilot, Lieutenant Vaughn, were wounded and their B-17 rose periously close towards Lieutenant G. Rojohn's, who had moved in after Webster's B-17 had gone down. Collision was unavoidable and there was a sickening thud as both aircraft shuddered and locked. McNab's engines were smoking and Rojohn and his co-pilot, Lieutenant W. Leek, frantically cut their engines to avoid a probable explosion. Still joined together Rojohn and Leek made a superhuman effort and managed to steer the mass of aircraft towards the coast. Only four men baled out of McNab's aircraft and seven from Rojohn's. Rojohn and Leek safely crash-landed their two aircraft pick-a-back in a German field. Altogether, the "Bloody Hundredth" lost twelve B-17s; half the total borne by the entire Third Division.

January 1945 marked the 8th's third year of operations and it seemed as if the end of the war was in sight. The Ardennes breakthrough was on the verge of failure and Germany had no reserves left. In the east the Red Army prepared for the great winter offensive which would see the capture of Warsaw and Cracow and take the Soviets across the German border. But there were signs that the Luftwaffe, at least, was far from defeated. On 1st January the First Air Division (this day the prefix "Bomb" was officially changed to "Air") encountered enemy fighters in some strength during raids on the tank factory at Kassel, an oil refinery at Magdeburg and marshalling yards at Dillenburg. The Magdeburg force came under heavy fighter attack while the Kassel force was badly hit by flak.

The following day the heavies once again pounded lines of communication and raids of this nature continued for several days until the position in the Ardennes gradually swung in the Allies' favor. There was no respite but for once the general "bitching" on the bases ceased when it was learned that General Ben Lear had been newly appointed to the ETO. Ground crews went about their daily chores with a new greeting, "Whaddya hear from Lear?," connecting the appointment with an announcement that ground personnel would be drawn from the bomb groups as replacement infantry for invalided men who fought in "The Bulge." This added to the administrative problems on the bases while the "ground pounders" began to realize that life in a bomb group was not so bad after all.

On 5th January the severe wintry weather over England was responsible for several fatal accidents during take-off for a mission to Frankfurt. Snow flurries swirled around the runways and at Mendlesham a 34th Bomb Group Fortress came to grief while attempting takeoff.

A period of fine weather, beginning on 6th January, enabled the heavies to fly missions in support of the ground troops once more. These were mostly against lines of communication, airfields and marshalling yards. Finally, the German advance in the Ardennes came to a halt and ultimately petered out. Hitler's last chance now lay in his so-called, "wonder weapons"; the V-1s and V-2s. The V-1 sites would only be rendered inoperative when they were overrun and swallowed up by the Allied advance but the V-2 would remain a dangerous threat for some time to come.

This long-range rocket flew too high and too fast to be stopped by conventional means although Allied counter-intelligence often misled the enemy into thinking they had found their targets when in fact they had fallen in open country. The nearest crews came to seeing a V-l was through the cross hairs of a bomb sight but, towards the end of the war some even saw V-2s being launched. On 13th January, when the 94th Bomb Group went to Mainz, Abe Dolim saw a V-2 leave Holland and soar to a tremendous height on its way to London. "Just recently I was a quarter of a mile away from one that exploded near Marble Arch in London. In my opinion this is the most sinister weapon yet invented."

Missions were flown to tactical targets throughout the remaining days of January but when the weather intervened the 8th mounted shallow penetration raids on "Noball" (V-1) targets in France. The 8th also attempted several tactical missions but the weather was so bad morale sagged as mission after mission was scrubbed, often just after takeoff. Cloud was a big problem and caused several abortive missions.

On 10th January, the conditions were responsible for a mid-air collision in the vicinity of Thorpe Abbotts. At around 0900 hours, not long after the 100th Bomb Group had taken off, ground staff heard the telltale sound of runaway engines. The sky was overcast and, "Suddenly," recalls Bill Carleton, the 351st Squadron Engineering Officer, "out of the sky loomed a B-17 in a dive of about forty-five degrees. The sentry at our bomb dump heard it and ran from his post, only seconds before it crashed into the dump. It had on board two 2,000lb bombs which exploded with a hell of a roar, throwing some debris all the way across the field." Men scrambled to the doors of their huts to see where the Fortress had fallen. They did not have to look far. From the area behind the base sick quarters rose a thick column of smoke, mushrooming skywards. Someone discovered a helmet in a field near the base. Then the concussion from the two 2,000 pounders set off the other bombs in the bomb dump and machine-gun fire was heard. The loudspeakers crackled out, "Every man for himself. Get off the base!" Men, some of them naked, ran for their lives across snow-covered fields while for the next hour and a half great clouds of smoke and debris cascaded on to the surrounding countryside. Bertie Piper, a farmer near the base, saw an American running for all he was worth, pushing a GI bicycle by the handle-bars. Bertie shouted out, "Why don't you get on it, boy?" Without stopping the perspiring Yank called back, "I ain't got time, I ain't got time!"

The pandemonium died down by 1130 hours and the smoke dispersed. At 1315, however, there were more explosions and it was feared that the fires might engulf the 2,000 pounders. Blackout blinds were drawn to prevent flying glass and the base waited. At 1500 hours the fires were out and the blackout curtains opened. Wreckage from the Fortress, verified as coming from another group, was strewn for hundreds of yards. Unfortunately, many of the men had taken the warnings to get off the base very literally indeed and local police had to comb the district telling personnel the danger had passed. George, the landlord of the Billingford Horseshoes, had never had it so good . . . !

Another incident occurred at Thorpe Abbots on 31st January, as Bill Carelton in the 100th Bomb Group, recalls.

"Heaven Can Wait, piloted by Lieutenant William Appleton, broke out of the clouds, heading directly for the control tower. To avoid crashing into it he banked to the right and crashed into two of the pyramidal tents that housed our maintenance crews. Fortunately, the only occupant in the tent was a black cat by the name of Jack, who evidently escaped injury but did not return for two weeks!

"The plane itself belly-landed, slid across the little public road that ran next to our tents and stopped in the field. The plane was on fire but it was possible for all of the crewmen to escape with no serious injury. The plane burned for possibly twenty or thirty minutes and then the bombs exploded. Although that area of the base had been evacuated, we were not able to get the airplanes out and three other aircraft were so badly damaged they had to be destroyed. One engine from the disabled plane was literally blown 300 feet into the air and landed on top of another."

On 3rd February 1945, Major Robert "Rosie" Rosenthal, flying his 52nd mission, led the 100th Bomb Group and the Third Division, to Berlin. General Earle E. Partridge approved the selection of a squadron commander to lead the division. Marshal Zhukov's Red Army was within only thirty-five miles of Berlin and the capital was jammed with refugees fleeing from the advancing Russians. The raid was designed to cause the German authorities as much havoc as possible. Just over 1,000 Fortresses were assembled and, although the Luftwaffe was almost on its knees, the flak defenses were as strong as ever.

A total of 2,267 tons of bombs rained down into the "Mitte," or central district of Berlin, killing an estimated 20,000 to 25,000 people. The German Air Ministry sustained considerable damage, the Chancellery was hard hit, and the Potsdamer and Anhalter rail yards were also badly hit. Reconnaissance photographs revealed that an area one and a half miles square, stretching across the southern half of the "Mitte," had been devastated. The 8th lost twenty-one bombers over the capital and another six crash-landed inside the Russian lines. Among them was Major Rosenthal, who put his aircraft down in Soviet territory. He and two others were picked up by the Russians while others were picked up by the Germans; one of whom was lynched by civilians. Of the bombers that returned, ninety-three had suffered varying forms of major flak damage. Among the losses had been *Birmingham Jewel* in the 379th Bomb Group, which had set an 8th Air Force record of 128 missions.

Three days later the 8th resumed its oil offensive with raids on synthetic oil refineries at Lutzkendorf and Meresburg. Bad weather forced all except one First Division Fortress to return to England while over the North Sea. Altogether, twenty-two bombers were lost in crash landings in England. The sole B-17 continued to Essen and dumped its load before returning home alone without meeting any opposition. Such an occurrence would have been unthinkable a few months before but now the Luftwaffe had been all but swept from the skies.

On 9th February the heavies returned to the oil refineries in the ever-diminishing Reich. Bombing was made visually. The following day saw the first raid using "Disney" bombs invented by Captain Edward Terrell of the Royal Navy. The 4,500lb bomb was powered by a rocket motor in

43-38125 of the 401st Bomb Group crashed near Saltby in England on 22nd January 1945, during formation assembly.

B-17G, 42-97976, A Bit O' Lace, *of the 447th Bomb Group, Rattlesden. The tail and wing tips were painted bright yellow in late January 1945 to assist identification in the air. Camouflage was no longer considered important.*

the tail and was designed to pierce twenty feet of concrete before exploding. Their weight prevented carriage in the bomb bay of a B-17 so, when nine B-17s belonging to the 92nd Bomb Group were dispatched to the E- boat pens at Ijmuiden in Holland on the 10th, they carried two "Disneys" under each wing. Colonel James W. Wilson, the CO, led the raid and strike photos were later to reveal a direct hit at the north end of the pens. Part of the E-boat shelters had also been hit where a final portion of the roof had not yet been laid, destroying a large section of the structure over three pens and damaging the north wall. Colonel Anthony Q. Mustoe, CO of the 40th Combat Wing, Captain Edward Terrell, Lieutenant Commander John B. Murray, RN, and the First Sea Lord, were at Podington when the bombers returned and later examined the strike photos. Both Terrell and Murray had worked closely in the development of the explosive. Although only one hit had been scored, the officers were shown what the "Disney" bomb was capable of and further trials were ordered. However, the Allies' sweeping victories in the Low Countries and the vast distance to suitable targets in Norway, brought the "Disney" missions almost to an end.

Again the 8th turned its attention to missions in support of the Russian armies converging from the east. At the Yalta Conference early in February 1945, Josef Stalin and his army chiefs asked that the RAF and 8th Air Force paralyze Berlin and Leipzig and prevent German troops moving from the west to the eastern front. Prime Minister Winston Churchill and President Franklin D. Roosevelt agreed on a policy of massive air attacks on the German capital and other cities such as Dresden and Chemnitz. These cities were not only administrative centers controlling military and civilian movements but were also the main communication centers through which the bulk of the enemy's war traffic flowed. Spaatz had set the wheels in motion with a raid on Berlin on 3rd February. Magdeburg and Chemnitz were bombed three days later but the most devastating raids of all fell upon the old city of Dresden in eastern Germany, starting with an 800 bomber raid by the RAF on the night of 13th February. Two waves of heavy bombers produced fire-storms and horrendous casualties among the civilian population. The following day, 400 bombers of the 8th Air Force ventured to the already devastated city to stoke up the fires created by RAF Bomber Command.

Flying his first mission this day was William C. Stewart, a ball turret gunner in the 92nd Bomb Group at Podington.

"I got up, dressed, proceeded through the darkness to the combat mess, and ate breakfast without much interest. The thought of flying the first mission was not conducive to having a good appetite. Walking into the enlisted men's briefing in a building near the flight line, I saw the room-size map of Europe on the front wall. There was a red ribbon on the map, held by pins, showing the route to be flown. The target on the map was Dresden. I had never heard of that German city before.

"We flew the dog-leg route over the Zuider Zee and into Germany. The weather under us was completely cloud-covered and I could not see the ground. I turned the turret, keeping watch for enemy fighters all the way to Dresden. When we neared the IP I turned the turret facing forward and could see the black bursts of flak directly in front of us at our level. We flew to that place in the sky where the flak was heaviest and I heard the bombardier shout, 'Bombs Away!' The plane rose in the air and settled back. We had dropped our bombs on Dresden, which from published reports was still experiencing fire-storms from the RAF bombing the night before. It was a long trip back to friendly territory and I finally got out of the turret when we were over France. By this time our fuel supply was growing short but we made it into AAF base right over the English coast. We landed and got sufficient gas to make it to Podington. However, the number one engine caught fire when started and had to be extinguished. We begged a ride back to the base with another 92nd crew who had also landed at the field. It was late in the evening when we finally reached our home base. Debriefing was held at the same time we were eating our evening meal. We were given one shot of whiskey before eating and I felt a little light-headed afterwards. The debriefing officer asked his questions and it was then that I learned, when the other crew members answered, that the flak was 'meager.' I thought it was worse

than that but this was only my first mission. The plane didn't get hit so this may have had something to do with it. I was to learn later on what 'intense' flak really was."

The 8th Air Force was to return to the pottery city of Dresden again in March and April 1945 on similar raids but the Allied air forces' top priority remained the oil-producing centers. On 16th February the heavies hit the *Hoesch* coking plant at Dortmund, estimated to be producing 1,000 tons of benzol a month. Bombing was completed visually and the Luftwaffe was noticeable by its virtual absence. But bomber losses continued to occur, mainly as a result of the bad weather, which often affected forming-up operations over England.

Marvin Barnes, a gunner in the 452nd Bomb Group at Deopham Green, recalls.

"It was 0600 hours on 17th February when the CO came in and awakened us for the mission. We dressed and went to chow and to briefing. After briefing and learning the target was Frankfurt, we went to the locker room and donned our flight suits. A brief Jeep ride took us to our plane, *Forbidden Fruit*, and we installed our .50 calibers and checked out the oxygen equipment. Everything seemed in order except the ball turret gunner, Staff Sergeant Gibson, was having a problem installing his guns so I gave him a hand. Harry Cross, the tail-gunner, asked me to help him adjust his parachute harness and then he helped me adjust mine.

"Our pilot, Joe Knoll, started the engines and taxied out for takeoff. The weather was terrible as usual for February and we had a pretty rough ride up through the overcast to 10,000 feet. When we finally broke out on top we

One of the nine 92nd Bomb Group B-17s that were modified to carry "Disney" bombs. "Disney" bombs weighed 4,500 lbs and were boosted in their descent by a rocket motor in the tail. Their function was to penetrate twenty feet of concrete before exploding. The first targets were the E-Boat pens at Ijmuiden. (Richards)

All 'er Nothin', *42-98017, of the 490th Bomb Group, came to grief on 23rd February 1945.*

spotted our formation at about the same altitude and passing directly in front of us, making the long left-hand circle waiting for us to join them. Joe Knoll made a slow left turn to catch the formation on the other side of the circle and at this moment the left wing dipped to ninety degrees, caused by severe prop wash. He pulled it back hard to the right and *Forbidden Fruit* did a barrel roll. Knoll pulled hard to the left and the plane did a slow roll and peeled off just like a fighter. It went into a flat spin and at this moment I kicked out the waist door. I had been pinned to the floor up to this point but the force that had me pinned gave up just long enough for me to jump. At that very second *Forbidden Fruit* couldn't take any more and she just disintegrated on her way down, spewing bits of silver metal everywhere.

"My 'chute opened and I landed in a wheat field just outside the B-24 base at Tibenham. After being picked up by some fellows from the base I learned that Harry Cross

and Sergeant Hawkins had been thrown clear and were lucky enough to have had their 'chutes on and were OK. Gibson's 'chute did not open and he lost his life, as did Joe Knoll. The navigator, togellier, flight engineer, and co-pilot also went down with *Forbidden Fruit*. This incident qualified Cross, Hawkins and myself as members of the 'Caterpillar Club.'"

On 22nd February, George Washington's birthday, the 8th launched Clarion, the systematic destruction of the German communications network. The strike was planned by Major General Orvil Anderson, 8th Air Force Chief of Operations, who said, "We could lose 300 planes today, but we won't." More than 6,000 aircraft from seven different commands were airborne this day and they struck at transportation targets throughout western Germany and northern Holland. All targets were selected with the object of preventing troops

B-17G 44-8355, a PFF ship in the 447th Bomb Group, took a direct flak hit on 24th December 1944. Eight of 2nd Lieutenant Miles S. King's crew were killed, but two survived and were taken POW.

being transported to the Russian front, now only a few miles from Berlin. It was all part of the strategy worked out at Yalta by the "Big Three" earlier that month.

Abe Dolim in the 94th recorded it thus.

"The bombing was carried out at extremely low altitudes and our targets were secondary rail junctions and marshalling yards in smaller cities not previously bombed. Just east of Ansbach, our target, we passed an enemy airfield and I counted ten Me 109s and other types on the field. We were only 5,500 feet above the ground but they did not fire at us. This was the first time that I felt the concussion of our own bombs and also the first time I saw boxcars tumble through the air. I felt we were unnecessarily exposed to light flak, which can be murderous at low altitudes and slow speeds. I feel uneasy when a boxcar attains almost as much altitude as our bomber."

Despite the low altitudes flown, the 8th lived up to Anderson's expectations and only five bombers were lost, including one to an Me 262 jet fighter. Next day only two heavies failed to return from the 1,193 dispatched. The flak batteries were being deprived of ammunition and gunners had to conserve their meager reserves. On 26th February even the normally notorious flak defenses in Berlin could shoot down only five bombers.

Clarion had ripped the heart out of a crumbling Reich and the following two months would witness its bitter conclusion. Even RAF Bomber Command could reduce its nocturnal role and join in the daylight war in harmony with the 8th Air Force. Teutonic legend tells of the Bavarian were-

wolf, which can only be killed by a silver bullet. Now the all-metal finish B-17s and B-24s were poised like silver bullets to deliver the final blow against the German werewolves while RAF Lancasters would overfly Hitler's mountain retreat at Berchtesgarden in Bavaria itself. The legend had come full circle.

Marvin "Peewee" Barnes holding the parachute with which he baled out over Tibenham on17th February 1945. He is pictured in front of the 728th Squadron barracks at Deopham, two hours after he baled out.

Chapter 17
Path to Victory

By March 1945 the Third Reich was on the brink of defeat and the systematic destruction of German oil production plants, airfields, and communications centers had virtually driven the *Luftwaffe* from German skies. Despite fuel and pilot shortages, Me 262 jet fighters could still be expected to put in rare attacks and during March almost all enemy fighter interceptions of American heavy bombers were made by the *Jagdverbande*. However, the German jets and rockets had arrived too late and in too few numbers to prevent the inevitable. On 2nd March, when the bombers were dispatched to synthetic oil refineries at Leipzig, Me 262s attacked near Dresden. Abe Dolim, who flew in the deputy lead ship in the 94th Bomb Group, saw them. "One of our bombers took hits from 30mm cannon fire. It all happened so quickly, only a few airmen saw the action." There appeared no immediate solution to the jet fighters of the dying Luftwaffe but flak batteries had lost much of their effectiveness thanks to shell shortages and extensive Electronic Counter Measures (ECM) equipment. Abe Dolim explains. "On the Leipzig raid we had an extra crewmember, an NCO, who handled the ECM equipment, called 'Panther,' designed to jam enemy radar transmissions." (This equipment reduced the effectiveness of radar-controlled flak guns.)

On 3rd March the largest formation of German jets ever seen made attacks on the bomber formations heading for Dresden and oil targets at Ruhrland and shot down three bombers. The Luftwaffe seemed to have found a temporary new lease of life for that night thirty Ju 88s attacked airfields in Norfolk and Suffolk. At Bury St Edmunds the air raid warning siren was sounded at 2300. "Crash alarm, Red bandits, take cover." But the Luftwaffe had not dared to attack the bases for a year and no one took much notice, as Abe Dolim explains.

"Our air raid shelter was only about fifty yards away but no one rushed outside to freeze in the cold, enemy or no enemy. Inside hut twenty-eight we were welcoming a new crew. Soon we heard the unforgettable rapid beat of unsynchronized twin-engined enemy intruders. I told the newcomers the enemy was overhead and if he followed the usual procedure he would cut his engines and glide into position as soon as he identified his target. Several bombs exploded some distance from Bury. The new crew felt we were 'putting them on.' Suddenly, the raider cut his engines and seconds later all hell let loose as the sound of hostile cannon fire destroyed the absolute quiet of the station. The rookie navigator, sitting on the bed across from me, clad only in his underwear and flying boots, darted out the door. An hour later, he returned from the air raid shelter looking somewhat blue."

Six of the attackers were shot down, two of them by RAF Mosquitoes. The attack on Bury St Edmunds damaged the control tower. Great Ashfield was bombed and strafed and Rattlesden, Lavenham, and Sudbury, were also attacked. The intruders returned again on the night of 4th March but damage to the bases was insignificant.

This day Abe Dolim flew his forty-ninth mission when his crew led a nine-bomber section to the assembly point at Troyes, France.

"This was a new assembly technique, which conserved a great deal of gasoline. The section leaders took off first and flew directly to 'Bunchers' in France where the assembly took place, instead of over 'Buncher 12' as usual. The enemy jammed hell out of the 'Buncher' at Troyes but I maintained position with the help of 'Gee' fixes from advanced transmitters in France. We bombed Ingolstadt using H2X. To date I'd flown with many bombardiers, most of whom usually said, 'Let's get the hell out of here,' after 'Bombs Away,' but one fellow I'll never forget said very quietly instead, 'Die, you bastards!' Like love, hate is a very personal emotion."

"On 8th March I flew as navigator of a B-17 transport which hauled twenty-seven officers and men from the 385th Bomb Group at Great Ashfield to Paris-Orly for forty-eight-hour passes. After a couple of hours in Paris we picked up a return load of 'happy warriors' from the 100th Bomb Group and deposited them at Thorpe Abbotts. Major Harry H. Crosby, group navigator of the 100th, helped me navigate on the way back. It was good to see him again. We had first met on the *New Amsterdam* on our return to England in September." The following day, Friday 9th March, Abe Dolim flew his fifty-first and final mission of the war when the 94th Bomb Group went to the marshalling yards at Frankfurt. He wrote of it later: "My last mission was a wingding. We refused to drop our bombs eight miles short of the target where the rest of the group unloaded. Deputy group lead bombardier Lieutenant Cearley was mad as a wet hen because the lead aircraft did not turn the bomb run over to us when they began to experience mechanical difficulties. Captain Reed was reprimanded for returning to base with a full bomb load, thereby reducing the group's tonnage for today's mission. The whole mess is ridiculous! Nobody seems to give a damn whether or not we hit the target anymore. What in blazes is tonnage worth if it does not hurt the enemy? Group is sore because we loused up their paper war - I'm glad. To hell with them - tonight I'll celebrate by getting plastered and forgetting the whole bloody war.

"Two days later my photograph was taken for the group records. One look at it and I saw the same look that I have seen so many times on others. A sort of weariness is apparent but most of all the expression is one of emptiness, features completely drained of emotion. I have lost fifteen

Mr Lucky, B-17G 42-38035 of the 385th Bomb Group, was being flown by 1st Lieutenant Charles Armbruster on 1st March 1945, when it was involved in a collision near Ostend. The tail section was severed, with gunner, Sergeant Joe F. Jones, trapped inside.

The tail section of Mr Lucky, *with the helpless Jones in the turret, landed near Henri Ryjkeboer, pictured here standing on the aircraft's tail with his family.*

Amazingly, Ryjkeboer got Joe Jones out of the turret alive, and six weeks later Jones was back at his base of Great Ashfield. Mr Lucky *was lucky for Jones at least.*

pounds since I started combat flying but none of my shirts fit me around the neck - it has expanded almost one inch within the last year. My nerves are not what they should be; I've become tense, irritable and unfit to fly or live with.

"Today I feel a sense of pride in having played a small part in the great drama of those days that truly belong to history. I formed friendships which have endured throughout the passing years with some of the finest men I have ever met. Many of our squadron mates suffered long imprisonment or gave their lives for our cause. As for the B-17, I am not ashamed to say that in 1944-45 I regarded her as a slow, flammable old lady who was really out of sorts among fast young friends and who became my potential enemy every time I flew a combat mission. Had it not been for the long-range escort fighter, the Luftwaffe would have driven us from the skies over Germany."

Abe Dolim, his second tour completed, returned home to Hawaii, while others continued accumulating missions in the hope that they too could soon go home. Paul M. Montague, an armorer-ball turret gunner in the 487th Bomb Group at Lavenham, flew his seventeenth mission on 15th March when the B-17s went to Oranienburg.

"This mission was another long haul into and out of Germany. Our crew in the *High Tailed Lass* had made it before. All went well until we approached the turning point toward the IP west of Berlin. We were flying at 24,000 feet when, suddenly, an accurate burst of flak hit our ship. The pilot was seriously wounded, one engine quit, the intercom only functioned sporadically and all the control cables on the port side, except the rudder, were severed. This caused us to bank to starboard at about thirty degrees. We dropped from formation, apparently unseen, lost altitude and turned toward Berlin. At only 12,000 feet over Berlin a second flak burst smashed part of the Plexiglas nose, stopped a second engine, ruptured the oxygen system, and started a fire in the bomb bay. Twelve 500 pounders stuck there would neither jettison nor toggle. Several crew members were hit by shrapnel. Our pilot gave us the alternative of baling out or staying while he attempted to ride the *Lass* down to a crash landing in Poland. As we gazed directly down at the Tiergarten, no one had the nerve to jump! The fire in the bomb bay was finally extinguished and we managed to jettison our bombs into a lake below. Thankfully, we were alone. No German fighters appeared. As we crossed the Oder river at only a few thousand feet, our Russian allies fired on us but no hits were sustained.

"Our pilot did a magnificent job of approach to what appeared to be a level field enclosed on three sides by woods. We had no flaps, gear, air speed indicator and many other vital instruments but all the crew survived the crash landing." The co-pilot and the engineer were later placed in a hospital for Russian wounded and the seven remaining crew were 'looked after' by their Russian Army hosts. The crew was disrobed by some Russian Army women who then proceeded to wash them with cloths and basins of water. Their uniforms were taken away and replaced with 'pajamas' (the type worn in concentration and prison camps). Paul Montague continues. "Little did we seven suspect that everything would be pantomime for two ensuing weeks and these pajamas would be our clothes. We were under constant guard. We were prisoners - not guests of our 'allies.' Just as we were falling asleep several of us heard the unmistakable click of the lock in our door.

"Next morning we had our first breakfast. I recall being very thirsty and I spotted a large cut-glass container of water in the center of the oval breakfast table. After pouring a glass-full, I took a large swallow and my breath was whisked away! Pure vodka at 0530! I tried to warn the crew members but was speechless. A few others made the same error. The Russians roared with laughter. For the next two weeks we used vodka in our cigarette lighters; it worked marvelously like an acetylene torch!"

Montague and his fellow crew members were finally transported to Poznan and on through Poland to Lodz where they continued to Kiev. They finally reached a Russian fighter base near Poltava where a Lend-Lease C-46 flew them nearer freedom. Paul Montague recalls.

"After flying for quite a time we noticed the co-pilot coming back to the area where the wing joins the fuselage. He unscrewed a cap of some sort, removed a rubber siphon from his jacket and proceeded to drink something. Could this possibly be de-icer fluid? Our pilot, his head still bandaged from our crash, remarked, 'My God! I may have to end up flying this plane.' After flying some hours at high altitude over some mountain ranges, we began our descent and finally made a very rough landing in Tehran, Persia. This was the last we were to see of any Russians. After spending a few days at the American base in Tehran we were flown on to Abadan by an American pilot in a C-47 transport. From then on it was shuttle hops by American pilots to Cairo, a nearly deserted base in the Libyan desert, on to Athens, Paris, and finally to Lavenham. Since we were due for R&R about this time, we were granted a week's leave and spent a most pleasant time in Girvan, Scotland, before returning to base to fly two more missions."

Not all crews were as fortunate as Montague's had been. Although German jets continued to pose a very real threat, losses from collisions and accidents were often higher than those caused by fighter attacks. On 17th March, the 490th Bomb Group was returning from a raid on Bittefeld when they encountered cirrus clouds which forced them to fly on instruments for thirty minutes. The Fortresses moved into tighter formation. Suddenly, a squadron in the 385th Bomb Group cut through the clouds into the 490th formation, causing one of the 490th ships, flown by Lieutenant Arthur Stein, to veer upwards. In no time at all it collided with another 490th B-17, flown by Lieutenant Robert H. Tennenberg. The radio room in the lower Fortress took the full force of the collision and the aircraft broke in two. All

The crew of High Tailed Lass, *pose with their Russian hosts. Paul Montague, the ball turret gunner, is second from left in the back row.* (Montague)

The Lord Mayor of London, Sir Frank Alexander, christened this B-17 of the 91st Bomb Group. The bottle contained Thames River water, and Sir Frank made the first flight of his life in the aircraft later in the day.

nine crew were killed. In Tennenberg's Fortress, Chester A. Deptula, the navigator, dragged the stunned nose gunner, John Gann, from the shattered nose to the radio operator's compartment. Despite a smashed engine, another partly disabled, a wing tip bent, the front of the nose knocked off, and the pilot's front view window broken, Tennenberg kept *Big Poison* airborne and managed to reach Belgium where he made a successful crash landing. The crewmen stepped out unhurt and surveyed the damage. Among the wreckage was the mutilated torso of a man later identified as the radio operator from the Fortress that had collided with them. He had been forced through the shattered Plexiglas nose of Tennenberg's aircraft on impact.

The following day a record 1,327 bombers were assembled for yet another raid on Berlin. It was the second mission to the German capital for William C. Stewart in the 92nd Bomb Group.

"The day was as bright and crisp as I have ever seen; more like a Technicolor movie than real life. There were a few small wisps of white cotton clouds interspersed through the picture but mostly it was clear. The sun glittered back from reflections of the shiny aluminum skin of the other ships in the formation. Before we reached the IP I could see the stretch of this great city. The streets were like a checkerboard beneath us and once in a while, an ant-like motor vehicle appeared on the streets. The movement of the scene below was unbearably slow and it seemed as though we were motionless. The black bursts of flak were also hanging ahead and right at our altitude the sky was completely peppered with the stuff. As I looked ahead I said to myself, 'And we're going to have to fly through that?'

"I turned the ball turret to the right, at about the 3 o'clock position, and could see the lumbering hulk of a Fortress, which was probably from another squadron, about 4,000 feet below us going in the opposite direction. Its nose was pointed downward with its right wing toward my left. Its right outboard engine was engulfed in red-orange flames streaking back about ten feet. There was no doubt that the plane was going down. I watched the scene transfixed and uttered silently to the crew of the plane, although really to myself, 'Get out. Get out!' As I watched one, two, three and then four small white blossoms appeared behind the craft. Some had made it out. I changed my gaze to one of the small white parachutes in the air with something hanging below; an airman, another American. As I watched small black puffs appeared around him as he slowly floated

Abe Dolim, far left, and the crew of Vie's Guys, *at Rougham.* (Abe Dolim)

downward. The Germans were shooting at him with anti-aircraft fire. They could have used the 88mm ammunition better by going after the rest of us still flying.

"As we proceeded over Berlin the ship lurched and twisted from impacts but we kept going and finally unloaded our bombs onto a railroad station in the heart of the city. Once away from the city, the flight back was uneventful. When I turned my turret to about 2 o'clock I could see strips of aluminum skin peeled back from the right wing. When we landed we found we had taken what must have been a 105mm anti-aircraft shell through the wing. It left a hole that a man could put his head through near the inboard end of the 'Tokyo' gas tank. There were

Major "Bucky" Cleven, shot down over Bremen on 8th October 1943, was among the many airmen to return from POW camps as they were captured by the Allies.

hundreds of smaller holes throughout the main body, wings and tail sections but no one was hit. I had learned what accurate and intense flak was."

Although flak was particularly hazardous on this mission the defensive honors went to the *Jagdverbande*. Thirty-seven Me 262s of the I and II/*Jagdverband 7* attacked the massive bomb formation and shot down sixteen bombers and five fighters (another sixteen bombers were forced to land inside Russian territory) for the loss of only two jets. The "Bloody Hundredth" lost four bombers this day, including one ship which was cleaved in two by Me 262 gunfire. By the end of the month the 8th was to lose thirty bombers to the German twin-engined jets. The jet menace became such a problem that, beginning on 21st March, the 8th flew a series of raids on airfields used by the *Jagdverbande*. The raids also coincided with the build-up for the impending crossing of the Rhine by Allied troops. For four days the heavies bombed jet airfields and military installations. On 22nd March, the heavies were requested by SHEAF headquarters to bomb the Bottrop military barracks and hutted areas directly behind the German lines. Next day the 8th struck at rail targets as part of the rail interdiction program to isolate the Ruhr and cut off coal shipping. Since the loss of the Saar Basin, the Ruhr was the only remaining source of supply for the German war machine.

On 23rd/24th March, under a sixty-six mile long smoke screen and aided by 1,747 bombers from the 8th Air Force, Field Marshal Bernard Montgomery's 21st Army Group crossed the Rhine in the north while further south simultaneous crossings were made by General Patton's Third Army. Groups flew two missions this day, hitting jet aircraft bases in Holland and Germany while the B-24 groups flew

As American troops pushed further into Germany they captured Luftwaffe airfields littered with aircraft abondoned by the retreating forces. This was one of the first Me262s to be found.

in much-needed supplies to the armies in the field. Soon the Wehrmacht was in headlong retreat. Bomber crews were now hard-pressed to find worthwhile targets and the planners switched attacks from inland targets to coastal areas. Beginning on 5th April, the weather over the Continent improved dramatically and the B-17s were dispatched to U-boat pens on the Baltic coast. On 4th April, the 92nd Bomb Group dropped "Disney" bombs on pens at Hamburg while other groups bombed Kiel.

Everywhere the Allies were victorious but while the enemy kept on fighting missions continued almost daily. Such was the 8th Air Force's superiority that the B-17s assembled over France on 5th April, before flying in formation for an attack on the marshalling yards at Nuremburg. However, on 7th April, during a mission to oil storage facilities at Hamburg, radios in the 100th Bomb Group formation came to life with shouts of "Bandits in the area!" Griswold Smith, a pilot in the 100th, recalls. "This had been called several times on other missions and we had begun to look upon it as 'crying wolf' but I called the gunners on the intercom and told them to be on the alert anyhow. Then I heard the groups in front of us calling for P-51s as they were being hit by Me 109s. Baugh was the first on our crew to see an enemy fighter. He reported them attacking and shooting down a straggler.

"The first pass was made from 7 o'clock low, up through 'C' Squadron and then on to us. Baugh and Russo were the first in the squadron to open fire. This Me 109 put a couple of slugs into us. One went through the nose and almost got Wilk and 'Turnip.' When this happened, Wilk said this was the 'real McCoy.' 'Turnip' started unlatching the nose guns and firing like hell. Wilk said that he started shooting at our P-51 escort and 'Turnip' maintained he was 'keeping the area clear.' The fighter went past us and turned back down at us. Wilk and Szalwinski were pouring .50s into him from their two turrets and O'Leary got a few from the waist. I think he was diving directly for us but he came just in front and knocked the left horizontal stabilizer off Lieutenant Martin's ship in front of us. That Me 109 diving into the formation spurting flames all over presented such a vivid picture that I shall never forget it. When he hit Martin's ship there must have been some sort of explosion as the nose and cockpit of our ship were filled with black smoke and dust. The Me 109's wing flew off and went over my wing, knocking Lieutenant Joe King's ship in the 'horizontal diamond.' (Both Martin and King managed to make it back to England and they were each awarded the DFC. Wilk and our crew got credit for that Me 109.)

The 390th Bomb Group, dropping supplies to the Dutch in May 1945. (Hans Onderwater)

"Another Me 109 came in from 5 o'clock high. Everyone said he was coming directly at us but our gunners put out so much lead that he diverted and crashed into a ship in the lead squadron. We saw both ships explode. The reason we got so many fighter attacks directed at us was because we were the top ship and the corner ship in the group and therefore around us was the least possible concentration of friendly fire. Ordinarily, fighters made their passes in a dive to get greater speed. The enemy fighters stayed with us for about an hour.

"We were at 15,000 feet as no flak was expected. However, there was plenty of accurate flak over the target. I never thought I would be glad to see flak but I was this day because it meant the fighters wouldn't 'come in.' We started out with ten ships in our squadron and on 'Bombs away' there were six ships. We were glad to return from this one. There were so many holes in the nose that Wilk nearly froze sitting up there on the way home. There was plenty of close support by the P-51s all the way back across the North Sea. I guess they finally found us. And to think, I met plenty of boys in London who completed an entire tour without seeing a single enemy fighter.

"After this mission the mental and physical strain was so much that I was too tired to keep up the log of my missions. Missions were coming every day with no rest in between. I would land from a mission and the pilots' truck would be waiting to carry me to the mission critique. From there I would stagger over to the mess hall and gorge myself. After that I would waddle over to my barrack and fall

in bed until the Alert Sergeant woke me the next morning for briefing. Following that schedule I didn't have much time to write notes on my missions. I planned to catch up on them in a couple of days while they were still fresh in my mind but somehow I never got around to it."

The following day, 8th April, the 8th was again out in considerable force, putting up nine groups from the First Division together with six groups of Mustangs. The Second Air Division put up nine B-24 groups with four groups of escorting fighters and the Third Air Division put up fourteen groups of B-17s with four groups of Mustangs. Griswold Smith flew in the 100th Bomb Group formation in the Third Division.

"At briefing, when they were pulling the curtain back from the map on which our route to the target was always marked with a red ribbon, it looked as if the ribbon was never going to stop. This was always a dramatic moment because no one ever knew where the mission was going until the lights were turned off and the curtain withdrawn. When the curtain was halfway drawn you could hear 'Berlin' whispered all over the room. My heart quickened a little. Finally, it turned out to be Eger, Czechoslovakia, to everyone's relief. Nothing happened on the raid except for the terrific nervous strain caused by the shout, 'Bandits in the area!' on one occasion. We really flew close formation and sweated it out. This was our Air Medal mission - we really had our fill of combat now.

"On 9th April, we hit Reim airfield five miles east of Munich. It was being used by German jets. The day was very clear and one could see many other airfields being hit by other groups. The object was to destroy airfields that could be used by jet planes in southern Germany. (Jet airplanes required an exceptionally long runway.) We could see where they were using their autobahns for that purpose. We let down to about 3,000 feet on the way home and could plainly see where the ground forces had been creating havoc. Passing over the Rhine we saw several destroyed bridges and two pontoon bridges.

"The 10th April mission to Burg airfield near Magdeburg was just about the worst of all. Again our target was jet aircraft. We were flying in the low squadron of the 100th Bomb Group, which was the worst place to be when the jets attacked. The jets usually made their attacks in twos and threes from 6 o'clock low or level, because from that angle they looked like P-51s with wing tip tanks and the gunners were afraid to shoot until they got in real close. They would coast in on a formation from the rear with their jets off, open fire, turn on their jets and vanish with terrific speed. They were armed with 30mm cannon.

"I remember they made several passes at us from 6 o'clock low. I distinctly remember two ships going down in flames. I believe a couple of others were crippled and knocked out of formation; one or two aborted earlier. Anyway, there were damned few left when we went over the target. Lieutenant Reeves, who was on his first mission, was flying in my squadron in front of me and a little higher. He burst into flames and a wing ripped off on one of the first jet passes. They put a few holes in us too but no one was hurt. I credited my life to Baugh and Russo, the tail and ball turret gunners, for putting out so much accurate fire that the jets diverted their attacks when they came in close. We were in the best position for them to attack.

"We had a toggelier flying with us this day who missed an excellent chance to destroy a jet. 'Turnip' said the toggelier 'just sat there and looked at it. That happened to a lot of people when fighters came in unexpectedly close. It is very astonishing and interesting: not to mention deadly. The papers said this was the biggest day yet for the 8th Air Force as it destroyed 205 enemy fighters. They also said that if the Germans had developed jets just a little earlier, the 8th would never have succeeded. I heartily agreed with this opinion. Our conventional fighters, the P-51 and the P-47, didn't have a chance of catching a jet in the air. When they shot one down it was because they were lucky enough to sneak up on one with his jets off and shoot him down before he knew what had happened, or if they came out of a cloud directly on top of one. Ordinarily, they would see one floating around with jets off and would start chasing

B-17s flying over Schipol, Holland, on their way to drop supplies. (Hans Onderwater)

him. He would sit around 'til they were almost in range, then he would turn on his jets and make them look as though they were sitting still."

The continual pounding of German airfields reduced the threat posed by the jets. However, other hazards sometimes caused casualties in the B-17 groups, as it did on 13th April when the 398th Bomb Group from Nuthampstead flew its

The Dutch show their gratitude for the supplies by mapping out "Many Thanks." (Hans Onderwater)

Another task given to the B-17 crews was to fly French civilians from work camps and concentration camps in Austria to Le Bourget, near Paris. 38,000 men, women and children were air-lifted in May 1945.

188th mission of the war, to Neumunster. Over the target a leading aircraft salvoed his RDX bombs in error. Two of them touched about 400 feet below, exploded and brought down six Fortresses in the 601st Bomb Squadron; five of which had to be abandoned on the Continent. RDX bombs were fitted with close proximity fuses and were most unstable at all times unless handled with great care. Bombing results were later described as "excellent," but at a high price indeed.

On 17th April, Dresden was again bombed. The German corridor was shrinking rapidly and the American and Russian bomb lines now crossed at several points on briefing maps. During the week 18th to 25th April, missions were briefed and scrubbed almost simultaneously. General Patton's advance was so rapid that at least on one occasion crews were lining up for takeoff when a message was received to say that General Patton's forces had captured the target the B-17s were to bomb!

The end came on 25th April when the 8th Air Force flew its final full-scale combat mission of the war, to the Skoda armaments plants at Pilsen in Czechoslovakia. To forty aircraft in the 92nd Bomb Group went the honor of leading the strike force. "Fame's Favored Few," was the oldest group in the 8th and this was its 310th and final mission. The total would have been greater had it not been for the group's role as a training outfit during the early part of the war, so other groups surpassed the mission total. The 303rd Bomb Group

at Molesworth chalked up the command record this day, flying its 364th mission, while other groups came close to equaling it.

Unfortunately, with victory so close, losses were experienced. Lieutenant Lewis B. Fisher's crew became the last in the 92nd to be shot down; struck by a flak burst. Their B-17 was last seen over Pilsen going into the clouds in a spin, trailing flame and black smoke. No parachutes were seen. Bombing was made visually but several runs were necessary because of the cloudy conditions in the target area.

The following day the American and Russian armies met at Torgau and the world waited for the inevitable unconditional surrender. Further bombing missions were cancelled and the bomb groups were stood down.

At Podington on 29th April the long-awaited, once-postponed, 300th mission (flown on 7th April) party, got into full swing. After a formal program in the morning in which the CO, Lieutenant Colonel James W. Wilson, and the guest of honor, Brigadier General Bartlett Beaman, Chief of Staff of the First Air Division, delivered speeches, the base was entertained by Mustangs of the 364th Fighter Group. The "Divisionaires" band of the First Air Division provided the music and celebrations continued late into the evening.

Over at Kimbolton, the 379th Bomb Group had good cause to celebrate. This group had flown more sorties than any other bombardment group in the 8th Air Force, had dropped more bombs on the enemy than any other group, and had the lowest abort rate of all groups in combat since 1943.

During the first week of May 1945 the German armies surrendered one by one to Montgomery at Luneberg Heath, to Devers at Munich, and to Alexander at Casserta and finally to Eisenhower at Reims in the early hours of 7th May 1945. The news of the Germans' final surrender was made known to the men at bases throughout eastern England on VE (Victory in Europe) Day, 8th May 1945.

Bill Carleton in the 100th Bomb Group sums up possibly the feelings of many at the war's end.

"All wars are senseless and yet, World War Two was unavoidable. We had gained victory, not necessarily through superior intellect but rather through the will to win and the belief that we were in the right. Like all human endeavors, we were fraught with frustration and, at times, saddled with stupidity, but the love of man and the love of our country brought forth accomplishments and sacrifices beyond man's own comprehension. The 100th Bomb Group was known throughout the land not because we were superhuman but rather because we were human. Our fame and notoriety spread not just because of Regensburg or Berlin or the Russian mission, but also because of our losses, and yes, even because of our 'faux pas.' We were famous and to some of the new flyers, infamous, both for what we did and what we gave. Mighty as we were with our seventy to eighty bombers and our 4,000 men, we were but a small fraction of the total force ultimately applied against the Axis powers. We contributed our part and it was our knowledge and belief that others were making an even greater sacrifice that assured us of ultimate victory."

When victory came the B-17 groups were assigned many tasks, such as flying Allied prisoners of war home from their camps in eastern Europe to France, and airlifting displaced persons from Linz in Austria to their homes in France, Holland, Denmark, and all other recently occupied countries. The B-17 crews airlifted troops from the United Kingdom to Casablanca where they continued on to the China-Burma-India Theater and also acted as "moving vans" for fighter groups going to Germany as part of the occupation forces there. In addition, "Trolley" or "Revival" missions were flown to bombed-out cities, the aircraft crammed with ground personnel to show them what destruction their aircraft had wrought. The flights ranged from 1,000 to 3,000 feet and the routes took passengers on what they described as a "Cook's Tour" of specially selected towns and cities which had been bombed by the 8th over the past four years. All these flights were important, but possibly the food drops to starving Dutch civilians were the greatest post-combat contributions made by Fortress crews. Among those taking part in the missions of mercy was Griswold Smith, who had flown his final combat mission with the 100th on 18th April.

"We flew three or four mercy missions to Holland until the end of hostilities, carrying food. One of them was before the Germans surrendered. They had promised us a

Sweet Chariot, 44-6888 of the 96th Bomb Group, crash-landed on 11th May 1945. Germany had unconditionally surrendered on 7th May.

corridor to fly across the country unmolested at low level. We could see German troops marching around in their black uniforms with swastikas flying.

"Our second mercy mission was on the day the Germans in Holland surrendered. We taxied out in the usual manner when the hydraulic system on the ship stopped working. The ship in front of us stopped and it looked as if we couldn't avoid running into her. Ancinolli, the bombardier, and Robascowitz, the navigator, were having a fit trying to get out of the nose. The co-pilot was madly stamping on the brakes and I was frantically reaching around trying to throw all the switches in the cockpit. Several gunners standing behind my seat were sweating blood. We finally restored the hydraulic system and stopped the ship in the last possible fraction of a second. Erwin Jones, a college classmate from my home town and a lieutenant in an air defense company at Thorpe Abbotts, was riding in the very front of the ship in the glass nose, oblivious to all our troubles. After we had finally stopped, he calmly turned around and innocently asked the navigator if we weren't awfully close. The navigator couldn't answer; he wasn't able to breathe yet!

"We went in at 200 feet, buzzing a small sail boat on the Zuider Zee and blowing it over. We had orders not to drop unless we saw crowds of civilians but the Dutch were lined up around the edges of the field, waving and cheering. They had really turned out. Flags were flying everywhere and the streets were packed with people. It was a great day for the Dutch. We dropped our 4,000lb of food after trouble with the improvised 'drop doors' in the bomb bay. We buzzed Amsterdam a couple of times. O'Leary, who was riding up front in the nose where he could get a better view of the town, called over the interphone, 'Church steeple coming in at 12 o'clock high!'"

Bill Carleton was another in the 100th Bomb Group who went across Amsterdam at rooftop height.

"I remember a little Dutch boy looking up and trying to race us on his bicycle. As we approached the target area, the Dutch had arranged stones to say 'Thank You' in large letters just as we crossed the field. There were planes ahead of us who made their drops and people were running across the target area to get the food, unmindful of the fact that they could be knocked to kingdom come with a can of spam. Planes all around us were starting to drop their food but our plane flew across the field without any salvo. The bombardier had gone to sleep! He awoke with a jerk and made the drop into the Zuider Zee. Such folly, but how typical. The best of intentions, the worst in execution. I hoped the forthcoming peace would be better than that!"

In the summer of 1945 the 96th Bomb Group was given the task of taking German POWs back to Germany after their interrogation. Ready to board this aircraft is none other than the ex-General der Jadflieger, Adolf Galland (inset), the man once in charge of defending the Third Reich against the 8th Air Force. (Hans-Heiri Stapfer)

Appendices

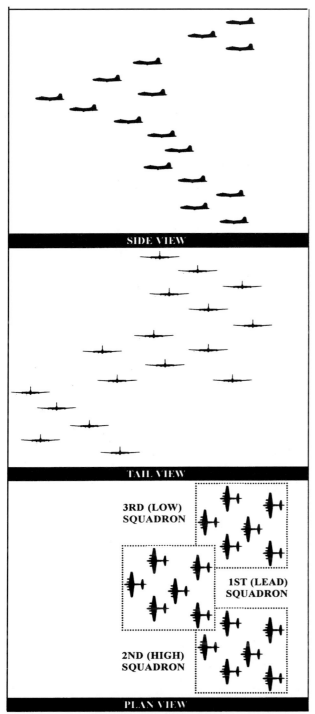

SIDE VIEW

TAIL VIEW

3RD (LOW)
SQUADRON

1ST (LEAD)
SQUADRON

2ND (HIGH)
SQUADRON

PLAN VIEW

Combat Box Stagger

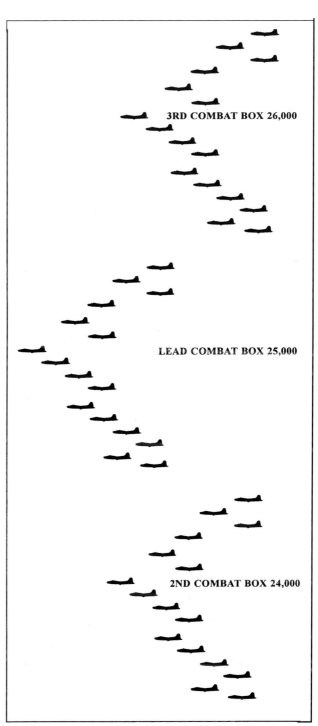

3RD COMBAT BOX 26,000

LEAD COMBAT BOX 25,000

2ND COMBAT BOX 24,000

Combat Wing-Three Combat Boxes

Final command and combat wing assignments, 8th Air Force, England, 1 January 1945

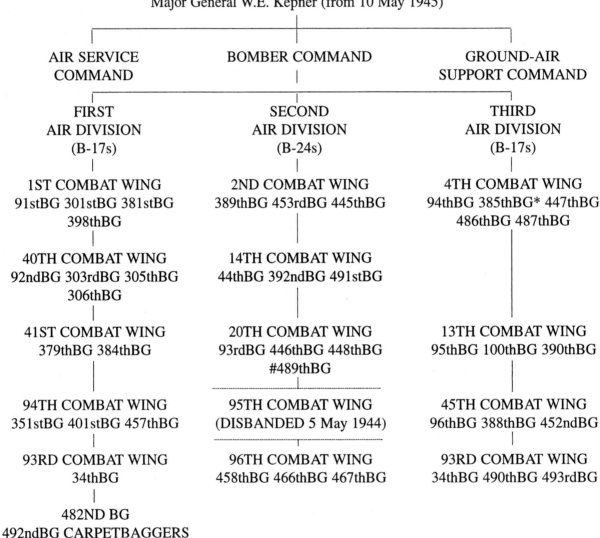

8TH AIR FORCE
Lieutenant General James H. Doolittle
Major General W.E. Kepner (from 10 May 1945)

AIR SERVICE COMMAND	BOMBER COMMAND	GROUND-AIR SUPPORT COMMAND
FIRST AIR DIVISION (B-17s)	SECOND AIR DIVISION (B-24s)	THIRD AIR DIVISION (B-17s)
1ST COMBAT WING 91stBG 301stBG 381stBG 398thBG	2ND COMBAT WING 389thBG 453rdBG 445thBG	4TH COMBAT WING 94thBG 385thBG* 447thBG 486thBG 487thBG
40TH COMBAT WING 92ndBG 303rdBG 305thBG 306thBG	14TH COMBAT WING 44thBG 392ndBG 491stBG	
41ST COMBAT WING 379thBG 384thBG	20TH COMBAT WING 93rdBG 446thBG 448thBG #489thBG	13TH COMBAT WING 95thBG 100thBG 390thBG
94TH COMBAT WING 351stBG 401stBG 457thBG	95TH COMBAT WING (DISBANDED 5 May 1944)	45TH COMBAT WING 96thBG 388thBG 452ndBG
93RD COMBAT WING 34thBG	96TH COMBAT WING 458thBG 466thBG 467thBG	93RD COMBAT WING 34thBG 490thBG 493rdBG
482ND BG 492ndBG CARPETBAGGERS		

GROUP ASSIGNMENTS, 8th AIR FORCE, ENGLAND - 6 JUNE 1943

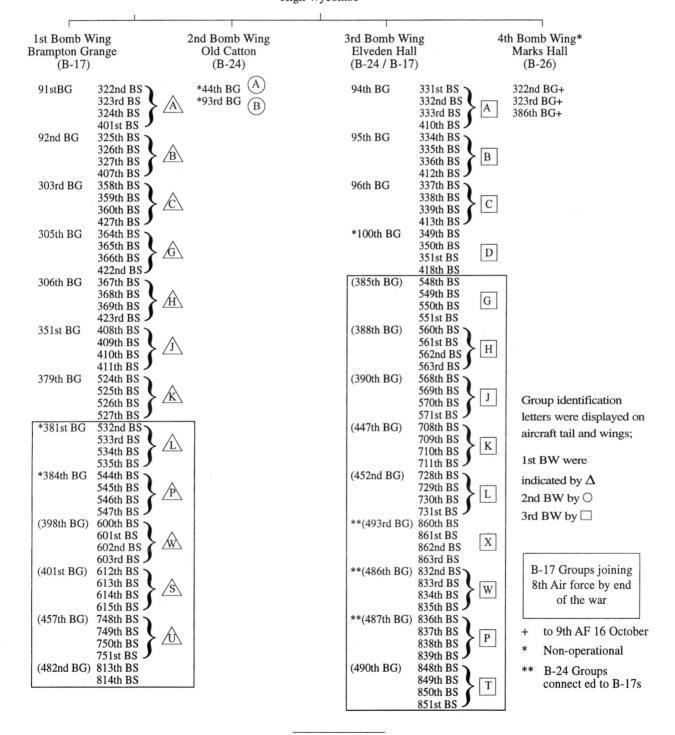

VIIIth AIR FORCE HQ
Bushey Park

VIIIth Bomber COMMAND
High Wycombe

| 1st Bomb Wing Brampton Grange (B-17) | 2nd Bomb Wing Old Catton (B-24) | 3rd Bomb Wing Elveden Hall (B-24 / B-17) | 4th Bomb Wing* Marks Hall (B-26) |

1st Bomb Wing — Brampton Grange (B-17)

91stBG — 322nd BS, 323rd BS, 324th BS, 401st BS △A
92nd BG — 325th BS, 326th BS, 327th BS, 407th BS △B
303rd BG — 358th BS, 359th BS, 360th BS, 427th BS △C
305th BG — 364th BS, 365th BS, 366th BS, 422nd BS △G
306th BG — 367th BS, 368th BS, 369th BS, 423rd BS △H
351st BG — 408th BS, 409th BS, 410th BS, 411th BS △J
379th BG — 524th BS, 525th BS, 526th BS, 527th BS △K
*381st BG — 532nd BS, 533rd BS, 534th BS, 535th BS △L
*384th BG — 544th BS, 545th BS, 546th BS, 547th BS △P
(398th BG) — 600th BS, 601st BS, 602nd BS, 603rd BS △W
(401st BG) — 612th BS, 613th BS, 614th BS, 615th BS △S
(457th BG) — 748th BS, 749th BS, 750th BS, 751st BS △U
(482nd BG) — 813th BS, 814th BS

2nd Bomb Wing — Old Catton (B-24)

*44th BG ⒶA
*93rd BG ⒷB

3rd Bomb Wing — Elveden Hall (B-24 / B-17)

94th BG — 331st BS, 332nd BS, 333rd BS, 410th BS ☐A
95th BG — 334th BS, 335th BS, 336th BS, 412th BS ☐B
96th BG — 337th BS, 338th BS, 339th BS, 413th BS ☐C
*100th BG — 349th BS, 350th BS, 351st BS, 418th BS ☐D
(385th BG) — 548th BS, 549th BS, 550th BS, 551st BS ☐G
(388th BG) — 560th BS, 561st BS, 562nd BS, 563rd BS ☐H
(390th BG) — 568th BS, 569th BS, 570th BS, 571st BS ☐J
(447th BG) — 708th BS, 709th BS, 710th BS, 711th BS ☐K
(452nd BG) — 728th BS, 729th BS, 730th BS, 731st BS ☐L
**(493rd BG) — 860th BS, 861st BS, 862nd BS, 863rd BS ☐X
**(486th BG) — 832nd BS, 833rd BS, 834th BS, 835th BS ☐W
**(487th BG) — 836th BS, 837th BS, 838th BS, 839th BS ☐P
(490th BG) — 848th BS, 849th BS, 850th BS, 851st BS ☐T

4th Bomb Wing* — Marks Hall (B-26)

322nd BG+
323rd BG+
386th BG+

Group identification letters were displayed on aircraft tail and wings;

1st BW were indicated by △
2nd BW by ◯
3rd BW by ☐

B-17 Groups joining 8th Air force by end of the war

+ to 9th AF 16 October

* Non-operational

** B-24 Groups connect ed to B-17s

Index